Yankee Reformers
In the Urban Age

hARPER ✝ τORChBOOKS

*A reference-list of Harper Torchbooks, classified
by subjects, is printed at the end of this volume.*

Yankee Reformers
In the Urban Age

Social Reform in Boston, 1880-1900

ARTHUR MANN

HARPER TORCHBOOKS   The Academy Library
Harper & Row, Publishers
New York

TO OSCAR HANDLIN

CONTENTS

PREFACE

Focusing on the Boston area, this work examines urban social reform in the seminal decades 1880–1900. My purpose is threefold: to demonstrate that the New England capital did not fall from liberal grace after the age of Emerson; to prove that modern liberalism owes its beginnings to the city as well as to the farm; to trace the origins of reform thinking to the character of a community, especially to the kinds of people in the community.

Only in its setting is this study local history. Boston was representative. The society by the Charles contained the essence of the social problem created by the urban and industrial changes remaking the nation in the last quarter of the nineteenth century. Boston had its share of strikes, poverty, slums, concentrated wealth, booms and busts, corrupt politics, debased values. It also confronted the older problems of prejudice against Catholics and women. How Bostonians attempted to square the ugly facts of inequality with the noble ideal of equality — for America as a whole and not just for Boston — is the theme of my book.

The history of social reform is the history of the perception of social evil and the will and the way to remove it. The duty of the historian of social reform is to explain why certain men were sensitive to evil and how this sensitivity shaped their thinking. This sensitivity I attempt to trace to the Bostonian's occupation, religion, ancestry, group traditions, role and status in the community, and the degree of his personal involvement in the problems of the day. The tale of Boston progressivism 1880–1900 is the tale of Protestant, Catholic, and Jewish religious leaders; of

professors, students, and free-lance intellectuals; of trade unionists and feminists. These categories are not arbitrary; the men and
women of that day thought they were real. I have defined Boston
as the city proper and its outlying communities, and Bostonians
as those who identified themselves with and participated in the
intellectual life of New England's capital.

It is far harder to define liberalism than it is to define Boston.
Contemporary opinion does not help, when Hubert Humphries
and Henry Hazlitt, Franklin Roosevelt, Jr. and Sherman Adams
claim to be true liberals. And the classic example of England —
of a nineteenth-century laissez-faire liberalism superseded by a
twentieth-century social welfare state liberalism — is not a model
for the historian of America. In this land the two streams have
coexisted, as in the New Nationalism and the New Freedom, as
in the First and Second New Deal. Any attempt to define American liberalism *a priori* without reference to the experience of the
American people is bound to mislead us.

In the American past there has been a type of person whom
we easily recognize, even if we cannot always "define" him, as a
social reformer. (For reasons of style I use interchangeably in my
book such terms as social reformer, liberal, progressive.) Social
reformers have not been of one piece, as I hope to show, but they
have shared a common approach to social problems. Of prime
importance, they have refused to acquiesce in the status quo,
but rather have objected to the what-is whenever it contravened
the what-ought-to-be. In this sense they have alerted the community to look after its values. Social reformers have also shared
the belief that, by tinkering with institutions, they could bring
out the good and suppress the evil of men in society. Finally,
they have characteristically dedicated themselves to improving
the position of disadvantaged groups. Beyond this tentative statement I do not at this point wish to go; the book tells the rest. If
this preliminary definition seems like a catchall which applies to
nearly every contemporary American, then it must be said in
defense that our generation has known but one dominant intel-

lectual tradition, the liberal tradition. It is my purpose to shed light on a neglected part of that tradition.

In examining one thread and one community, I was fortunate in receiving help from Professor Oscar Handlin of Harvard University. By example, he has demonstrated that strand history need not be parochial nor local history antiquarian. Rather the first allows for an understanding of the whole social process if the single part is related to the other parts; and the second permits studying the milieu in all its significance. Professor Handlin suggested the topic, criticized the manuscript, encouraged me from beginning to end. Knowing a first-rate scholar and first-rate man, I have experienced the drive and stimulation that compensate for the drudgery of research — for the necessary but foreboding excursions into chaos — out of which, one hopes, meaning and pattern will emerge.

ARTHUR MANN

January 6, 1953
Cambridge, Massachusetts

ACKNOWLEDGMENTS

At various stages of the manuscript I have profited from the coöperation of the surviving participants of the reform movements of the 1880's and 1890's and their descendants and friends. Dr. John Haynes Holmes of the Community Church of New York gave me his particularly fine insights into the characters and thought of Francis Greenwood Peabody and Minot J. Savage. The late Philip Davis, the late Ralph Albertson, and Mrs. Hazel Albertson — all of whom knew and worked with Frank Parsons — gave me their insights into the life and thought of Professor Parsons. Mrs. Claire Schindler Hamburger provided me with a number of personal details about her father, Solomon Schindler, and placed his papers at my disposal. Miss Elizabeth Hodges, librarian of the Episcopal Theological School, explained certain aspects of the career of her father, George Hodges, to me. She also dug his heretofore unused papers out from the basement of the School. Mrs. Eleanor H. Woods was kind enough to lend me the stray papers of her husband, Robert A. Woods, and was especially helpful in placing Mr. Woods in his proper context. Miss Florence Converse and Miss Vida D. Scudder relived their reforming days with me, read and criticized Chapter IX, and allowed me to use their papers.

Certain of my colleagues and teachers were generous in their time and criticism. These I wish to thank: Professors Edward Neal Hartley, John M. Blum, C. Conrad Wright, and Karl Deutsch of the Massachusetts Institute of Technology; Professors Arthur M. Schlesinger, Arthur M. Schlesinger, Jr., and Frederick Merk of Harvard University; Professor William Leuchtenberg of Columbia University. I also wish to thank the librarians of Yale, Radcliffe, the Boston Public Library, Widener, Andover, Boston Horticultural Society, Andover-Newton Theological Seminary, Dartmouth, Massachusetts Institute of Technology, Haverhill Public Library, and the Essex Institute. I owe a debt to those who typed the manuscript from the impossible hieroglyphics of my drafts. These include Miss Alma Leavis, Mrs. Fred Alexander, and the fine secretarial staff of the Massachusetts Institute of Technology's Department of English and History: Miss Virginia M. Butler, Miss Bernice M. Bianchi, Miss Elizabeth Cameron, Miss Nancy Horne, and Miss Mary Jane Wade. I also wish to thank Mrs. Eugenie Kaledin, Mr. Frederic L. Holmes, and Mr. Jack Neusner. Finally, I am indebted to Mrs. Marion L. Hawkes of the Harvard University Press for expert care in getting the manuscript ready for the printer.

My wife, Sylvia Blut Mann, already knows how much I owe to her.

A. M.

We are told every day that great social problems stand before us and demand a solution, and we are assailed by oracles, threats, and warnings in reference to these problems.

— William Graham Sumner
What Social Classes Owe to Each Other
(New York, 1883)

. . . where lies the road to Utopia, which strong men, not ashamed to confess their love for the ideal, may take with modest confidence, and follow to profit?

— Nicholas Paine Gilman
Socialism and the American Spirit (Boston, 1893)

yet bigness mushroomed in all sectors of the economy. The nation prided itself on self-government; yet everywhere rose the complaint of corporation rule. The United States boasted a classless society; yet Pittsburgh, Coeur d'Alene and Haymarket, Pullman and Homestead revealed antagonisms strikingly like those of Europe. Immigration, fertile soil, and agricultural machinery turned the West into the granary of the world; yet farmers cried out that they were being crucified. The cities qualified as centers of culture and convenience; yet numerous poor knew only the brutality and inconvenience of the slums. Expansion in population, industry, and agriculture raised America to a position of world power; yet the federal government used its power for purposes of imperialism. The central paradox was growth without progress; moral and material poverty amidst expansion. On a small but significant scale, Boston faced those problems of industrial, urban, and population growth that Americans must overcome to remain faithful to the democratic ideal.

While Boston did not undergo the revolution in heavy industry that characterized post-Civil War America, its economic difficulties were a typical statistic in the business life of the nation. An investment center of first rank, the Hub was affected by the boom of the 1880's and the bust of the 1890's, as the expansion and collapse of its brokerage houses and banks testified. Financiers "died like flies under the strain, and Boston grew suddenly old, thin, and haggard," observed Henry Adams of the Panic of 1893. Five hundred and fifty-five strikes in the "great uprising" of the mid-1880's upset the stable labor relations in the half-century-old manufacturing establishments of the city; and in the awful winter of 1894 a contingent of the city's jobless reinforced Jacob Coxey's ragged army advancing on Washington. Franchise scandals raised the question, debated throughout the land, of the merits of privately owned utilities as against publicly owned ones. Finally, by the early 1890's, ruinous competition from the sweatshop forced Boston's clothing factories to the wall, resulting in the displacement of well-paid factory operatives and

the exploitation of impoverished immigrants in the dismal tenements of the North End, the city's worst slum.[3]

Troublesome, too, was the question whether the melting pot
would melt, and Boston's experience in the past with the Irish
had not been good. By 1880, immigration, especially from Ireland
and since the 1840's, had so altered the Protestant and Yankee
character of the community that the foreign-born and their children comprised three-fifths of the 362,839 populace; in 1900,
with Boston's population at 560,892, the newcomers outnumbered
the descendants of colonial stock by nearly three to one. Sufficiently numerous by 1885 to elect Hugh O'Brien as one of their
own for mayor, the Catholic Irish contended with the Protestant
Yankees over the school system, modernism in religion, the control of the police department, discrimination in employment.
The Jewish community, which expanded from 10,000 to 30,000
with the coming of coreligionists from the Russian and Austro-
Hungarian empires, formed a third angle in the triangle of ethnic-
religious relations.

Complicating the process of accommodating alien cultures was
the cleavage that developed between native skilled workers and
immigrant unskilled laborers, as the latter made inroads in the
clothing industry. There was also the matter of the adjustment of
the uprooted of diverse stocks to one another. It was apparent to
all who visited the larger ghetto of the slums that there were
smaller ghettos of immigrant groups living in compact units
among themselves. They were distinguished by speech, mannerisms, dress, religion, location of residence, and held together
by the desire to be among people of like kind and the fear of a
prejudiced and hostile world. By 1900 more than twenty-five
nationalities had come to make the North End their home,
strangers to one another as well as strangers in a strange land.[4]

To the liberal generation brought up on London's Charles
Booth, Chicago's Jane Addams, New York's Jacob Riis, and Boston's Robert A. Woods, the slum was the microcosm of the evils
which beset Western civilization. The blighted areas of the city

revealed the meaning of unemployment, racial and religious prejudice, spiritual and physical want, class oppression, filth, disease, prostitution, drink, and corrupt politics. Boston had its slums, the Concentrated District, of which the worst were the South Cove, Ward 12 in South Boston, Ward 10 in the West End, Wards 11 and 19 in the South End, and the North End. Social workers knew the section last named as "Boston's classic land of poverty." The eighteenth century's "court end," it had become, since the 1840's, the first place of settlement for the poorest immigrants, who, on prospering, sought more desirable quarters in the city. As fast as the prosperous moved out, the depressed from overseas crowded in.[5]

The tenement houses, some constructed as multiple dwelling units but most converted from the single family homes of an earlier day, were filthy, evil smelling, overcrowded, and poorly ventilated. It was the rule rather than the exception for several families to share promiscuously common privies, water closets, and washrooms. Alleys and passageways, which often served as dumping grounds, ran into narrow, crooked, and dirty streets. The lofts, sweatshops, factories, and stores, bounded by the waterfront and the main commercial street of the city, disclosed that the North End was more properly a business center than a place for human habitation. The very wretchedness of the area attracted gamblers, pimps, prostitutes, sailors out on a spree, paupers, and human wrecks of one kind or another. Surrounded by such conditions North Enders suffered high rates of disease and mortality.[6]

Whereas Boston North of the Common was squalid, the South End was dreary. This was the city's largest working-class quarter, with inhabitants who were skilled and superior workers: its immigrants were once removed from poverty and on the way up the economic ladder. While there were overcrowded and unhygienic conditions in some of the tenements, the neighborhood was better known for the monotony and dinginess of its architecture, of red bricked houses stretching endlessly from lower

Roxbury to the city. To dreariness was added the garishness of a little Bowery at Dover and Washington Streets, where were found cheap theaters, dime museums, saloons, pool rooms, and easy women.[7] Something about the South End suggested a wasteland, and caused one Boston writer to call it a "social wilderness" and another, the "city wilderness."[8]

As the immigrants of Catholic and Jewish persuasions settled the West and South Ends, the well-to-do native Protestants retreated to the suburbs and the Back Bay, giving geographical borders to the ethnic and class cleavages of the community. Its first streets thrown open in 1872, the present Back Bay filled up in the next thirty years, and became equal to Beacon Hill in the status that it conferred on inhabitants. Its air of Victorian prosperity and gentility made the North End appear even more squalid and the South End even more dreary. Brownstone-front private houses made their appearance in the 1880's, Romanesque came to dominate the 1890's, and along the genteel and broad streets rose imposing churches, luxurious hotels, and obviously solidly constructed clubs. At spacious Copley Square and within sight of the historic Common, were McKim's Public Library, Richardson's Trinity Church, the Museum of Fine Arts, and the New Old South Church. They testified, in Romanesque and Gothic arch, stained glass, statue, and mural, to the final removal of culture and wealth from the ancient court end North of the Common.[9]

Social critics perceived that Boston's social problem was writ large in the contrast between the obvious meanness of the Concentrated District and the manifest prosperity of the Back Bay. There "are lessons in political economy in bricks and stones," wrote the liberal journalist, Walter Blackburn Harte; and from stately Commonwealth Avenue he derived the following lesson: "the aggregate cost of the mere luxuries of the table consumed in this one street, would be sufficient to properly house the poor, stifling and degraded in the filthy tenements of Boston." In a sensationalist exposé of conditions in the North End, *Civilization's*

Inferno, Benjamin Orange Flower, the dean of American muck-rakers, hammered home the point that "within less than an hour's walk of palatial homes on Commonwealth Avenue," in "cannon-shot of Beacon Hill . . . are hundreds of families slowly starving and stifling . . . " His conclusion was: *"Appreciation of the magnitude of the peril, and concerted action* — these are the supreme needs of the hour." [10]

The abolitionists had willingly involved themselves in the question of Negro slavery in the far-off South, but their descend-ants in the urban, capitalist, and polyglot community by the Charles were involved, whether they willed it or not, in the prob-lems of the machine culture. Their way of life depended on how they responded to the challenge of the business cycle, the unequal distribution of wealth, conflict between labor and capital, racial and religious antagonisms, and the role of government in the economy. So thought the official economists and statisticians of the Massachusetts Bureau of Statistics of Labor, as they rolled off a volume a year on the well-being and ill-being of the Com-monwealth and its cities. At the same time, Bostonians perceived that their problems were different only in degree from those of American and Western industrial society at large. The social crit-ics agreed, by omission and admission, that Pennsylvania's strikes were more savage, that London's slums were meaner, that New York's parvenus were more vulgar and numerous than their own.[11] The milieu of Bostonians then was more than Boston. The Hub of the Universe had become a state of mind: urban man's ideas of adjusting himself to the cosmopolitan forces remaking the Western world.

Bostonians adjusted to rapid social change in either of two ways, through democratic reform or aristocratic recoil. The liber-als, conscious of the radical tradition of their city and mindful of progressive movements in Europe and the nation at large, at-tempted to resolve the social problem with characteristic nine-teenth-century optimism. Many proper Bostonians, their backs to the wall on the other hand, despaired of directing society, and withdrew into themselves to shut out a world in which they refused to live.

II

The recoil of fashionable Boston took the form of an Anglophilism that would have warmed the Federalist heart of Fisher Ames. The purpose was to exclude the new peoples coming to Boston from the traditions denied them by birth. Under Phillips Brooks, the Anglo-Catholic church became a symbol of the devotion of the well-to-do to the homeland of their ancestors. The descendants of the generation that had led the nation in the public school movement chose to educate their own progeny at St. Paul's and Groton, where British names, sports, and methods of instruction were aped. The Back Bay resembled fashionable England, and, to make sure of the intended identity, its inhabitants gave its streets, hotels, and apartments such names as Clarendon, Exeter, Wellington, Hereford. More directly, Society closed its doors to the newer rich with the death of John Lowell Gardner, the last of the China merchants: inherited wealth from commerce had become the badge of the aristocracy. In the absence of a coat of arms, wealthy Bostonians hunted up ancestors with properly remote origins, "grandfather on the brain" assuming the proportions of a cult with the founding of patriotic and genealogical societies. The multiplication of trusts signified that Boston's upper classes also had lost economic nerve.[12]

As wealth showed no signs of concern with the welfare of the many, so culture revealed no faith in the will to mold society. George E. Woodberry, George Cabot Lodge, and Charles E. Norton shared Barrett Wendell's pessimism: "We are vanishing into provincial obscurity . . . America has swept from our grasp. The future is beyond us." Francis Parkman, who had thrilled to the struggle of winning a continent and taming its resources, concluded with Godkin of the *Nation* as well as with fellow Bostonians of his class that the American experiment had failed. In contrast to the robustness of Emerson's "Self-Reliance," there poured forth a number of morbid novels describing a dying Yankee people, of lonely men and women, run-down families, and neglected buildings. To his students Charles Eliot Norton lectured that it would have been better "had we never been born in this degenerate and unlovely age . . . "[13]

When the brothers Brooks and Henry Adams became scientists in gloom and doom it was truly a sign that the blood of Boston's most gifted sons was running thin. The first Adams had been a constitution maker, the second an architect of American foreign policy, the third a crucial influence in keeping England neutral during the Civil War. But the members of the fourth generation chose to take masochistic pleasure in telling themselves that they were not meant for their world and equally sadistic delight in lecturing the American people on their impending collapse. Shortly before Brooks published *The Law of Civilization and Decay* in 1896, he explained to Henry his pessimistic perversion of Darwin's optimistic theory of evolution and concluded: "It is time that we perished. The world is tired of us." [14]

From his illustrious ancestors, Brooks had "inherited a belief in the great democratic dogma," as he had inherited his pew in Quincy's church. He lost faith in America when he came to believe that the bankers ran the nation. In 1892, in "The Plutocratic Revolution," he noted with alarm that capital controlled the country through the trust and the tariff. During the panic of 1893, when Adams faced the loss of his livelihood, he looked back wistfully to the American past to see how the country had erred. He found the "apex of democratic civilization" in George Washington, who tried to give unity and purpose to American life. The great father failed, and John Quincy Adams attempted to revive Washington's dream, only to lose out in the fateful election of 1828 to Jackson and his mean and selfish crowd. This was the last great conflict between a higher moral force and man's selfishness; and the higher moral force went down to defeat.[15]

America could do nothing to reverse the process of degeneration, for Brooks Adams was convinced of "the exceedingly small part played by conscious thought in moulding the fate of men." Men act according to instinct, and in nineteenth-century capitalism and democracy, according to the instincts of greed and selfishness. Western civilization had reached its last peak during the military and religious age of the medieval world, when men valued courage, honor, the family, religious devotion, and sexual passion, and produced inspired architecture and art. With the development of commerce, industry, and finance after the thirteenth century, Western society began to decay. Prose replaced poetry, the sexual appetite atrophied, the family declined, and art and architecture became materialistic. The past had belonged to the warrior, priest, and artist; the present and the future to the banker and his "usurers' paradise." Henry, after reading the manuscript, agreed with his brother that "man . . . could be nothing but a failure." [16]

When Henry Adams returned to America after the Civil War he believed in progress and American democracy. His inheritance and his contact with the liberals in England during his father's ambassadorship had led him to dream it "to be possible that a democratic republic could develop the intellectual energy to raise itself to that advanced level of intelligence which had been accepted as a moral certainty by Washington, his own grandfather, and most of his grandfather's contemporaries." In 1891 he finished the last volume of his *History of the United States of America During the Administration of James Madison.* The American people, he noted, had progressed during the first critical decade of the nineteenth century. Their character was fixed, their economic development predestined, their ingenuity established. In the next century, Adams asked, would Americans carry on successfully? [17]

Adams had answered that question eleven years earlier in his novel, *Democracy;* and the answer had been no. His first doubts had come when he was cruelly disillusioned by the corruption of the Grant administration. This disillusionment he poured into his novel. Through the eyes of Mrs. Lightfoot Lee, a cultivated and intelligent widow of gentle Philadelphia birth, Adams examined Washington politics. Mrs. Lee was a humanitarian; she had, like Henry Adams, read Taine, Ruskin, Comte, and Mill, and was interested in charities and schools. She went to the nation's capital "to see with her own eyes the action of primary forces; to touch with her own hand the massive machinery of society; to measure with her own mind the capacity of the motor power. She was bent upon getting to the heart of the great American mystery of democracy and government." [18]

Madeline Lee learned, as Henry Adams had presumed to discover in 1870, that democracy runs according to man's corruptibility and greed. Senator Ratcliffe, the symbol of the American politician, is coarse, uncultivated, hostile to literature, platitudinous, and hungry for power and patronage. Madeline is tempted to marry the senator, who is destined to be president, and through him reform the nation's political life. At the last moment she withdraws. Exhausted by her efforts, she cries: "I want to go to Egypt . . . democracy has shaken my nerves to pieces. Oh what rest it would be to live in the Great Pyramid and look out for ever at the polar star." [19]

From the "Great Pyramid" of his withdrawal, Henry Adams found his "polar star" in medieval France. Shortly after the publication of *The Law of Civilization and Decay* in 1896, Henry began to search for a scientific principle to explain the famous century which had produced St. Thomas Aquinas, Chartres, and Mont-Saint-Michel. He had come to believe that modern civilization, as a result of lack of unity, had shown "its movement, even at the centre, arrested." In the years 1150–1250 he discovered unity of purpose deriving from the adoration of the Virgin Mary. That age was the high point of Western society, which, since then, had been running down, losing energy as its unity disintegrated. There could be no hope for a revival because, as Henry Adams explained, the Second Law of Thermodynamics applied to human cultures as well as to the physical and natural worlds. For Darwin's cheery hope for everlasting progress and Newton's concept of a perfect machine-universe held eternally in balance, Adams substituted Thompson's gloomy determinism that the cosmos would one day wear out.[20]

III

The social physics of Henry Adams expressed the pessimistic side of Boston; the spirit of Ralph Waldo Emerson as embodied in the survivors of the age of newness spoke for the hopeful side of the city. Still very much alive, active, and articulate were Wendell Phillips, the Reverend Dr. Edward Everett Hale, Franklin Benjamin Sanborn, Thomas Wentworth Higginson, Julia Ward Howe, Mary Ashton Livermore, and Abby Morton Diaz (a student of Margaret Fuller). They were living evidence that the Hub City had once been the cradle of Unitarianism and Transcendentalism, the public school movement and feminism, temperance and prison reform, abolitionism; while their liberal activities in the 1880's and 1890's gave proof, to all who chose to see it, that the humanitarianisms of the pre- and post-Civil War eras were but two sides of the same struggle against unfreedom and misery. Well-known, highly cultivated, free from eccentricities, and respectable in terms of ethnic lineage and social status, the products of the New England Renaissance were a recognized power for good in the community.[21]

Because they were proper, the old-timers' criticism that proper Society was less than proper carried weight. Julia Ward Howe, who, like Wendell Phillips, was a Beacon Hiller and one of the few Bostonians who met European standards of aristocratic bearing, complained: "English manners are affected by those among us who mistake the aristocracy of position for the aristocracy of character." Mrs. Howe had traveled much abroad, and in the company of titled nobility, but her experiences overseas had confirmed her democratic Americanism. Therefore, she resented those "society-men . . . so depolarized in their tastes and

feelings, as to be at ease nowhere but in Europe, and not much
at ease there . . . who return . . . and ape the display of European grandees as far as their fortunes will allow." As for fortunes,
Edward Everett Hale implied, in a Boston University Commence-
ment address, that they were, so to speak, vicariously acquired.

> The leaders in Massachusetts sixty, seventy, eighty years
> ago were the men who had done something. They had dis-
> covered the Columbia River or traded for furs with the In-
> dians, or split ice off an iceberg in Labrador and sent it to
> Havana or Calcutta . . . the leaders of society now, whose
> most prominent business is to unlock a safe in a safety de-
> posit vault and cut off the coupons from their bonds and
> carry them to be cashed . . . do not, to my mind, compare
> favorably. . .[22]

As Hale and Howe pointed up the lack of originality of Society,
so Thomas Wentworth Higginson and Wendell Phillips inveighed
against the "cowardice of culture." It was an old malady, wrote
Higginson in an urbane, witty, and yet angry essay; Alexander
Hamilton, Chancellor Kent, and Boston's own Fisher Ames had
been educated weak sisters, like their modern counterparts, in
priding themselves that they were not meant for the democratic
world and in prophesying social degeneration. A highly cultivated
gentleman whose books reached a wide reading public, Higginson impatiently snapped: "If all the scholar's education in a republic gives him no infallible advantage over the man who cannot read or write, let the scholar have the manliness not to whine
over the results of his own inefficiency." Where Higginson used
the rapier, Wendell Phillips used the battle-axe. In his memorable
(fashionable society thought it notorious) Phi Beta Kappa address at Harvard in 1881, he defended his lifelong radicalism,
further scandalized cultivated Harvardians by praising the Nihilists, rebuked educated men for having refused in the past to join
the army in social reform struggling for a better world, and dared
the scholar to turn out and do battle against the giant corporation.[23]

The lives of the old-time reformers stood out all the more affirmatively alongside the negations of the faint-hearted. Their capacity for work was enormous. Higginson left behind a list of writings that took forty printed pages to catalogue; Hale's collected works fill a library shelf; Sanborn took upon himself the job of doing biographies of Samuel Gridley Howe, Bronson Alcott, John Brown, William Ellery Channing, and Michael Anagnos. They were doers, these liberals. Higginson had stormed the Boston Court House to rescue the fugitive slave Anthony Burns, had fought in the Civil War as a colonel in the first Negro regiment. Phillips had braved physical violence as an abolitionist; Sanborn had edited the militant anti-slavery sheet, the *Boston Commonwealth*. In summing up her life, Mrs. Howe asked posterity to remember her for her efforts in prison reform, women's rights, abolitionism, and education of the blind. Mrs. Livermore, in her reminiscences, took pride in describing her activities against slavery, intemperance, and female inequality, and her labor in the Sanitation Commission. Boston's grand old man, Edward Everett Hale, had identified himself with so many causes for good that he was known in the 1880's and 1890's, in the words of Edwin D. Mead, editor of the *New England Magazine*, as "the incarnation of the Boston spirit." [24]

It is doubtful whether the men and women of the age of newness could have been content without agitating against evil and for good. Children of the Enlightenment, they had imbibed in the pre-Civil War days the happy optimism that "all things are possible to one who believes." Their optimism fed on challenge, and the more serious the challenge the more significant the reform. Mrs. Howe observed that the history of progress was the history of protestants: of Moses, Jesus, the Puritans, the revolutionaries of 1689 and 1789, William Lloyd Garrison, and Lucy Stone. "No one," she explained, "has any reason to be surprised at any new manifestation of human folly." Phillips expressed the theory that "Republics exist only on the tenure of being constantly agitated"; and Higginson went so far as to think of liberalism as

a kind of moral weight-lifting. Shortly after Appomattox he wrote
with sorrow of the "probable excess of prosperity, and . . . the
want of a good grievance" in the America of the future. He felt
pity for those "likely to have no convictions for which they can
honestly be mobbed." [25]

Scornful of proper Society, optimistic, belligerent yet respectable, and activist, the products of New England's Renaissance
threw themselves into the ferments of the 1880's and 1890's. They
felt particularly at home in movements where the sole issue was
a moral issue, where good will sufficed to judge right. Wendell
Phillips, who minded his wife's injunction not to "shilly-shally,"
agitated for Irish Home Rule, and with Thomas Wentworth Higginson, championed civil service and equal rights for women. A
member of the General Court at the age of fifty-eight, the Colonel backed bills to abolish the poll tax, remove the stigma from
atheist witnesses, protect public school children from reading
the Bible against their parents' wishes. A Mugwump and a free
trader, Higginson also shared honors with Edward Everett Hale
in the anti-imperialist crusade and the movement for world peace
through arbitration. Behind all of these activities lay the motto
of the author of *Ten Times One Is Ten* and *In His Name*: "Look
up and not down; look forward and not back; look out and not in;
lend a hand." [26]

The pre-Civil War reformers were also comfortable in causes
that put their personal recollection of New England's traditions
to a test. Thus when Thomas Wentworth Higginson appeared
before the General Court to back a bill providing for the municipal ownership of electric, gas, and street railway utilities, he
cited the Boston water works as a precedent. Edward Everett Hale
denounced extreme laissez faire as "un-American," such had been
the nation's experience during his own boyhood with the public
ownership of schools and libraries, roads and canals, lighthouses
and docks, the post office. He noted that, even in the private
construction of canals, railroads, and turnpikes in the first half of
the nineteenth century, the corporations that undertook their

construction did so as public agents, much in the same way as the great English chartered companies had functioned in overseas colonization. The "friends of strong government," he concluded, were therefore "acting on the lines of our best traditions." Similarly, Frank Sanborn, whose experience as a social worker had taken him into state hospitals and asylums, denounced the "chimera of non-interference by government, — the Franco-Britannic specter of *laissez-faire*, — which has been conjured up so many times to thwart wise statesmanship and a decent public policy, in the ethical relations of government." Herbert Spencer, doctrinaire in his anti-statism, was dismissed as a fanatic.[27]

In endorsing the younger generation of doers of good, certain of the older liberals were more than generous; and any fledgling progressive organization felt secure with the appearance of the names of Boston's old-timers on the masthead of its stationery. Therefore it was a triumph for the Christian Socialists when Mary A. Livermore and Abby Morton Diaz joined their ranks, and a plum for Edward Bellamy when the Reverend Dr. Hale and Colonel Higginson became members of the First Nationalist Club. Although the two men feared that complete collectivization might destroy individual liberty, they believed, in the words of Higginson, that "the tendency of events is now towards Nationalism — or State Socialism if you please," and they became, so to speak, fellow travelers, happy that the Nationalists had created a "sort of 'half-way covenant' or 'anxious seat' in their new tabernacle, for the reception of those who are not full converts, but simply looking Zion-ward." They did not stay long, but when the first issue of the *Nationalist* appeared, an obscure radical sheet of uncertain reception, it contained a poem dedicated to Edward Bellamy by Cambridge's distinguished man of letters, Colonel Higginson:

> Some day, by laws as fixed and fair
>   As guide the planets in their sweep,
> The children of each outcast heir
>   The harvest-fruits of time shall reap.

> The peasant brain shall yet be wise,
> The untamed pulse grow calm and still;
> The blind shall see, the lowly rise,
> And work in peace Time's wondrous will.[28]

Such faith as derived from mid-century optimism — and which was vindicated by the emancipation of the slaves and the success of numerous reforms — was often negated by certain of the memories that the older agitators retained of their youth. No man surpassed the moral passion of Wendell Phillips to promote progress, yet he would step back to go forward. The first of his generation to perceive the menace of concentrated wealth, he ran for governor in 1871 on a combined labor and temperance ticket. He lashed the plutocracy with the fervor he had employed against the slavocracy and asserted that only workers organized for political and economic purposes could check capital and thereby save the republic. A socialist, Boston's veteran agitator had in mind the "overthrow of the whole profit-making system" through coöperative enterprise; but a Bostonian with mid-century ideals, he yearned for a return to the Massachusetts village. His "ideal of a civilization" remained a "New England town of some two thousand inhabitants, with no rich man and no poor man in it, all mingling in the same society, every child at the same school, no poorhouse, no beggar, opportunities equal, nobody too proud to stand aloof, nobody too humble to be shut out." [29]

This longing for a day gone by was given concrete form by Edward Everett Hale in his *How They Lived at Hampton*, a utopian novel set in an overgrown Yankee village. The communitarianism of Hale was a blend of practical Christianity and the principles that had underlain the whaling industry. In the mill, labor received wages, capital interest, and management salaries, while such profits as obtained after operating costs were divided equally among the three. The factory hands strained to do their best, for they were paid by the piece, and were encouraged to buy stock in the business so as to become capitalists as well as workers. The eight-hour day prevailed, and because the wage-earner never reached the point of exhaustion that made drink necessary, Hamptonites enjoyed total abstinence. Each man owned his own home, which he purchased from the bank on easy terms, as well as his own garden to raise food for the family. This combination of self-reliance and coöperation, of independence and interdependence, Hale likened to St. Paul's concept that society is organic and depends for health on the harmonious functioning of its parts. The Reverend Doctor's predisposition to solve the social problem in the dimensions of a small community led him to believe that a clergyman assigned to every thousand persons in the city would put an end to pauperism and intemperance.[30]

Such was the tenacity to cling to mid-century concepts that philanthropy was identified with social reform. Edward Everett Hale gave up the *New England Magazine* to Edwin D. Mead, who made it a reform journal of first rank, while Hale devoted his editorial energies to *Lend a Hand*, a monthly clearinghouse for benevolent activities that merged in 1897 with the *Charities Review*.[31] Immediately after Appomattox Frank Sanborn helped organize the American Social Science Association to teach "the responsibilities of the gifted and educated classes toward the weak, the witless and the ignorant." He worked tirelessly to reclaim the pauper, the criminal, the alcoholic, and the insane, and to give "eyes to the blind, feet to the lame, voice to the dumb," and shelter to the foundling. Lecturer at Cornell University (1885), editor of the *Journal of Social Science* for thirty years (1867–1897), member of the State Board of Charities, and founder of one philanthropic institution or another, Frank Sanborn achieved distinction as the leading social worker of the day.

Active in Boston but living in Concord, whose rural character had not been destroyed by industrialization, Sanborn believed, at bottom, in self-help except for the obviously defective or degenerate. The questions raised by big labor, big business, big cities, and big government either eluded or angered or confused him. After the Haymarket Affair he wrote that there was no an-

tagonism between capital and labor but only minor grievances
between "Ownership and Exertion." He inveighed equally against
the heartlessness of the wage-fund theory and the disturbances
of the Knights of Labor. In 1894 after a trip to England, he discovered with pleasure that respectable British "gentlemen" espoused socialism, and declared that he, too, was a socialist since
he "sought . . . modifications of the existing order . . . [for]
the good of society as a whole." However, he warned against the
bureaucratic dangers of municipal socialism and mocked the
superficiality of Nationalism. In 1900, Frank Sanborn, who had
believed that gentlemen of good will could restore outcasts for
society, confessed that "a grasping and pretentious plutocracy"
and a threatening "up-rising of popular wrath" confused him as
to the way out for America, save that it must follow the moral
passion of his generation.[32]

Thomas Wentworth Higginson alone of the pre-Civil War
reformers comprehended from the outset that enthusiasm for
good would not suffice to set the urban age right. Whereas at
mid-century, faith in democracy, love for mankind, and belief in
natural rights served adequately as intellectual weapons for the
abolitionist, the post-Civil War humanitarian required a knowledge of the law, economics, sociology, and political science that
would lay bare the workings of his complex industrial culture.
This knowledge the old-timers never acquired. As Higginson
summed it up in his essay on Phillips in 1884: "you could not
settle the relations of capital and labor . . . by saying, as in the
case of slavery, 'Let my people go'; the matter was far more complex. It was like trying to adjust a chronometer with no other
knowledge than that won by observing a sundial." [33]

Yet it mattered little that the ante-bellum reformers had no
labor theory, that their philanthropy proved inadequate, that
their wish to recreate the village was unrealistic, that they scattered rather than concentrated their efforts. It was more important that they reaffirmed and transmitted to the younger generation of progressives the ideals cherished by the enlightened folk
of the New England Renaissance. Remember that "the voice of

Massachusetts . . . bade the Greek, the Mexican, the Hungarian, the Cuban, struggling for independence against odds, to take courage by our example," declared one veteran progressive. Another rebuked and broke off relations with William Jennings Bryan for such "ignorance . . . [of] American History" as to believe that "no man or party has advocated social equality between the white . . . and the black . . . The simple fact is that no man concerned in the great anti-slavery movement . . . advocated anything else." Students who asked this abolitionist how best to become expert in public speaking were told: "Enlist in a reform." [34]

With the death of Wendell Phillips in 1884 (the others survived amazingly long into the twentieth century), the younger generation of liberals had a saint as well as a religion to follow. It was suggested in 1890 that a temple of reform be built in honor of Phillips and his friends with stained glass windows and bas-reliefs to depict the scenes of their abolitionist struggles. At his memorial the old crusaders gathered with new, and on the shoulders of John Boyle O'Reilly, then in his prime as "the poet of humanity," fell the honor of paying proper poetic tribute to the prodder of Boston's conscience. O'Reilly's poem, one of his best and quoted many times, sang of Phillips' message to liberals.

> Come, workers; here was a teacher, and the lesson he taught
> was good:
> There are no classes or races, but one human brotherhood;
> There are no creeds to be outlawed, no colors of skin debarred;
> Mankind is one in its rights and wrongs — one right, one hope, one guard.
> By his life he taught, by his death we learn the great reformer's creed:
> The right to be free, and the hope to be just, and the guard against selfish greed.[85]

From such awareness there would be no severance with past ideals, as contemplated by proper Society, but continuity of Boston's will to achieve democracy.

IV

The task of proposing schemes of social reconstruction so as to achieve democracy in the urban age fell to the younger folk of the latter part of the century. Apart from Francis Greenwood Peabody and Vida D. Scudder, every youthful progressive of importance originated from outside Boston — from New England, the Middle States, the West, and from faraway Ireland, Germany, and Denmark. They came to New England's capital because they regarded it as a center of culture and liberal aspirations; Boston to them was the Mecca of the Tea Party and the *Liberator*, of Brook Farm and the Over-Soul. (Benjamin Orange Flower, for example, a Midwesterner by birth, felt compelled in his reminiscences to write about Emerson and his generation as if they had been his immediate ancestors.) [86] With the steadfastness and zeal of converts the new Bostonians kept the faith.

They started with the basic assumption that America was not living up to its ideals and then labored to square the fact with the ideal, to make promise and fulfillment one. As social critics, they singled out for attack the venal politician, the vulgar rich, the grasping monopolist, the bigoted native, the complacent citizen, the chauvinistic imperialist, and the socially indifferent minister; while they commiserated with the slum-dweller, immigrant, worker, and unfree woman. Except for feminism, which concentrated solely on the problems of the fair sex, the liberal mind isolated the canker of society in concentrated wealth, to which it traced the brothels and town houses, the bought legislatures and strikes, the Social Register and unemployment rolls, the North End and Beacon Street. As social reconstructionists (and their numbers grew from 1880 to 1900), they proposed schemes of all sorts which, however different on specific points, were alike in the attempt to wed ethics and science to make the promise of American life realizable for the masses of men.

The ethics were the rich fund of idealism in the American creed, in which, as the older reformers had demonstrated, Americans of all political shades other than the most convinced reactionaries believed. Progressives in the Hub City inherited the proposition that the nation was dedicated to extending rights and privileges to ever-widening groups of men and women. They also built on what Lord Bryce had shrewdly observed as characteristically American: "a sort of kindliness, a sense of human fellowship, a recognition of the duty of mutual help owed by man to man, stronger than anywhere in the Old World . . . "[37] They were heirs of a belief discovered by the Greeks, revived by the Renaissance, strengthened by the Enlightenment, but most widely accepted by America because it was the land of plenty and free of a feudal heritage — the dignity of the individual human being — which is the first axiom of the geometry of reform.

The science was social and, whenever it suited the purposes of the liberal, biological. All progressives of every stripe were Darwinians in the sense that they believed in progress. With Professor Strong in Henry Adams' *Esther* they asked: "If the soul of a sponge can grow up to be the soul of a Darwin, . . . may we not all grow up to abstract truth?" In Boston, the doctrine of evolution was particularly important in the climate of ideas as John Fiske, in domesticating Darwin and Spencer, taught that the sciences of nature and mankind gave unshattering proof for the doctrine of unlimited progress. Furthermore, as the evolutionary hypothesis, Biblical criticism, and the study of comparative religion cracked the supernatural structure of institutional religion, ministers were obliged to defend the Judeo-Christian heritage by applying the ethics of the Gospel to the social problem.[38]

Of particular significance, the liberals made use of political economy and sociology, terms so interchangeable in the reform mind that Marx and Comte seemed to be masters of the same discipline.[39] The name of the subject mattered not at all so long as the subject provided empirical proof to refute the deductive dogma of Manchester-Spencerian laissez faire that paralyzed human will. Such proof reached Boston through scholars who were studying government and economy as they existed and had existed and who were describing what was being done to solve the social problem. New Zealand, Australia, Great Britain, and Europe, ahead of the United States in trials of schemes of social reconstruction, were laboratories for the social scientific-minded liberal.[40] At the same time, Boston's craft unionists interpreted the laissez faire of Herbert Spencer so as to argue against the monopoly privileges of big business.

Boston's intellectual resources made it possible to assimilate and contribute to the new learning. Within its own territorial boundaries and in neighboring suburbs were Harvard, Wellesley, Radcliffe, Andover Seminary, the Cambridge Episcopal Theological School, Tufts, and Boston University. The city, state, private, and school libraries ranked with the best in the nation. Although by 1900 New York outstripped it as a publishing center, Boston was adequately represented by Houghton Mifflin, Little, Brown, Ginn and Company, D. C. Heath and Company, the Arena Publishing Company, Roberts Brothers, and many lesser houses. A number of religious journals were issued from the city, as well as secular magazines and newspapers. To Boston's thriving musical life was added the Symphony Orchestra in 1881. Its literary men and women in 1887 numbered more than twoscore, and by the end of the century the figure had not diminished. The writers of the classical age who lived in the 1880's and 1890's were reminders that there had been only one American Athens: Emerson and Longfellow lived until 1882, James Freeman Clarke and Bronson Alcott until 1888, Lowell until 1891, Whittier until 1892, Francis Parkman until 1893, and Oliver Wendell Holmes and Elizabeth Peabody until 1894. While such men as William Dean Howells left the Hub City for New York, others, for example, John Boyle O'Reilly, Frank Parsons, Solomon Schindler, Edwin D. Mead, Hamlin Garland — all reformers — were drawn to Boston because of its intellectual vitality.[41]

Out of the urban and industrial revolutions, the then contemporary science, and the promise of American life came a fresh crop of Bostonians to fashion conceptions of social reform for the machine age. The smelting pot of the common milieu made them speak the same language of rendering life more meaningful for the underprivileged. However, they also thought within distinguishable frameworks of reference of their own, which derived from their respective traditions and positions in the community of Boston. Among the earliest and most articulate of progressive leaders were the Irish Catholics, John Boyle O'Reilly and James Jeffrey Roche, who spoke for a people confronting racial and religious prejudice, intemperance, and poverty.

Chapter Two

IRISH CATHOLIC LIBERALISM
The Spirit of 1848

I will conduct the *Pilot* as becomes an Irishman, a Catholic,
and a gentleman. — John Boyle O'Reilly

The Irish blood is the gulf stream of humanity.
— Katherine Conway

Socialism is the hope of the People. — John Boyle O'Reilly [1]

In 1875 the Irish were well on the way to becoming the
most numerous element in Boston's population. As yet, however,
they remained outside the liberal traditions of the city; they were
faithful to a church that opposed the nineteenth-century rationalism and optimism upon which rested aspirations for social reform.
As a result of the revolutions of 1848 and the loss of sovereignty
over the Papal States, Pius IX (1846–1878) sought to strengthen
the Church. In 1870, a council summoned to Rome proclaimed
the dogma of Papal Infallibility. Six years earlier the Pope, in his
Syllabus of Errors, had condemned public schools, socialism,
communism, "Clerico-Liberal Societies," religious toleration, nat-
uralism, and rationalism. His concluding words in denouncing
the main streams of nineteenth-century thought were: "It is an
error to believe that the Roman Pontiff can and ought to reconcile himself to, and agree with, progress, liberalism, and contemporary civilization." [2]

Boston's Irish Catholics had anticipated Pius IX in scorn for
mid-century humanitarianism. They brought from Ireland a per-

vading pessimism and entrenched conservatism, which, in the Puritan city, drew nourishment from foul living quarters, wretched working conditions, and racial and religious prejudice. Irish journalists denounced penal reform as violating the basic law of punishing him who needed punishment, ridiculed abolitionism as "niggerology," opposed the public school movement, sneered at reform third parties, and condemned utopian socialism. For the aspirations of European subject nationalities for freedom in the years 1848–1850, they showed wavering sympathy, then hostility. Unlike the native Protestant Bostonians who believed that man could manipulate the environment to make life better, the Catholics dogmatized that human will could not and should not change the social order.[3]

By 1880 the Boston hierarchy had institutionalized time-honored practices for society's wards: philanthropic agencies for orphans, young working boys, abandoned infants, wayward girls, and the sick and the aged. These charities served the dual purpose of uplifting and keeping within the Church unfortunates who might otherwise seek relief in non-Catholic institutions. Only in caring for wayward girls did the Church attempt reform — but of an individual, not social, kind; fallen women did penance for their sin and learned a trade to support themselves honorably. The environmental determinants of prostitution were left untouched.

Concern with society's underprivileged did not once spur the Boston hierarchy to remove the social causes of underprivilege. In the age of Bessemer the clergy still clung to the dogma that economic inequalities were divinely ordained and that Christian charity kept the social organism in equilibrium. Voluntary poverty was thought a religious virtue, while involuntary poverty sprang only from disobedience of God's law. In no case were the poor poor because of defects in society. Indeed in expounding Catholic orthodoxy, a Boston priest warned reformers who wished to abolish want that they were conspiring against divine plan. "If the rich man," the Reverend Father William G. Byrne explained in 1880, "could find no poor in regard to whom he could exercise the virtue of charity by way of alms-giving, I fear it would be utterly impossible for him to enter into heaven." Equally important, a liberalism that contemplated the rearrangement of institutions was irreligiously cold. Charity, on the other hand, promoted warm, Christ-like human relations and prevented violent frictions in the body politic: "It is through . . . alms-giving on the part of the wealthy and . . . gratitude on the part of the poor, that we are saved . . . the dry rot of communism or a war of classes. . ." [4]

Rendered passive by the doctrine of Christian charity, the Archdiocese of Boston failed to send a single priest into the army of social reform, which recruited so many Protestant ministers during the period 1880–1900. The sole exceptions were those who supported the temperance movement. Here, though, there was little similarity between Catholic and non-Catholic thought, for the former opposed government enforcement, as it had done during the 1840's, while the latter hoped to either regulate or stamp out the saloon through statutory action. Characteristically, in the anti-drinking campaign, the priests stressed regeneration through individual and not collective effort. [5]

The Catholic laity took no more to social reform than men of the cloth. The politicians, whether ward bosses like Jim O'Donovan or of more distinguished rank like Hugh O'Brien, were Irish Democrats aspiring to win elections against Yankee Republicans. The handful of literary folk (Robert Dwyer Joyce, Henry Bernard Carpenter, Imogen Guiney, Mary E. Blake) wrote fables, composed verse on medieval France, and sang nostalgically of old Ireland. The mass of transplanted peasants, whose numbers increased with immigration, were mute. As for the small Irish middle class risen from immigrant status, they wished to belong to society, not to revolutionize it. Indeed because the Pope's European foes were often left of center, liberalism was readily identified with antipopery.

Such come-outism as existed was channeled into and syphoned

off by agitation against the ancestral enemy, England. In this case the Boston Irish recognized the social roots of sin and proposed serious changes in government and economy. However, while militant on home rule and land reform for Ireland, the laity was content with the philanthropy of the St. Vincent de Paul Society for Boston. Founded in 1861 and headed by Thomas F. Ring in the last quarter of the century, this organization worked on a parish level to uplift released prisoners, poor immigrants, unmarried mothers, and neglected children. All were taught industry, foresight, a trade, and the necessity of keeping the Catholic faith. In 1883, Pope Leo XIII summed up the philosophy behind such efforts in the following oral message to the Society: "Christian charity . . . unites the rich and poor by sweet bonds of holy affection." [6]

II

With different roots in the Ireland of Fenianism were two Irish-born intellectuals, John Boyle O'Reilly and James Jeffrey Roche. Inspired poets and journalists, they placed a radical stamp on American Catholic social thought which, until the strictures of orthodoxy embodied in *Rerum Novarum*, the Encyclical of 1891, compared to the come-outism of the Protestant Social Gospel.

John Boyle O'Reilly was born June 28, 1844 in Dowth Castle, County Heath, four miles above historic Drogheda on the River Boyne. His father, William David, was a schoolteacher, and his mother, Eliza Boyle, a cultured descendant of Colonel John Allen, who had served with distinction in the Napoleonic wars. John grew up learning his three R's from his father and roaming the historic countryside, where he imbibed the poetry of the old ruins and natural beauty of the region. At the age of eleven he was apprenticed to a printer in Drogheda. Four years later he joined an aunt in Preston, England, where he became a typesetter and reporter. He led a gay, carefree life until 1863, when he was moved by the Fenian drive for independence from England. He joined the British army as a cavalryman with the purpose of organizing Irish soldiers in the king's employ to overthrow English rule. Boyle O'Reilly liked the military life, especially the glamour of the uniform, and confessed to his biographer that often he would go out of his way to pass "a certain great plate-glass window, in which he could behold the dazzling proportions of himself and his steed." [7]

The plans for an Irish uprising were smashed in 1866. O'Reilly, tried and convicted for treason and sentenced to death, received a commutation to twenty years' imprisonment. For two years he rotted away alternately in Millbank, Chatham, and Dartmoor, and then was sent to Australia to serve the remainder of his term. One year after his arrival O'Reilly made a daring escape through the help of a friendly Irish-Australian priest, who arranged to have Captain Gifford, skipper of a whaler putting out from Nantucket, pick up the Fenian outside the three-mile limit. O'Reilly spent several months at sea, narrowly missed recapture, and thoroughly enjoyed the strenuous and adventurous hunt for whales, although he nearly lost his life when a "bad whale" upset a boat in which he was riding. In 1869 he arrived in Philadelphia, a free man and a hero of the Irish abortive revolution. Settled in Boston at twenty-six, he soon became the city's most influential and colorful Catholic intellectual.

Until death cut his life short in 1890, O'Reilly enjoyed every success America could confer. A reporter for the Boston *Pilot* in 1870, he became editor-in-chief and co-partner with Archbishop Williams by 1876. In New England, where poets were men of standing, O'Reilly became a poet, praised by Oliver Wendell Holmes, Colonel Thomas Wentworth Higginson, John Greenleaf Whittier, Julia Ward Howe, and called a genius by Richard Watson Gilder. To this young Irishman went the distinction of composing appropriate verse for the memorial of Wendell Phillips in 1884, the dedication of the Crispus Attucks monument in 1886, and that of Plymouth Rock in 1889, honors which ordinarily only the most proper native Protestant would have received. He wrote two novels, *Moondyne* and *The King's Men,* the latter in collaboration with Robert Grant, Frederic J. Stimson, and John T. Wheelwright; edited *Poetry and Song of Ireland;* and prefaced George Makepeace Towle's *Young People's History of Ireland,* Justin McCarthy's *Ireland's Cause and England's Parliament,* and J. Ellen Foster's *Crime Against Ireland.* Well-built and lover of the strenuous life, O'Reilly was admired as an athlete; he refereed at Harvard, boxed with the great John L. Sullivan, and canoed New England's rivers. These experiences he described in *Athletics and Manly Sport,* published in 1890. He was friendly with Wendell Phillips, Whittier, General Benjamin F. Butler, Walt Whitman, Emerson, Robert Grant, and a host of others, and was president of the famous literary Papyrus Club. O'Reilly was clearly, as one observer pointed out, "the most distinguished Irishman in America." [8]

Personal success did not render John Boyle O'Reilly less sensitive to social evils; it gave him an opportunity to use his prestige for reform. By the time he set foot on United States soil, the transplanted Irishman was already a reformer cut from the mold of nineteenth-century romanticism. His unsuccessful exploits as a revolutionary led him to believe most ardently in self-sacrifice. His experiences as a son of Erin, despised by the English for his Irishness and his Catholicism, placed him on the side of those fighting against racial and religious prejudice and for a universal humanity. British monarchy, aristocracy, and landlordism made him a foe of class exploitation and inequalities and a votary of republicanism and liberty. As a soldier, sometime whaler of four months, and cavalryman, he rejoiced in the active life. Growing up in rural Ireland, among historic and picturesque surroundings, he grew to love nature, simplicity, the outdoors, and a golden age of virtue. To these traits John Boyle O'Reilly added an emotional nature Rousseauan in its worship of the feeling rather than the thinking man. "The strength of a man," he wrote, "is in his sympathies. . . A man without sympathies . . . is an Australian flower, either over or underdeveloped, scentless — selfish as a living fire without heat for the cold hands of children." [9]

Because he was a man of sympathies John Boyle O'Reilly was a loyal son of the Roman Catholic Church. He loved its "sacrificial, devotional faith," its art, music, color, spirit, mysticism, and symbolism. He ridiculed the rationalism of Unitarianism — "this . . . religious freezing to death" — and denounced the Reverend Dr. Edward Everett Hale for denying the supernatural apostolic succession and the Reverend Dr. Minot J. Savage for humanizing the nativity. Owing to his Irish experience O'Reilly regarded Catholicism as on the side of liberty and the oppressed. This was crucial for the former Fenian — he was a passionate spokesman for the subjugated common folk. To an unidentified friend he wrote: "Put your ear down to the rich, good earth and listen to the vast gurgling blood of Humanity, and learn whither it strives to flow, and what are its barriers. Love and hope and strength, and good are all in the crowd." [10]

Through the novel, the poem, the lecture platform, and the editorial page of the *Pilot*, John Boyle O'Reilly criticized the worst evils of Western society. Because of his European birth, the universality of his church, and his constant preoccupation with English imperialism and Irish discontent, he regarded humanity, not just America, as his proper concern. Indeed, Katherine Conway noted that Boyle O'Reilly wrote his best poetry on man in the abstract, rather than on a single man or national group.[11]

Boyle O'Reilly's verse records the making of a social critic. Where his first volume of poems, published in 1873, sang romantically of whales, storms, Australian aborigines, and rural Ireland, his second and third volumes, which came out in 1881 and 1886, rang with stanzas of social significance. The Paris Commune, the Russian Nihilists, the Irish peasant anti-rent demonstrations, the Pittsburgh riots, English imperialism, racial prejudice — these provoked the ex-Fenian to accuse the rich of exploiting and then consoling the poor with the promise of heaven. In the "City Streets," he protested against the shameful contrast of the elegant town house and the squalid slum tenement; and in "From the Earth a Cry," his lyrical heart went out to the death-tired men of "mines and mills," to the beastlike peasant, to the "Pale-faced girls and women with ragged and hard-eyed children." With a love for the common clay reminiscent of Walt Whitman, but with a venom traceable to Fenianism, the Irish poet exclaimed: "The bluest blood is putrid blood . . . the people's blood is red!" [12]

Such was his rejection of the principles behind Christian charity that he uttered

> A cry to the toilers to rise, to be high as the highest that rules them,
> To own the earth in their lifetime and hand it down to their children!

And such was his antagonism toward "Emperors . . . Chancellors . . . Landlords . . . Lawlords . . . Tradelords" that he warned them that unless they changed their ways

> . . . The crust on the crater beneath you
> Shall crack and crumble and sink with your laws and rules
> That breed the million to toil for the luxury of the ten —
> That grind the rent from the tiller's blood for drones to spend — [13]

These exhortations and threats derived not only from the revolutionary's Irish past but from his comprehension of the meaning of America and Christianity. In "Promethus-Christ," he asserted that the Nazarene loved the lowly, and that to be Christ-like, men must create a society that would be just, merciful, honest, and free. At Plymouth Rock, he recited that the Pilgrim fathers, who "fled from feudal lords," would be betrayed were we to "retrograde To lucre-lords and hierarchs of trade." Crispus Attucks, the Negro who fell in the Boston Massacre, knew that America must be independent; and Wendell Phillips, who preached fraternity, also taught that

> It is not enough to win rights from a king and write them down in a book.

New men, new lights; and the father's codes may never brook.
What is liberty now were license then: their freedom our
    yoke would be;
Each new decade must have men to determine its liberty.[14]

Apart from imploring college men to restore to mankind the rights enjoyed in a state of nature, O'Reilly's verse contained no program for reform. His poems were a vehicle for criticism, for the Irish man of letters thought that poetry should be "the soul cry of a race" — the protest of humanity against social sins. These sins were cloaked in generalities because the former Fenian believed that it was a function of poetic greatness, such as the greatness of the Irish, to deal in generalities rather than facts. For the Anglo-Saxon, who could handle only facts, O'Reilly had contempt.[15] But in Boyle O'Reilly's novels and editorials in the Boston *Pilot* one finds concrete indictments of concrete evils and, except where the official Catholic position made him ambivalent, concrete solutions.

Boyle O'Reilly's first novel, *Moondyne: A Story from the Underworld*, published in 1879, was dedicated "To all who are in prison for whatever cause." It is the tale of an escaped British convict who had been sent to jail for stealing in time of hunger (the author considered this stealing rightful). Under an assumed name the hero amasses a fortune in Australia and, with the aid and admiration of Queen Victoria and the British Parliament, reforms the penal systems of India and Australia. Several passages in the novel are hackneyed. O'Reilly reads character by the "ugly sneer in the muscles of the nose," his women are tender, pure, and long-suffering, his men either desperate curs or stout manly souls. The book, whatever its literary defects, reveals the author to be a social reformer intent on rearranging society to conform to God's immutable laws of justice, not to man-made unjust ones.

The basic assumption in *Moondyne* is that man is inherently good — indeed capable of perfection — and that the proper environment can bring out the best in him. O'Reilly's hero revamps the British penal system to re-educate hardened criminals to take

their places in society as productive citizens. Prisons, the former
Fenian wrote, are "meant for reformation not for vengeance."
O'Reilly's most radical suggestion for penal reform — and here he
opposed orthodox Catholic doctrine — was to eliminate poverty,
which, he asserted, produced crime and therefore the need for
prisons. This he would achieve "by burning the law books" and
"by burning the title deeds." By this he meant that Great Britain
revolutionize its economy by the purchase of uncultivated lands
of the aristocracy and the distribution of them for the purpose of
creating a nation of small and prosperous farmers. He took special pains to point out that religion and charity among the rich
could not and should not solve the British social problem. Directly
contradicting Catholic orthodoxy he wrote:

> Charity among the rich simply means the propriety of the
> poor being miserable — that poverty is unfortunate, but not
> wrong. But God never meant to send the majority of mankind
> into existence to exercise the charity and the religion of the
> minority. He sent them all into the world to be happy and
> virtuous, if not equal; and men have generated their evils by
> their own blind and selfish rules.[16]

Five years later, in *The King's Men: A Tale of Tomorrow*, John
Boyle O'Reilly wrote another radical novel. The story concerns
the struggle for power between radical, liberal, and reactionary
groups in an England of the future. In 1889 the people in Great
Britain — finally enraged by "the shameful monopoly of land, the
social haughtiness of the titled classes, the luxury and profligacy
of the court" — elected a Parliament which immediately confis-
cated the estates of the aristocracy and King Albert. The latter
was given a salary and served as a figurehead, until the elector-
ate decided on a republic twenty years later. Donovan O'Rourke
was elected the first president.

After him came undefined "demagogues" who led the country
into ruin and who were opposed by former royalists plotting
counterrevolution. In the 1940's George V, Albert's son and pre-
tender to the throne — brutally satirized as fat, ludicrous, cow-

ardly, and lascivious — kept a threadbare court in a South End
hotel in Boston waiting for an opportunity to return to power.
The problem was to steer a middle course between the leftism of
Bugshaw ("a woman hater as well as an atheist") and the royal-
ism of Sir John Dacre. Richard Lincoln, "a liberal," arranges a
coalition of well-meaning former nobles and responsible com-
moners and establishes republicanism on a firm basis. This theme
of reconciliation is summed up in the concluding lines of the
novel, when John Dacre, leader of the royalist faction, and Mary
Lincoln, daughter of the leader of the liberal group, are buried
side by side in a cemetery. "I tried to think of it as a symbol of
what is to be . . . theirs is the first alliance in the reconciliation
of the few and the many on which the hopes of posterity depend." [17]

The social criticism and specific proposals for reform in *Moondyne* and *The King's Men* applied only to Great Britain and were
therefore anachronistic for an America which had neither monarchy nor hereditary aristocracy. An American critic and crusader
had to contend with the problems of urbanization and industrialization. These problems the former Irish revolutionist attempted
to solve in his capacity as editor of the Boston *Pilot*. Their solution was particularly urgent to O'Reilly because he was, as Count
Plunkett explained, a self-appointed spokesman for the Irish peasants who "swarmed from the West of Ireland directly to Boston
. . . penned in, as in a Ghetto." [18]

America, according to the editor of the *Pilot*, was part of world
history. In the past, under feudalism, kings and nobles had oppressed the people. The industrial revolution shattered feudal
society, only to create "a new monster, even more terrible, more
selfish, more insatiable and more powerful." In the name of progress and the religion of laissez faire, capitalists drove the workers
to produce more and more without regard to their living and
working conditions. By the middle of the 1880's O'Reilly had
come to believe that the United States in this respect was little
different from Europe.

The king, the noble, the aristocrat have yielded to the railroad magnates, the great incorporated owners of mines and mills and factories, the speculating capitalists. The law of the monarch's will is substituted by the law of the bribed legislature. The people are ever the prey, ever the dazed workers in the valley, the voiceless ones. There is no change, except in the masters.[19]

Boyle O'Reilly's analysis of the labor problem, which he regarded as the central problem of capitalism, was socialist in spirit and source. Of Karl Marx he wrote: "no socialist reasoned closer. . ." In an obituary on the author of *Das Kapital*, the editor of the Catholic *Pilot* stated that Marx was correct in his labor theory of value and in his view that machinery conferred benefits only on capitalists, never on workers. In a review of W. H. Mallock's novel, *The Old Order Changes*, O'Reilly quoted approvingly the socialism of the following line: "capital is simply the thief's name for accumulated labor." Bellamy's *Looking Backward*, because it portrayed the exploitation of the wage-earner, led the crusading editor to proclaim it the " 'Uncle Tom's Cabin' of the industrial slavery of today." In an editorial on a strike in Lowell in 1884 the journalist asked: "How long . . . will the very many who toil consent to accept the terms of their labor from the very few who reap all the profits of toil?" [20]

In his defense of labor, O'Reilly attacked big business. He ridiculed Mrs. Leland Stanford for buying a $100,000 necklace, called Vanderbilt and Gould "financial corsairs," denounced the telegraph and telephone monopolists for high rates, reprobated Congress for giving lavish land grants to railroads, and heaped calumny upon calumny on the Pinkertons and their plutocratic employers. During the Chicago meat strike of 1886, the editor of the *Pilot* wrote: "There is something worse than Anarchy, bad as that is; and it is irresponsible power in the hands of mere wealth." At the same time that O'Reilly contributed to the stereotype of the bloated capitalist, he fought the stereotype of the vulgar worker. In two vigorous editorials he criticized such a portrayal of labor in John Hay's *The Bread-Winners,* and lamented that one who had been so close to Lincoln could look down on the poor. As for the Social Darwinist rationalization that poverty was the inevitable lot of the unfit and prosperity the natural fruit of the fit, O'Reilly retorted that the latter were only more "adroit, selfish, bold, avaricious, hard, unscrupulous — and in many cases dishonest, cruel and villainous." The former revolutionist warned the Spencerians that, if they persisted in their "unchristian science of the day," the workers would rise up and "cast off the restraint of law and religion as devices of the enemy, and prove themselves fittest to survive by crushing the logic choppers." [21]

The dissatisfaction of the American worker, as well as the British peasant, Boyle O'Reilly contended, could never "be removed by the organized charity of a section of the wealthy classes." Thus he objected to a North End workingmen's center. The former Fenian agreed that the center would combat the saloon, and thought well of the plan to provide loans at generous rates of interest. However, this philanthropic institution, like all others, either overlooked or assented to the inequity of gross disparities in wealth. The average laborer "knows that God made the world as much for him" as for capitalists, and he will no longer make the "profit-taker rich . . . while he and his children live meanly. . ." If the well-meaning rich persist in charity and ignore the possibilities of a "larger equity," O'Reilly warned, "the social congestion . . . growing worse every year . . . will end in inflammations." [22]

The "larger equity" was socialism. However, the Vatican's condemnation of that system made O'Reilly blow hot and cold on its customary forms. He agreed with Father Hecker's statement that right-thinking and well-meaning persons should be socialists but that Catholics ought to follow the ethics of their church. He disapproved of Marx's godlessness and of the atheism of his continental followers, yet at one point at least concurred with the British Marxist, Hyndman, that England could and should have a communist revolution. He admired Bellamy's vision of utopia,

thought well of his ideal of industrial coöperation, yet denounced
Nationalism as "paternalism run mad" with the state as "universal
teacher, employer, landlord and provider." Despite this mass of
tergiversation O'Reilly stated that "Socialism is the hope of the
People." However,

> To this world movement, (socialism), there is only one safe-
> guard, the Catholic Church . . . for the revolution must be
> spiritual as well as intellectual. . . How deep the crime of
> those who have made the word synonymous with Atheism
> and disorder. The shallow reasoners of Europe who have dis-
> associated Socialism and Religion have committed an almost
> unpardonable sin. With the deepest equities underlying social
> order, the Catholic church must always be in the deepest
> sympathy.[23]

O'Reilly's fear of big government poses the problem of what
he meant by socialism. Shortly before his death he summed up his
political creed in an editorial in the *Pilot* in which he claimed
that he was a votary of "Jeffersonian Democracy." He opposed
centralization and believed, as he thought Jefferson had believed,
in "the least government for the people." [24] O'Reilly distrusted
the state because, as a Catholic, he feared secular encroachment
on religious areas. Moreover, he had suffered under alien rule
from Westminster, and had seen the Yankee Massachusetts legislature deprive the Boston politicians of his nativity from appoint-
ing policemen (act of 1885). Caught between his loyalties to his
church and countrymen, on the one hand, and his understanding
that statutory action was essential to curb capital and promote
the interests of labor, on the other, O'Reilly never quite made up
his mind where he stood with regard to the social welfare state.

Labor, he thought, should unite and improve conditions of life
and work through self-help and legislation. He admired T. V.
Powderly, joined forces with the liberal wing of the hierarchy in
defense of the Knights of Labor, and rejoiced when Cardinal
Gibbons prevailed upon the Pope not to declare the Knights
anathema. A unified trade unionism, he prophesied, would "de-

stroy the merciless law of supply and demand. . ." Because capital controlled the court and the legislature, O'Reilly urged the
arbitration of workers' grievances. However, he also favored the
strike and was encouraged by the success of Knights' strikes of
1885 and 1886. He urged his unskilled countrymen, who crowded
into America's worst slums, to settle on the prairies. The eight-
hour day movement, as well as the need for legislation outlawing
alien contract labor and protecting women and children, met with
his approval. When T. V. Powderly proposed workers' producer
coöperatives, O'Reilly wrote: "'A plan for coöperation through
which the workingman may control the machine he operates must
one day supersede the present system.'" [25]

The special labor correspondent for the *Pilot*, who signed himself Phineas, muckraked as vehemently as O'Reilly, but was more
radical in proposing direct political action as a solution for the
social problem. His columns preached class consciousness and,
in some instances, class hatred; labor's "interests and the interests
of the capitalistic class," he insisted, "are antagonistic." When
William Graham Sumner, America's leading champion of Spencerian sociology, declared trade unions unnecessary, Phineas retorted that Sumner was but the "social attorney" for "New England factory lords." "The Irrepressible Conflict" between the
slaves and masters of capitalism could be resolved only when
labor formed a third party. The plutocracy, Phineas explained,
has the church, the press, and the two major political parties on
its side, and thus controls the government. A workers' party would
be sure to win, since it could count on two-thirds of the vote.
The radical columnist did not specify what the new party should
stand for, but wrote vaguely that it could prepare the country
for a "social reformation" by demanding that the government
consider the wretched conditions of the wage-earner. On one
occasion he called for legislation for accident insurance and the
eight-hour day, and laws against speculation in land and against
property qualifications for the franchise.[26]

From time to time O'Reilly urged Washington to regulate big

business. In 1880 he appealed for a federal law to prevent speculation in grain. During the telegraph strike of 1883 he proposed
government ownership of the telegraph to free the nation from
the "insolent despotism" of Jay Gould. He approved the passage
of the Interstate Commerce Act. The use of Pinkertons in a Pennsylvania coal strike of 1888 angered him enough so that he demanded the nationalization of mines. During the Haymarket
Affair O'Reilly denounced the anarchists, but asserted that Pinker-
ton aggressiveness had provoked them, and warned workers
against solving the problem of vested wealth through violence.
In 1888 the editor of the *Pilot* confessed that, if the trusts continued to grow in number and size and greed, he would consent
to the paternalism of nationalization rather than allow the nation
to fall prey to "insatiable monopoly." [27]

The two major political parties being little more than contend-
ers for power and patronage, it was necessary to realize reform
through a third party. This O'Reilly was loath to do; he was an
unswerving Democrat. His devotion to the Democratic Party derived from his belief that it was the party of the masses, whereas
the Republican Party was that of the classes, and, even worse,
the inheritor of the anti-Irish and anti-Catholic prejudice of
Know-Nothingism. In city, state, and national elections, he urged
the readers of the *Pilot* to vote *en masse* for Democratic nominees,
although he had the very awkward task of explaining away Cleveland's anti-parochial school bias. When Benjamin F. Butler, the
idol of the Irish in Massachusetts, bolted the Democratic Party
and ran for President in 1884 on the Greenback and Anti-Monop-
oly ticket, the Irish editor warned his people that a vote for the
General would be a vote lost to Cleveland and hence one for
Blaine, the leader of the anti-Irish party. Yet O'Reilly admired
Butler to the point of idolatry and approved his platform: ally-
ing small businessmen, farmers, and workers to prevent the granting of public lands to corporations, and to achieve the direct election of senators, a graduated income tax, and the regulation of
big business.[28]

Toward Henry George's third party Boyle O'Reilly showed sympathy, then hostility. Although he never became a Single-Taxer, the former Irish revolutionist admired the California crusader more than any other reformer. Hailing him as "a great man," he scolded a critic for not including him in a list of forty literary immortals. O'Reilly sided with George when the latter wrote a polemic against an Englishman who had criticized *Progress and Poverty*, and favorably reviewed George's *Social Problems*, which exposed America's unfair concentration of wealth. He agreed with George "that the fruits of labor belonged first to labor," and that the poor should not stay poor and be given "the prospect of heaven to console them." [29]

In the opening months of New York's mayoralty campaign of 1886, O'Reilly supported George against Abram Hewitt and Theodore Roosevelt. He interpreted the contest as one between honest labor and crooked Wall Street; George, if victor, would give "fair play and democracy," although O'Reilly doubted and seemed happy that he would not be able to carry out his "equitable social principles." The Californian's defeat O'Reilly attributed to the "money-class," which wickedly (he never stated just how) swung the election in its favor. The ardor of the Catholic journalist cooled to hostility when Father McGlynn, the New York priest who had campaigned actively and openly for George, was suspended and excommunicated by Archbishop Corrigan, and then refused to appear in Rome when summoned. O'Reilly editorialized that the priest submit to his superior, for Archbishop Corrigan had episcopal authority in the Church which " 'is the guardian of God's unchanging truths. . .' " He rebuked George when George scolded Corrigan. As time went on, the editor of the *Pilot* attacked the land reformer's social theories; he asserted that George wanted to confiscate property without compensation (O'Reilly had done the same thing in *The King's Men*), and stated that the Single-Tax would leave nonagricultural monopolists and speculators free to wax rich. On February 18, 1888 O'Reilly concluded that McGlynn should have stayed in his pulpit and George with his books instead of venturing into "the marshy wilderness of practical politics." [30]

While his Irish and Catholic loyalties made him equivocate on the social problem and direct political action, those same loyalties made O'Reilly unequivocal in denouncing racism. He came to America when some natives were beginning to lose faith in the melting pot. Where Emerson had philosophized that America would forge a new culture and a new race out of the diverse stocks flocking to these shores, the would-be creators of a new nationality asserted that ours was a fixed Anglo-Saxon culture into which only Northern European Protestants might fit. This attitude was little different from what O'Reilly had struggled against as a Fenian, and the fact that he found its American supporters to be of English parentage convinced and infuriated him the more that it was almost a fixed element in the English personality.[31]

The former Irish Fenian became the champion of the Negro. A true romantic, he loved the freedmen for their gaiety, music, dancing ability, unquestioning religious faith, and closeness to a former natural life. He criticized Edward Grady, editor of the *Atlantic Constitution,* for believing that the Negro was congenitally inferior to the whites. He urged Negroes to vote only for those who would win economic and political rights for them. He defended Cadet Whittaker when he was dismissed from West Point, rejoiced when a Negro policeman was appointed in New York in 1883, and hailed Governor Butler's nomination of George L. Ruffin to a judgeship in Charlestown. He looked upon unchurched Negroes as potential Catholics, noted with pride that the Catholic church made no distinction as to race or nationality, and hoped that Negroes would one day intermarry with whites and thus be smelted down in the American tradition.[32]

Anti-Semitism, such as it existed, also aroused Boyle O'Reilly. There was very little in Boston and America, and the Irish editor had to look for it to fight against it. He wrote impassioned editorials against Jew-baiting when it appeared in violent form in

Russia, Germany, and Austria. *The Jew,* an obscene book written by Telemaque T. Timayenis, a teacher of Greek at Harvard, angered O'Reilly to white heat. When the editor of the *American Hebrew* objected to what he considered to be an anti-Semitic passage in Howells' *Silas Lapham,* O'Reilly agreed with Howells that the remark was not intended to be anti-Semitic, but also agreed with the editor and Howells that it should be deleted in future editions so that it would not be misunderstood. When a Mrs. Jacoby was refused admission to a Staten Island hotel, O'Reilly criticized that resort. For all his ardor against anti-Semitism, however, the former Fenian had to confess that "there is no wide spread anti-Semitic feeling in this country, while there is anti-Catholic. . . "[33]

At the beginning of the 1880's the Irish Catholics were still not welcomed by native Boston. Between the sons of the Puritans and the sons of Erin there were numerous conflicts which reflected the division between the two: the refusal of state aid to Catholic charities, the presence of Protestant chaplains in state institutions, and the inspection of parochial schools by public officials. As late as 1880 the Irish could lament that no politician of their nativity had been elected congressman from, or mayor of, Boston. Throughout the eighties organized nativism was sparked by British Americans, Protestant Irishmen, and Fundamentalist ministers. Boston's papers carried such advertisements as "WANTED — Young ladies of Anglo-Saxon parentage." On occasions passions ran so high that Boyle O'Reilly received obscene letters of which the following is representative.

> John Boyle O'Reilly: — The following is a sentence that is as true as you are a mick: Rum, Romanism, and Rebellion. Eat it, swallow it, but it is going to live. Hoping the day is not far off when you and your broilers will be boiled in hell. Hurrah for the Queen. Damn the Irish.[34]

Against the cult of Anglo-Saxonism and the worship of English blood O'Reilly waged relentless war. He pointed out that there never was an Anglo-Saxon in the past, that properly speaking

England had been invaded by the Angles, Saxons, and Jutes; furthermore the product was barbarous, selfish, nonartistic. He acidly editorialized against Henry James, the "dirty bird" who preferred English aristocracy to American democracy. For the Northern Irish in America who distinguished themselves from Southern kinsfolk by calling themselves Scotch-Irish, he had the contempt reserved only for renegades. America, the Fenian asserted, was diverse in its ethnic sources, not homogeneous, and must return to original principles: "We are gathering and boiling down here all the best blood of Europe — the blood of the people. Not to build up an Anglo-Saxon or any other petty community, but to make the greatest and the strongest manhood that God ever smiled upon." [35]

By 1890, as a result of O'Reilly's unflinching war against racism and his own appealing personality, the cleavage between Irish Catholic and Yankee Puritan in Boston had become less pronounced. At a memorial service for the Irish Fenian, reformers of the Hub City gathered to pay him homage. Thomas Wentworth Higginson, the abolitionist who knew the meaning of racial democracy, eulogized that O'Reilly had "chiefly a mission of love and reconciliation," particularly "the reconciliation in this community between the Roman Catholic Irishman and the Protestant American." [36]

"In some ways, Boyle O'Reilly was not enough of a reformer for me," explained Thomas Wentworth Higginson. Therein lies the key to the Irish Fenian's place in American liberalism; he was a radical among Catholics and a moderate among non-Catholics. O'Reilly condemned monarchy at a time when the Pope defended it; he was a stanch advocate of religious toleration when the Vatican opposed it; he supported the Knights of Labor when such officials as Archbishop Corrigan and others denounced it; he had contempt for Christian charity when orthodox Catholics asserted that it was the only remedy for the social question. He reversed the Boston *Pilot*'s policy of ignoring secular literature by reviewing, oftentimes favorably and in full editorials, the works of such reformers as Prince Kropotkin, Karl Marx, Edward Bellamy, Laurence Gronlund, Henry George, and many others.[37]

Although O'Reilly believed that literature should be socially significant he refused to identify himself with the schools of realistic fiction then developing in Europe and America. Indeed he was sometimes hostile to them. He spoke unkindly of Ibsen, was indifferent to Howells, patronizing to Garland, and repelled by Zola. Once he remarked that literature, if captured by the realists, would become "as exciting as a market review." On the question of woman suffrage he parted from fellow Boston reformers by insisting that the woman's place was in the home. He was a socialist but never worked actively with the Nationalists or the Society of Christian Socialists, as did other Bostonians who believed in socialism. In 1890, when progressives wrote systematically on the social welfare state, O'Reilly declared himself a 1790 Jeffersonian.[38]

However, to his successor, James Jeffrey Roche, he willed a valuable legacy: criticism of the worst effects of urbanization and industrialization; an unequivocal rejection of Christian charity; a demand for a racial democracy in the tradition of Emerson's smelting pot; the need for an equitable solution for the labor problem; and the dream of a nonmaterialistic culture founded on the principles of Jesus Christ. For O'Reilly this was Christian socialism — the only kind that one as Irish and as Catholic as he could accept.

III

James Jeffrey Roche was born May 31, 1847, in Mountmellick, Queens County, Ireland. When he was quite young his parents emigrated to Prince Edward Island, where his father taught school. James was first educated by his father and then entered and received a degree from St. Dunstan's College. He came to Boston in 1866 and, attracting the attention of John Boyle O'Reilly, joined the staff of the *Pilot*. By 1883 he had risen to the position of assistant editor; and on the death of his friend and ad-

viser seven years later, succeeded to the editorship and became
the leading spokesman of Boston's Catholic intellectuals. Like
O'Reilly he was honored with the presidency of the St. Botolph
and Papyrus literary clubs.[39]

To John Boyle O'Reilly, James Jeffrey Roche dedicated his first
volume of verse, *Songs and Satires*, published in 1887. In "Netchaieff" he wrote sympathetically of Russian Nihilism. Netchaieff
was a Russian Nihilist who had been imprisoned by the Czar.
Denied pen and ink he let one of his nails grow until it was long
enough to use as a pen. With his blood he then wrote his story
of suffering in the margins of a book. His tale was smuggled out
of prison and published. Although the Pope had denounced the
Narodniki, Roche was clearly, like his good friend, Boyle O'Reilly,
on the side of the Russian revolutionary and against the Czar.

In "The People," Roche was frank in developing the surplus
theory of value. The workers — the "hewers and delvers," the
"common clods and the rabble" — labor for their exploiters who
give them little recompense. The masses, cried the poet, long for
a change.

> We want the drones to be driven away from our golden
>   horde;
> We want to share in the harvest; we want to sit at the board;
> We want what word or suffrage has never yet won for man, —
> The fruits of his toil God promised when the curse of toil
>   began.

Christ, he continued, laid down His life to save humanity in the
here and now, to make possible the "kingdom . . . of the Lord."
Whether under monarchy, republicanism, or aristocracy, the
workers' lot had been poverty and hunger. To the oppressors the
poet issued a warning striking similar to that which Edwin Markham would later issue.

> Ye have shorn and bound Samson and robbed him of learn-
>   ing's light;
> But his sluggish brain is moving, his sinews have all their
>   might.

Look well to your gates of Gaza, your privilege, pride, and
caste!
The giant is blind in thinking, and his locks are growing fast.

Roche had no solution for the labor problem but, as the Catholic
critic Walter Lecky pointed out, left the reader to determine how
to right the evil.[40]

The Catholic Church, the Democratic Party, and John Boyle
O'Reilly were James Jeffrey Roche's guiding spirits in running the
Pilot. Like OReilly, he frowned on third party reformers and
therefore criticized the Populists. They were right, he said, in denouncing corporate rule but their platform was made up of
"'crank' resolutions." However, when William Jennings Bryan
and the Silverites of the Democratic Party took over the platform of the People's Party in 1896 and 1900, James Jeffrey Roche
turned the *Pilot* into an organ for Bryan. In both elections, although Roche regarded silver as financially unwise, he wrote
that the issue was "the classes . . . against the masses," to realize
the "emancipation of the people from the rule of money bags,
from the dictation of Wall Street." McKinley's victory in 1896
Roche interpreted as "triumph for gold, of gold, by gold"; in 1900
the "Dollar beats the Man." [41]

Roche's apprenticeship under O'Reilly is clearly seen in his attitude toward racism. He objected to a proposed Virginia bill to
revive the whipping post as punishment for Negro offenders. Discrimination against the Irish had declined in the 1890's but the
editor of the *Pilot* did not overlook the fact that Boston's banks
refused to hire Irish clerks. He opposed the Lodge literacy test of
1897, which was intended to restrict immigration from Eastern
Europe and Catholic countries, because he thought it was anti-
Semitic and anti-Irish. He campaigned against American imperialism on the grounds that it was undemocratic for one nation
to rule another, and feared that his adopted country would form
an alliance with the arch-enemy, England.[42]

The Boston *Pilot* continued throughout the 1890's to support
the cause of labor against capital. The editor called for a law out-

lawing the Pinkertons, "the mercenaries . . . of arrogant capital
. . ." During the Homestead Strike, when management defended
its lockout by saying that under the doctrine of freedom of contract the workers could go elsewhere, Roche retorted that because
of their poverty the workers were immobilized. During a strike in
Lattimore, Pennsylvania, in 1897, he opposed the use of the injunction. Like O'Reilly he supported the eight-hour day movement. He also muckraked against the "coal combine . . . sugar
syndicate . . . oil ring . . . other irresponsible monopolies." [43]

Like his predecessor, Roche favored government ownership at
times. In an editorial of 1897, he came out for the municipalization of public services. He noted that critics of American government had proved that Birmingham was the best governed city in
the world because it owned and managed basic utilities. Roche
agreed, although it was hard to do so, Birmingham being an
English city, and urged Boston to follow the lead of that metropolis. The Hub could reduce rents through public housing, lower
interest rates through generous government loans, and eliminate
the capitalists who fixed legislators and manipulated stocks and
profited from public franchises.[44]

On June 13, 1891, the *Pilot's* special correspondent in Rome
wrote that "Leo XIII has chosen this fateful hour to teach the
world's contending forces the social gospel." That same day Roche
devoted a special supplement to *Rerum Novarum*, editorializing
that it was the "greatest utterance of the Statesman Pope . . ."
On the surface the encyclical was a radical document. The Bishop
of Rome denounced Manchester economics and predatory capitalists as unchristian, while sanctioning government legislation to
prevent excessively long hours, low wages, and foul working conditions. He encouraged the formation of Catholic trade unions
without disapproving entirely of non-Catholic labor organizations.
However, Leo XIII made it unmistakably clear that the primary
purpose of life was salvation in the hereafter, and that the toiling
masses could hope for no permanent resolution of the social problem since man must toil in pain as punishment for original sin.

Nor could one tinker with divine plan. Because private property was ordained by God, state socialism was therefore ungodly. Workers, the Pope commanded, must practice thrift so as to accumulate property; and the rich, as the stewards of God's wealth, should attain to the Christian virtue of charity.[45]

With these axioms and their deduced conclusions Boston's leading Catholic weekly did not take issue. Indeed Roche retracted his own as well as O'Reilly's root ideas. Whereas "The People" and *The King's Men* foresaw a rough kind of economic equality, the *Pilot* was forced, after 1891, to note: "it is vain to hope that while sin and its consequences remain in the world poverty can ever be legislated out of existence." In the 1880's Roche and O'Reilly had described the Son of God as a reformer; after *Rerum Novarum* "the worker . . . [was told] to remember that the Divine Christ chose to labor with his hands during the days of His earthly life, and to be a Man of Sorrows and acquainted with infirmity." Prayers, patience, faith — these the laborer would "need while time endures" for his "material advancement" and for "the most effective checking of the monopolist in land or other material possession." All this, the *Pilot* rejoiced, "the great Leo XIII pointed out in his Encyclical on Labor . . ."[46]

Retracted, too, was the labor theory of value, which had lain at the heart of O'Reilly's social criticism and his championing of the producer coöperatives proposed by the Knights of Labor. In an editorial review of M. D. Cronin's "The Economic Aspects of Socialism," Roche wrote: "Karl Marx . . . insists on labor as the source and standard of economic value in the world, whereas the practical experience of life forces upon us the fact that not labor but the utility of its products is the source of value." Just before the close of the century, the editor of the *Pilot* declared that there was to be no final solution for the industrial problem, coöperatives or otherwise. Heaven was finality, life but a "way-station." Let the proletariat wisely learn a trade, be thrifty, and gladden their hearts and enrich their minds with literature, music, poetry.[47]

Christian charity, which Boyle O'Reilly had regarded as both an opiate and a symptom of social disease, was recommended in accordance with *Rerum Novarum* as a God-given medication. The "obnoxious traits of the poor . . . are deliberately chosen for them," it was explained, so that the rich will overcome their repulsion for the poor and, through Christian sacrifice, uplift them. Some twenty years after John Boyle O'Reilly had flaunted the personalistic philosophy behind Boston's philanthropies, Roche glowed over the activities and purpose of the St. Vincent de Paul Society. Alms-giving, he triumphed, brings out the best in the haves and prevents the have-nots from embracing an "irreligious and destructive socialism." [48]

Roche's excursions into imaginative literature during the 1890's show a like retreat. His novel, *Her Majesty the King, a Romance of the Harem*, published in 1899, was a gentle satire against monarchy. The story is laid in the East, and Roche scoffs, rather than bristles as O'Reilly did, at kings and kingcraft. His *Ballads of Blue Water and Other Poems* (1895) and *The V-a-s-e and Other Bric-a-Brac* (1900) contain only subjective poetry. However, the editor of the *Pilot* defended Edwin Markham's "The Man with the Hoe" against the attacks of that "eager Hessian of the stock jobber and capitalist, the *New York Sun* . . ." [49] Roche's anger was in keeping with *Rerum Novarum*, which denounced irresponsible capitalists for promoting *needless* misery.

Catholic thought in Boston had come nearly a full cycle. Roche, under the influence of the Pope's Encyclical on Labor, reversed O'Reilly's and his own radical assumptions to return to the passive doctrines which flowed from the doctrine of Christian charity. However, the *Pilot*, while easing up on the labor question, became more aggressive politically as the party of its allegiance, the Democracy, became more aggressive. Thus in 1900 the *Pilot's* editor preached the moderation of Rome, and at the same time, thundered with Bryan against the trusts, the blacklist, the injunction, imperialism, and for the direct election of senators, a graduated income tax, and labor arbitration.[50] Roche found no difficulty in following the Bishop of Rome and the fundamentalist from Nebraska; for *Rerum Novarum*, while warning against a final secular outcome for history, spoke out strongly against predatory capitalism and for government legislation. If the wage-earner could not hope to achieve utopia in this world, he was nevertheless encouraged to deflate the bloated capitalist. Boston's leading Catholic weekly played this theme without variation throughout the 1890's, thereby preparing its readers for the progressivism of the Democratic Party of the twentieth century.

IV

Victims of prejudice, the Irish made a significant contribution to the liberalism of the 1880's and 1890's in expounding the principles of racial and religious democracy. The *Pilot* attacked the myth of Anglo-Saxon superiority and spoke out against the maltreatment of Negroes, Jews, and Catholics. At a time when such poets as Thomas Bailey Aldrich sang in racist tones, John Boyle O'Reilly's verse reminded Americans of their heritage of the melting pot. In this context, Katherine Conway's boast that the "Irish blood is the gulf stream of humanity" has meaning. Yet, however much he sympathized with oppressed peoples, O'Reilly opposed the feminist movement, which, like his own idealism, purported to make American life just for everyone irrespective of birth. The Catholic part of his Irish background thus set limits to his progressivism.

In confronting economic problems, John Boyle O'Reilly and James Jeffrey Roche sidestepped and backstepped to keep in line with policy made in Rome. Shortly before he died, O'Reilly was working on a manuscript on the American social problem, which subsequently has been lost. One wonders whether the Irish revolutionist would have proposed reforms as drastic as those he presented in *The King's Men*; for he had been uncompromisingly radical as regards England but moderate with respect to the United States. Nothing in the experience of the Irish in Boston encouraged him toward radicalism. The poets of his day were indifferent; the politicians cared only for the ballot box; Archbishop Williams was not known to have any marked social views; no younger priest stepped forth like New York's Father Edward McGlynn; and the mass of transplanted peasants were the prey of opportunistic ward bosses.

If the Irish uprisings of 1848 and 1865 were part of the same revolution, then John Boyle O'Reilly, the dashing cavalryman who plotted against the King of England, was the most prominent Celtic Forty-Eighter to come to these shores. Like most of the Forty-Eighters, he was a romantic, full of feeling, proud of his emotions, unashamed to proclaim his allegiance to such abstractions as truth, beauty, goodness, justice, manliness, virtue. He imparted his idealism to James Jeffrey Roche, and together they placed the romantic husk of Irish Fenianism on the conservative core of Boston Catholicism. In having little support and less inherited liberal ideals from Boston's immediate past, they were like the solitary figure attempting to formulate a Jewish Social Gospel — Solomon Schindler.

Chapter Three

JUDAISM
Premature Radicalism Aborted

It is the mission of modern Judaism to educate the Jew for his position as a citizen in the community in which he lives by removing all . . . prejudices . . . [and] all those superstitions which he himself has artificially built up in order to save himself from the rough contact with a world that never loved and merely tolerated him. — Rabbi Solomon Schindler

Religion is the endeavor of mankind to bring all the realities of life into the nearest possible relationship with their ideals — that is with mankind's latest conceptions of God and the universe. — Rabbi Solomon Schindler [1]

T he mass of European Jews who settled in Boston in the last part of the nineteenth century were similar to the Irish in bringing from the Old World a deep sadness and immense resignation. The majority of the Jews were immigrants, whose numbers increased from 1880 to 1900, and their religion was orthodox. The Old Testament contained the ringing social criticism and social reform of the Prophets; but more important were the Five Books of Moses. The latter, with the Talmud and traditions accumulated through the centuries, required Jews to follow unquestioningly modes of dress, ritual, and diet so as to distinquish Israel from other peoples and thereby make her sons and daughters acceptable to God. The Enlightenment and nineteenth-century science had not as yet touched the core of Orthodoxy.

Like the Irish, the majority of the Jews were humble folk uprooted from Old World villages and deposited by chance in Boston. Already familiar with alien rule and poverty, the immigrant Jew and Irishman, in settling the appalling slum of the strange city, alike found confirmation of an ingrained belief: that always they must be the poor and the stranger until delivered through divine agency. As the Catholic dockhand looked forward to the Day of Judgment to begin heavenly bliss, so the Jewish sweatshop toiler awaited the Messiah to lead God's children back to the Promised Land. The Jews of the North End knew by heart the rabbinical saying, "This world is like a vestibule before the world to come." Meanwhile, in the time and place of exile, one must get by as best one can, as one's ancestors had done before; and one must retain the more the old rituals and familiar festivals lest all be lost in the trans-Atlantic crossing. Resigned to the evil created by men and all too often the recipients of charity, the poorer Jews of Boston were, with their Irish neighbors, alien to the Yankee optimism that "all things are possible to one who believes." [2]

The small number of prosperous Jews who had escaped from the slum were either too insecure or grateful to question the institutions of their adopted land. Still awkward, they hoped desperately to do what was right so as to achieve middle-class respectability: to be graceful in Boston mannerisms, speech, dress, outlook, and religion. There was no anti-Semitism, as there was anti-Catholicism, to block social acceptance; and so there was neither alienation from, nor anger with, what was. Indeed certain of the older Americans encouraged the Jews to take their place in the city, as had Leopold Morse. Leaving the ghetto via trade, discarding Orthodoxy, marrying well, dispensing charity, and attaining a seat in the United States Congress, Morse was a model for well-to-do Jews seeking adjustment to Boston.[3]

A political refugee enabled certain of the Irish to face outward, and so it was the case for the Jews. Driven from Germany, as John Boyle O'Reilly had been from Ireland, Solomon Schindler arrived in Boston in 1874, four years after his Celtic contemporary.

The two men, with much in common, became close friends. They
had learned in the Old World that their peoples must speak out
against the status quo. Each was a rebel who had given up a life
of personal ease to risk reputation and safety for a moral cause.
Neither descended from either peasant or proletarian families but
from professional and learned parents. In the Hub the two men
edited newspapers and wrote utopian novels; and where O'Reilly
achieved distinction as poet and athlete, Schindler attracted
attention as linguist and religious innovator. It mattered little
that O'Reilly was a nineteenth-century romantic and Schindler an
eighteenth-century neo-rationalist, for their respective presuppositions led alike to social reform. The Irish O'Reilly and the Jewish
Schindler were, by Boston standards, assimilated.

Solomon Schindler was until death a nonconformist. Born in
1842 in Silesia as the eldest son of an Orthodox rabbi, he flouted
custom and parental authority, after training for the rabbinate,
by refusing to follow his father's calling. He was the first of his
family to take to secular learning (anathema to the Orthodox
Hebrew), graduating from the gymnasium and normal school.
Settled as a teacher with a wife and three children, Schindler prepared to live out his life as a first-generation emancipated German
Jew. However, objecting to the annexation of Alsace-Lorraine, he
"delivered a scathing and denunciatory speech against Bismarck"
on the very day that the triumphant Prussian armies returned to
Berlin. For this speech he had to flee from his native land.

The Schindlers arrived penniless in New York in 1871. Too
proud to ask assistance from his spouse's wealthy relatives in
New York and El Paso, Solomon fed his family by peddling
shoelaces. Within several months poverty in America accomplished what custom and training had failed to do in Germany:
it forced the rabbi's son to become a rabbi. Hard-up and dis-
couraged, Schindler grabbed at the opportunity to become the
leader of a small Orthodox synagogue in Hoboken, New Jersey,
and remained there for three years.[4]

In 1874, the businessmen of Boston's Temple Adath Israel,

seeking a leader to reform services, engaged Solomon Schindler as "Reader, Teacher and Preacher . . . with a yearly salary of $1500." [5] As head of this congregation, he pursued his early ambition for a secular career outside the ghetto. The synagogue, which in the villages of Central and Eastern Europe had been simply a prayer house without a minister (the rabbi was a state official of the community), was in the process of becoming a Jewish church complete with pastor and pulpit. The ex-schoolteacher perceived that his people wished to discard embarrassing alien customs so as to end the *apartheid* that had cursed Israel through the centuries. In twenty years Temple Israel caught up to the Enlightenment. However, Schindler's radicalism went beyond the modest aspiration of his people for respectability, and isolated, he left the temple and Judaism for the religion of social reform as propagated by Edward Bellamy.

Throughout his tenure at Temple Israel, Schindler felt more at home with non-Jews than with Jews. The former were of a special kind, the rebels who had liberated themselves from the values of their parents — Schindler's kind. He was attracted to the Free Religionists, as they were to him; both Jew and Calvinist were attacking a cosmology that rested on the literalism of the Old Testament. With Hamlin Garland, who fled the intellectually unfertile life of the prairies, Schindler researched the unseen spiritual world for the American Psychical Society, a fad for the intelligentsia of that day. Benjamin Flower, who traveled from fundamentalism to the Social Gospel, welcomed the rabbi to the *Arena* crowd, the apostles of newness; and the Nationalists considered it a triumph when New England's first Reform rabbi joined their ranks to translate Edward Bellamy's *Looking Backward* into German, and write his own sequel (in English) to that novel. Schindler's closest friend was Minot J. Savage, the first American clergyman to reconcile Christianity and Darwinism. Savage, as his autobiographical novel revealed, went through a grueling emotional experience before he could throw off the fire and brimstone orthodoxy of his boyhood. In the twentieth century Minot J.

Savage would lay the foundations for the Community Church of New York.[6]

Mixing easily with humane and literary Boston, Solomon Schindler was a bridge between the Jewish middle classes and their non-Jewish neighbors. When he brought out an *Illustrated Hebrew Almanac for the Year 5641*, his good friend John Boyle O'Reilly gladly contributed a poem to it. When Boston wanted a representative Jewish opinion, it went to Temple Israel's rabbi. The leading journals published his opinions on education, immigration, racial relations; and the lecture halls often called upon him. Schindler explained Christianity to his congregation, and expounded Judaism to interested Christians. By the middle of the 1880's as many non-Jews as Jews flocked to his sermons at Temple Israel. So well did Solomon Schindler fit that Boston took pride in the fact that he was the first person in the city's history to be nominated by both political parties for the School Committee.[7]

II

Sensitive to the possibility of a *rapprochement* between liberal Christians and Jews, Solomon Schindler devoted his energies "to educate the Jew for his position as a citizen in the community . . ." The men who engaged him as rabbi wanted, at the outset, little else than to make their services similar to the dignified Protestant mode of worship. But Temple Israel's congregation did not know what measures to take or how far to go. Their rabbi capitalized on this yearning for an Americanized Judaism. By destroying the old forms and preaching a theology of humanitarianism, he sought to bring the Hebrew faith "abreast with the time and to win for it the respect of the Gentile world." [8]

The first reforms exploded like a bombshell. When Schindler introduced the family pew, choir, organ, vernacular prayer book, and male worship without hats, fifteen of his congregation of forty withdrew in protest against what seemed to them brazen steps toward Christianity. Schindler did not mind. These measures were

calculated to attract the assimilationists among the younger and
well-to-do Jews who could not bring themselves to belong to any
of the Boston synagogues. The calculation proved correct. By the
middle of the 1880's, Temple Israel increased its numbers threefold to include the "100 of the richest and most influential
Hebrews in the city," among them Congressman Leopold Morse.
In 1885, Schindler's people moved from their modest quarters in
downtown Boston into a newly built temple in a still fashionable
part of the South End. At the dedication ceremony, there were
addresses by the Reverends Minot J. Savage, Brooke Herford,
Edward Everett Hale, and Phillips Brooks. Once in the new building, Solomon Schindler persuaded his flock to take "the so much
dreaded step of . . . Sunday services" on the grounds that the
business obligations of the men made it impossible to observe the
Saturday Sabbath. This drastic innovation failed to get the congregation out in full, but by rejecting the ancient Hebrew Sabbath, Rabbi Schindler severed the last connection with the
old forms and achieved his purpose of making the "Jew like the
Gentile . . . in ceremonials . . ." [9]

Worshiping like the Unitarians whom Schindler admired, Boston's Reform Jews were still in need of a modern theology. They
went to Jewish church on Sunday and prayed without hats, but
as yet they had not formally given up the idea that Israel was
God's chosen, that the Messiah would come one day, and that
Gentiles were pagans or worse. Further, there was still the Jewish
as against the Christian conception of Jesus. Wishing to minimize
theological as well as ritualistic differences between Jew and non-
Jew, Schindler created a synthesis not unlike that of a James
Freeman Clarke or a Minot J. Savage. Happily, the climate of the
then contemporary science enabled him to embrace modernism.
In particular, he made Judaism come to terms with the study of
comparative religion, Biblical criticism, and the evolutionary
hypothesis.[10]

The rabbi of Temple Israel, as he later told, knew that the spot-
light was on him and that he had a large and sympathetic audi-

ence. His first series of sermons, *Messianic Expectations and Modern Judaism,* were delivered in 1885 in the temple to a numerous throng of which, Minot J. Savage wrote, "more than half . . . was Christian . . ." What Bostonians could not hear they could read in the daily and Sunday papers. So keen was their curiosity in what Schindler had to say that one Boston newspaper drummed up yearly subscriptions by offering Schindler's sermons free of charge. "No literary papers in *The Globe,*" wrote that journal, ". . . have caused so wide an interest as those of Rabbi Schindler on MODERN JUDAISM AND ITS BELIEFS." Similarly, the otherwise unspirited *Transcript* spiritedly urged its readers to follow the rabbi's discourses; for "the enormous influence which the Hebrew race has exerted . . . in the history of the world makes it interesting to know where the present representatives of that wonderful nation stand in the turmoil of . . . modern intellectual life." [11]

The rabbi corrected misconceptions of Judaism that earlier had led to prejudice. In his popular "Jesus of Nazareth," delivered before Congregationalist and Unitarian audiences, he noted that the Romans not the Jews had crucified the Nazarene; for neither the method of execution nor the trial was part of ancient Hebrew legal practice. Schindler also broke through the separateness of Orthodoxy by commenting on the relationship of Christianity to Judaism for the *Globe,* which asked him to write on the accuracy of a play set in the synagogue of Jesus' day. The rabbi's observations on moot points concerning the origins of Christianity were less significant for their contents than for the fact that a Jewish minister would discuss Jesus in public. No Orthodox rabbi had done so before. Schindler showed, by example, that liberal Jews were interested in, and could view rationally, the religious traditions of their Christian neighbors.[12]

Similarly, Temple Israel's leader hoped to dissipate Jewish misconceptions of Christianity. "We must learn," he preached, "to understand our neighbor . . . for at present we do not know him and our ignorance . . . breeds . . . prejudice . . . against him . . ." He inveighed against the exclusiveness of Orthodox Judaism. The study of comparative religion makes foolish "the notion that one religion only can be the right one." Indeed, "all religions appear like flowers in the garden of humanity." He reminded his people that Christianity was not a homogeneous whole, that forms and theological differences separated various sects, and that the Unitarians, because they were returning to the "Jewish conception of God," had more in common with liberal Jews than with orthodox Christians. He advised his flock to give up the medieval fear that the Hebrew faith would die if they recognized the validity of Christianity, that the younger Jews would give up their religion for the other. An up-to-date Judaism, he asserted, would have the vitality and strength to survive.[13]

Under the influence of the new school of Biblical criticism and the theory of evolution, Solomon Schindler cast off the Jewish belief in a personal God and the divine origin of the Bible. The concept of the Creator had evolved through several stages: "from a household god into a tribal god, then into a national divinity, finally into the god of the Universe." God was First Cause and Clockmaker. He was not the capricious, jealous Jehovah who had chosen the Hebrews as His special children; nor could He intervene personally on their behalf. "To seek him," Rabbi Schindler said, "will mean to enter into the spirit of His laws, of the justice and wisdom of which the whole universe will be acknowledged to be one grand manifestation." The fact that God did not dictate the Old Testament from on high reduced neither His stature nor the merits of the Holy Book: indeed it reveals, said Schindler, the essential wisdom of the early Hebrews and proves, moreover, the evolutionary thesis that each age fashions religious beliefs for its own needs.[14]

If there was no Jewish God, no chosen people, and no infallible book, then there could be no basis for the belief in a Messiah. With the evolutionary hypothesis as his instrument of analysis and history as his laboratory, Rabbi Schindler traced the origin, development, and frustration of the hope for a Hebrew Savior.

He pointed out that the notion originated during the Babylonian captivity when the Jews yearned for a political-military leader who would throw off their yoke and restore the Hebrew state to the old glory of David's kingdom. Five hundred years later, while under the domination of the Romans, a handful of the Jewish masses regarded Jesus as such a leader, but the bulk of the Palestinians ignored Him. After the introduction of Christianity and the Jewish Diaspora, the original Hebrew concept of a warrior-Messiah evolved into another form. In the misery and isolation of the ghettos, and under the influence of the Christian conception of the Savior, Israel's scattered tribes developed the idea of a God-sent spiritual leader who would gather up the dispersed Hebrews, take them to Zion, and establish a universal order of peace and brotherhood with Jerusalem as the center.[15]

The belief in a Hebrew Savior, said Schindler, died with Jewish emancipation following the American and French revolutions — and properly so, he thought. Ideas to him were like biological organisms: he believed, like Darwin, that only the fittest survived; and in a free, democratic country like America the hope for a Messiah could hardly compete with the ideal of assimilation. In the United States the Hebrews had freedom of religion and speech, enjoyed the ballot, could aspire to political office, and enjoyed equal privileges of citizenship. Why then return to Palestine, an insignificant, poverty-stricken land on the Mediterranean? The Messianic hope, moreover, was out of step with nineteenth-century conceptions of representative government. The Savior, after organizing the trek to Palestine, would no doubt wish to rule Zion by himself; and no rational democrat — Jew or Christian — could accept such a government. Finally, the wish to set up Jerusalem as the world capital, with Judaism in the driver's seat, was in conflict with the basic idea, propagated by the study of comparative religion, that all religions were equally valid. If American Hebrews insisted on yearning for a future religious uniformity let them note that: "The religion of the future will be neither specifically Jewish nor Christian nor Mohammedan. It will be an entirely new system, in which the immortal parts of all the present religions will be represented, but at the same time so equally balanced that none will dare to claim superiority." [16]

For the ancient hope of a personal Savior unfit to survive in the competitive world of ideas, Rabbi Schindler substituted the nineteenth-century concept of scientific and mechanical progress. Jesus of Nazareth and Bar Kockba of Biblical fame, Solomon Molcho, David Reubeni, and Sabbatai Svi (sixteenth- and seventeenth-century pretender-Messiahs) had not improved the world; they grew out of the misery of their times and left their societies in exactly the same condition in which they found them. But the scientists, the inventors, the scholars — they were "the real saviors of humanity." They broke down class distinctions, made possible representative government, and improved the standard of living. Above all, their "rails and electric wires have tied humanity into one large community, and through their agency all human beings have learned to regard one another as brethren, and to share the joys and woes of their fellow beings from pole to pole." [17]

Rabbi Schindler's rejection of the Messianic conception derived not only from his intellectual convictions but from his desire to Americanize Judaism. Although an internationalist in his socialist beliefs, he wished to sever all ties between the American Jews and their place of origin — remote or otherwise. He believed that so long as the Hebrews desired a return to Palestine, they would be distrusted as foreigners lacking in patriotism. Similarly, he had little patience with the Orthodox Jews in the North End, who did not understand the "spirit of Americanism" and who wished to perpetuate "European traditions and customs." Insisting that a "man cannot have two countries at the same time," he asserted that the Jew "will never be a good American citizen who always dreams of a return to the country from which he came, and who delights only in the customs and usages of the fatherland." [18]

If Judaism did not rest on the literal interpretation of the Bible, the belief in the Messiah, the Saturday Sabbath, the orthodox ritual, and the faith in a personal God with the Jews as His chosen people, what was it then? In his *Dissolving Views in the History of Judaism*, Rabbi Schindler pointed out that from its very inception the Jewish faith had gone through a process of evolution, changing its form in response to the pressures of the environment: Moses, Isaiah, Maimonides, Mendelssohn, Wise — all had put their stamp on the faith. But always there remained a changeless core, for Judaism, according to Schindler, had ever been "the religion of humanity." In the far-off future, Rabbi Schindler foresaw a reconciliation of Christianity and Judaism, when racial prejudice and the belief in the divinity — and in the case of the Unitarians, the uniqueness — of Christ would be no more. For the present, however, the American Hebrews had to adapt their faith to the rational, tolerant, progressive milieu; break down the parochial barriers dividing coreligionists of diverse European backgrounds; become Americans by nationality and Jews by religion; accept the fatherhood of God and the brotherhood of man; and work for the ever upward progress of mankind "on the ladder of civilization." This was essentially the creed of the Pittsburgh Platform, the declaration drawn up by sixteen Reform rabbis in 1885. Schindler endorsed their principles, but he came to his conclusions independently, and significantly, at the same time.[19]

Behind Rabbi Schindler's efforts lay the thought that his kind of Judaism would win respect from emancipated Gentiles. He was not disappointed. As he anticipated, orthodox Christians and Jews alike inveighed against him for rejecting the concept of a personal Messiah. But from Harvard's Divinity School came "praise to the Reform for the vigor with which it is carrying on its work, for its intellectual clearness and its ethical activity." The *Transcript* was pleased to note that the Jews in turning their backs on Palestine had proved that they are "as American as any of us can be." Schindler particularly delighted in the unqualified endorsement of the Unitarians, whom he admired for doing to Christianity what he was doing to Judaism. The Index Association published his sermons in pamphlet form, and wished

for "a few thousand dollars [to print] . . . a large edition
. . . in handsome style . . ." while Minot J. Savage, in the
preface to *Messianic Expectations*, hailed the rabbi's ideas as
a sign of the age that the "Christian's ceasing to be a Christian,
and the Jew's ceasing to be a Jew." In a similar vein, the Channing Club rejoiced that they and Schindler had "few, if any . . .
theological differences" and agreed on the need for ethical striving. Their conclusion: "The liberal Jew and the liberal Christian
. . . meet today on common ground. . ." [20]

As Newtonian physics and Lockean epistemology earlier had
undermined the foundations of Calvinism, so the Biblical and evolutionary science of the late nineteenth century smashed the
chassis of Orthodox Judaism. Unitarian and Reform Jew alike
believed that God was one and rational, and that man was perfectible. Where early Unitarianism had made room for revelation
and miracles, so the first liberal temple in Boston retained certain
of the holy days in the Hebrew Calendar; there was only partial
emancipation. In the slums, though, there was no emancipation.
The numerous synagogues in the North End, added to by immigration, were little different from what they had been like in
Russia, Poland, and Austria-Hungary — a fact of which Solomon
Schindler was painfully aware. Indeed the Orthodox, who outnumbered by far the Reform, regarded the views of the latter
with intense bitterness, and thought no better of the one temple,
Ohabei Shalom, that was midway between Orthodoxy and Reform. In short, Adath Israel was the exception to the norm of
Boston Judaism. And its rabbi, in embracing the secular radicalism of Nationalism, was an exception grafted onto an exception.

III

The road to Edward Bellamy's philosophy of Nationalism was
easy for Solomon Schindler to take. Like his Boston contemporaries, Edward Everett Hale and William Dwight Porter Bliss,

Unitarian and Episcopalian respectively, he saw in Edward Bellamy's brand of socialism the perfect expression of "the religion of humanity." Many elements in Bellamy's thinking corresponded with Schindler's religious principles. The Nationalist creed asked all people, regardless of class, creed, race, or origin, to join hands to work for the brave new world. The utopia described in *Looking Backward* was founded on science, reason, and material comforts for everyone. Above all, Bellamy's hope for a better society rested on the one assumption that was basic to the rabbi's thinking: the possibility of the limitless improvement of the human race. All my life, wrote Schindler, "my nature has ever led me to believe in progress." [21]

Schindler brought to these general principles a logical, learned mind, unhampered by blocs that would make him reject, like so many liberals of the day, the necessity of socializing the economy. Having cast off the dogmas of the oldest surviving religion in Western civilization, he was mentally prepared to blast the comparatively young capitalistic devotion to private property, free enterprise, and competition. His German background convinced him that the nationalization of such basic utilities as the railroads was practicable and profitable. Schindler hated war but admired the efficiency and discipline of the Prussian military force; hence Bellamy's industrial army, working for peaceful ends, appealed to him. Because he accepted without qualification the American democratic creed that the people is the government, he saw no dichotomy between authority and liberty — between those who governed and those who were governed. And free from the Protestant ethic, he could and did believe that the state, and not the individual, was responsible for a man's calling.

The rabbi of Adath Israel was a high priest of Nationalism who labored zealously for his faith with pen and voice. In 1888 he accepted the invitation to join the First Nationalist Club in Boston and, in the same year, made a contract with Bellamy to translate *Looking Backward* into German; in 1890 the Riverside Press published the translation under the title of *Ein Rückblick*.[22] But he was more than a foreign echo of his master's voice. He wedded Spencer, Darwin, the Industrial Revolution, and monopoly capitalism to his own "religion of humanity." By this dialectical feat he made a synthesis of the forces that were remaking America and, at the same time, provided himself with a bludgeon against capitalism and a weapon for Nationalism.

Individualism and competition, the twin pillars of the capitalist system, Solomon Schindler found both irrational and unethical. He was acid in denouncing the Social Darwinists for giving sociological approval to the "competitive struggle for existence . . . in the form of the doctrine of the survival of the fittest. . ." It is contrary to religious justice, he asserted, to give "the big fish the legal right to swallow the small one on no other ground than that he happens to be big." He was equally vigorous in his criticism of the ethical individualism of Henry George. In a stout article for *The Arena* Hamlin Garland, leading exponent of the Single-Tax in Boston, attacked Bellamy's socialism on the grounds that it would destroy freedom of action which, he agreed with Spencer, was the final and best product of the evolutionary process. B. O. Flower, editor of *The Arena*, and stanch believer in free inquiry, called upon the rabbi, whom he believed to be one of the "ablest nationalistic thinkers in America," to answer the son of the Middle Border. Schindler replied that evolution was on the side of the Bellamyites. He argued that society, in its early, primitive stages, had been individualistic — that each man had satisfied his needs solely through his own efforts. As the world progressed, however, increased knowledge, improved methods of transportation and communication, and the division of labor broke down the early atomism and made men dependent on one another. Individualism, thus, was synonymous with barbarism; the modern interdependence of mankind was the real mark of progress.[23]

Like other progressive clergymen, Solomon Schindler rejected Spencer's laissez faire but used the latter's organic theory of society for purposes that the Englishman "would have sternly disapproved." To the Jewish minister and to the author of *Social*

Statics the social order was a gigantic organism. But whereas the latter argued that it was folly to tamper with the economy, the former asserted that the collective body would have to be regulated for the good of the organic whole. Nationalism, the preacher wrote, was the "logical consequences . . . of the nineteenth century," of the roundabout method of production that made civilization "a plant of which . . . individuals form the cells." From these axioms, Schindler deduced the principle of economic equality:

> Mankind being the unit, a place must have been reserved for every person in which to become useful. A man cannot do more than nature has fitted him for, if he does that conscientiously . . . no more can be required of him, but for contributing his share, for filling the place which nature has assigned him, he becomes entitled to an equal share of the products turned out by the grand machinery.

Schindler did not fear that economic equality would produce a nation of slackers: once freed from the "fear of starvation," man would "strain every nerve unselfishly for the welfare of society at large." [24]

To convince the "lazy and torpid masses" that socialism could work, the Jewish minister pointed to the success of public ownership of utilities in Europe and America. Schindler took the opportunity, while serving the *Boston Daily Globe* as special European correspondent during the summer of 1889, to write glowing reports about Bismarck's social welfare state. What "we . . . call in America Nationalism . . . may be studied best here in Germany." The government-owned railroads, telegraph, schools, post office, war factories, and express business were efficient and profitable; they made the nation as a whole more prosperous than he previously had known it; Germany was truly on the road to a "communistic Brotherhood." And what about our own America? Our cities and states educate the people, put out their fires, supply them with water — why not then extend the socialization of the means of production and exchange to all goods and services? [25]

Convinced that Nationalism was marching to the fife and drums of science and history, Schindler threw himself into his most ambitious project: the writing of *Young West: A Sequel to Edward Bellamy's Celebrated Novel LOOKING BACKWARD*. The rabbi's book, which appeared in 1894, three years before the publication of *Equality*, Bellamy's own sequel, was more radical than the latter's two volumes. Bellamy's reaction to the work is unknown. Even the format of *Young West* was revolutionary: the Arena Publishing Company, a liberal house, believing that the conventional black and white page caused eyestrain, printed Schindler's utopian novel "at an increased expense" with colored margins. Into the yellow, blue, and green bordered pages, the author poured all his radicalism, finding solutions for the liquor, capital — labor, education, feminist, slum, and sundry other problems. Before he got halfway through his story, the rabbi talked himself right out of Judaism into an agnostic socialist humanism.

Solomon Schindler used the framework of *Looking Backward* as the starting point for his own volume. Edward Bellamy took leave of Julian West (the nineteenth-century Bostonian who awoke from a mesmerized sleep in the utopia of the twentieth century) with the understanding that the hero would live happily ever after. In the rabbi's sequel, Julian dies two years after his arrival in the land of the all-perfect. His son, Young West, born out of Julian's marriage with Edith Leete, is the central figure of the book. We follow his career from his birth until he becomes President of the United States, the supreme achievement in Nationalistic America.

The major outlines of Schindler's society are those of Bellamy's. There is compulsory education from six to eighteen. Everybody serves as a private in the industrial army from eighteen to twenty-one, and after that takes up a chosen occupation and labors until the retirement age of forty-five. A regulated state capitalism has supplanted private enterprise. Men still compete — for "rivalry is the spice of life" — not out of the desire to destroy one another, but to serve their state. Economic equality is the foundation of the new social order, but ranks corresponding to army grades are used to distinguish extra meritorious service. The President is at the top of the class pyramid.[26]

There are several significant differences between *Young West* and Bellamy's two novels. *Looking Backward* and *Equality* are characteristic of all utopias in that they describe essentially static societies. The people experience neither pain nor sorrow; strife and conflict are unknown; progress is at a standstill, for like Marx's dialectic in the communistic stage, Bellamy's evolutionary process ceases to operate in the Nationalistic phase of human development. Everything is in a blissful state of nirvana. Schindler, however, escapes these common failings. The regulated economy founded on economic equality solves the major social problems — labor, capital, slums, and so forth — but Young West suffers the pangs of unrequited love; and his first sweetheart, although thoroughly well-fed, well-housed, and well-clothed, and a world famous musician, lives a miserable life because of successive divorces. Julian's son, moreover, knows the meaning of struggle, for he wins the presidency only after a strenuous campaign. And, for the rabbi, the ever-upward progress of humanity does not grind to a halt with Nationalism: his hero, after leading a completely gratifying life in an ideal society, remarks that "my faith is firm that mankind will advance and reach a still higher plane of culture. . . "[27]

Equally important are the different roles that Schindler and Bellamy assign to religion. The latter, like the former, the son of a minister, was deeply religious; he believed in God, that the Creator had planted the divine in human nature, and that all men would return to their Maker after death. There are no denominations in *Looking Backward* or *Equality,* but there is a minister, the Reverend Barton, who, significantly, in his radio sermon, compared nineteenth-century to twenty-first-century civilization on the basis of Christian principles. In *Young West,* the author puts the Bible and other holy books in the library to gather dust. When his hero is troubled by the mysteries of life and death he consults his science teacher, who tells him that the first cause is unknown, that the conception of a personal God grew out of the misery and insecurity of predatory capitalism, and that the belief in the hereafter can neither be affirmed nor denied. Schindler clearly had become an agnostic, for in the eighties he believed in God and, although he could not prove it, in a life after death.[28] In his brief flirtation with spiritualism in 1892, the rabbi failed to find scientific evidence for the immortality of the soul, and in *Young West* he announced his new position.

Minor differences between the two Nationalists are also apparent. Mechanically, Bellamy was the more ingenious of the two; in *Looking Backward* he described what has since become the radio, and in *Equality* he rhapsodized over the "electroscope" — television. Schindler, on the other hand, was fascinated by the aeroplane, which Bellamy introduced in his first novel. Whereas the founder of Nationalism believed that socialism would come first to America, the rabbi prophesied that Europe, because of its head start in the municipal ownership of utilities and the experience in discipline it derived from its standing armies, would adopt it first. Finally, Bellamy did not envision the end of national states. Schindler did; his future world would be organized on the basis of the five continents, and because of his devotion to "race amalgamation," he foresaw the wholesale intermarriage of Europeans.[29]

Not content merely with criticizing capitalism and with describing the glories of Nationalism, the Boston rabbi suggested concrete measures to usher in the future. Because he believed that the social organism grew with geological slowness, he rejected the class conflict and the use of force. He had faith in the creative minority of intellectuals and therefore regarded education as the great engine of social change. Rich and poor, and above all, the conservative petit bourgeoisie — the backbone of America — had to be instructed in the logic and inevitability of socialism. He would encourage the growth of trade unions in order to train the workers in the discipline necessary for the industrial army. Monopoly capitalism he regarded a blessing, and therefore urged the growth of trusts until they controlled the entire economy, at which time it would "require nothing more than the necessary legal actions to nationalize them." As immediate measures he advocated the national ownership of railroads, telegraph, telephone, and banking systems, and the municipalization of street railways, gas, and electricity on the grounds that since they were the nervous ganglia of the social organism they should belong to the community at large. He was particularly interested in socializing the insurance companies because he felt that, aside from giving the bureaucrats experience in handling public business, insurance against accidents, sickness, unemployment, and death would teach the principle of Nationalism that society was responsible for the individual from "the cradle to the bier." [30]

Like the progressive movements of New England half a century earlier, Boston liberalism in the 1880's and 1890's received fresh winds of doctrine from the Old World. For his liberal contemporaries, Solomon Schindler interpreted German economic experience and English sociology to meet the needs of America. But even here the Jewish clergyman was sensitive to American currents, for he comprehended that the history of the United States economy was not one of pure laissez faire, that the citizens, in their collectivity, had put into public hands the fire, water, roads, postal, and educational systems. Objective, and without formal training in economics, he realized better than many of the academic economists that the American economic system, even then, was a mixed one.

IV

Fundamentally a cosmopolitan in his social and economic thinking, Schindler was, in his religious beliefs, fiercely American. As the leader of an immigrant church whose adherents felt that their individual futures were linked to the future of their adopted country, the rabbi labored to make Judaism conform, in spirit and form, to the dominant liberal faith in Boston — Unitarianism. There is nothing in Schindler's writings, or in the individual backgrounds of the members of his congregation, to suggest that Reform Judaism was a German importation. On the contrary, it was indigenous to this country, a product, on the one hand, of the desire to Americanize the ancient Hebrew creed, and on the other, of the contemporary science that was shattering traditional modes of thought in Western civilization.

Solomon Schindler gave his congregation what it wanted: a modern Judaism suited to the needs of the prosperous immigrant and native-born members of Temple Adath Israel. Yet in the end, while succeeding as a theologian, he failed as a rabbi. In 1893 he was dismissed, and Rabbi Charles Fleischer took his place.[31] The outward cause for his leaving was the lax attendance of services. Schindler's flock, which earlier had taken pride in his ability to draw the Boston non-Jewish intelligentsia to services, now disapproved of him. He simply was not American enough. Between 1874 and 1893 a new generation born in Boston came of age who found fault with Schindler's accent, his Old World didacticism, his lack of tact, and his somewhat foreign appearance. Fleischer, in contrast, was handsome, personable, an eloquent speaker; he was in the tradition of the then American pulpit. Ironically, Americanization backfired on the pioneer in Reform Judaism: Schindler opened the window of American life to the immigrants, and their children closed the door on him.

He was even more grieved that his congregation refused to follow him into Nationalism. He failed to understand that economic equality did not appeal to a generation which had wrung success from the American economy through hard work and self-reliance. Wholesalers and retailers, for the most part, they had little contact with the working classes and therefore did not know their problems or feel that they were exploiting them. Moreover, Nationalism primarily attracted intellectuals and, excepting a bare handful of younger folk, there were no college graduates and certainly no writers or artists in Schindler's congregation.

Finally, because they were of such recent origin to Boston, his flock did not have the Puritan sense of obligation to the community, except as it applied to their own people. Therefore, public-spirited Jews found an outlet for their desire to do good in Jewish charities. Federated in 1894 and with aid from the Baron de Hirsch Fund, the United Jewish Charities pioneered in placing needy immigrants in jobs outside Boston, eschewing the almsgiving which made the poor even less self-supporting.[32] In short, Schindler's religious inspired radicalism was premature, for his congregation lacked a reformist tradition such as had the middle-class Protestant community in Boston.

estant pulpit rallied as it sought solutions for the problems of the machine age.

The traditions inherited by the Boston ministry of the last part of the century were conducive to social Christianity. From Roger Williams to Theodore Parker there had emerged a distinct type of clergyman: educated, high-minded, activist, sensitive to social problems, receptive to secular ideas, and willing to dissent. Men of God had played an important role in the Revolution as well as in the reform movements of the first half of the nineteenth century.[3] The Hub City had had its quota of conservative pulpits in the times of Jefferson and Jackson, but to the generation of 1880–1900, the composite of William Ellery Channing, Theodore Parker, James Freeman Clarke, and Edward Everett Hale seemed to bespeak the authentic Boston clergyman. As in the past, the ministers of the last two decades of the nineteenth century counted for much in the community; and they knew it. Custodians of the Christian ethic — and with the pulpit, newspaper, magazine, and book available to them as means of communication — they could instruct fellow Protestants, if they so desired, on the ends and means of social reform.

By the 1880's the decay of orthodoxy was almost complete. As a consequence, Boston's ministers — whether Unitarians or Bushnellians, Free Religionists, Broad Churchmen, or Millennial Calvinists — shared modernist conceptions of God, man, and society. Society was not a collection of atoms struggling for individual salvation; it was an organic body tied together by the Christ. Man did not sin entirely out of inner wickedness; sin also sprang from the wickedness of the environment. The atonement did not end at Calvary; it was continuous reconciliation with God through brotherly service. By the time of the Haymarket Affair, few ministers questioned that Jesus' gospel was social as well as individual, that it contained the essence of brotherly service. The humanitarian ethic of Jesus became all the more important as evolution, Biblical criticism, and the study of comparative religion stripped Christianity of its supernatural clothing. Deprived by science of its unscientific bases, Protestantism defended its role in American life in terms of social effectiveness. The numerically unimportant Swedenborgian, German Lutheran, Presbyterian, and Greek Orthodox churches resisted modernism. But from the Episcopal Bishop Phillips Brooks to the ultra-Unitarian Minot J. Savage, from Congregationalist Andover to Methodist Boston University, the Hub's Protestant clergymen demanded that the church do its worldly duty. And this was as God wished. He was not the capricious Hebrew tyrant of a Jonathan Edwards. He was kindly, tolerant, interested in progress. God had become an American democrat.[4]

How to achieve democracy was of personal concern to Protestant ministers. In the last twenty years of the century, urban Protestantism, including that of Boston, was too often the religion of the businessman and the professional. Equally important, Protestant churches were located almost exclusively in Yankee and fashionable neighborhoods, in the ghettos of the wealthy. With the arrival of Jews and Catholics in the older sections of the city, prosperous Protestants of Puritan pride fled to the suburbs or to the Back Bay. They left behind coreligionists of the lower classes; and church buildings were often converted into charitable agencies. Certain clergymen, who refused to or who could not give up their churches, also remained, such as the Episcopalian Philo W. Sprague. He was a Christian Socialist. More commonly, however, the minister followed his congregation to the new and pleasant neighborhood. In this respect, the Reverend Dr. Edward Everett Hale, who moved his pulpit from the South End to Back Bay's Exeter and Newbury Streets, was typical.

Religious leaders who read statistics were quick to note that the Protestant church was not reaching the masses. Trade union leaders were equally quick to accuse the ministry of apologizing for the misdeeds of capitalist vestrymen. Indeed it was reported that, at their meetings, trade unionists applauded at the mention of Jesus, but hissed at the reference to Christianity. Rightly, reformers among the clergy were apprehensive lest Protestantism contribute to a permanent hardening of the arteries of class and ancestry. They would revive the idea that the church must be an organic body harmonizing the needs of all classes, not a divisive force strengthening the position of the prosperous.[5]

What to do? Past experience in philanthropy was of no help. The methods of uplifting such obvious social defectives as Indians, freedmen, and prisoners did not apply to the industrial problem. Even the new charity, which eliminated overlapping agencies and helped the poor to help themselves, by-passed the causes of poverty for the effects. The same was true of the church-sponsored organizations that mushroomed after 1865 — the Y.M.C.A., the Mission, the Christian Endeavor and Lend a Hand Societies. More significant was the impediment of the Protestant ethic. For decades clergymen had been brought up on Francis Wayland's works, which explained how laissez faire was the agency through which Divine Providence maintained the equilibrium of society. However, such optimism seemed incredible in the face of the sweatshops of the North End. Clergymen who read the Reverend Louis A. Banks's muckraking account of that tenement district learned that the sweater would continue to sweat others unless the government stepped in and said no. Knowingly, the Reverend William J. Tucker observed that Protestant ministers needed to slough off their faith in both charity and economic individualism in order to achieve "social justice."[6]

Socialism acted as a vigorous stimulus on the Protestant search for social justice, attracting some and frightening others. "Socialism," wrote the *Christian Register*, "is the burning question of the day." Throughout the period it meant all things to all men, as is suggested by Webster's definition of it: "A theory of society which advocates a more precise, orderly and harmonious arrangement of the social relations of mankind than that which has hitherto prevailed." In the Websterian sense, many Social Gospelers regarded themselves as socialists. To some, especially in the 1880's, socialism signified Marxism and anarchism, evoking horrible images of violence, atheism, the Commune, the Haymarket Affair, and the despoiling of the Protestant business community; and ministers hastened to devise alternative reforms to head off radical upheaval. In the 1890's, the domestic socialisms of Laurence Gronlund, Edward Bellamy, and W. D. P. Bliss, which claimed both peaceful and Christian intentions, attracted a number of clergymen, and while repelling others, did so for reasons of logic, not panic. In short, socialism was a challenge to Protestant Christianity; the drift of the Boston Social Gospel was to beat off a socialism hostile to Protestantism by espousing one that was akin to it.[7]

In 1880, there was only a handful of Social Gospelers in Boston — Edward Everett Hale, James Freeman Clarke, Jesse H. Jones, and Joseph Cook. By 1892, W. D. P. Bliss counted nearly two-score,[8] and the figure increased by the turn of the century. The aims, the methods, and the basic assumptions of Boston social Christianity were as varied as interested clergymen were numerous. Anarchy being the rule in Protestant polity, there was little agreement, save by coincidence. It is possible, however, to divide Boston's reforming men of God into two groups: the moderates, who wished to Christianize capitalism; and the radicals, who wished to socialize Christianity. The two camps turned to the Bible and secular theory, trying to splice the Christian ethic with appropriate means of social regeneration.

II

The moderate Social Gospel had four basic themes: a fear of Marxism and Nationalism as well as Spencerian sociology and Sumnerian economics; a marked desire for instruction in the facts of American economic life; a readiness to adopt meliorative reforms rather than drastic changes; and a willingness to back honest reformers with Christian brotherliness. The basic assumption was that capitalism was not organically evil or unworkable, but rather a good economic system suffering from explosive yet easily removable unchristian practices. Therefore, the middle-of-the-road Social Gospelers sought to reconcile the hostile factions of capital and labor within the framework of the existing economy. Accepting their responsibility as leaders of the churched middle-classes, the ministers appealed to the business community, to their Christian humanity and to their good sense, to quiet discontent and head off a possible revolution from below.

The theory and consequences of unrestricted economic individualism struck the ecclesiastical mind as being both unchristian and unAmerican. Immediately after the bloody strikes of 1877, the *Unitarian Review* noted that the critical problem of the age was how to distribute the enormous wealth created as a consequence of the Industrial Revolution. The practice of each man for himself had resulted in making many men poor and a few men rich; and "Vast fortunes," thought the *Review*, ". . . are at variance with the fundamental principles of Christianity and of a free government." As for William Graham Sumner, the chief American theoretician of laissez faire, the *Christian Register* found him "flippant," "repellent," "arrogant," and "superficial," an intellectual and moral pigmy as compared to the scholarly and humane economist, Richard T. Ely. Competition, it was conceded, might be just if all men were equal, but they are not; and the struggle for life therefore becomes cruel, unjust, and illogical. Nowhere in the systems of orthodox economics or Spencerian sociology did the moderate Social Gospel mind find mention of the Christian principles of sympathy, coöperation, and helpfulness. As the *Unitarian Review* summed it up: "There is no remedy for our social burdens but to acknowledge our entire interdependence, — we are members one of another. . . The true Christian communism is that community of interests which binds man to man in sympathy, and man to God in obedience." During the 1880's church spokesmen also inveighed against socialism, which they reasoned would destroy Christianity and its precious ethic of the free individual.[9]

Antagonistic to extreme collectivism and economic individualism, the moderates looked for enlightenment on what to do and how to do it. Whatever "reforms pertain to the growing science of applied Christianity," wrote the *Congregationalist*, should be published; and as an example, it solicited articles from Richard T. Ely on trade unions, coöperatives, and the role of the church in social reform. The *Unitarian Review* suggested that clergymen study the labor problem by reading Karl Marx on socialism, Sedley Taylor on coöperatives, A. J. F. Behrends on social Christianity, and Godin on welfare capitalism. The Unitarian minister John Graham Brooks returned to Boston after studying social theory in Germany to write for and lecture to church audiences on the new economics, the glibness of Herbert Spencer, and the humaneness of John Ruskin. In 1891, the Episcopalians launched the *Church Social Union* to study the social problem with the purpose of helping labor. Five years later the *Christian Register* opened a section under the direction of Edward Everett Hale to acquaint people with the "practical improvements which the Christian religion is making in the affairs of the world." With the exception of the Reverend Louis A. Banks, who made a sensational exposé of the sweatshops in the North End, Boston's clergymen studied the economic and political questions of the day soberly.[10]

Knowledge of society led to the endorsement of meliorative measures. Protestants stood together in backing clean government and opposing racial bigotry: they approved of civil service reform and the good government societies aiming at removing the saloon and the boss from politics; and they spoke out against the maltreatment of Chinese immigrants, Negroes, and Indians. With respect to the industrial question, however, solutions varied. Julius H. Ward and George Batchelor never got beyond the point of stating that something must be done. Phillips Brooks and Louis A. Banks were content to urge businessmen to be more Christian toward their laborers. The Free Religious Association satisfied itself with prophesying a glorious coöperative future for mankind without proposing anything concrete. None

of the older church journals came to a systematic liberal program, although on one occasion the *Christian Register* advocated
coöperatives, arbitration, profit-sharing, and the sliding scale.[11]
It is to the Reverends Joseph Cook, Minot J. Savage, and Nicholas Paine Gilman that one must turn to find the chief system-
makers of the moderate Social Gospel.

Joseph Cook, the outstanding representative of moderate
reform among Evangelical Christians, attempted to steer a middle course between collectivism and individualism. After the
labor violence and the forming of the Socialist Labor Party in
the late 1870's, he felt compelled to beat off the peril to property
and religion "from susceptibility to communistic and socialistic
disease." Holding forth in his Boston Monday Lectures at the
Music Hall in 1880, he quoted from Marx, Lassalle, and Proudhon to prove the godless intentions of socialism, and threatened
the Socialist Labor Party with a battle at the barricades if it
succeeded in the mad and leveling desire to get an income tax
law passed. State Socialism, he argued, was unworkable, would
lead to corruption, and eventually breed Caesarism. The task for
the wealthy and cultured Protestant was to devise Christian
plans for social reconstruction to eliminate the honest grievances of labor and thereby thwart the vicious demagogues who
would repeat the Commune in America. "In pleading for the
poor," Cook explained, "I do not attack the rich but defend
rather the interests of wealth. . ." However, the Congregationalist minister had no sympathy with unchristian businessmen
("fleecers of the poor") and, because he recognized the suffering
of the poor, wished to improve their conditions. No "socialist,
but . . . a labor reformer," he proposed: consumer, productive,
and building association coöperatives; slum clearance through
the private construction of model tenements by honest Christian
businessmen; and state legislation for temperance, the inspection
of factories, the enforcement of the Sabbath, and the arbitration
of labor-capital disputes.[12]

Wishing to reach a wider audience than that contained in the

Music Hall, Cook, in 1888, started publication of *Our Day: A Record and Review of Current Reform*, a monthly "to unite Evangelical Christianity with Practical Reform." Because of the peaceful declarations of Edward Bellamy and Terence V. Powderly, Cook was no longer consumed with the dread fear that labor and socialist leaders would repeat the Paris uprising of 1871 in the streets of Boston. Indeed the social criticism of *Our Day* was as sharp as that of the Socialist Labor Party, as it attacked the exploitation of women and children, the denial of equal rights to Southern Negroes, and the persecution of Jews in Russia. Edward Bellamy's Nationalism, the journal criticized, would destroy individual liberty; but even more reprehensible were the "Christian men . . . in haste to join the hue and cry raised by politicians and capitalists against the Knights of Labor." *Our Day* stood behind the program of the Order: a graduated income tax, coöperatives, postal savings banks, the regulation of trusts, and the government ownership of the telegraph, telephone, and railroads. From a fear of state socialism and a liking for the free market Cook had come to believe that the ideal community would be a "combination of competition and coöperation. . ." [13]

While the Reverend Joseph Cook spoke for Evangelical Christianity, the Reverend Minot J. Savage represented the radical Unitarian theologians of the Free Religious Association. On the whole, the Association displayed little interest in immediate urban and industrial problems, so much so that in 1882, Felix Adler, its president, resigned in protest. They were more concerned with freeing the human spirit from hoary superstitions, a concern which left little energy for other reforms; and too often they made such long-range prognostications of mankind's destiny that they immobilized themselves for frontal assault on nineteenth-century evils.[14] Minot J. Savage, by birth a strict Calvinist but by choice a militant convert to advanced Unitarianism, suffered from this orientation until the compelling realities of the depression of 1893 brought him down to earth.

The fountainhead of Minot J. Savage's social thought is his

theology. In his *The Religion of Evolution,* the first systematic reconciliation of Christianity and Darwinian biology written by an American clergyman, he reasoned that the knowledge of evolution shattered the central doctrine of Christianity, the fall of man, and therefore invalidated the orthodox conceptions of God, man, revelation, the atonement, heaven, and hell. The Divine Being was not outside the universe but immanent; man was not contemptible but had proved himself perfectible; Christ had not died to save man from the Devil but to instruct him in the love and self-sacrifice necessary to achieve the earthly Kingdom of Heaven; and God's will was not revealed in the Bible but in natural law. According to Savage's logic, it followed that the Christian must be a reformer; he must "obey the laws of God . . . until the ideal humanity is reached. . ." The leading disciple of Herbert Spencer in the Boston ministry, Minot Savage declared that the principles of the Creator were individualism and competition. Together, they would perfect the human species and lead it to "socialism." Then men, free from poverty, ignorance, disease, and drudgery, would coöperate with one another, ignoring the barriers of race, nationality, class, and religion. Neither the Marxians nor the Bellamyites should conduct us toward the desired end, Savage wrote; for they violated the divine law of slow social change, gave undue emphasis to material comforts, and hoped to reduce the race to the enervating level of economic equality.[15]

Following the hard times of 1893, the Unitarian minister discovered weaknesses in the philosophy of Herbert Spencer. Previously having had little respect for the ordinary person, he now wrote: "We could spare Jay Gould . . . better than we can spare the common man. . ." "If you trace the methods by which most . . . millionaires . . . have come into possession of their millions, you will find them touched, tainted, with dishonesty, with injustice, with selfishness, with cruelty, somewhere." He thought, but rather vaguely, that monopoly was God's way of making the economy "blossom out into coöperation." Somehow, wrote Savage, there must be a "way by which wealth can be more equally distributed." As remedial measures for the poor he proposed legislation against the tenement house, child labor, the sweat-shop, and the saloon. Like Cook, Savage did not attack middle-class businessmen; in fact, he urged them to throw out the bosses and institute good government.[16] Minot J. Savage never went beyond this point of groping for concrete means of social change, and in 1899, he left for New York to take an even more radically religious church than his Boston one.

In contrast to Savage, who reasoned from cosmic principles into confusion, the Reverend Nicholas Paine Gilman, a Unitarian, argued from experience into a systematic social philosophy. He resided in Newton, but had no pulpit, reaching his audience through the Unitarian journals, of which he edited the *New World*. He was of Ohio birth, proud of his New England and Anglo-Saxon blood, yet not so provincial as not to master French and German and the economic, sociological, and historical works in those languages. He was pragmatic, tough-minded and fact-conscious, but a humanitarian and therefore appalled by both the cynicism of Spencer and the well-meaning tyranny of the Nationalists. In his *Profit Sharing*, published in 1889, and *Socialism and the American Spirit*, 1893, he took up arms against the extreme right and the extreme left, surveyed American character with the help of Henry Adams, Lord Bryce, and Alexis de Tocqueville, and deduced from it moderate, middle-class reform measures suitable to the American temper.

The essential characteristic of the American, wrote Gilman, was a distaste for theoretical systems, such as individualism and collectivism, and a penchant to adopt institutions through trial and error. A century's development of winning and taming a continent had produced a people with beliefs in equality of opportunity but inequality in station; in liberty for the individual but authority for the state; in fraternity without utopian communistic living. Americans display individual initiative in trading, farming, manufacturing, and in acquiring property; yet they have also made it a community responsibility to carry the mail, fight wars, put out fires, educate the young, and police the streets. Neither Karl Marx nor Herbert Spencer dictated the choice in achieving the balance between "individualism" and "socialism"; Americans did what they did because they wanted to satisfy their needs. The conflict between labor and capital, which threatens the existence of society, Gilman wrote, must likewise be settled by the New World pragmatic genius — by choosing what to do after studying "the teaching of the past and trial in the present." [17]

Profit-sharing, having been started by M. Leclaire in France and tested by experience in French, English, Continental, and American factories, appealed to Gilman as being the most equitable and practical alternative to the baleful wage system. By removing the dichotomy of interest between labor and capital, Gilman hoped that society, employers, and employees would enjoy economic prosperity and peace. Capitalists, he explained, would make more profits through the increased productivity of workers, for the latter, knowing that they would share in the profits, would take excellent care of tools and produce to the fullest capacity. With both sides content, society would be free from strikes, and capitalist and worker would again know the happy and peaceful relations of the handicraft system, when master and journeyman worked harmoniously with the single purpose of providing the community with the goods it needed. Gilman thought it impossible to abolish classes, quixotic to work for utopia, and unwise to depend on an omnipotent government as the agency of social change. He addressed his plan to Christian-minded factory owners, insisting that they, as Christians and businessmen, be humane and wise by giving labor a higher standard of living so as to head off industrial warfare. Shy of monistic schemes of social reconstruction, the Unitarian minister also favored the government regulation of trusts, consumer cooperatives, the municipalization of electric light plants, the nine-hour day, and trade unions.[18]

For Nicholas Paine Gilman the facts of industrial life were the test of liberal plans, but the ethics of Christianity were the propelling force for good. "Continuous social reform in the name of the Most High God of the actual universe," he wrote, "is the religious commandment for our age." Although the Unitarian clergyman abhorred the tyranny of Marx's collectivism, he preferred the German communist, because of the latter's interest in the coöperative ideal, to William Graham Sumner and Herbert Spencer, the spokesmen for the jungle and therefore anti-Christian economy. Gilman thought his own plans added up to "socialism," that they harmonized, in a manner palatable to Americans, the interests of the individual and of the community, as well as those of the capitalist and worker. For him the concept that "We are all members of the body of Christ" was pregnant with meaning for Protestants who wanted to be Christ-like during the week and not just on Sunday. Behind the statistics, case histories, and economic theory of Nicholas Gilman lay the ruling idea — stated so often as to be redundant — that "the commercial spirit should be tempered by the Christian feeling of the brotherhood of man." [19]

By 1893, when Gilman's *Socialism and the American Spirit* appeared, the moderate Social Gospel in Boston was worked out, and it did not change in the next seven years. None of its reforms threatened the position of the solid middle-class businessmen of Protestant persuasion in the Hub City. Rather the moderates made it clear that unless the owners of wealth took an active interest as leaders of social reform they might one day face ruin through revolution. This *noblesse oblige*, intensified by the urgency of the times and fed by self-interest, is the crucial element in the moderate social Christianity of Boston. In appealing to wealth and culture, ministers of the Gospel were carrying on the Puritan tradition of going to prominent persons when society needed looking after. In the past, charity had been the remedy for the consequences of economic disequilibrium. In the 1880's and 1890's the means changed, to coöperative schemes of one sort or another, but the spirit of chasing out evil and promoting good as God's stewards remained the same.

The ministerial makers of the moderate Social Gospel functioned entirely as educators, refusing to alter the rule of separation of church and state by suggesting direct political action as the means to attain their reforms. As educators they were successful. None of the older church journals failed during the eighties and nineties, and four new ones were added: the *Unitarian* (1886), the *New World* (1892), *Our Day* (1888), and the *Church Social Union* (1891). Minot J. Savage filled his large church every Sunday, his sermons were all published (collected from 1879 to 1896 they fill seventeen volumes), and his ideas reached out over America through his contributions to the *Arena*. Joseph Cook's Monday Lectures became a Boston institution, while Nicholas Gilman's reputation as a social scientist led Pennsylvania's Meadville Theological School to establish a special chair in sociology for him. Even the young were affected; the Sunday School primer by the Unitarian minister, Charles F. Dole, went into ten editions by 1898. *The Citizen and the Neighbor; or, Men's Rights and Duties as They Live Together in the State and in Society*, as Dole's book was entitled, was strong on social criticism but vague on reform proposals. It espoused "Moral or Christian Socialism [which] does not aim to remove inequalities — which is impossible — but to make men friends with each other." [20] In sharp contrast to this view was that of the radicals who, believing it impossible to remove class antagonisms in capitalism, attempted to find God, economic prosperity, and social peace in the fraternal milieu of the public ownership of all productive property.

III

Central to the radicalisms of Boston's Protestant clergymen was the Christian belief in a glorious and final outcome for history disclosed through revelation. Apart from Herbert Newton Casson, the leading radicals were either Episcopalians or Millennial Calvinists who viewed the world in terms of the traditional eschatology of mankind fallen and then miraculously redeemed by Christ. This eschatology applied to society as well as to the individual. Christ died at Calvary to assure individual salvation in the hereafter, and lived to show wherein lay the road to collective redemption in the here. The road, as revealed in pentecostal society, was communism. Unlike the moderates, who looked to Jesus solely for inspiration, the radicals regarded the communitarian example of Christ and his disciples as a literal commandment to live a like life. In no other way could men absolve themselves from the original social sin of private property and the profit motive. Indeed for one man, Jesse H. Jones, communism in this world was the vestibule through which men must pass to attain the other world.

Jones, the first socialist clergyman in the Boston area, was brought up on the mid-century come-out fundamentalism of Charles G. Finney. The latter had sparked the Oberlin abolitionist movement as well as numerous utopian communist Christian communities of the burned-over district of New York. In Finney's sermons ran the theme that mortal men could not compromise with divine commandment, that they must perfect society so as to prepare for the Second Coming of God's only and miraculously begotten Son. Expecting an imminent return of Jesus Christ, such followers of Finney as Jones scorned the patchwork reforms of Nicholas Paine Gilman. Jones spoke for God, and not, like Gilman, to the businessman.

The Civil War intensified Jones's millennial fervor. Ordained in the Congregationalist ministry in 1861 at the age of twenty-five, he immediately enlisted in the Union army as a chaplain. However, he was so full of hatred for the Satanic evil of slavery and so longed for the gore of the battlefield that he resigned his commission for a captaincy in the infantry. Characteristically, he reproached himself, on an occasion that his company was decimated, for being so notoriously deficient in duty as to have been absent on his honeymoon. This intense moral zeal to battle for the Lord as a Christian soldier unto death ruled the clergyman's life. There was in this zealot something of the fanaticism and masochism of John Brown, something of the latter's fascination with blood and struggle, something of the yearning to bear a personal cross. The two men thought of themselves as prophets of the Old Testament uncompromisingly meting out justice to the unregenerate. After the collapse of the slavocracy the unregenerate were the plutocracy; and Jones, returned to the ministry, inveighed against them as "total depravity itself organized into the institutions of society." "Wall street, and all that belongs with it," he thundered, surely will be "cast down into the bottomless pit forever." [21]

Like other mid-century pentecostalists, Jones spoke of Americans as having supplanted the Hebrews as God's chosen people in the modern age. Also, as a good Yankee, he accepted without qualification the idea that New Englanders were the selectest of the select. As the ancient Jews had received the Law, so the modern Americans, especially the people who inhabited the region of Boston, must execute It. Already the Puritans had followed divine commandment by establishing democratic forms in local town government. To complete their appointed mission of democratizing the world, Americans must abolish poverty through owning wealth in common and compensating workers according to need and not ability. This was as God intended, for why else had He sent His Son to live the communist life? Once established as a Christ-like society, America would stimulate the nations to follow suit. Then the Messiah would return as religious and secular leader of the world to terminate the woe of history and begin the glory of the millennium.[22]

The desire to prepare the way for a Christian *deus ex machina* led the zealous clergyman into several organizations. All of them failed. His society of Christian Socialists and two journals of the 1870's, *Equity* and *Labor-Balance*, expired quickly for want of support, except for "two or three personal friends . . . and . . . a

Negro minister in Arkansas. . ." In the 1880's, Jones pinned his hopes on the Knights of Labor, and here too he was shortly forced to abandon his activities. He spoke of founding a model community in the vicinity of Boston, but that enterprise never came off. Finally, by 1890 his radicalism so enraged his North Abington congregation that they refused to renew his contract. "Perhaps in all the land," he wrote, "there is not a pulpit open to me." This last must have been a bitter pill for one who had all the prerequisites for success in the New England pulpit — for one who was a Phi Beta Kappa, a Harvard man, a war hero, a writer, for one who had been described by Joseph Cook as the most promising freshman minister he knew.[23]

Yet one suspects that a career blighted by unfulfilled promise and rejection was a source of joy. Modeling his life after Him who died on the Cross, Jones embraced personal failure in the present as the means to redeem mankind in the future. This pleasure in suffering for others, as well as the faith that only Jews and Yankees understood God's revealed truth, Jones wrote into his chief work, a semi-fictionalized autobiography entitled *Joshua Davidson*. The New England clergyman, lamenting that he had no Jewish blood, endowed Joshua with a Yankee father and a mother who was part Jewish; Joshua was as Jesse "might have been, but for certain 'constitutional defects,' to use his own words." Descendant of the two chosen peoples, and instructed in the Old Testament by his Jewish maternal grandfather and in the New Testament by his Puritan minister father, Joshua took to the public forum at the age of thirty as a layman, like Jesus. He preached the communism of pentecostal society, winning the love of the poor but enraging the rich. The story closed as Jesse H. Jones would have liked to close his own life could he have arranged it: a lynch-mad mob of workers led by capitalists, the modern Pharisees, gave Joshua sweet martyrdom by hanging him.[24]

Bitter-sweet as was his rejection, the Yankee Jesus succeeded in breaking ground for radical Christianity in Boston, providing a precedent for and joining the Society of Christian Socialists (formed in 1889). William Dwight Porter Bliss, a thirty-three-year-old Episcopalian clergyman, dominated the group, editing its organ, the *Dawn*, and after a disagreement with the Society in 1890, financing it out of his own pocket. More worldly than Jones, he was born abroad, and was well educated at Constantinople's Robert College, Phillips Academy, and Amherst. Graduated from the Hartford Theological Seminary, he was ordained in the Congregationalist ministry, but entered the Episcopal church because it was leading the Protestant world in social reform. Bliss read voraciously in social and intellectual history, far more than Jones, and managed to put down what he read in innumerable pamphlets, essays, two books, a social science series, and a fat encyclopedia. Particularly familiar with English thought, he started editing in 1896 the *American Fabian*, which rehashed the ideas of Shaw and Webb, Wells and Besant. Also an enthusiastic joiner, Bliss played important roles in the Knights of Labor, the Union Labor Convention, the Church Association for the Advancement of the Interests of Labor, and lectured for the Church Social Union in England, Canada, and "almost every state of the Union." Despite this outward show of secularism Porter Bliss equaled Jesse Jones in evangelical zeal, and displayed the same Christian compulsion to wear the hair shirt. The Congregationalist minister yearned to be a Joshua Davidson; the Episcopalian clergyman identified himself with John Ball, the English priest who had been gloriously crucified for preaching "medieval Christian Socialism" in the peasant rebellion of 1381.[25]

Theologically a Broad Churchman, Bliss did not preach the imminent Second Coming. However, like Jones, he anticipated a final resolution of man's historical struggle with poverty. He accepted, with Finney's disciple, the pentecostal communism of Jesus Christ as a commandment for Christian civilization to obey; "In man's relations to man, [Christ's] . . . disciples must be socialists." Again like Jones, and unlike a Gilman or a Savage, he believed, with a footnote to Karl Marx and Thorald Rogers,

in the increasing degradation of the proletariat since the advent
of capitalism. The depression of the 1890's confirmed this belief,
and convinced Bliss that the misery of economic collapse was
the prelude to the revealed golden age.[26]

The Boston Society of Christian Socialists attracted both lay
and clerical persons who, like their leader, thought in terms of a
millennium. They included the Marxians, Laurence Gronlund
and Daniel De Leon; William D. Howells, the writer of utopian
novels; Vida D. Scudder, the Anglo-Catholic with apocalyptic
socialist visions; Hamlin Garland, who championed the social
magic of the Single-Tax; and George E. McNeill, the high priest
of the producer coöperative. As for the ministers who joined
forces with Bliss, they were a Methodist lay preacher, several
Baptists and Methodists, an Episcopalian, and Jesse H. Jones;
there were no worldly Unitarians such as a Nicholas Paine Gilman. The moderate Social Gospel of profit-sharing, because it
would strengthen private property and the profit motive, was
anathema.[27]

Herein lay the core of the Society's social criticism — that private wealth subverted Christian morality. The essence of Jesus
was selflessness, and not selfishness. His life and death revealed
that man was created for self-sacrificing service, the very antith-
esis to capitalist gain. Jesus had lived in holy coöperation with
His disciples, without profit and without property; and the Christians who understood Him knew that His doctrine propounded
the oneness of all who belonged to His body. Was not that true
of St. Paul and St. Augustine, who alike taught that the social
world was organic and not atomistic? And was it not equally
true of the Anglican Church, which claimed to embrace, yes to
unify, all believers? True ministers of the Gospel were like John
Ball, Frederick Denison Maurice, Charles Kingsley, who advocated the coöperative as against the competitive ethic in the name
of God's Son. To the point of redundancy, the Christian Socialists maintained that a literal reading of Scripture compelled the
Christian to reject economic individualism for collectivism.[28]

In citing secular theoreticians who supported their social analysis, the Socialists revealed this same ecclesiastical penchant for textual exegesis. A *Handbook of Socialism, The Encyclopedia of Social Reform,* and *The New Encyclopedia of Social Reform* were written to convince Americans that, from the Greeks down, the most eminent men in Western civilization had condemned capitalism. With Ruskin and Carlyle, Morris and Webb, Bliss and his colleagues isolated private property and the profit motive as the sources of drink, prostitution, crime, slums — and the poverty that underlay them all. Richard T. Ely, Edward Bellamy, and Lester Ward provided arguments to refute the dogmas of laissez faire. More important than the social scientists were certain metaphysical or cosmological thinkers. The Christian Socialists claimed Thomas Huxley, for he got the best of Herbert Spencer in proving that individualism was destructive of the social organism. As for Karl Marx, he was declared great among modern philosophers because he founded the movement that would unquestionably finish capitalism. Materialism in history and literalism in Scripture led alike to the expectation of the end of economic time.[29]

The Society, however much it admired Marx, refused to become a section in the Socialist Labor Party. Rather Bliss and his co-workers hoped to put an end to the squabbling among contending social reformers, and unite them in one grand Christian socialist reformation. It was for this reason that he had withdrawn from the Nationalists, when the latter fell to quarreling with other socialists and Single-Taxers. Already these very Nationalists agreed with the Socialist Labor Party, the Knights of Labor, the Grangers, the Prohibitionists, and the American Federation of Labor on the need to extend government ownership. If only they would put aside their respective differences and come together through Christ, they would be ready to strike when the day came. At "almost any moment," Bliss expected that a "panic, a crisis, a bad crop might drive men together into an invincible Reform party. . ."[30]

The desire to rally liberals of all shades and colors led the Boston clergymen to define socialism in vague and neutral terms. They sometimes referred to it as an anti-individualistic philosophy, at other times as an altruistic movement to do good, and not infrequently as the spirit of self-sacrifice exhibited by Jesus. Such vague pronouncements led a hostile critic, Nicholas Paine Gilman, to crack that Bliss and his followers were "something like a society for the propagation of virtue in general." The tendency to avoid being doctrinaire even confused the members of the Society itself. "We of the Christian Socialists have come to be Christian Socialists by such various paths," wrote Jesse H. Jones, "that it is not quite certain we mean just the same thoughts by the same words, though there is general agreement." [31]

The systematic works of Philip Moxom, Philo W. Sprague, and W. D. P. Bliss overcame only in small measure the vagueness attributed to their school of thought. However, on three points they were specifically clear: an economic order based on the public ownership of productive wealth, equal compensation to be reached slowly, and coöperation. Unwilling to defend a detailed blueprint for the future, they refused to describe the precise form of collectivization. That was a matter for experience to suggest. However, whatever the form, it must, Bliss insisted, vest authority in the people and "conform to a beneficent free and divine order." On one occasion that the head of the Christian Socialists hazarded a glimpse ahead, he wrote: "*In some way* (my italics) the local organization of business both in production or distribution, will democratically control its own affairs and yet through its chosen representatives be united with other local organizations into State and National Trade Boards and Federations — these finally being bound into one federated industrial state." As first steps toward the desired goal, Bliss borrowed the following from the Nationalist program: the Australian ballot, the eight-hour day, the nationalization of the railroads, telephone, and telegraph, the municipalization of public utilities, and prohibition.[32]

Christian Socialism was defended on the grounds that it promoted the Christian and democratic traditions of Western civilization. Economic equality, which would take time to evolve, would broaden the meaning of individual freedom; it would liberate workers from poverty, capitalists from materialism, women from bondage, ministers from slavishness, artists from commercialization. Coöperation would make real the Christian principle of brotherly love, and the people's control of productive wealth would extend the principle of democracy to the economy. Individualism would not perish in a society free from want, but would assume "a higher and less material form"; in place of money, "men would contend . . . for . . . attainments in the arts, in science, in learning, in character." Nor would the coöperative commonwealth destroy evolutionary progress; Bliss assured his readers of "a renaissance in art, a revival in learning, a reformation in religion." [33] At no time did the Christian Socialists regard material well-being and economic security as ultimate ends, but rather as means to achieve the spiritual life.

The *Dawn* monotonously repeated the ends of the desired society from 1889 until its demise in 1896, neither changing nor clarifying its views. The means of social change, however, shifted from education to direct political action. In the first year it was hoped that the churches, by organizing classes in "Social Christianity," would serve as educational cells to propagate the cooperative commonwealth. With this in mind the Society engaged Laurence Gronlund, Edward Bellamy, Francis Bellamy, P. W. Sprague, W. D. P. Bliss, and James Yeames to write pamphlets on the literature of soical reform to be used as reading materials. Abhorring class warfare, Bliss hoped that the church study groups would draw all who "are interested . . . statesman . . . merchant . . . farmer . . . mechanic . . . miner. . ." Between 1890 and 1892 the *Dawn*, thinking the educative process too slow, looked for a union of clergymen, intellectuals, farmers, and laborers to make socialistic gains through the People's Party. After a trip through the country after the election of 1892, Bliss concluded that America was not ready for his advanced ideas, and he reverted to education as the means to attain the good life. As late as October 1895, he remarked that "Socialism . . . simply needs a knowledge to be accepted." His own Church of the Carpenter, comprising all classes and teaching the gospel of Marx and Webb as well as administering the creed of the Thirty-Nine Articles, reveals how Bliss would have liked to see all churches organized.[34]

In 1896, the Episcopal clergyman left Boston to do organizational work for the Church Social Union, and with his departure came the end of the *Dawn* and the Christian Socialist Society. Numerically, the Society had little effect; it numbered less than two dozen at the outset, considerably less at the end. Bliss published the *Dawn* irregularly for want of outside financial aid, and often he complained that because he could not afford an assistant he could neither prepare articles with leisure nor proofread them. No other reform journal in Boston shows such haste in being put together. On the credit side, the Society took the atheist onus out of the word socialism, helping to dispose the public toward a more rational approach to it. Bliss played an active role in the anti-sweatshop campaign in Boston, which led to the regulation of making clothing in the North End tenements. Also, as a worker in the Church Social Union, he educated fellow Episcopalians in socialism, the causes of poverty, and the desirability of trade unions. Admired by certain leaders of the Knights of Labor, and stimulating to such middle-class intellectuals as Robert A. Woods, William Dean Howells, and Vida D. Scudder, he was thought, however, something of a socialist nuisance by the trade unionists of the American Federation of Labor.[35]

Ironically, it was not a Bliss or a Jones who banded together modern pentecostalists, but a clergyman who disbelieved in the divinity of Jesus and who broke with institutional Christianity: Herbert Newton Casson. Born in Canada in 1869, and ordained a Methodist clergyman twenty-one years later, he left the ministry shortly thereafter to devote himself to socialism. He was convinced that institutional religion had "become an opiate"; that it supported the business community against laborers, and that it was false to the communist principles of Jesus, the "most famous and influential of all workingmen." In 1893, Casson appeared in Boston, where he agitated for public works for the unemployed, and enrolled many of the latter in Coxey's Army. One year later he established in industrial Lynn, on the English model, the first Labor Church in America.[36] Until he left for New York in 1900, Casson spoke in his pulpit on subjects ranging from the historical role of Jesus to that of William Jennings Bryan, spicing his sermons and pamphlets with venomous shafts against Christianity and Christian Socialism, Jews and moneylenders, political bosses and plutocrats — the oppressors of the poor.

The Labor Church was unaffiliated with any religious institution in America. Only workers belonged to it, as once only workers had belonged to the labor church of Jesus. Its purpose was to destroy capitalism and its ally, Christianity, and institute the coöperative life. Casson believed in God, the Father, but Jesus was a historical figure. The young radical established the creed of himself and his followers in his own "Ten Commandments." The "shalt nots" added up to a war against private property, the profit motive, the wage system, and competition; the "thou shalts" enjoined Cassonites to "seek thine own welfare in advancing the welfare of all" through the common ownership of property. Casson never made clear the details of his socialism, but he believed that God was for it, as He had been for abolitionism.[37]

Through the working masses, the Lynn preacher hoped to achieve the desired end. He hated the Pharisees and Sadducees of the middle and upper classes, whether they were W. D. P. Blisses or Mark Hannas, believing with single-minded fanaticism that workers were God's children. He hoped that trade unionism would bring the socialist triumph, but in 1896 he pinned his hopes on William Jennings Bryan. Tillman, Altgeld, Debs, Bryan, and the people, he wrote, are out for the "aristocrats and monopolists who have again and again hounded the laboring people to starvation and death." And behind the enemies of the people stood international Jewry: "After centuries of contempt, the money-lending Jew is at last having revenge on the world. Once his trade was the most disreputable in Europe, but today he is master of nations." [38]

Radical social Christianity did not have a large following, and by 1896 it was dead, excepting the lone and vitriolic figure of Herbert Newton Casson. However much W. D. P. Bliss dressed up Karl Marx and Sidney Webb in Christian attire, he could not sell the abolition of private property to the Protestant business community. And Jesse Jones's concept of the noble and Herbert Casson's stereotype of the vile Jew were simply out of place in Boston, where there was neither anti-Semitic nor pro-Jewish feeling. One wonders indeed if the radicals really wanted to succeed; for throughout their writings runs the theme of sacrificing oneself, as did Jesus, for a noble cause. Bliss recorded with pleasure, in a reminiscing mood, how tragedy went hand in hand with reform, how he suffered from lack of money, how his wife endured loneliness and poverty to stand by her husband. The relative unconcern with detail also suggests that the radicals did not thrive on success. Bliss gave space to a coöperative clothing store in his community center, but he failed to follow its activities — and it turned into a sweatshop! [39] The otherworld aspect of the radicals suggests that they regarded a reform tract as an act of communion; public rejection as a reënactment of Calvary.

IV

The unique development of American Christianity in the last part of the nineteenth century was the Social Gospel, and the Boston experience did not differ from that of the nation at large. It neither led nor followed the movement; its Washington Gladden was Nicholas Paine Gilman; its George Herron was W. D. P. Bliss; its Josiah Strong was Joseph Cook. However sharp their differences, both radicals and moderates agreed on the need for some kind of coöperative society to take the place of predatory individualism. Aside from its straight reform proposals, social Christianity in Boston also embraced the institutional church (especially the Universalists and the Congregationalists), which represented a wiser philanthropy, rather than a reforming agency.[40] Throughout the period strode Edward Everett Hale, throwing his Unitarian weight behind projects for good; in having this venerable figure from the past, Boston boasted of a personality not available in other eastern cities or in Gladden's midwest.

The works of W. D. P. Bliss and Nicholas Paine Gilman represent respectively the most fruitful products of the radical and moderate Social Gospel. As editor of the *Encyclopedia of Social Reform*, 1897, Bliss made a first-rate compilation of the progressive ideas of the 1880's and 1890's; and as editor of the Social Science Series, he brought out the works of John Ruskin, Thomas Carlyle, William Morris, and Thorald Rogers, thinkers significant for their social criticism. All this led Richard T. Ely to remark: "The Christian Socialists display much zeal in the dissemination of useful economic knowledge." [41] At his best in presenting the ideas of other men, W. D. P. Bliss's own thought, however, was often vague, obscure, superficial, and imitative. In contrast, Nicholas Paine Gilman wrote the chaste, clear prose of the best stylists of the day and, while not the originator of profit-sharing, presented a forceful and lucid defense of it. His *Socialism and the American Spirit* is a major synthesis of both moderate social Christianity and United States character. The product of careful research, it is at the same time the most ambitious, systematic, and original tract written by a Boston clergyman in the last two decades of the nineteenth century. Gilman's predilection for a mixed economy — of government regulation of big business, of trade unions, of the state ownership of some productive property and, above all, of welfare capitalism — anticipated the liberalism of the 1930's and 1940's.

The moderates succeeded where the radicals failed because they came to terms with secularism. The first looked to Jesus of Nazareth solely for ethical inspiration (Christ was a sacred "poet," not a "professor of economics," as Nicholas Paine Gilman put it); [42] the second regarded pentecostal society as containing the eternal laws of divine political economy. The one backed reforms capable of immediate realization; the other preached atonement for sinful capitalism through self-mortification. Where Nicholas Gilman hoped to realize his plans through the leadership of the business community, Jesse H. Jones exorcised the modern Pharisees, and W. D. P. Bliss counted on dissident clergymen to make a socialist reformation. Significantly, the Unitarians, who felt most at home in urban and secular Boston, were the leading moderates; whereas the orthodox Jesse H. Jones, who looked upon the modern city as painted harlotry and Babylon, shared with Bliss the leadership of the radicals. Jesse Jones would have been at ease with Jesus and his humble supporters, or so he thought, and perhaps with the English Levellers of the seventeenth century and the mid-century religious utopian socialists; in the Boston of 1880–1900, he was simply an anachronism. Porter Bliss, who converted to Episcopalianism, also felt out of place in America, which, unlike England, had no established church, and therefore no ecclesiastical officers independent of laymen to lead the way in Christian Socialism. For all his secular learning, the rector of the Church of the Carpenter was medieval in his idealization of the joys of simplicity and poverty.[43] In general, the following rule and its converse held true for the Boston Protestant Social Gospel: the less modern the theology, the more radical the sociology.

In the years 1880–1900 the Protestant ministry in Boston failed to form an organization to unite Social Gospelers so as to give cohesion to liberal aspirations.[44] Yet, however sharp their differences, Protestant clergymen had more in common with one an-

other than with the overwhelming majority of Catholic priests
and Jewish rabbis, whose traditions precluded the recognition
and removal of the environmental determinants of sin. Secularized, Protestantism traced individual and collective wrongdoing
to maladjustments in society. The Catholics, essentially Augustin-
ian, regarded evil as almost entirely the consequence of the taint
inherited from Adam and Eve. The Jews, not even excepting
Solomon Schindler, did not think in terms of sin; they could not,
as their heritage did not embrace the Christian cosmology of the
creation, the fall of man, the incarnation, and salvation. Catholic
resistance to secularization prevented the formulation of conceptions of God and man conducive to the sociological idea of evil,
while Solomon Schindler's liberalization of Jewish orthodoxy resulted ironically in giving his congregation a necessary appurte-
nance for middle-class living, not presuppositions for the removal
of economic injustice.

The respective positions of the three religious communities in
Boston also conditioned their response to urban and industrial
problems. Of longer residence in the city than the immigrant
Jews and Catholics, the Protestants regarded themselves as rightful leaders of society in time of crisis. The Puritan conception of
stewardship fortified this attitude, and the simultaneous decay of
orthodoxy and the inadequacy of charity stimulated the Protestant
clergy to justify Christian leadership by creating a social order
compatible with the ethics of the Sermon on the Mount. The tradition of the Boston clergy encouraged this high-minded activism.
To the perception of evil, the conception of stewardship, and the
heritage of activism, one must add a final and compelling factor:
the Protestant clergyman's sense of guilt. Unlike Catholic priests
and Jewish rabbis in ministering almost entirely to the prosperous
members of a society judged unchristian because of its predatory
individualism and class cleavages, Protestant men of God grieved
that it seemed as if they were sanctioning the worst consequences
of capitalism. In their reform activities then they attempted to
absolve themselves as well as society from sin.

Boston's minority of old stock Americans of Protestant persuasion contributed more ministers to the progressive movements of the 1880's and 1890's than the more numerous Catholics and less numerous Jews. The reformers considered John Boyle O'Reilly, James Jeffrey Roche, and Solomon Schindler as prizes — as liberal exceptions to the norms of their respective faiths. But the Protestant Social Gospelers appeared perfectly normal to the social reform mind, in fact, not radical enough for the taste of a W. D. P. Bliss. As the sons of Puritan stock predominated among the progressives in the church, so they enjoyed a monopoly among the intellectuals, and especially in the Protestant-oriented centers of higher learning.

Chapter Five

THE HIGHER LEARNING
The Inductive Method and the Gentleman's Burden

One cannot justify education today except in terms of social welfare. — Professor Francis Greenwood Peabody

Social science is not, like geology or astronomy, a science which has its results only in the progress which comes from conforming exactly to data which will be practically the same whether we conform or not; social science includes within its data the constructive and reconstructive energy of the conscious mind. It is the science of social nutrition and hygiene, of social pathology and therapeutics. — Robert A. Woods [1]

With no thought of being Positivists, the reformers of the eighties and nineties had faith in the capacity of social science to translate ethics into action. They hoped to find in social science, not merely a description of society, but the means of social change for democratic ends. In the last two decades of the nineteenth century academic sociologists and economists promised to provide such a body of information. They were to the reform mind of the 1880's and 1890's what John Keynes was to the liberals of the New Deal. The professors seemed to hold the key to unlock the treasures of industrialism and distribute them on a wide and just basis. They were the social engineers of their day.

This faith in social science derived from the complexity of American life as it assumed its industrial and urban forms. The

work of the abolitionist was done once he perceived the wickedness of slavery; the task of the post-Civil War reformer began
with his comprehension of economic injustice. From there he had
to puzzle out how a rich and equalitarian culture bred paupers
and millionaires, slums and mansions, booms and busts, corrupt
politics. Given that knowledge, he could then hope to find ways
of improving the nation. So thought a handful of professors with
a social conscience in Boston's institutions of higher education.
In the seminaries and in the departments of economics and philosophy in the liberal arts colleges, they introduced and taught
either institutional economics or social science of their own making. They compounded academic knowledge with Puritan duty,
expounding at the same time the principles of modern society
and the responsibility of the college man to the community.

These ideas were superimposed on an academic tradition which
by 1875 was alien to the concept of education as preparation for
social change. The chief end of both the college and the professional school was to prepare men and women for success in the
world as it existed. On the undergraduate level a curriculum that
had changed little since the Renaissance operated to create "a
separate and Brahmin class, who could be called gentlemen."
Certain of these gentlemen went on for further study in bread
and butter subjects so as to achieve specialized competence in
the law, medicine, architecture, dentistry, engineering, or the
ministry. Louis Brandeis learned his law lessons so well that he
became a millionaire by the time he was forty. With equal ex-
pertness Theodore Roosevelt grasped the meaning of Harvard
Yard when he dismissed the more than a dozen socially improper
students who outranked him academically. "Only one gentleman
stands ahead of me," he crowed. When Brandeis and Roosevelt
came to champion the progressive cause early in the twentieth
century, they did so only after reëducating themselves. The one
created a sociological brief such as had not been taught in Lang-
dell's day, while the other acquired an understanding of central
planning from the Comtean Herbert Croly, whose ideas, Roose-

velt noted, the college of 1880 would have "treated either as un-
intelligible or else as pure heresy." [2]

Harvard's future trust-busting President of the United States
was not the only one to complain that "there was very little in
my actual studies which helped me in after life." Even ethics,
which supposedly got at moral living, was taught in such a
wretched rote way, Owen Wister recalled, that the frivolous and
the serious alike considered it as unrelated to actual life as the
square root of two. The divinity schools were no better, with
courses that never went beyond dry-as-dust church history, homi-
lectics, Hebrew grammar, and textual exigesis. Many a Boston
minister who taught himself the Social Gospel reminisced bitterly
that his seminary training impeded his coming to terms with the
city, or at best left a vacuum that had to be filled. The latter was
also the case for the high-minded Mary Kingsbury Simkhovitch,
founder of Greenwich House, who departed from Boston University with "a thesis on the supine in U as a dative. . ." Doubtless
the lamentations of the *Education* were a form of both masochism
and boasting, but Henry Adams was typical of the men who went
to college before the 1880's in his failure to be instructed in the
ways of the city and the machine.[3]

Up to 1880 a Bachelor in Arts or Science left the campus without the opportunity to take a course in the Industrial Revolution.
At Harvard there was a Bowdoin Prize for the best essay on "The
History and Economic Effects of the Metayer System of Farming," but no prizes for either a historical or an inductive study of
the effect of the factory upon the worker. The political economy offered at Boston's colleges led students to believe that the
factory was an unqualified blessing. Established as an academic
discipline by the 1870's, economics taught hallowed laissez-faire
doctrine through the orthodox works of Mill, Cairnes, and Bastiat.
The chief axiom was the economic man, the major theorem was
let alone. The method was deductive, and the conclusions were
drawn *a priori*. It was assumed, as was fitting for rational men,
that the economic machine was like the physical-world machine:

harmonious, self-regulating, complete, and governed by natural law. The wise and benign described the machine, only the unwise or vicious dared tamper with it. When, in the 1870's, Herbert Spencer's pontifications were joined to Manchester encyclicals, professors had an almost sacrosanct base from which to fend off welfare economics. Snapped M.I.T.'s President: laissez faire "was not made the test of economic orthodoxy, merely. It was used to decide whether a man was an economist at all." [4]

On the day laissez faire triumphed "Satan won a great victory and there was joy in hell," cracked an irreverent young economist. In the universities and seminaries there was merely lethargy, among students and professors alike. Fortifying this lethargy was a tradition which held that college men who went social reforming were "amazing if not vulgar." Such had been the experience of Wendell Phillips. He lost his gentleman status upon embracing abolitionism, and further ouraged proper classmates in supporting Benjamin ("Beast") Butler for the governorship. In his Phi Beta Kappa Address at Harvard in 1881, Phillips sought vindication. He accused the college man of being worse than vulgar in shutting himself up in an ivory tower. What was the good of learning when the university turned its back on the temperance, feminist, prison, and abolitionist movements — "the great social questions which stir and educate the age"? His final peroration commanded the audience to support labor so as to defeat a money-grubbing business class such as had "wrecked the Grecian and Roman States." But it is doubtful that Phillips thought he could persuade the assemblage at Harvard Yard that all along he had been right and they had been wrong. Such American tory radicalism as had existed had been extinguished by the failure of the Liberal Republicans and the almost incredible grip of the boss on politics. One of Phillips' hearers dismissed his discourse as "delightful . . . but preposterous from beginning to end." [5]

The school had first to reform itself before it could reform American society. The handful of Boston educators after 1880 who responded to the challenge of the urban age comprehended the necessity for an inductive social science, one that described life as it was really lived. They knew, too, that the college must understand that its "vocation" was neither "the breeding of elegant dilettantes . . . nor the manufacture of efficient breadwinners," but the preparation for men for social service. Apart from Francis Amasa Walker, President of the Massachusetts Institute of Technology, these educators were ministers who returned to the seminary to give the younger generation that training which they had failed to get. One returned to Andover, one to Harvard, and one to Cambridge Episcopal Theological School.[6] Their fruits were numerous writings, pioneer courses in social science, a few gifted disciples, and the social settlement. The story of campus liberalism is thus the story of two generations, of those who were graduated from college before 1870, and those who learned from them and others like them in the 1880's and 1890's.

II

The pre-1870 group numbered four: Francis A. Walker, of M.I.T., William Jewett Tucker, of Andover, Francis Greenwood Peabody, of Harvard, and George Hodges of the Cambridge Episcopal Theological School. They were not like the Young Turks who stormed the walls of academia in the 1890's and the first part of the twentieth century. They drank neither the socialist brew served by the faculties of Germany, as did an Edward Ross, nor the intoxicant fermented on Populist prairies, as did a J. Allen Smith. Nor were they the sort of root thinkers that were Charles Beard and John Dewey. They were settled in their careers, endowed with positions of responsibility, rooted in the community. They were not the stuff radicals were made of. Rather they were the stuff college presidents, deans, and professors of applied Christianity (who kept their jobs) were made of. Convention calls them deridingly — at best condescendingly — patrician or genteel reformers. Normative judgments aside, they were the predecessors of the institutionalists and pragmatists, a quartet among the first generation of academic dissidents.

They were born in the 1840's and 1850's, too young to participate in mid-century reform movements, yet old enough to remember their families' participation in them. Walker grew up under the influence of a father who had been a typical middle-class universal liberal in his involvement in feminism and abolitionism, the peace and temperance movements. Ephraim Peabody was minister of King's Chapel, a position that enabled his son Francis to meet and associate with abolitionist Boston. Tucker, an orphan, was nurtured in the household of a minister uncle, where the Puritan virtue of high thinking had not as yet been severed from plain living. George Hodges' family started him on Gibbon at six, and at ten he was already enrolling neighborhood boys in the "Hodges Temperance Society." Each inherited from his immediate forebears the mid-century Yankee passion for minding the moral business of others; and this "bequest of the Puritan conscience," as one put it, "was not something to be accepted or denied: it was to be taken at its full value and put to immediate use." [7]

The three clergymen-academicians played prominent parts in reëxamining the gospel so as to provide a Christian sanction for social service. Tucker was a Bushnellian Congregationalist, Peabody a Unitarian, and Hodges a Kingsleyan Episcopalian, but all shared the idea that the proper duty of theologians was not "gloss upon gloss, comment upon comment," but the teaching of the idea that the religious life must be "crowded with fraternal deeds." Due partly to their efforts, Andover, Harvard, and Cambridge Episcopal taught theology historically and comparatively, not as dogma made respectable with age and custom. None of the three men expected humans to be angels on this earth, yet they hoped with a Robertson and a Kingsley and a Bushnell that a good environment would make it difficult for men to be bad. They also agreed that society was tied together by the living Christ, and that men must serve one another in order to serve

Christ. Therefore, their credo was: the divinity student "should be instructed in theology, but more in sociology." So blurred did the lines become between Unitarian Harvard and Congregationalist Andover that their divinity schools merged early in the twentieth century, ending the rift begun in 1804. As for Cambridge Episcopal, a lady parishioner withdrew in a huff from St. John's Chapel because "Dean Hodges was a Unitarian, Dr. Nash an atheist, and Mr. Drown impossible!" [8]

Criticism even worse than this could not intimidate. Boston's quartet belonged, each man enjoying a commanding stature. Walker succeeded brilliantly in everything he undertook; he was a Civil War brigadier general at twenty-five, a statistician of international reputation at thirty, an economist of first rank at thirty-five, President of M.I.T. at forty. Peabody rose steadily at Harvard, from lecturer in 1880 to full professor in 1886 to Dean of the Divinity School in 1901. Hodges during the 1880's was rector of the most important church in Pittsburgh, turned down the presidency of Kenyon College and the position of Bishop Coadjutator of Oregon, and came to Cambridge Episcopal as Dean only after the most ardent persuasion on the part of Robert Treat Paine, Boston's leading Episcopal layman. As for Tucker, he won recognition as a brilliant clergyman, inspired a generation of Andover students, and capped his career by becoming President of Dartmouth in 1893. Situated as they were, the quartet knew everyone who counted in academic, literary, and philanthropic Boston, knew the sort of Brahmins celebrated by Oliver Wendell Holmes.

Such persons rejected the concept that the millionaire was the bloom of civilization and should rule simply because he was a millionaire. Their values were not of the market place, of the *nouveaux*. Peabody was accustomed to wealth, and considered money-grubbers outside the refined traditions of Boston. Walker, who gloried in his military exploits, cared as little for men motivated solely by economic gain as his friends John Hay and Henry Adams. (After a particularly gory encounter which his Union

division won, Walker wrote: "Ah, Kate don't you wish you were
a man and could fight?") Hodges' Pittsburgh church had included
the wealthiest steel men of the city, among them Henry Frick,
but the rector preferred ministering to the unfortunates in the
mission. He read prodigiously in Ruskin, Kingsley, and Carlyle,
in whom he discovered the social problem for the first time, and
concluded with them that economic individualism destroyed
Christian idealism. A Lowell Institute audience, which had forgotten slave-trading and smuggling ancestors, appreciated the
indignation of his lecture over men who "undersell their neighbors, pay starvation wages, maintain sweatshops, adulterate goods,
bribe . . . , lie and cheat and steal and commit murder, for love
of money." At a time when clergymen and educators applauded
Andrew Carnegie for wishing to give away his fortune to philanthropic agencies, Tucker took Carnegie to task for accumulating too much fortune to begin with.[9]

State socialists were as repellant as plutocrats. As a proponent
of ethical competition, Walker abhorred the monolithic Marxian
and Nationalist governments. As disciples of Christ, the clergymen-professors recoiled from the atheism of Marxism and that
part of the catechism which stated that personality and idealism
derived from a materialistic base. At the same time it was understood that workers, with legitimate grievances, were attracted to
Marxism and might smash "the prosperity and permanence of our
social life. . ." Tucker lectured on the "dangerous classes," Peabody noted the large number of converts to German Social Democracy, and Hodges observed that "when property is in the
hands of the few and power in the hands of the many," the day "is
a day of peril." They sympathized with the worker, as had Jesus
and Kingsley, but they did not want him to follow a Socialist
demagogue. He might, however, unless Christians, through "sentiment applied to science," solved the social problem before it was
too late.[10]

The sentiment was there, in Christianity; the science had to be
created. The first task was to demolish the dismal science of clas-

sical economics. As early as the 1870's Walker pioneered in putting political economy on a historical and inductive basis. In his
Wages Question he proved statistically that labor was not compensated by a fixed capital fund, as the Iron Law of Wages postu-
lated, but by the productivity of its own work. He destroyed the
abstraction of the economic man, which did not square with such
observed facts that patriotism, ignorance, superstition, and solici-
tude for labor often operated in the market. Above all, he claimed
that there was not a single piece of evidence to support the thesis
that the economic order was like a machine. Such a conception
had derived from a false eighteenth-century "natural theology"
whose priests unfortunately understood only the "*a priori* and
deductive." [11]

Walker attacked orthodoxy as a professional and dispassionate
economist, the clergyman-professors assaulted it as Christian
humanists. Sympathetic with workers, they "refused to obey the
mandate of the old political economy, and leave the individual
to the fortune of the market-place." Tucker's course, Social Economics, required students to read Toynbee's *Industrial Revolution,* which painted a canvas of working-class misery in bold and
black strokes; Peabody's students in Social Ethics read Ruskin
and Carlyle, who decried the ugliness of planless capitalism. And
in his Lowell Institute Lectures, Hodges pointed to the slum as
a chief consequence of blind economic growth. The three men
agreed that there was an *observed* need to eliminate poverty, the
boredom of machine-tending, child and female labor, the tenement, class stratification. This was the lesson of history, and the
orthodox economist who claimed economic equilibrium was either
a pedantic fool or businessman's tool. After comparing the growth
of the factory system with the theory of Manchester science,
Hodges concluded bitterly that the latter rightly had come "to
be thought as the science of extortion, the gentle art of grinding
the faces of the poor." [12]

The statistical Walker and the Christian trio combined to
create an academic dissent such as led to the founding of the

American Economic Association in 1885. The leaders, young social scientists returned from Germany, chose the forty-five-year-old Francis Walker as first president: "we looked upon him as a champion and emancipator," wrote Richard T. Ely. From the beginning, Tucker accepted articles from the members of the Association for publication in his *Andover Review,* articles which propounded a new political economy. Its essence was a combination of what Walker and Tucker and Peabody had been saying for at least a half dozen years. Such rights as property and such theories as laissez faire were neither absolute, nor divine, nor universal, nor eternal, but products of a particular stage in history. From this it followed that the economist must know the institutions of past and present before generalizing economic experience. Equally important, he must consider Christian ethics as having a bearing on economic policy and be ready to give the state wider powers whenever laissez faire proved to be cruel and inefficient. Concluded one professor: "Contemporary economists have become social scientists, philanthropists, political philosophers." [13]

The big question in the new social science — whether called institutional economics or social ethics or social economics — was not what is, but what ought-to-be. By the very nature of the question, the answer called for social experimentation of one sort or another. Walker, who thought that competition worked well in America, proposed only such legislation as affected the solvency of banks and the hygienic well-being of factory hands. He also supported the rising trade union movement because it "curbed the authority of the employing classes. . ." Peabody urged businessmen to raise wages, shorten hours, erect model tenements, and proposed that the government provide parks, playgrounds, and rapid transit to the suburbs. Together good businessmen and wise government would improve the material well-being of the working class.

Andover and Cambridge Episcopal were more militant than Harvard and the Massachusetts Institute of Technology. Tucker and Hodges, as Bushnellian Congregationalist and Kingsleyan

Episcopalian, believed more in the organic society and the immanent God than Peabody and Walker. Therefore, they were theologically receptive to the concept of planning. The Andover professor wrote hopefully that profit-sharing, coöperatives, the income tax, and a legal eight-hour day might recover for society
"wealth as may now be wrongfully or wastefully in the possession of the few." However, he immediately added that he did not
know which of the "experimental methods for distribution of
wealth" would work best. Hodges paraphrased approvingly
Albert Shaw's arguments for municipal socialism on the model of
Glasgow and Birmingham. If the city undertook to supply itself
with light, gas, and tramway service, it would remove the corrupt
politician and greedy capitalist who colluded to make the utility
franchise the curse of the city. Equally important, a planning
board would tear down slums and build sanitary apartments,
provide gymnasiums and baths. Above all, the municipal government, with important and expanded functions, would attract as
officials men of good will and talent rather than the usual seeker
for power and patronage.[14]

The four pioneers at Harvard, Andover, Cambridge Episcopal,
and the Massachusetts Institute of Technology assume significance
as transitional figures. Their works stand between the cold-blooded
deductive volumes of Francis Wayland and the humanitarian
fact-larded tomes of John R. Commons. Their demolition of
laissez faire is recognizably modern, but certain of their concepts
either jar or seem curious. Walker, a prominent racial snob, wrote
disparagingly of immigrants and warned ominously of Anglo-
Saxon race suicide. Peabody's Social Ethics and Tucker's Social
Economics contained units on prisoners, paupers, drunkards, Indians, freedmen, and divorced persons — hangovers from the social science of the post-Civil War decade. Both men stumbled into
their courses. Tucker started out to acquaint seminarians with
city conditions, and Peabody hit on the inductive method in order
to change the traditional way of teaching ethics at Harvard
through memory of text.[15] Only Walker did original research in

economics. The others lacked his professional training, and their energies were almost completely devoted to discrediting the Manchester School. When the quartet's conceptions of social reconstruction were definite, they were usually mild; when they were militant they were often tentative — and derivative.

As educators and as administrators in education the four achieved solid success. Walker, while President of Massachusetts Institute of Technology, introduced courses in economics, sociology, and history in a technical school for the first time, thereby beginning the long and arduous task of humanizing the engineer. Tucker's Social Economics, first offered in 1880, attracted considerable attention at the end of the decade and was adopted in several colleges and divinity schools. Hodges popularized social Christianity in nine volumes of sermons, innumerable articles, and thirty-four books. As Dean of Episcopal Theological he was the first of his denomination to make room in the curriculum for Christian sociology. Peabody gave the first course of its kind in a seminary, and by 1900 was holding a graduate seminar in the "Christian Doctrine of the Social Order." From the beginning both collegians and seminarians took his elective, and in 1906 Social Ethics was elevated to a full-fledged department in the university. Joyfully, Edward Everett Hale observed that, whereas his own college generation had been interested in literature, "the fashion of the young men to-day . . . is social science. They ask how man is to be improved, how the black spots are to be washed off, how the world is to be made better." [16]

The Boston four broke down in part the Renaissance ideal of the gentleman as a cultivated lounger, which had lain uneasily on the Puritan conscience. As Peabody put it: "One cannot justify education today except in terms of social welfare." However, they did not destroy the idea of the gentleman. Rather they appealed to a class consciousness in students deriving from high social standing and Anglo-Saxon parentage. They pointed to the model of that fraction of English university men who, accustomed to the responsibilities of wealth and culture, were in the 1880's

attempting to soften the effects of capitalism. They endowed the
Boston seminarian and collegian with the idea that he stood between the plutocrat and the proletarian, that he was neither
grasping nor degraded, but altruistic and refined, and with social
science know-how. The burden was clear: to safeguard society
against subversion from extreme and antithetical elements. To
this burden of the gentleman they added a comfort, however. The
clergymen-professors pointed out that in a materialistic and selfish age an educated young man could make life personally meaningful only by helping others.[17] Here we have it. The major educational accomplishment of the Boston four was to teach the
younger generation the gentleman's burden and the gentleman's comfort.

III

In the 1860's Russian students, ashamed of the sterility of mere
learning and mere luxury, fled comfortable surroundings to live
among and uplift an illiterate and impoverished peasantry. "V
Narodnye!" ("To the People!") was their cry. In the 1880's English university men, similarly motivated, invaded London's White-
chapel and East End. In the 1890's Boston's educated younger
generation took to the field. For a decade Professors Tucker and
Peabody had been preparing students for such a venture. The
two teachers, in order to show firsthand how the other half lived,
guided students through reformatories, prisons, asylums, factories,
trade union headquarters. What was missing was an institution
to house mill hand and campus product together so that the latter could begin — in the words of the *Harvard Advocate* — the
"lifting up of degraded humanity." [18]

The first venture was the Prospect Union. Established in 1891
by Peabody and a small group of workingmen and Harvard students, the Union was a combination workers' college and club.
There came together in brotherhood and for mutually helpful
contact "white and black, Hebrew and Gentile," laborer and

scholar, rich and poor. Students and faculty of Harvard who served as instructors enjoyed living outside the bounds of class and race, and a few spoke of "a certain joy and buoyancy in self-sacrifice that those not engaged in it can't understand." As for the workers, Peabody explained, they had a substitute for the saloon. They discussed their own problems, pursued the higher things of the mind under an able faculty, and learned too the pleasure in association transcending social barriers. Improver and improvee were alike uplifted. The project "would have seemed to the college man of a generation ago amazing, if not vulgar," was the boast.[19] Yet the Union was but another expression of the charitable impulse, and failed to attack the causes that made for classes in the first place. The task of removing disparities in wealth by the wise application of Christian social science fell to Professor Tucker's protégé and Boston's male Jane Addams — Robert Archie Woods.

Robert A. Woods was born December 9, 1865, in Pittsburgh, of middle-class, Scotch-Irish parents. Intellectually arid, his natal city was mercantile, hard-headed, and Calvinist, reflecting the values of the British-American business community which dominated the life of the Pennsylvania town. From his serious and morally rigid Presbyterian upbringing, Robert learned the meaning of duty; but it was not until he enrolled at Amherst in 1882 that he entered upon the world of ideas and ideals. The western Massachusetts college was then exposing undergraduates to the new learning in religion and science. The Pittsburgh student got "safely away from the doctrinal aspect of his Calvinist environment" without losing his faith in religion and the moral passion of Puritanism. He listened to lectures which derided the theory of individualism and which substituted for it that of the organic conception of society. He heard, as guest preachers, Lyman Abbott and Henry Ward Beecher, leaders of the Social Gospel. He remembered long after he left Amherst that President Seelye "In one of his most solemn utterances . . . declared that no career could be of higher service to the nation than that of the educated man who should go among the people and in largeness of mind and heart join with them in working out the labor problem."

Prepared thus to embark on a career of public good and service, Woods, on being graduated from Amherst in 1886, was not sure where he could do his best work. He did not wish to pledge himself prematurely to the ministry, and therefore decided to go to Andover for graduate study, where he could learn the lessons of applied Christianity that would be of value for any future work he would choose to take up. Professor Tucker was then inspiring his students with his message, so much so that "the fellows make a regular pope out of him," Woods wrote to his mother. The Amherst graduate imbibed the tenets of Progressive Orthodoxy, read widely in constitutional history and political economy, served as special correspondent of the *Christian Union*, and studied on the spot utopian societies, trade unions, and reformatories. As a member of the advanced class, he was permitted much study of his own choice, which he did under the direction of Tucker. In Calvinist earnestness the twenty-three-year-old wrote to his mother of his selected project: "I am trying to find out what has been done in the last five centuries to make men, especially poor men, better and happier." [20]

Shortly before his twenty-fifth birthday Robert A. Woods came to a philosophy which would guide him throughout his life. A compound of Progressive Orthodoxy and applied social science, it was serious, severe, single-minded, and both pragmatic and mystical. He pledged himself to ignore theories and ideas which did "not promise to actively contribute to the artistic sacramental living of life . . . "; to "learn by experience . . . "; to find God and His purpose in the world; to reach the Almighty by taking up the "calling" of serving fellow men. That Robert Woods could not return to Pittsburgh, as his mother hoped, was clear. To her he wrote that, "I am compelled to feel as if nothing less than the world was to be my home." A rationalist and a social scientist, Robert Woods was also child of the 17th-century Puritans in the belief that God was the prime mover of history:

God is striving to realize some great thought in the history of mankind. We can know that thought only by working together with God. There is a mighty purpose working out in the life of humanity and of every man. I commit myself absolutely to this fact and to the movement of this purpose. I will learn to test every suggestion by this motive. God must have infinite activity as well as infinite repose. I know the law of my being. I will follow it absolutely.[21]

In 1891 Professor Tucker sent his favorite student to England to study Toynbee Hall in order to found a similar establishment in Boston. Woods spent less than a year abroad, examining trade unions, institutional churches, settlement houses, the conditions of the poor, and familiarizing himself with literature of social reform. He met William T. Stead, the muckraker, Professor Marshall, the economist, Graham Wallas and William Clarke, Fabian Socialists, the Reverend Mr. and Mrs. Barnett, leaders of Toynbee Hall; and he discovered the inspiring social criticism of John Ruskin. He saw pauperism at its worst and reforms at their maturest; he returned to America firmly convinced of the need of getting men to believe more in the collective salvation of mankind on earth and less in the individual journey to heaven. Of this field trip to industrial England Robert A. Woods wrote that it marked "the end of the first stage in my career" — his education.[22] Thereafter, he interpreted British humanitarian thought for his countrymen and developed into the philosopher and tactician of the university settlement.

In describing the many-faceted endeavors for social betterment in Great Britain, Woods represented the trend of the new social science to describe actual, observable conditions of life and work. His *English Social Movements*, the first systematic treatment of its subject in American scholarship, contained his observations for the year 1891, while his subsequent book reviews, articles, and lectures informed interested Americans of the very latest developments. He revealed to his countrymen that England, having awakened to the seriousness of poverty and rigid class stratification, was bent on achieving social democracy through as many regenerative movements as there were segments in English life. Businessmen were building model tenements in the slums and making exhaustive studies of London's blighted neighborhoods, while Anglicans and Non-Conformists were establishing institutional churches. Artists were turning to radical panaceas in the hope of destroying the materialism of capitalism, and workers were being organized into industrial trade unions by Tom Mann and John Burns. Local and city governments were taking on the ownership and management of public utilities, whereas members of the refined and cultivated classes were declaring themselves in favor of Fabian Socialism. And the universities were sending their young men out to live with the poor in the slums. If Englishmen were disagreed on the means to achieve the desired society, and perhaps on the ends, they were one in believing that they must live according to the spirit of Christianity.

The time is past, insisted the Andover alumnus, when Americans can ignore England's progressive ferments in the smug belief that the United States has none of the economic evils of the former mother country. The New York slums are as bad as those in London; and the "American aristocracy is more powerful and dangerous than the English." At one time America was better for the workingman than the Old World, but today in the North of England the coal miners have strong trade unions, coöperative stores, the eight-hour day, and university extension courses, whereas their counterparts in Pennsylvania go from bad to worse as a result of immigrant competition. As for class snobbery, America has its evil if less open share, and we are not doing enough to overcome it. Clearly, thought Woods, America must profit from English experience by choosing from it what best satisfies the needs of the nation.[23]

For his own part the earnest scholar of reform chose to dedicate himself to the university settlement, although at the outset he admired the Fabian Socialists. Graham Wallas and William Clarke, with whom he had traveled much in Great Britain, had impressed him with their learning, integrity, and zeal. "I was, so to speak, brought up in the school of Fabians," he remarked later in life. The gradualist socialists were admirable, he thought, for pioneering as "a new school of economists" through such works as Charles Booth's *Labor and Life of the People*; and they believed in "possibilism and permeation. . . ," not utopia and revolution. But Woods thought even more highly of the work of the Reverend Mr. Barnett at Toynbee Hall, which offered the most practical way of bringing runaway capitalism in line with Christianity and democracy. On his return to America in 1891, the Andover House Association was founded, with Woods as Head Resident and his teacher, Professor Tucker, as President. On January 1, 1892, the doors of 6 Rollins Street in the South End were thrown open to the surrounding poor and interested humanitarians.[24]

The philosophy of the college settlement movement was religious, for, like Tucker, Woods believed that society, tied together by the living Christ, was organic. In the cities the poor lived apart from the rich, in different neighborhoods, separated by education, tastes, and values. The two classes suffered thereby, the workers failing to get the refinement that association with the cultivated could give, the upper classes missing the experience of knowing how their less fortunate brothers lived. The bringing together of classes was the major problem of industrial civilization, as nation building was for feudal culture, and only the colleges could do it; for a "university . . . stands not only for a knowledge of the whole world as it is, but . . . the . . . troubles of society ought to be most keenly felt there." That American students and teachers should fail to take up the challenge would be absolutely sinful.[25]

Unlike existing philanthropic organizations, the settlement house required its members personally to identify themselves with the life of the poor by living in their neighborhoods as permanent residents. Benefits were to accrue to both the college man and his neighbors. The former would be happy in knowing that he was doing his duty, not in any romantic or martyr sense, but in the knowledge that "to live within the limits of a class belittles man-hood." He would elevate the neighborhood by bringing to it art, literature, music — the refinements of a cultivated home. More important, he was to study the conditions of life and work of the area, acquaint himself with regenerative agencies in operation, and learn how to eliminate poverty and drudgery: he was to be a social engineer. If settlement-house workers and laboring class neighbors coöperated, they would create a sense of community from which would come the desire to improve the community. The exact methods of social reconstruction were to be left for experience to suggest, for Woods, frankly an opportunist, ab-horred doctrinaire and monistic reforms. The founders of Andover House hoped that they would train and export a steady stream of social reconstructionists to other needy communities.[26]

The tactics of the Andover House are a story in pragmatism. Instead of immediately embarking on the ambitious scheme of in-vestigating and removing poverty, Woods found, at the outset, the need to take boys off the street; and so he organized clubs for them. When he discovered that the hopelessly degenerate, the alcoholics, pimps, and prostitutes, were lowering the tone of the honest working-class neighborhood, he asked the city to remove them. Throughout the first decade he grew wise in raising money and selecting personnel. During the years following the panic of 1893, he discarded the grandiose notion of eliminating want on a permanent basis and satisfied himself with relief measures; he proposed public works, helped to pressure the General Court in setting up a commission on the unemployed, and was instru-mental in having a five-cent restaurant opened. He was appointed a member of the Central Labor Union, served on arbitration committees, spoke in behalf of unionization and profit-sharing, and threw his House open to lectures by Harry Lloyd and Jack O'Sullivan, labor leaders. He also coöperated with the business-men of the Public Franchise League, which purported to prevent utility corporations from cheating the city.[27]

In politics, as in the labor problem, Robert Woods was "always the possibilist." He scorned the reformers of respectable birth and position who thought that the millennium would come by throwing out the bosses and getting honest businessmen to run the city. The local politician, noted the social worker, was powerful because he represented people of his own kind; and national and religious ties simply could not be broken. Moreover, the question was not who ran the government but how it was run; the crucial municipal issue was to extend political functions to satisfy the needs of the poor, to give them baths, gymnasiums, sanitary tenements, parks, playgrounds, clean streets, industrial education. The ward leader, being strategically placed in the slum, would respond to public pressure because he wanted to please. On this theory, Robert A. Woods coöperated with the South End's "Honorable Jim" Donovan. Josiah Quincy was of the same realistic political views as the head of Andover House, and when he was elected Mayor of Boston in 1896 he appointed Woods to a committee to study the enlargement of municipal duties.[28]

Ten years after Robert Woods opened Andover House, Dean George Hodges of the Episcopal Theological School wrote of him: "He is today one of the strongest influences for good in the city of Boston. . ." The settlement was firmly established, and Woods was about to be married with plans to settle down with his bride in the South End. He and his staff had achieved the goal of investigating the slums of Boston on the model of Charles Booth, the results of which appeared in the *City Wilderness*, in 1898, *Americans in Process*, in 1902, and numerous articles and pamphlets. As the associate of John Donovan, Josiah Quincy, Louis Brandeis, Harry Lloyd, and Jack O'Sullivan, Robert Woods achieved his "ambition . . . to be an unofficial, untitled statesman."[29] Yet a decade had made the settlement-house worker less ambitious. In place of the goal of discovering the causes of poverty and removing them permanently from American life, he had come to believe in piecemeal reform, in patching the existing social order and not in changing it drastically. Knowledge of society and men reduced the settlement house to a scientific kind of philanthropic agency from which came the modern field of social work.

The founding of settlement houses summed up the inductive and humanitarian drift of the social science of the Hub City. In a paper read at the Chicago World's Fair in 1893, Robert A. Woods defended "the usefulness of university settlements as laboratories in social science. . ." Their technicians were expected to specialize in housing, or intemperance, or labor relations, or local politics, or education by studying the "crowded neighborhood . . . [as] a microcosm of all social problems. . ." Similarly, the University Settlement, established by the School of Theology of Boston University, was to be to the School "What the clinic is to the school of medicine, [what] the physical or chemical laboratory [is] to the technical school. . ." [30] This quest for knowledge of observed conditions of the social and economic order distinguished the social science of the 1880's and 1890's from the abstract and deductive political economy of the 1870's.

Behind the inductive method lay the Christian urge to do good and an imported English class consciousness. The young people who went into the slums considered themselves missionaries of a sort (only in the case of the Boston University settlement, however, was there evangelical work). Of the middle and upper classes, they held themselves responsible to uplift the poor. As sinners both repel and attract evangelists, so the dwellers of the slums repelled and attracted certain of the settlement workers. Frederick A. Bushée, the demographer of Andover House, for example, wrote about Jews, Negroes, Italians, and Irish with a mixture of contempt and sympathy. The resident of the settlement believed that he had not only to raise the worker to civilized standards of life and labor but to Americanize him as well, a task that widened the gulf between those who belonged and knew it and those who did not fit into American life. Unlike the liberals of the 1930's who idealized the Okies and industrial proletariat, the residents of the university settlements looked upon North Enders and South Enders as an inferior breed of peasants in whom the human light had all but gone out. In time the residents would propose restricting immigration, and the gentleman's burden would become, like the White Man's Burden, an oppressive racism.[31]

IV

The spirit of social service swept the seminaries but made headway in the liberal arts colleges only in the departments of economics. Boston College made no concessions to social science and continued the classical tradition as interpreted by the Jesuits, while Tufts expanded its courses in economics hardly at all. The departments of economics at Harvard and Boston University underwent the greatest changes. At the first, the works of Cairnes, Bastiat, and Mill had been standard for 1880, but by the middle of the 1890's a large number of electives were being offered on the history of economic thought and institutions, the labor problem, statistics, demography, sociology, the public ownership of utilities. One elective dealt with "Ideal Social Reconstructions from Plato's Republic to the Present Time." Professor Laughlin, the orthodox economist, had retired, and his colleague, Professor Dunbar, taught banking and finance; the leaders of the department were younger men, William J. Ashley, Edward Cummings, John Cummings, Frank W. Taussig, and Hugo Richard Meyer. In 1898 a special course was given by Dr. Cunningham of Trinity College on the Industrial Revolution in England.[32] The inductive method had come to Harvard.

In 1895 Boston University appointed F. Spencer Baldwin to the department of economics, and he promptly revolutionized it. Of the new school, he did his Ph.D. in Germany under Professor Brentano on the history of coal mine legislation in Great Britain. His conclusion was: "trade unions and legislation in the interests of workingmen . . . supplement each other and the . . . result . . . has been the elevation of the English miner from a condition of deepest physical and moral demoralization to the high economic standard he now enjoys." An institutional economist, Baldwin taught E. B. Andrews' *Institute of Economics* in his introductory course and gave electives on the history of economic thought, applied social problems, modern socialisms (the texts were Richard T. Ely's *French and German Socialism* and Thomas Kirkup's *History of Socialism*). As at Harvard there was a "historical view of various theories of the state and social ideals from Plato to the present time." Interested in direct observation wherever possible, Baldwin supplemented lectures and discussions with visits to the "almost numberless reform associations and conventions in the city." Boston, in the words of the university catalogue, was a first-rate laboratory: "To the student of economic and sociological problems . . . Boston offers unsurpassed opportunities . . . from the beginning it has been a community of ideas, a lover of new methods, a most fruitful mother of reforms, a champion of popular rights, a leader in world-wide charities." [33]

Like the seminaries, the social science of the liberal arts colleges emphasized the obligation of the middle-class student to the nation. Professor Baldwin, for example, hoped to educate a generation of college men to take posts of responsibility in the courts, the legislature, and the colleges, and thereby raise the tone of American life. He approved the annexation of the Spanish possessions in 1899, for as India had trained a noble corps of selfless English servants, Baldwin explained, so American imperial needs would "raise up by the side of the now dominant aristocracy of mercantilism, absorbed in the ignoble pursuit of private gain, a new aristocracy devoted to the honorable career of public service." The crux of Baldwin's philosophy of education was his faith that democracy could survive only with "a government for the people by their real superiors," not by demagogues or plutocrats but by university men "competent to grapple with the problems of American life." [34]

The professors with a social conscience in Boston were all middle-of-the-roaders, and not one of them was dismissed as were the more radical academicians at Marietta, Kansas State Agricultural, Brown, or Chicago. Professor Baldwin, while hostile to the plutocracy and the sociology of Herbert Spencer, thought Bryanism quackery and attacked the "wild-cat sociology of the present day . . . a result of the over-addiction to social reform which besets students of society." The scientist, he thought, must be interested in the application of his findings but he should not twist the facts to serve a preconceived theory. William J. Ashley took a lively interest in the Church Social Union, the Episcopal study group; his pamphlet on the Homestead strike shows him to be a well-meaning but cautious scholar. Hugo Meyer, while an institutional economist, wrote four solid books on the history of public ownership to prove that "Industrial Development [is] due to Individual Initiative." [35]

The seminaries and departments of political economy and sociology in the colleges did not contribute systematic studies to the literature of economic nationalism. Their faculties were more concerned with inculcating students with a sense of *personal* responsibility to the poor. Boston's representative of the economics espoused by Richard T. Ely, Edwin Seligman, and Simon Patten was Frank Parsons. A lecturer in the Law School of Boston University, where he taught insurance, he was denied a position in the economics department because of his radicalism. Engineer, lawyer, and ardent devotee of applied Christianity, he made prodigious researches of the economy. Through his prolific writings, he provided contemporary liberals with factual indictments of monopoly capitalism and briefs for the social welfare state.

Chapter Six

FRANK PARSONS

The Professor as Radical

I am strongly tempted to give up my position in the university and my writing of legal textbooks, and devote my life to showing the people the way out. — Frank Parsons

. . . among the coterie of silent leaders who have led in the serious constructive and scholarly work that must precede a successful onward movement, no man has wrought more effectively or convincingly than Professor Frank Parsons, who, as educator, economist, and author, has carried forward the cause of coöperation and the public ownership of public utilities in such a manner as to challenge thoughtful attention from friend and foe alike. — Benjamin Orange Flower [1]

The key to Frank Parsons' philosophy is the man himself. He was attached to no religious denomination but his writings are saturated with Christian principles. Foremost in the Boston radical's makeup was a sense of duty. He regarded life as the fulfilling of the calling of proper living, which, when translated into action, meant the striving for noble, serious, and selfless ends. Early in the nineties, when the country was stirred by the aspirations of the Populists for social democracy, Parsons gave up a lucrative and respectable job of textbook writing in order to devote more time to the profitless task of working for the common man. He never married, took little time out for play, lived in Tolstoyan simplicity, and labored incessantly in two rented rooms in downtown Boston, which overflowed with piles of books, magazines, newspapers, and galley proofs. Characteristically, he wrote on the "mathematical demonstrability of the wisdom of righteousness," laughed little but lectured on the "laws of laughter," and could declare with utter seriousness that it was a "moral duty to perspire at least once every day." This stern devotion to high-minded pursuits drove Parsons to an early death. After a serious illness in 1907, he returned to his reform activities against the advice of his physician, and then literally killed himself with overwork the following year. He died penniless.[2]

Frank Parsons was born in Mount Holly, New Jersey, on November 14, 1854. His family, an amalgam of English, Welsh, and Scotch-Irish strains, dated back to the American Revolution and, on his mother's side, boasted a long line of doctors, teachers, and lawyers. A brilliant and precocious student, Frank entered Cornell University at the age of fifteen and was graduated three years later at the head of his class with a bachelor's degree in civil engineering. He lost his first job, that of engineer with a railroad in western Massachusetts, when the depression of 1873 bankrupted the company. After several trying months as a common laborer, he became a public school teacher in Southbridge, Massachusetts. Convinced by friends that his talents were best suited for law, he took the bar examination in 1881 after one year's private preparation "and passed an examination which the examiners said showed the best grasp of the subject, in all its bearings, that had been displayed by any candidate who had appeared before them in the twelve years of their term as an examining board." But the New Jersey boy, endowed with a weak constitution that would plague him throughout his life, broke under the strain of cramming three years' work in one. He was obliged to spend three years in New Mexico to recoup his strength.

From the land of little culture in the Southwest the lawyer came to Boston to seek his fortune. He set up his own office but private practice did not appeal to him. Little, Brown and Com-

pany engaged him as a writer of legal textbooks, and from his
pen came revisions of *May on Insurance, Perry on Trusts,* and
Morse on Banks and Banking. His scholarly achievements won
him recognition in the form of a lectureship at the law school of
Boston University, a position which he held from 1892 until 1905,
when his excessive research projects forced him to resign. A
born teacher, Parsons was extremely popular among the students,
impressing them with his fairness, honesty, and prodigious memory. In addition to his legal writing, Frank, who was amazingly
well read in the classics, augmented his income by lecturing on
English literature before various groups in the city. In 1889 Little,
Brown and Company brought out his literary reflections in *The
World's Best Books,* a slender volume which won generous praise
from Francis Parkman and Phillips Brooks.[3]

In the 1880's Frank Parsons gave up scholarship for scholarship's sake to turn his knowledge over to the cause of reform. In
the Industrial Revolution he saw both the promise and the degradation of American life. The magnificent inventions of the
nineteenth century bade fair to raise the standard of living of
the average person to unbelievable heights. But the age of the
Carnegies and the Morgans — torn by strikes, polluted by money
in politics, cheapened by the commercialization of values, and
festering from the open sores of the slums — convinced the Boston
professor that science and industry were conferring benefits only
on the plutocracy.[4] This contrast between what was and what
could be catapulted him into a multitude of movements which
aimed at placing the machines and the monopolies in the service
of the common man.

Frank Parsons' capacity for work was enormous. In addition
to the one volume on literature and the three works on law, he
wrote ten books, several of them stout tomes which number
seven hundred pages. After the campaign of 1896, in which he
supported William Jennings Bryan, he met Dr. Charles Fremont
Taylor, a wealthy Philadelphia physician and editor of the liberal
journal, *The Medical World.* With the aid of Parsons, Taylor

brought out another magazine, *Equity*, to which Parsons was the chief contributor. Ultimately, the Philadelphian published the latter's works in book form: *Rational Money* in 1898, *The Telegraph Monopoly* and *The City for the People* in 1899, *Direct Legislation* in 1900, *The Story of New Zealand* in 1904, and *The Trusts, the Railroads, and the People* in 1906. Parsons, because he was a respectable reformer, had other publishers for *Our Country's Need* (1894), *The Heart of the Railroad Problem* (1906), *Choosing a Vocation* (1909), and *Legal Doctrine and Social Progress* (1911). The last two appeared posthumously under the preparation of Ralph Albertson, the Bostonian's literary executor.

Pamphlets, newspaper articles, magazine essays, speeches, and special reports were still other vehicles of expression for the professor turned reformer. His pamphlets number more than half a dozen and were widely read and distributed. He contributed more than 125 pieces to the leading journals, most of them to the *Arena*, of which his good friend and stanch admirer, Benjamin Orange Flower, was editor. William Dwight Porter Bliss, the founder of Christian Socialism in America, printed his contributions in the *Dawn* and in the *American Fabian*. In 1896 Parsons became one of the contributing editors of the latter magazine. By 1906 the Bostonian's reputation as an expert in public utilities was so well established that the National Civic Federation commissioned him to study the municipalization of tramways in England as part of a bigger project on the public ownership of natural monopolies; and Parsons' report, made after a visit to Great Britain, is one of the most important in the multivolume publication of the federation. In the midst of this activity Parsons somehow found time to write "The Capture of Fort William and Mary, December 14 and 15, 1774" and to run a poor third in Boston's mayoralty campaign of 1895 on the radical ticket.[5]

When Parsons was not writing he was teaching. Because his lectureship at Boston University engaged him only part of the year he was free to teach at other colleges. In 1897 he joined the staff of Kansas State Agricultural College where, because of the Populist victory that year, a liberal administration came into power under President Thomas E. Will, a stanch advocate of the Social Gospel. Among the newly appointed faculty members were Professor Edward Bemis, dismissed from Chicago because of his radical leanings, and Helen Campbell, an outstanding Eastern progressive. Professor James Allen Smith, having been dismissed from Marietta College, was invited to join the staff but turned down the offer at the last minute to take a position in Washington. Admired by both his colleagues and students, Parsons taught political science and history, interjecting into them his belief in progress through evolution and the general welfare state. In 1899 the Boston radical and his fellow colleagues were dismissed by the newly returned Republicans on the grounds that the College was teaching more about the distribution of wealth than its production. Following his dismissal Parsons helped to organize the Ruskin College of Social Science, the center of the Oxford movement of America, and became Dean of the lecture extension division.[6]

At the time of his death the Boston reformer was deep in a number of projects. Through his closest friend, Ralph Albertson, he became interested in settlement-house work; and in 1905 he organized Breadwinner's College in North End's Civic House in imitation of Toynbee Hall's Workingmen's Institute. Together with Albertson and an ardent coterie of Harvard and Massachusetts Institute of Technology students as aides — among them young Morris Raphael Cohen — the professor brought enlightenment and culture to the dwellers of the slums. Three years later he secured the financial backing of Mrs. Quincy Shaw, the well-meaning daughter of Louis Agassiz, to open a vocational guidance center in Civic House with branches in several institutions in the city.[7] His personal papers reveal that he was working on several books when he died.

For all his self-sacrificing and prolific activity Frank Parsons has been consigned to relative oblivion by historians. His liberal contemporaries, however, mourned his death as a serious loss to the progressive cause. He was compared to Edward Bellamy, Henry Demarest Lloyd, and Governor John P. Altgeld. "Every earnest scholar respected him," noted Edwin D. Mead, editor of the *New England Magazine*, and everyone recognized him as "a 'worker together with God' in the long and painful process of transforming human society in this old earth of ours into some reflection and bailiwick of the kingdom of God." [8]

II

Like many another reformer of the late nineteenth century, Frank Parsons drank deep of the European and native American currents that were remaking the intellectual life of the nation. From his friend, Oliver Wendell Holmes, Jr., Parsons derived the concept that the law should be guided by the needs of society and not by the dead hand of precedent. The Social Gospel, in general, and his spiritual mentor, Bishop Phillips Brooks, in particular, inspired him with the idea that Christianity was "a life not a creed." America's economic nationalists, Professors Richard T. Ely, John R. Commons, Edwin R. A. Seligman, and others, strengthened Parsons' own belief in the social welfare state. It was Herbert Spencer, though, the intellectual giant of the age, who most influenced the Boston reformer. Although Parsons was to take issue with the Englishman's devotion to laissez faire, he built his own system in the "foothills" of Spencer's massive sociological structure, taking from him philosophical materialism, the organic conception of society, the conflict theory of progress, and the evolutionary stages in human development.[9] By a brilliant *tour de force* Professor Parsons turned the last three elements, which were essential to the inert determinism of Social Darwinism, into powerful arguments for social reform through a regulated economy.

Out of these diverse intellectual forces and his own moral bent Frank Parsons compounded an original synthesis. His first taste of social philosophy was at Cornell where, like many another college student of the day, he studied the economics of laissez faire. The college textbooks disturbed him, for they described only what was, instead of predicting what could be, and treated the creation of wealth without reference to morals. With the passage of time he came to believe with John Stuart Mill that the crucial problem of political economy was the reconciliation of "individual liberty with public ownership of the means of production and equal division of the product." [10]

The former engineer was obviously in search of a blueprint for the future, and there were at least two he could choose from. He rejected Henry George's panacea on the grounds that the Single Tax would leave the financial, industrial, and transportation monopolies untouched. Although in 1889 Parsons had remarked that only "blissful ignorance" could call *Looking Backward* a great book, by 1892 his devotion to the ideals of brotherhood and industrial democracy, which Bellamy stressed, had made him a "thorough going nationalist." Two years later, however, he broke away because he thought that the discipline of the industrial army and the nationalization of the entire economy would destroy individual liberty.[11]

If the economics of David Ricardo and the socialism of Edward Bellamy could not solve the problem of freedom and authority, then Frank Parsons had to create a system that would. In "The New Political Economy" he urged economists to study the production and distribution of goods and services, not as ends in themselves, but in relation to their furtherance of "manhood" and happiness — the true measure of wealth. Because his economic science would center in the welfare of man, he wished to coördinate it with relevant data from the sister social studies. Finally, he would replace the older discipline which assumed "existing conditions to be right and eternal" with a bold and experimental economics which could devise a plan for "coöperation or socialization" to be "tested under conditions that will give it a reasonable chance of success." [12]

Mutualism was the name which Parsons gave to his plan for the coöperative commonwealth. As early as 1890 the Boston liberal had begun to grope for an original synthesis; but four years passed before his ideas appeared in systematic form in *Our Country's Need* and in "The Philosophy of Mutualism." The basic principle of mutualistic society is brotherly love, which, as Parsons pointed out, was simply the ideal of mutual help which lay at the foundation of family life. Specifically, the social engineer's vision of the future would rest on a planned economy in which the government would possess and manage public utilities but would leave manufacturing and agriculture to voluntary coöperatives owned and operated by the workers.[13] By this mixed economic system Parsons hoped to eliminate the waste and conflict of competition and the evils of private monopoly, and to avoid the perils of bureaucratic state socialism.

The controlling principle was freedom from want, not so much as an end in itself, but rather as a means to enable man to pursue the higher things of life. Like Herbert Spencer, Frank Parsons believed that "sudden changes are apt to be injurious," and therefore proposed a slow growth into economic equality. For the immediate first step he urged that the government set a "Subsistence annuity," an annual minimum wage guaranteeing basic comforts to the laborer. Proper education would prepare the people for the second stage, the equal division of wealth, when men would work for honor and prestige in their chosen fields rather than for the profit motive. The final product in the evolutionary ascent would be "Familyism" — from each according to his ability and to each according to his needs — and would be attained when "human nature has evolved to . . . perfection," when men would labor out of love for society.

Part of Mutualism's defense is couched in the language of Spencer's sociology, which Parsons used in ways which the Englishman would have denounced. The Bostonian pointed out that his vision for the future met the Englishman's criteria of progress: cohesion, flexibility, power, and symmetry. It was necessary — society being organic — that the government provide for economic equality, since the equitable distribution of wealth was to the "Social Organism what the circulation of blood is to the individual body." Parsons agreed with the British philosopher that civilization had evolved from lower to higher forms through the conflict between antagonistic forces and that it would one day reach a perfect state of equilibrium; and then added that Mutualism could best promote that equilibrium. Finally, in accordance with the "historical parallel," which stated that all institutions were governed by the same laws of evolution, Parsons argued that since government and religion had achieved democratic forms, then despotic capitalism would have to follow suit by giving way to an "Industrial Republic."

Parsons also defended his system of thought by attacking the passive determinism of Herbert Spencer. If history was demonstrably on the side of Mutualism, it was proper to direct the course of events rather than wait for the future to work itself out blindly and automatically. He was acid in pointing out that the struggle for existence did not provide for the survival of the fittest but more often for the supremacy of the most cunning, selfish, and unscrupulous. Moreover, in the race for life the truly gifted frequently fell behind; slyly the professor noted that Spencer was the "Shakespeare of Science," yet his books did not sell as well as pulp literature. Because the future civilization would rest on perfect individuals, Parsons would produce the desired type, not through the haphazard methods of natural selection, but through the predictable "intelligent selection" of the biologist. "Life can be moulded," the reformer asserted, "into any conceivable form. Draw up your specifications for man . . . and if you will give me control of the environment and time enough, I will clothe your dreams in flesh and blood." [14]

Spencer's formulation of the problem of liberty and authority the Bostonian found both inadequate and inaccurate. The Englishman wrote that man was at liberty to do what he wanted provided he did not infringe on the "equal freedom" of another to do the same thing. Parsons replied that Spencer's law was a mockery, for class inequalities ruled out equal opportunities for action. Further, Spencer's deduction *en vacuo* that government existed solely for restraint — to enforce the "law of equal freedom" — did not square with the empirical evidence of the Common Law and nineteenth-century industrial history, which gave abundant evidence that government also existed for economic enterprise. The Boston reformer passionately believed in the free individual, but "subject to the limitations as the good of the community requires"; and the government could do all that the people wanted it to. In a passage that bears striking resemblance to Nikolay Lenin's formulation of the withering away of the state, Parsons said: "As a coöperation of all for the restraint of each, governmental activities will be needed less and less as humanity approaches perfection; but as a coöperation of all for the service of each, I hope to see the functions of government continually grow." [15]

In the 1890's Parsons was undisturbed when called a socialist because socialism was then, in spite of Daniel De Leon, a respectable asylum for sensitive souls who condemned competition and who advocated the coöperative society through peaceful means. After 1900, however, the growing strength of native and European Socialist parties tended to identify the movement with class hatred and uncompromising ends; and the professor found it necessary to distinguish his creed from doctrinaire Marxism. He condemned the Marxists for their violent language and for their unwillingness to compromise on ultimate aims. Their omniscient bureaucracy, in charge of all sectors of the economy, he noted, would leave no room for voluntary coöperatives and would destroy individual freedom. Whereas Eugene V. Debs and company drew inspiration from dialectical materialism, Parsons explained that Mutualism rested on the belief that the "Golden Rule ought to be the basis of business life as well as of life in the church and the home." [16]

III

Once satisfied with the validity of his philosophic system, Frank Parsons devoted the rest of his life to make it a reality. According to his rigid laws of historical determinism, Mutualism "would come whether we lift a finger to help it or not." But the professor was bent on giving the future a push. Because he believed that human beings first had to be prepared for new institutions, he regarded education as the great engine of social change. Essentially a Fabian in his outlook, he tried to convert all classes, but he believed that the motor power for progress would come largely from "the great middle classes of the people who are not unbalanced by misery . . . or the fever for wealth and mastery." In his campaign to enlighten the American *petit bourgeois*, the Boston reformer championed a wide range of practical measures, which, in their entirety, would ultimately lead to the coöperative commonwealth.[17]

In the nineties Parsons became vitally interested in the money question. He attributed the "booms and busts" of the late-nineteenth-century American economy to the contriving of the private bankers to manipulate prices through their control of the volume of specie and credit. The power to produce prosperity or panic, which drastically affected the economic life of the nation as a whole, Parsons declared, was "an attribute of sovereignty and ought to belong to none but the sovereign people." He ruled out Greenbackism as leading to unregulated inflation and declared that Free Silver was only a "temporary palliative."

Under the professor's plan the Secretary of the Treasury, with the advice of a staff of economists, was to maintain a constant price level by regulating the volume of currency and credit. In times of stringency, when private bankers were most loath to make funds available, the Postal Savings Bank was to lend money at reasonable rates of interest. Parsons proposed that America go off the gold standard and adopt a national unconvertible currency. The Secretary of the Treasury was to regulate its value by pegging its volume to the volume of several hundred basic commodities, keeping the ratio constant at all times. In this way the dollar would no longer fluctuate with the international price of gold and silver.[18]

The wretched condition of labor disturbed the Boston reformer. As a lawyer he looked upon the savage railroad and coal strikes of the day as the modern, economic counterparts of feudal trial by battle, and therefore suggested the judicial remedy of compulsory arbitration in which the trade unions would have a voice. Shocked by the rookeries of the North and South Ends, the professor called for government slum clearance and model tenements for workers. Following the Panic of 1893 he urged that the unemployed be provided for by "public works, making good roads, planting forests, digging canals, building ships, establishing schools, etc." In 1905 Parsons organized a national campaign in support of the eight-hour day on the grounds that it would promote "a longer life, more opportunity for self-development, a higher citizenship and a nobler manhood." [19]

Like many of his liberal contemporaries Parsons saw grave perils in unrestricted immigration. Part of his animus derived from the belief that foreign workers undercut their American brethren, but more fundamental was his fear that the Eastern European would pollute the Anglo-Saxon blood of America. Steeped in the racism of Social Darwinism he identified the American "race" with the English-speaking peoples who had led the world in democracy and declared that further progress was impossible if the United States lost its "heroic blood by the foul admixture of serfhood . . . pouring in from Europe." Echoing the Know-Nothing sentiment of a half century earlier, he proposed that immigrants pass an English literacy test before admission and that they wait twenty-one years for naturalization papers.[20]

The specter of monopoly capitalism haunted every reformer of the 1890's, and Frank Parsons devoted the major part of his life to put the trusts in the hands of the people. He resembled his good friend, Henry Demarest Lloyd, in his passion for facts, his ardor for muckraking, his emphasis on morality, and his insistence on the socialization of the natural monopolies. But whereas Lloyd achieved competence in only one industry, oil, Parsons was an acknowledged expert in several fields: railroads, telegraph, tramway, telephone, gas, and electricity. Further, his legal training gave him fresh insights into government ownership, and in recognition of this talent Edward Bemis had the Bostonian write a chapter on "Legal Aspects of Monopoly" for *Municipal Monopolies*, a basic textbook in reform.

Parsons ruled out both the smashing and the regulating of the monopolies as remedies. Supervisory and rate-fixing commissions, while affording some relief, failed to alter the unfair concentration of wealth, and in some cases actually intensified the need of big business to corrupt politics. In pamphlets, magazine articles, and finally in two stout tomes, the Bostonian pointed out that even as late as 1906, in spite of government prohibitions, the railroads were still charging unfair and discriminatory rates. The solution was not the return to smallness and competition by way of the Sherman Anti-Trust Act, for unlike his friend, Louis D. Brandeis, Parsons looked upon monopoly as inevitable and considered it superior to the waste and conflict of a competitive economy.[21]

Public monopoly was the only way out. Parsons pointed out that it was legally mandatory for the government to own utilities operating under franchise, for monopoly carried with it the taxing power, and the legislature, as agent for the people, could not consign that power to private sources. Further, the tenor of the Constitution required that the government make the telegraph and the telephone parts of the post office as instruments for the "transmission of intelligence." Public ownership, Parsons noted, by removing the dichotomy of interest between producer and consumer, would shower economic blessings. He declared that private monopolies were inferior to nationalized and municipalized plants with respect to service, treatment of labor, use of new inventions, and fairness of rates. These assertions he backed up with statistics, financial statements, charts and graphs culled from his readings, and interviews with Continental, English, and American businessmen and officials. Germany's railroads, Switzerland's telegraph, Berlin's telephone, and Glasgow's tramways and gas and electrical works were but a few of the examples he used with telling effect. For nonmonopolistic big business, Parsons, who was afraid of too much government control, proposed voluntary coöperatives to be owned and managed by the employees.[22]

Direct legislation was another reform that Frank Parsons championed. It had been one of his interests in 1894, but it was not until six years later that it became crucial for his entire program. He agreed with Wendell Phillips that progress never "came from the upper classes" and felt that his proposals would be hammered into the statute books only when the "common people" controlled the government. Hence he advocated the initiative, referendum, recall, direct primaries, proportional representation, and woman suffrage. The Boston reformer prophesied that without these measures there would be a revolution. "Anglo-Saxon manhood," he warned, "confined beneath the pressure of accumulating injustice, is the most dangerous explosive known to history." [23]

In 1899 Frank Parsons made a significant contribution to the cause of municipal reform. *The City for the People* was a heavy book, replete with the aims and achievements of the crusaders for urban progress, and bulging with the legal and technical data that the lawyer and engineer took delight in. Throughout, however, there is the same stress on moral ends that characterizes all of the Bostonian's works. In a sense the book ranks as Parsons' major synthesis. Within the framework of Mutualism he brought together his favorite causes to focus more sharply on "the problem of the city," which, because it was the center of population and of wealth, had become "the problem of civilization."

Anticipating Lincoln Steffens, he told the story of the shame of the cities. City by city he traced the history of corruption, pointing out that even in staid Boston such scandals as the West End Railway and Bay State Gas Company affairs were not uncommon. Clearly the central issue was whether the citizens would "own the city . . . or . . . be owned by the politicians and monopolists." Parsons' solutions were three: public ownership of utilities, direct legislation, and municipal home rule. The last was the *sine qua non* of his program, for in accordance with American practices of local government, the city was the creature of the state, having little and in some cases no autonomous jurisdiction over its economic life.[24]

The social science of Frank Parsons came complete with a laboratory, for like fellow academicians turned reformers, he sought proof for his theories in what Benjamin O. Flower euphemistically called "Foreign Experiment Stations." [25] Parsons found his in England and Europe, but above all, in New Zealand. Henry Demarest Lloyd encouraged Parsons to write *The Story of New Zealand,* for Lloyd's own work was an account of contemporary conditions, whereas the Bostonian planned a "story of cause and effect" — a history of the origins and practices of progressivism on the island. Parsons' book, the product of a prodigious amount of research and personal correspondence with New Zealand politicos, is poorly organized, dull, rambling, and over long (eighty-two chapters and eight hundred pages). Although poor history, it is nonetheless important for its underlying assumptions, its scattered and unsystematic generalizations, and the type of society that the Boston reformer portrayed as a "Co-operative Industrio-Political Combine."

The New Zealand social welfare state had set up "Manhood as king." The inhabitants, of "the same stock . . . as ourselves, the good old Anglo-Saxon," had solved the crucial problem of liberty and authority by making the former "yield wherever the public good required it." Under this formula New Zealand had accomplished the following: public ownership of coal mines, railroads, telegraph and telephone, and voluntary coöperatives in several fields; the restriction of immigration, government life insurance, old age pensions, the eight-hour day for most industries, suburban working-class homes, public works for the unemployed, and government loans to farmers at reasonable rates of interest; direct elections, woman suffrage, and municipal home rule. These gains, Parsons was especially careful to point out, were achieved without the aid of either a Carlylean great man or doctrinaire socialists. The "common people" — farmers, workers, and small businessmen — simply voted in a liberal slate in 1890 and then worked out the best measures by trial and error, having learned that "in politics and industry as in science, experiment is the best method of arriving at the truth." [26]

IV

Frank Parsons ranks with Lester Ward, Henry George, and Edward Bellamy as a major critic of Social Darwinism and as a chief proponent of progress through social experimentation. Mutualism is as systematic as either Nationalism or the Single Tax, and if it failed to make many converts, it was only because it did not rest on a single, catch-all slogan. In a sense, Frank Parsons went beyond the other three men; for whereas they were merely architects of a model society, he was both architect and builder. By the middle of the nineties the dreamers had done their work, and the future of American liberalism lay with the patient, hard-headed specialists who could dig into the facts, come up with concrete as well as moral indictments of monopoly capitalism, and suggest, through model city charters and the like, the how and wherefore of specific measures. Professor Parsons, by tempering his legal and engineering training with liberal doses of applied Christianity, met that task with admirable efficiency.

We live today in the shadow of many of Frank Parsons' ideas. John M. Brewer, the historian of vocational guidance, credits the Bostonian with being the founder of that movement; and out of

Parsons' Vocation Bureau developed the idea, and ultimately the practice, of the scientific hiring of personnel.[27] The initiative, referendum, recall, direct primaries, and woman suffrage have become realities, and several American cities now own their own public utilities. Long before the New Deal hammered them out into the statute books, Parsons advocated the eight-hour day and public works for the unemployed. Herbert Hoover's Reconstruction Finance Corporation operates on Parsons' principle that the government should lend money to industry in times of stress; and Harry S. Truman's three-man board of consulting economists is reminiscent of the Bostonian's financial commission working for the Secretary of the Treasury.

We also live in the shadow of racism — and that, too, is part of the professor's legacy. As a person, he was above all prejudice and bigotry. He was sincerely devoted to his immigrant students at Breadwinner's College; and his colleagues, for the most part of Eastern European origins, admired and respected him.[28] However, as a social engineer, he believed that he could create the coöperative commonwealth only if he could choose the stock to go into it as well as the environment to mold that stock. Blood was important to Parsons, for like the biologists of the day he thought that acquired characteristics were inherited. Hence he attributed the superiority of Western over Eastern Europe — in the face of the new immigration — to the hereditary traits of the residents of the British Isles. Unwittingly then Parsons and other well-meaning scholars joined hands with the not so well-meaning to forge the myth of Anglo-Saxon superiority.

Probably few of the common people read the professor, but his books and ideas reached strategic places. He won over his good friend, Bishop Phillips Brooks, to his philosophy of Mutualism, and James Russell Lowell, although too old to embrace a new cause, approved of Parsons' blueprint of the future. President Thomas E. Will of Kansas State Agricultural College stated that the turning point in his life came when he read *Government and the Law of Equal Freedom*, Parsons' polemic against Herbert

Spencer. Liberal politicos invited Parsons to state his views on public utilities before the Industrial Commission; Senator Marion Butler had *The Telegraph Monopoly* placed in the *Congressional Record;* and Senator Richard F. Pettigrew presented two of Parsons' papers when arguing for the nationalization of railroads. By far his most widely circulated book, *The City for the People,* was a veritable bible for reformers. Eugene Debs, Governor Hazen S. Pingree of Michigan, Mayor Samuel M. Jones of Toledo, Josiah Strong, Edward Everett Hale, Washington Gladden, Henry Demarest Lloyd, Felix Adler, Professor John R. Commons, and a host of others who read like the Who's Who of reform heaped lavish praise on the volume. Finally, as President and organizer of the National League for Promoting the Public Ownership of Monopolies, the National Referendum League, and the Massachusetts Referendum Union, Parsons brought together such reformers as Bellamy, Samuel Gompers, Thomas Wentworth Higginson, George P. Herron, "Golden Rule" Jones, Lloyd, and many others to give cohesion to liberal aspirations.[29]

The most advanced of the middle-class reformers of the day throughout America rejoiced in the liberal social engineering of Frank Parsons; but the academic community of Boston rejected him. Unlike Richard T. Ely, Edwin Seligman, Simon Patten, and John R. Commons, Parsons did not teach in the economics department of a major institution. His career at Kansas State Agricultural College was brief, and Boston University thought him safe teaching insurance in the law school (he would have been as safe teaching mathematics) and so kept him there. Francis Greenwood Peabody disagreed with Parsons; perhaps Professor Baldwin had Parsons in mind when he inveighed against "wild-cat sociology." Significantly, Frank Parsons enjoyed highest academic prestige as Dean of the extension division of the Ruskin College of Social Science. A kind of Rand School of its day, it was located far away from Boston — in Trenton, Missouri.

Parsons felt at home with the free-lance intellectuals who

admired him and with whom he worked for the good society. They referred to him as "professor" before he taught at Kansas State Agricultural College (he was only a lecturer at Boston University), which suggests that they considered an academic title as enhancing their causes. The most radical of the Boston reformers were the free-lance intellectuals. Having no fear of displeasing deans, college presidents, boards of trustees, and heads of departments, they wrote and thought what they pleased. They were anarchists, Single-Taxers, Theosophists, Marxian socialists, Nationalists, spiritualists — experimenters with all sorts of new ideas at war with the existing order of things.

tradictory, aimed at remaking people in the image of themselves and the heroes they had read about.

With few exceptions they were not native Bostonians, which suggests that they had rebelled against the mores of, or at least had not felt at home in, the towns and villages of their birth. However, the intellectuals hardly fitted into the community by the Charles, either Irish or Yankee Boston. They had no family ties, and itinerants, they came and went as job opportunities beckoned, thus striking no roots. For the most part, they arrived as unknowns, and distinction as radicals did not open doors to them, except those of the older liberals. Writers of reform tracts by avocation and more often by vocation, they seemed to have no regular place in the industrial and urban order. As for religion, they were Free Religionists, spiritualists, Theosophists, agnostics, deists, atheists, again on the edge of the norm. They were a society among themselves, saved from Bohemia by their activist urge to do good for mankind.

They could not do good, however, through recognized and institutionalized channels. They occupied neither pulpit nor university chair, and the established journals, such as the *Atlantic Monthly*, and the older newspapers, such as the *Transcript* and the less august but mildly liberal *Globe* and *Advertiser*, were not open to crusaders.[2] As men who acted, or wrote, or painted for a living, the intellectuals were workers, but they did not consider themselves as such. Therefore, unlike their radical counterparts of the 1930's they did not join trade unions in the belief that laborers of the brain and the machine were proletariat slaves of the same wage system. In a sense, they were their own employers, yet they were not like the businessmen who owned factories, mines, railroads, stores. As a consequence, they did not share the businessman's zeal for the good government societies to clean up politics by teaching civics and throwing out corrupt officials (Edwin D. Mead, who fitted into Boston better than others, was the chief exception). Since the trade unions, businessmen associations, colleges, pulpits, and established newspapers and magazines denied the intellectuals means of expression, they found ways of their own. They formed their own societies and publishing houses, from which came pamphlets, monthlies, fortnightlies, novels, poems, treatises of one sort or another. And with none of the responsibility of those who operated within the older channels, the free-lancers were free to be as radical as they pleased.

At the same time they wanted to belong; they had a mission and a message that might succeed if presented with the right credentials. Where the conservatives Charles Eliot Norton and Henry Adams turned their backs on the Boston past, the freelance intellectuals, as immigrants to the Hub City, identified themselves with the heritage of Emerson and his generation: with abolitionism, with Brook Farm, with the Over-Soul. They insisted in lecture, book, and magazine article — which poured forth in an endless stream — that the scholar as reformer filled an old and respectable Boston role.[3] Edwin D. Mead, the New Hampshire-born editor of the *New England Magazine,* and the Midwesterner Benjamin Orange Flower of the *Arena* in particular wrote about the men and women of the age of newness as if they had been lineal ancestors. Buoyed up by this respectable legacy, the intellectuals pressed for new standards in government, economy, art, literature, religion, sex.

Many progressives carried on in a manner to suggest the over zealous, the very moral, the too demanding minister who forces himself upon an unwilling congregation. In part, this evangelical quality derived from the liberal's conception of being the marginal man who leads society in time of crisis. It also grew out of a personal need to find a substitute for the decaying Calvinist orthodoxy. Social reform became that substitute.[4] In many instances, the reformers combined secular causes with spiritualism and Theosophy. The latter preached the brotherhood of man without the contradictions of stern Calvinism, spiritualism promised to prove the existence of an after life, and both emphasized the primacy of the spirit and the mind over the material. Descendants of the Puritans, the intellectuals still thought in terms of the this-world evils and the other-world virtues, larding their broad-sides with such terms as sin, Babylon, Mammon, the Kingdom of God. Against orthodoxy, they were still of the religious temper and mind. The intellectuals were priestly keepers of society's conscience.

In unstratified nineteenth-century America, intellectuals claimed the role of being society's conscience without fear of usurping anyone's authority. The nation was young, its traditions un-formed, its population as yet not ethnically fixed, its religions not permanently cast, and its literary and artistic forms by no means decided. The generation of 1880–1900 believed with Emerson and Whitman that literary folk should seek to enlarge opportu-nities for more and more people. When the sudden appearance of a plutocracy after the Civil War threatened the equalitarian ideal, the intelligentsia refused to acknowledge the business leaders as the leaders of America. To do so would have meant abdicating to a foreign agent in the democratic blood stream; and, if need be, they would stand alone, like their heroes, Hugo, Carlyle, Zola, Ruskin, Tolstoi, Ibsen, Whitman, and the Boston abolitionists. Throughout the writings of the intellectuals as re-formers in Boston in the last two decades of the nineteenth century runs this self-conscious theme of staying at the steering wheel come what may.

The intensity of reform thinking among intellectuals in Boston can be plotted on a graph that shows a curve starting at a low point in 1880, gradually rising through the decade, suddenly shooting up in 1888, and skyrocketing thereafter. The 1880's is the period of groping; the 1890's the period of maturation. Until Edward Bellamy, Edwin D. Mead, and Benjamin Orange Flower appeared late in the eighties, the task of reform fell on William Dean Howells, the only polite writer to make the transition from art for art's sake to art for humanity's sake, Benjamin R. Tucker, the Dartmouth-born anarchist, and Laurence Gronlund, the Danish-born Marxian. Schematically the pattern of social regen-eration falls into four parts, centering around the realism of

Howells, the anarchism of Tucker, the socialisms of Bellamy, Gronlund, and Morrison I. Swift, and the eclecticism of Mead and Flower.

II

Ohio-born, but of New England stock, William Dean Howells had won his literary laurels by 1881, when he stepped down from the office of editing the *Atlantic Monthly*. Thereafter his work showed much concern with the social question, whereas before it had not. Howells came to his progressivism through reading Tolstoi, who quickened his sympathies for the common man, and Laurence Gronlund, William Morris, and Edward Bellamy, who taught him the socialist way out. In *The Minister's Charge; or the Apprenticeship of Lemuel Barker*, published in 1887, he portrayed the life of factory girls sympathetically. In *Annie Kilburn*, published in 1888, he declared that charity was no remedy for the social question, for the rich, being the chief beneficiaries of the capitalist system, injure the poor and cannot therefore help them. In 1889, Howells left Boston for New York, where *A Hazard of New Fortunes*, which came out in 1890, takes place. Here Howells dissected the new urban social structure, its old and new rich, its professional and middle classes, its poor and immigrants. The author's sympathies are clearly with the latter, who are spoken for by Lindau, a German Forty-Eighter and socialist.[5]

At the same time that Howells was adding socialism to the realistic novel, Benjamin R. Tucker was pioneering in the field of the radical magazine. "LIBERTY," he wrote in launching his journal in 1881, "enters the field of journalism to speak for herself because she finds no one willing to speak for her." Born of a Quaker and banking family in 1854, and originally educated as an engineer at the Massachusetts Institute of Technology (1870–1872), Tucker, during the 1880's, was a journalist, doing rewrite work for the *Boston Daily Globe*. In 1872, while a student at M.I.T., he met Josiah Warren by chance, who showed him the "Source of

Light" by converting him to anarchism. This marked the end of the nonconformist student's groping for a systematic philosophy. Tucker, by the age of eighteen, having read Darwin, Spencer, Mill, Buckle, Tyndall, had been alternately "an atheist, a materialist, an evolutionist, a prohibitionist, a free trader, a champion of the legal eight-hour day, a woman suffragist, an enemy of marriage, and a believer in sexual freedom." After his meeting with Warren, Tucker went abroad, where he read Proudhon, and returned to Boston with the desire to promulgate the Frenchman's views. In 1877, he brought out his first anarchist sheet, *The Radical Review*, which contained articles by him and the veteran anarchists Lysander Spooner and Stephen Pearl Andrews. The magazine collapsed in a year, and in 1881 Tucker began publishing *Liberty*, removing its office to New York in 1893.[6]

Liberty was an eight-page fortnightly, financed almost entirely out of Tucker's savings and earnings from the capitalist *Boston Daily Globe*. It very rarely carried news items, except for such explosive events as Homestead and Haymarket. Rather it consisted of logic-chopping articles on the meaning of socialist anarchism; Tucker's philosophy was deductive and not empirical. A good part of the journal was given over to reprints of the works of Josiah Warren, William C. Greene, Proudhon, and Lysander Spooner; translations of European novels of social significance; letters to the editor; and extended polemics among members of Tucker's staff and between Tucker and such hated adversaries as John Most, the communist anarchist. There was such little agreement between Tucker and his followers that by the end of the 1880's the former was left with only two faithfuls to carry on. He antagonized them when he became the unqualified disciple of Max Stirner, the arch-Nietzschean egoist. Cold, aloof, uncompromising, and fanatical in his single-mindedness, Tucker had, Victor Yarros remembers, "few, if any, intimate friends." [7]

So passionate was Tucker in his desire to remove coercion of any kind on the "non-invasive" person that he wrote: "Anarchism implies the right of an individual to stand aside and see a man murdered or a woman raped." His philosophy being deductive rather than empirical, he started with the Josiah Warren and Lysander Spooner axiom that the individual's natural right was to be absolutely sovereign, and concluded that God, marriage, the public school system, and, above all, the state violated the sovereignty of the individual. This overwhelming concern with personal liberty has led students to identify the Boston radical as the foremost exponent of individual or philosophical anarchism in this country.[8]

Tucker, however, preferred the term "Anarchistic Socialism," using it as Proudhon had. Socialism meant to him a just economic system in which labor-time would be the sole determinant of cost; anarchism was *"the doctrine that all the affairs of men should be managed by individuals or voluntary associations, and that the State should be abolished."* These two concepts derived from Proudhon's theories that labor was the source of value and that the state was the instrument of the ruling classes (Tucker boasted that Proudhon anticipated Marx). By destroying the state, Tucker would uproot the monopolies it fostered in land, currency, banking, tariff, patents, and copyrights — the causes of poverty. In the resulting society mutual banking would enable many to become small businessmen, free land would allow others to be farmers, and unrestricted competition would assure laborers that goods and services would be exchanged at labor-time value. There would be no end of classes, or economic equality, but simply equal opportunity.[9]

In wishing to return to the purest laissez faire, Tucker and his band asserted that they were "simply unterrified Jeffersonian Democrats." Indeed, the Boston supreme individualists regarded William Graham Sumner as a distant kinsman, who, if he followed logic, would be in their camp if he once denounced *all* state activities. Of Herbert Spencer they read much, profiting from his views, until late in the 1880's they accused him of selling out to the bourgeoisie. The closest thing to socialist anarchism in action that Tucker observed was the Irish Land League which, through passive resistance to rent and the British Parliament, embodied his ideas of resisting the tyranny of the state and the landlord through peaceful means.[10]

Anti-state to the point of being a fanatic, Tucker inveighed against other reformers who desired to use the government as a welfare agency. He particularly concentrated on Karl Marx, John Most, and Henry George; the Greenbackers, Christian Socialists, Nationalists, and the trade unionists also drew his fire. Equally repugnant to Tucker was the use of force to achieve the desired society, which accounts for his almost violent hatred for Most. The means of social change for the Boston anarchist was passive resistance. If "one-fifth of the population" refused to support the state, to pay taxes, to attend the public school, to be drafted, the government would wither away. Only in such extreme cases when the government was excessively oppressive, as in Russia, did Tucker countenance violence. He defended the Chicago Anarchists only because he regarded them innocent of the charges brought against them; he refused to contribute to the defense of Alexander Berkman, who shot Henry Frick after the Homestead Strike.[11]

A tireless scholar with roots sunk deep in European intellectual life, Tucker enriched the reading matter of American radicalism. He translated Proudhon's *What Is Property* and his *System of Economical Contradictions* as well as novels of social significance by Zola, Tolstoi, and others. Among the "Tendency Novels," as he called them, was Felix Pyat's *The Rag Picker of Paris*. It was advertised in the columns of *Liberty* as a

> vivid picture of the misery of poverty, the extravagance of wealth, the sympathy and forbearance of the poor and despised, the cruelty and the aggressiveness of the aristocratic and respectable, the blind greed of the middle classes, the hollowness of charity, the cunning and hypocrisy of the priesthood, the tyranny and corruption of authority, the crushing power of privilege, and finally, of the redeeming beauty of the ideal of liberty and equality that the century has produced.[12]

Clearly, as American public relations chief for the French novelist, Tucker was trumpeting his own wares, indeed generalizing on the contents of *Liberty* from 1881 to 1893.

A popularizer rather than an innovator Tucker was known both in this country and abroad as the chief spokesman for social anarchism. George Bernard Shaw, who had little respect for supreme individualism, nonetheless conceded that *Liberty* was the best journal of its kind. But Tucker had little support, and certainly not among the working classes, attracting rather a few nonconformist intellectuals on both sides of the Atlantic. The Boston Anarchist Club numbered less than a dozen members; and when Lysander Spooner died in 1887, they raised barely forty dollars for his memorial fund. Tucker was not incorrect in describing *Liberty* as a "journal edited to suit its editor, not its readers." [13]

III

At the other extreme of the anarchists stood the socialists, Morrison I. Swift, Edward Bellamy and his disciples, and Laurence Gronlund. The latter, born July 13, 1846 in Denmark, emigrated in 1867 to America, where he turned first to teaching, then to law, and finally to lecturing and writing on socialism as a full-time occupation. As he spent his time traveling to whatever cities would give him an audience, Gronlund was not a permanent resident of Boston. But he was closely identified with its intellectual life. He was a member of the Nationalist Club, contributed articles to the *Arena* and the *Dawn*, and had his chief works published by a Boston firm, Lee and Shepard. Such a veteran socialist as W. D. P. Bliss regarded the Danish-American as having made "the first full statement of modern socialism published in this country. . ." [14]

The Coming Revolution: Its Principles, published in 1878, was Gronlund's first work, but he was known chiefly through *The Coöperative Commonwealth*, which came out in 1884. He wrote the volume out of the conviction that "a crisis *of some sort* is impending, no matter if it is likely to burst out now or in ten or fifty years from now." Our society, he wrote, is like Augustan Rome in its materialism, extremes of wealth, demagoguery, class rule, and skepticism of high ideals; and unless we improve conditions, we shall have a revolution as bloody as that of 1793 and end up with a Napoleon. To head off violence, upheaval, and dictatorship, Gronlund addressed his book to a minority to instruct the masses on the peaceful socialist way out -- a minority to consist of "reflective minds of all classes," but especially of "many, very many literary men and women, very many lawyers, very many physicians and teachers. . ." [15]

The Coöperative Commonwealth introduced the American reading public to the Marxism of the German Social Democracy. For Americans, Gronlund stripped Marx's principles of class hatred, and noted that socialism rested on empirical evidence, not the *a priori* principles of Spencerian sociology or French egalitarianism. He accepted the entire Marxian critique of capitalism: the labor theory of value and surplus value, the principle of increasing misery of the proletariat, and the interpretation of business cycles; the law of capital accumulation, the pauperization of the middle class, and monopoly control. He also presented Marx's view that history had passed from slavery to feudalism to laissez faire to monopoly capitalism, and would evolve by necessity to socialism. To Marx he added Thomas Huxley, who turned Spencer's own metaphor against him: since society was organic it therefore had to be controlled by an intelligent overseer, the state, to function well. Through education and direct political action Gronlund hoped to achieve the common ownership of productive wealth; and in 1888 he became a member of the executive committee of the Socialist Labor Party.[16]

But the Marxian social theoretician was by no means doctrinaire, joining both the Nationalists and the Christian Socialists, although later withdrawing from the two. For both groups he prepared works to plead that socialism was both in the American and the Christian traditions because it would promote a higher life and brotherhood, whereas corporate rule subverted both ends for the masses of men. At the time of the Populist upheaval, Gronlund, still seeking a way to realize the desired society, formed the American Socialist Fraternity, which would enroll college students to agitate for the coöperative commonwealth. He died in 1898, never gaining foothold in an agency that would have made his dreams come true.[17]

From the West, in 1893, came an eccentric ex-college professor, Morrison I. Swift. He was a free-lance writer, contributing to the *Andover Review*, the *Unitarian Review*, and the *Dawn*. In 1893 he led a Boston contingent out of the city to join up with Coxey's army in its march on Washington. While in Boston, and the itinerant rebel did not stay long, he wrote a utopian tract called *A League of Justice* (1893), which was as revolutionary as it was quixotic. Capitalism, asserted Swift, means exploitation; only socialism, by providing for economic equality, can make people happy. A league of justice is formed which, by robbing the rich like modern Robin Hoods, establishes a newspaper to instruct the poor on the necessity of rebelling. After fourteen years the people rise up, cow the government into reorganizing along coöperative lines, and enter on the utopian plan of living. Swift, impatient and atheistical, scoffed at the Christian Socialists for believing that the churches could prepare the nation for socialism.[18]

Swift had no followers, Gronlund was recognized as the leading American Marxian, but it was Edward Bellamy, the literary man from Chicopee Falls, who rallied the literati around the socialist principle. It is debatable why Edward Bellamy wrote *Looking Backward*. In 1889, he asserted that he started out to write a fantasy, not to become a social reformer; in 1894, he declared that his purpose was to solve the industrial question. Critics have accused him of plagiarism; Arthur E. Morgan has defended him against this charge. Perhaps Bellamy had no particular society in mind; Morgan asserts that he was thinking of ancient Peru as his model. What is unmistakably clear is that the Chicopee Falls writer poured into his novel his past experience and idealism: his admiration for the military, his compassion for the poor, his dream for a better world, his philosophy of the unified human race, his prodigious readings in science, history, philosophy, and literature, and his attractive literary style.[19]

As a youngster, Bellamy had a passion for generals, battles, and wars. His keenest disappointment came when he failed to make West Point because of physical deficiencies. Shortly before his death he used to amuse himself by playing with toy soldiers. In 1867 Bellamy went abroad, where he encountered poverty for the first time and was awakened to economic inequality. As editor of the *Penny News,* he wrote sympathetically of the working classes in Springfield, and in the *Duke of Stockbridge,* published in 1879, a novel on Shays's Rebellion, he took the side of the debtors against the creditors and scheming lawyers. At the age of twenty-four he wrote the *Religion of Solidarity,* a mystical and metaphysical piece on the indestructible ties that men have to one another, of their duty to live for each other. In the *Duke of Stockbridge, Mrs. Ludington's Sister,* and numerous short stories, Bellamy developed a style of high craftsmanship, which made his *Looking Backward* more readable than the more than twoscore utopian novels to appear in the third part of the nineteenth century. As a book reviewer for the *Springfield News,* he read omnivorously on eugenics, evolution, technology, and history. He knew no Marxism, wrote before the *Fabian Essays* appeared, disliked Webster's innocuous definition of socialism, and abhorred class warfare. In short, the novelist and journalist, on the eve of writing *Looking Backward,* was a humanitarian, spasmodically interested in social regeneraton, but by no means a professional reformer.[20]

The society of 2000 A.D., in which Julian West of *Looking Backward* awakens, is founded on economic equality. Technology has so revolutionized human life that there are radios, time-saving gadgets in the house and the factory, rapid transportation through the air, food, clothing, and shelter for everyone, and permanent umbrellas over the streets to keep off rain. The government is organized like the general staff of an army, owns all the means of production and exchange, and runs the economy through an industrial army organized on a hierarchical basis. Discipline is severe, but men are free from want, and women are equal in every respect to men. At the age of forty-five, the citizen quits the army, at leisure to cultivate whatever hobbies his tastes incline him to. Society has solved the problem of freedom and authority by submerging the individual in the group, as Bellamy's *Religion of Solidarity* called for. Through intelligent mating, suggested by Bellamy's knowledge of eugenics, the best offspring are reproduced. The end results of Nationalism appealed to the author of *Looking Backward* as being the final product of man's ascent from the slime; and they were achieved peacefully and legally.

Others thought so too, especially literary folk in and around Boston. Edward Everett Hale, Thomas Wentworth Higginson, William Dean Howells, and two journalists, Sylvester Baxter and Cyrus F. Willard, approved of the book enthusiastically. The latter two wrote to Bellamy in 1888, shortly after his volume appeared, suggesting the formation of Nationalist clubs around its principles. Bellamy approved, two clubs were formed, and the Nationalist movement was on, spreading to New York, Philadelphia, Washington, and across the country as far as California. In Boston the clubs consisted largely of intellectuals, but also had at the outset retired army officers, women, and clergymen. A good many members were Theosophists, notably Willard and Baxter, who saw in Bellamy's social vision the realization of human brotherhood; Bellamy was specific in insisting that Nationalism would smelt down all races and classes in the socialist amalgam. Among the more important Boston intelligentsia who supported the movement were the poets, Henry Austin Willard and Sam Walter Foss; the novelists, William Dean Howells and Hamlin Garland; the social economists, Laurence Gronlund and

Frank Parsons; the journalists, Baxter and Willard; the publicist, Thaddeus B. Wakeman. The Boston Nationalists' names numbered more than three hundred.

The First Nationalist Club, dominated largely by the Theosophists, put out the *New Nation* from 1889 to 1891, of which the editor was Cyrus F. Willard. It eschewed politics, wrote on the outlines of the society to come, pointed out the relationship of the philosophy of Madame Blavatsky and Edward Bellamy. It carefully distinguished between Nationalism and Marxism, condemning class warfare and appealing to all classes to work for the co-operative commonwealth. The Second Club, made up by people who wished to realize immediate gains, rather than wait for the millennium in the distant future, appealed more to Bellamy. When in 1891, the *New Nation* ceased publication because of financial difficulties and internal dissension among the elect, Bellamy with the aid of the Second Club brought out the *Nationalist*. In it he campaigned for a number of immediate reforms: the initiative, referendum and recall; graduated income tax; the national ownership of the telegraph, telephone, and railroads; the municipalization of electricity, gas, and tramways; an eight-hour day. Boston's Nationalists, seeing eye to eye with the farmer Populists, in 1892, and again in 1894, supported the People's Party, indeed making up the Massachusetts end of the Party.

In 1894, the *Nationalist* came to the same end as the *New Nation*. The causes for failure were many. For one thing, the Populist Party absorbed the Nationalists. For another, the Nationalists were not unified; such people as Higginson, Garland, Howells, Gronlund, Bliss, and others going their separate ways. Finally, Nationalism was simply not attractive to enough Americans, who were neither ready nor disposed to sanction the complete collectivization of the economy. By 1895 Nationalism was dead and Bellamy, becaue he was not a silver man, refused to recognize Bryan, as did other Populists, as the legitimate heir to his principles.[21] In 1897, in his *Equality*, a sequel to *Looking Backward*, he continued his analysis of the future, adding to it only a more detailed account of the means of social change, through education and political action. He died in 1898, his works to be a stimulation to social reform, rather than a blueprint.

IV

Between the socialists and anarchists, on the one hand, and the staid *Atlantic Monthly*, on the other, stood two resolute doers of good, Benjamin Orange Flower and Edwin D. Mead. They edited respectively the *Arena* and the *New England Magazine*, both started in 1889. The two men were eclectic in their reform tastes; they championed a wide range of progressive measures popular in the 1890's, unwilling to commit themselves either to a monistic diagnosis or prognosis of society. Here the similarity ends. Flower, bombastic, emotional, argumentative, and religiously dedicated to better every aspect of life in Western civilization, devoted practically every issue, every article, every editorial in his journal to the cause of social regeneration, rapidly winning for the *Arena* the reputation of being the outstanding organ for newness in America.[22] Mead, in contrast, a gentleman with impeccably good taste and above polemics, wished to have a magazine that would appeal to all New Englanders of refinement, reformers as well as those who were not. In his journal, therefore, he published not only material on liberal movements in America and abroad but also articles on the level of those in the *Atlantic Monthly* dealing with literature, art, history, travel, and various aspects of New England life. He spoke out on public issues in "The Editor's Table."

Of New Hampshire birth, Edwin D. Mead was a Puritan and a Bostonian by conviction and choice. After four years at Cambridge and Leipzig Universities, he arrived at Boston in 1879, where his cousin through marriage, William Dean Howells, secured a position for him in the countinghouse of Ticknor and Fields. Due to his connection and background, Mead had easy access to the older generation of intellectuals, at Mrs. Ticknor's salon, at Longfellow's Dante Society, at Bronson Alcott's Concord School of Philosophy. In the 1880's, the New Hampshire scholar lectured on Kant, Plato, and Transcendentalism, wrote on the *Divine Comedy*, and, after 1887, headed the Old South historical activities. Trained in history, Mead venerated Boston's past, the moral seriousness of its Puritanism, the revolutionary ardor of its Seventy-Sixers, the fecundity of its intellectual life. His heroes were the men of Emerson's generation; he admired their optimism, their faith in themselves, their country, and the common man. What most appealed to him was the example they had shown of the scholar in reform, a tradition which, after his fling at literature for literature's sake in the 1880's, he conscientiously and consciously emulated as editor of the *New England Magazine*.[23]

The major causes to which Edwin D. Mead devoted his reform energies were international peace, good municipal government, and the elimination of poverty. As a bookish man he took his cue on liberal measures from other writers. Mrs. Lynn Linton, in her *Joshua Davidson*, an early English Social Gospel novel, defined the economic problem for Mead in sharp moral terms. Davidson, recreated as a modern Jesus, is born into a Cornish worker's family, participates in the Commune, returns to England to agitate against the rich for the poor, and dies a martyr's death. Mead, who was President of the Free Religious Association, sympathized with the portrayal of Jesus as a "social reformer" and declared that those who believed in Jesus must stand "for more social and political reform than the Christ-men of the past." The crucial problem was to eliminate the "tyranny of the rich" over "the poverty of the poor" lest civilization perish from violent upheaval. And the solution would not be easy; "the Garrisons and Phillipses of this time must expect to meet their 'mob of gentlemen'. . ."[24]

Henry Demarest Lloyd's *Wealth Against Commonwealth* taught Edwin D. Mead the facts of life of industrial America. In a long review of the book, the Boston reformer made a précis of it, agreeing with Edward Everett Hale that it was "the 'Uncle Tom's Cabin' of the present crisis." Turning muckraker for the moment, Mead asserted that it was perfectly true that the plutocracy was subverting the republic through its control of the courts, churches, legislatures, and schools. He was particularly alarmed over the manner in which the corporations were strangling academic freedom. Three years after he reviewed Lloyd's volume, Mead wrote an impassioned editorial against big business for forcing President Benjamin Andrews out of Brown University because of his views on free silver. As a remedy for diminishing the power of privileged wealth, the Boston journalist proposed the nationalization of the railroads, citing as precedent the public ownership of roads. When Lloyd's book on English coöperatives appeared in 1897, Mead championed its ideas. Like the Chicago crusader, the Boston liberal hoped for "industrial equality"; but he did not make clear what he meant by it, nor did he propose how to achieve it.[25]

In political reform Mead was both a "goo-goo" and a militant. He and his wife, Lucia Ames, stood resolutely for the immediate enfranchisement of women. To improve municipal government he radically urged his own Boston to adopt the Swiss initiative and referendum as a measure to assure the people a voice in government; the Danish system of proportional representation as a means to encourage interested men to run for office; and the Birmingham plan of municipal tenements, parks, and public utilities as ways of keeping big business out of politics and providing the poor and the public with needed and good services. The Chicago World's Fair showed Mead the benefit of city-planning; and he proposed that Boston set up a "Board of Beauty" to consist of engineers and architects to plan Boston's growth so that it would become a modern Athens. With respect to enlarging the functions of city government, Mead readily confessed that he was a socialist.[26]

However, the Boston reformer also approved of the British scheme of "philanthropy and 5 per cent," the businessman's reform of building workers' tenements and suburban cottages at reasonable profit. Moreover, he supported the polite and wealthy doers of good in the Massachusetts Society for Promoting Good Citizenship and Municipal League of Boston, who fulminated against boss rule and gave lectures on civics. Finally, Mead believed that if rich Protestants and loyal Catholics would desert their private schools and send their children to public school, the young would learn tolerance, democracy, and public virtue and thereby save the republic.[27]

Immanuel Kant, Dante, and Samuel Gridley Howe were Edwin Mead's mentors in international affairs. As Howe earlier had solicited for the Greeks, so Mead inveighed against the Turks for persecuting the Armenians. With the eighteenth-century German *philosophe* and the medieval Italian poet, Mead believed in world peace through world government. He devoted his entire life to Kant's idea that progress would lead ultimately to a world federation of republics and, as a first step, favored an international court of arbitration.

Throughout the 1890's opposing war, he condemned the jingoists during the Venezuela crisis, criticized McKinley for engaging the nation in war against Spain, and took a leading part in Boston's anti-imperialist movement. So avid was Mead's desire to prevent America from building an empire that he supported Bryan in 1900, having refused to follow him in 1896 because of the silver issue. At the turn of the century Mead prophesied that global peace would be the consuming interest of the future. He noted:

> The world is to be organized, not to keep nations peaceful in orderly arbitrament and protected separateness, but for constructive and coöperative life. That life will come as nations see that they are not their own, but all of them members of one another, with common inheritances, with common obligations, and with a common destiny. . . Some great enlightened, chosen nation — shall it not be this federal republic — will see it, and the vision will make it a centre of union . . . and so . . . the organization of the world will come.[28]

What then is the significance of the *New England Magazine*? For one thing, it made reform respectable. Edwin Mead was eminently respected in the Boston community, and his articles and books on Emerson, Channing, Hale, Parker, and Phillips demonstrated that Boston's most honored citizens had been and were liberals. His editorials were always sober, with the moral passion of an Emerson, but never sensational. Second, he encouraged young writers, such as Sam Walter Foss, the poet, and Walter Blackburn Harte, the essayist, who contributed to his journal. Third, he championed a number of liberal ideas acceptable to middle-class Americans dissatisfied with the status quo, but who did not want to break radically from the past. Fourth, he published articles, whose views he did not share but wished to be known, on Fabian Socialism, Nationalism, Christian Socialism, and the Single Tax. Fifth, he joined with others in insisting that the churches do their duty in social reform.[29] Above all, through his writings on Boston's past, he demonstrated the continuity between the fighters against George III and colonial oppression and Henry Frick and war. To the extent that he rooted the *New England Magazine* in the local past, he made of it a more liberal version of the *Atlantic Monthly*, differing thereby from Benjamin Orange Flower.

When B. O. Flower began editing the *Arena*, he was already a veteran journalist of nearly ten years' experience. Born in Albion, Illinois, October 19, 1858, a town founded by his paternal, English-born grandfather, he grew up in Evansville, Indiana, and was educated at Kentucky University. His father and brothers were orthodox ministers, but while at college Benjamin became a Unitarian. From the outset he desired a career as a writer; at the age of twenty-two he was editor of the *Albion Sentinel*. In 1880, the young Midwesterner came east, to Philadelphia, where he remained for five years, doing odd journalistic chores. In 1885, he turned up in Boston, where he brought out the *American Spectator* in 1886, which merged three years later with the *Arena*. Just over thirty, then, Flower became head of what was to be the first successful muckraking magazine in America. He attracted other young intellectuals who, sensing like him that America was at a moral crossroad, turned reformers. Buoyed up by this support, the youthful editor wrote: "The destiny of this great civilization lies largely in the hands of the rising generation — our young men and women . . . a splendid minority in the struggle for human progress." [30]

As a philosopher of social reform Flower became a latter-day Wendell Phillips. He was in a strict sense a professional agitator, a full-time employee in the service of progress. He believed that a handful of such full-time employees, moreover, could lead civilization upwards. In his adoration of the heroic and creative minority of liberal intellectuals, Flower was both Platonic and Christian. With Plato he believed that in "great transition periods there are always a few children of genius who, . . . ascend the mountain of the ideal and catch glimpses of the coming dawn"; these prophets announce the eternal truths of right living, only to be immediately denounced by the inert masses who will later accept their ideas. Flower was Christ-like in his desire to sacrifice himself, his fortune, his well-being, his reputation, to serve the *eternal verities*. As other heroic examples he pointed to Socrates, More, Savonarola, Hugo, Hampden, Massey, Whittier, and Mazzini. In this conviction he was especially attracted to Ruskin who, Flower delightedly wrote, gave up his beloved wife so that she could marry her lover.[31] There was in Flower a most obvious kind of masochism, which he called martyrdom, to be borne, according to his philosophy, by everyone who intended to improve the world.

And the world, at least its western part, not just Boston, was his home. The editor of the *Arena* read and wrote history, his eye on the lookout for men and events that would demonstrate both the parallels and continuity of past and present, the "subtle but conspicuous kinship among the luminous periods of history." In *The Century of Sir Thomas More*, Flower pointed out the similarity between his own age and the Renaissance. The sixteenth century was like the nineteenth century in groping for new forms in government, religion, art, literature, and science. Da Vinci and Michelangelo, Raphael and Correggio, he wrote, are examples of "what heights the soul of man might soar. . ." Machiavelli demonstrates how wicked man gets when he follows "*self-interest* instead of *conscience*. . ." And the Italian republics are a lesson for us today, for the plutocrats of their day, the Medicis, seized power; "republics have nothing to fear so much as vast accumulations in the hands of the few." Lay evangelist of social democracy that he was, Flower drove home the point, with his usual penchant for moral generalities, that: "Sincerity, justice, morality and integrity are the only sound foundations for human character or human society. . ."[32]

Flower found few men interested in these qualities in his own America and again he turned to the past for an answer. American civilization, he wrote, started out gloriously with a bold stroke for freedom during the Revolution. Jackson and Lincoln preserved democracy, and up to the Civil War the new nation served as a stimulus to the Old World countries to free themselves from despotism; this was our mission. After Appomattox, the United States fell on evil days. Giant corporations grew up and bought up the natural resources, the labor, and the land, and controlled the government. America must defeat the owners of privileged wealth, asserted Flower, and reclaim for itself the mission of republicanizing the world.[33]

America suffered not only from corporation control, thought Flower, but from other institutions and values which violated good sense and conscience. In the pages of the *Arena*, Flower and his staff muckraked against the more conspicuous evils. Women were denied the ballot, they suffered from the ignominy of the double standard of values, and were forced into corsets distorting their figures. American literature languished for want of realists to interpret the native scene. The churches were, on the whole, more concerned with ritual than ethics. Government had become impersonal, removed from the people, and therefore irresponsible. The worst shame of America was the slums, where cold-blooded capitalists bled their operators white, where unchristian landlords fleeced their tenants, where the poor drank themselves blind, and where the rich satisfied their lust for prostitutes. And the agricultural slums in the West were not better. These drawbacks in American life were evil, not only in themselves, but in a moral sense: to Flower they signified that man had still not wiped out the ape in him. And it was to the elimination of the ape in man that he dedicated his life.[34]

However formidable the obstacles to the improvement of the human race, and the *Arena* painted them in the blackest colors, Flower and his staff approached their task optimistically. For was not progress, the great God of their age, on their side? Flower admired the English naturalist, Alfred Lord Russell, who in *The Wonderful Century*, forecast that science, technology, and altruism would transform mankind as natural selection already had done. The Boston editor did not believe that the dialectic of progress would work itself out automatically, indeed it needed guidance, but its march would be irresistible. From Wallace, Flower also accepted the theory that man's spirit had also evolved, from selfishness to altruism; and that the final struggle for existence would be the battle between the selfish and altruistic spirits for control of society.[35]

As a spiritualist, Flower gave a special twist to evolution. The perfect human product, he believed, would come after death, when men, free from the degrading bodily cares and wants, would live in the rarefied atmosphere of art, music, literature, and good conversation.[36] To prepare men for that state, Flower would cleanse them of lust, ignorance, envy, selfishness, ambition, greed, dishonesty, and materialism, substituting for them their opposites as well as appreciation for the divine muses. Social reform for the editor of the *Arena* was thus a means toward a twofold end — the end of good living in the here and the hereafter. Unlike Bellamy, who quite often regarded bodily comforts as ends in themselves, Flower wanted to free men from daily cares so that they could be Victor Hugos, Michelangelos, John Greenleaf Whittiers — or at least be fit company for them.

Rooted in the compounded social philosophy of biology, history, and pseudo-science of Benjamin O. Flower, the *Arena* looked both forward and backward. One function was to point to the past to indicate lines of progress; the other was to look ahead to square tactics with strategy. At all times Flower and his aides exposed the evils of their society. Believing that improvement came through free discussion, Flower published articles presenting new ideas which, because of their unconventionality, could not find space in the more respectable journals.[37] By 1900, the Boston magazine had become the champion of a new society, of a new art, a new religion, a new economy, a new government, a new education, a new sexual ethic. However bold the exclamations of Flower and his staff, they were embedded in the traditional secular and religious meaning of American life, of expanding opportunities for the many.

Quite early the *Arena* developed into a kind of family magazine, consisting of a core of specialists in one reform, or perhaps two. The expert in government was W. D. McCrackan; in education, Joseph Rhodes Buchanan; in religion, Minot J. Savage; in literature, Hamlin Garland; in economics, Frank Parsons; in sex, Flower; in art, William Ordway Partridge; in women's affairs, Helen Campbell; in the drama, James A. Herne. Flower also solicited articles from Count Tolstoi, Felix Adler, Robert Ingersoll, Edward Bellamy, Laurence Gronlund, and Henry George, who presented their pet social philosophies. J. J. Enneking, friendly with Flower but not a very active contributor, was a landscape artist who, after studying the park system in Vienna, returned to Boston to play a leading part in beautifying the Hub city.

Flower, Hamlin Garland, J. J. Enneking, W. D. McCrackan, and James A. Herne were Single-Taxers, but the *Arena* was not known as a Henry George journal, but as an eclectic one. W. D. McCrackan, after spending five years in Switzerland, was invited by Flower, on Garland's suggestion, to prepare articles on the initiative, referendum, and proportional representation. These measures, McCrackan wrote, would restore American democracy on the town meeting model and allow for minority representation. In education, Joseph Rhodes Buchanan proposed moral and manual as well as intellectual training, on the theory that the entire child be educated. Frank Parsons advocated the public ownership of utilities and corporations as a way of crushing the plutocracy. Flower inveighed equally against prostitution and the male tyranny of the marriage bed on the grounds that a child conceived in a moment of lust would become, if a woman, a prostitute, if a man, a conceiver of children in lust. He argued for the absolute equality of the sexes, the female the controller of her sex, purse, vote, and vocation. Minot J. Savage, joined by the Reverends Carlos Martyn, George C. Lorimer, and Cyrus A. Bartol, urged the church to turn its back on dogma and work for human improvement.[38] Behind all of these reforms lay the idea that, by the proper tinkering with the environment, one could raise mankind to the high material and moral standard of life promised by the Industrial Revolution.

The *Arena* stood against art for art's sake; for art for humanity's sake. Flower's own heroes were Victor Hugo, Gerald Massey, and John Greenleaf Whittier, on whom he wrote understandingly and lovingly. Of his own generation of writers, he praised William Morris and Joaquin Miller. Two of his staff, James A. Herne, the playwright with a penchant for realism, and Hamlin Garland, the spokesman for Veritism, embodied Flower's favorite ideas. Both men, like him, were Single-Taxers, interested in social problems, and in recreating life as it existed. Flower and Garland helped Herne produce *Margaret Fleming*, a daring play in its day. The theme was that the double standard in marriage was immoral, that fidelity was required of both husband and wife.[39]

Garland was first introduced to the reading public through the *Arena*. He came to Boston in the 1880's, taught school to eke out a living, and spent most of his time in the Public Library reading Darwin and Spencer, Howells, Zola, and Ibsen. From the evolutionists Garland fortified his rebelling nature in believing that literary and artistic forms, like all forms of life, must change with each generation. From the American and Continental realists he marshaled arguments in favor of writing fiction that took life as it is really lived for its subject. From his own memories of the heartbreaking experiences of his family in the Great American Desert he learned to identify himself with the common folk of the land. The gentility of Boston letters and the squalor of Boston's slums convinced the erstwhile farm boy that conditions in the city needed as much improvement as those on the prairie. He was the *Arena* bridge between city and agrarian radicalism.[40]

Fiction, according to Garland's theory of Veritism, should portray the ugly aspects of life to show people what to get rid of. All that was sordid in American life, wrote Garland, could be traced to the economy: big business corrupted government, and poverty brutalized both mind and body. He asserted that the artist should be most sensitive to raising the standard of living; when "men have enough to eat, they turn to art and literature." And men could only be happy with leisure to think and read and dream. Garland's fiction followed his theory. In *Under the Wheel*, a drama in six acts, published in 1890, he exposed the poverty of Boston's North End and the North Dakota farms, driving home the point that land speculation was the sole cause for making and keeping people poor. As a disciple of Henry George, he argued that a single tax on unearned increment would remove the "North End rookery, with its overcrowding, and the settler's shanty, with its loneliness and despair." Like his mentor, Henry George, Garland also believed that the state was the instrument of the ruling classes and, in *A Spoil of Office* (1892) and *A Member of the Third House* (1890), he inveighed respectively against the collusion of capitalists and politicians in the West and Massachusetts.[41] In the two novels the heroines are modern, Ibsen-like women and the heroes scholars in politics.

The *Arena* stood for direct political action, thereby differing from the *New England Magazine*, which ignored partisan battles. In 1892 Flower came out in support of the Populists. Against socialism because it would destroy personal liberty, Flower wrote that the People's Party stood for just the right amount of government strength to allow for freedom and yet curb the owners of privileged wealth; he approved their platform of postal savings banks, the government ownership of natural monopolies, the initiative, referendum, and recall. In 1896 the Boston journalist hailed William Jennings Bryan as a demigod come to save the republic. As Sam Adams had slain Toryism, Jackson monopoly, Lincoln slavery, so Bryan would lay low "the double-headed party of plutocracy and centralized wealth." [42] The Nebraskan was Flower's type, an evangelist in politics, and the editor of the *Arena* prophesied that he would win. One year after the election of McKinley, Flower left Boston for reform duties in Chicago, but the *Arena* continued his policies under his successors, John Redpath and Paul Tynor. It was moved to New York in 1899.

Benjamin Orange Flower's radical magazine was sent to the principal editorial offices of the nation and also had a wide circulation among the literate middle classes. Flower's special contribution to the ferments of the 1890's was his message that the country was in a crisis, indeed faced with revolution unless cured by peaceful and democratic reform. In *How England Averted a Revolution of Force*, a laboratory study of British liberalism in the 1830's and 1840's, he concluded that social change could be promoted best by the effective organization, leadership, and education of social reformers. The crusading editor was also influential in making every issue a moral issue; such words as truth, beauty, goodness, virtue, manhood, altruism were stock words in his editorial vocabulary. His penchant for evangelical social democracy led him to sum up the causes of the unrest of the 1890's as "that trinity of evil: poverty, rum and masculine immorality." [43] In his literary style he was as much the gentleman as Edwin D. Mead; he never became a vulgar sensationalist. He was simply more impatient, more emotional, almost female in his shock at degrading conditions. Whereas Mead's reminiscences contain dispassionate, critical afterthoughts, Flower's abound in the first judgments of the controversialist.

V

Every intellectual in reform in Boston from 1880 to 1900 stood by his liberal aspirations with the notable exception of Walter Blackburn Harte. A Canadian by birth, he came to Boston to seek a literary career. Harte assisted Edwin D. Mead on the *New England Magazine*, wrote for the *Arena*, and when he was still under thirty emerged as one of the more distinguished essayists in Boston. He read widely, especially in realistic fiction, but was most attracted to Walt Whitman, who, he wrote glowingly, was "an evangel of a new gospel of humanity . . . a tonic and impulse for this generation." Just what happened is not clear, but by 1895 he ceased contributing to Boston's liberal journals, indeed sneering at the *Arena* for trying to improve the world. Together with Jonathan Penn, L. Lemmah, Olga Arnold, Claude Fayette Bragdon, and other young writers he began to edit the *Fly Leaf*, which lasted but one year (1895–96) for want of support. Its contributors sang of the delights of Bohemia, scoffed at reformers, inveighed against Philistinism, attacked polite literature, and condemned immigrants ("barbaric scum of Europe") for polluting journalism by their taste for sensationalism. The joy in living, wrote Harte the erstwhile Whitmanite, is to be found in the company of "Nature's aristocracy" of the intellect who, free from the debasing influence of the mob and the market place, dwell with the muses of pure ideas.[44]

While Harte and his associates retreated to Bohemia, Boston's other intellectuals organized themselves to steer society in time of crisis. Because the older radical clubs were moribund, the reformers founded their own. Professor Frank Parsons enrolled many of his fellow-liberals in the League for Promoting the Public Ownership of Monopolies, the National Referendum League, and the Massachusetts Referendum Union. In 1894 Benjamin Orange Flower, with the assistance of Hamlin Garland, Parsons, and Thomas Elmer Will, founded the Union for Practical Progress. Within a year branches sprouted in Baltimore, New York, New Orleans, and other large cities. These were federated into a National Union which, through the *Arena*, planned the agitation against and solution for such problems as child labor, corrupt municipal politics, intemperance, sweatshops, tenement houses.[45]

In 1893 Edwin D. Mead organized the city's leading progressive literary and artistic men into the Twentieth Century Club. Approached by William Ordway Partridge, the sculptor, to form a group of liberals for good talk and comradeship, Mead reacted by suggesting that a center be established "for free and frank discussion of social reform. . ." His idea won out. He asked John Fiske to become the first president, but the latter feared the "socialist proclivities" of the Club; and Mead himself was elected head. Established on Beacon Hill, the Twentieth Century people invited William Dean Howells, Keir Hardie, Richard T. Ely, William Clarke, Henry Demarest Lloyd, George D. Herron, Jacob A. Riis, and other luminaries in social betterment to lecture to them. In 1897 the Club hired Harold Estabrook to study the condition of Boston's slums; and his *Some Slums of Boston* paved the way for giving the Board of Health wider powers in condemning unfit tenements. On December 31, 1899, the Twentieth Century Club sponsored a mass meeting attended by 20,000 people at the State House to usher in the new century. Edward Everett Hale presided, embodying for the moment the idea that the younger generation had kept his faith in doing good.[46]

The coming together of liberals in organizational work to give greater force to their ideas reveals both the strength and weakness of the Boston intelligentsia as reformers. They were realistic in believing that they had to organize as effectively as their opponents, the monopolists and corrupt politicians. But they had little association with the working masses, choosing instead to address one and another of the middle-class intellectuals capable of conversion. Both Mead and Howells appealed to Americans of refinement, moderate wealth, and taste; Garland spoke for the dwellers of agricultural and city slums but not to them; Flower, Tucker, Gronlund, and Swift operated on the principle that a creative minority might somehow lift the people out of their indifference and ignorance; and the Nationalists, excepting their experience with Populism, cultivated a socialism of the salon. Only in admitting women to their ranks, who were really as literary as they, did the intelligentisia labor side by side with those they wished to aid.

Frank K. Foster, Boston's leading trade unionist, recognized that the intellectuals did not coöperate with labor for the simple reason that they did not care to. In part the character of organized working-class liberalism was responsible for this. By the time the free-lancers appeared late in the 1880's the Knights of Labor had nearly passed from the scene and the American Federation of Labor took its place. The latter distrusted intellectuals and did not include them in their ranks, whereas the former welcomed the aid of all well-meaning persons provided they were not bartenders, lawyers, or bankers. Led by Frank K. Foster and other tough-minded trade unionists, the Boston workers did not seek, like the intelligentsia, a radical change in society. They accepted the existence of classes and, within the framework of capitalism, attempted to raise standards of life and labor through shorter hours and higher wages. Foster, while a humanitarian, thought little of the practicality of the advanced schemes of social reconstruction of the writers and artists, and even less of their flirtations with and conversions to spiritualism and Theosophy. Finally, he disapproved of the direct political action advocated by the *Arena* and the Nationalists; the trade union was a bargaining agency.[47]

More important, the intellectuals did not think highly of the working masses, thereby differing from the cultists of the proletariat of the Depression decade. The trade union movement was numerically weak and did not promise to be a bulwark against concentrated wealth. Furthermore, the journalists and magazine editors and novelists knew only the outcasts of the slums who, because they were so uttterly depressed and ignorant, were inert. The masses thus were to be helped, to be taught, to be led; they were not to be the spearhead for an army of liberals fighting the plutocracy. Hamlin Garland, who descended from the common folk, for example, sympathized with the people, he seemed to say that they were the salt of the earth, but, in his books, they could not solve their own problems. In *A Member of the Third House*, the hero was obviously a gentleman and a scholar, with the right clothes, the right accent, the right manners, the right college degree. He was the proper chief of the progressive cause, apart from and yet a part of the working and business classes: he was above them. The intellectuals wanted to believe that they were classless, as befits the persons who assume the priestly function of exhorting the many to renounce the evil world. In sharp contrast, the workers belonged to society — and they desired to belong even more.

Chapter Eight

THE WORKERS

Coöperators and Collective Individualists

This Preamble [of Knights of Labor] demands . . . measures
be provided for the distribution of products and opportunities
. . . by and through the wage-system, until the moral and
social wisdom and the increased wealth of the masses shall
ultimate in co-operation. — George E. McNeill

The job of making over worlds is . . . easy to tackle by platform and by resolution, but the trade union walks into the region of accomplishment and gets more bread and butter, and
clothes, and other things worth having. Hence its stability and
assured perpetuity as a factor in social progress.
                                        —Frank K. Foster [1]

W orkers, in contrast to reformers of pulpit, press, and
university, did not look in on the social problem from the outside: they were the social problem. From personal experience
they knew the toll of strikes and lockouts, of excessive hours and
low wages, of depression. At stake for middle-class intellectuals
was personal fulfillment in a materialistic age. At stake for men
who earned less than four hundred dollars a year and toiled more
than sixty hours a week was a higher standard of comfort and
leisure. Social reform among workers was thus a species of self-
help, an example of a disadvantaged class seeking a place in the
economic sun. What saved this class from a grasping and narrow
selfishness was the inheritance of the motif of the pre-1880 labor
movements, which had voiced an abstract protest against injus-

tice as well as a program for a particular group. This motif continued to operate in the 1880's and 1890's. Labor demanded not
only for itself but for all Americans other than plutocrats the
right to enjoy a life enriched by industrialism, promised by democracy, but thwarted by predatory men. The first demand was
for the producer coöperative.

The coöperators were the shoe workers, who plied their craft
less in Boston than in the outlying communities of Milford and
Lynn, Stoneham, Haverhill, and Brockton. They were casualties
of a technological revolution completed in ten swift years. By
1870 the manufacturing of shoes came of modern age, as the
productive processes were harnessed finally to the machine and
housed under the single roof of the large factory. Early in the
1860's the Mackay stitcher made obsolete the trade of the turner
and the handwelter, and the large manufactory replaced the
small shop. Shortly thereafter came the pegging machine, button-
fasteners, polishers, heel-trimmers, and numerous other machines
in bewildering and quick profusion. Apart from lasters, artisans
who had once prided themselves on skills laboriously learned
either left the mill or toiled side by side on hated power-driven
tools with once-scorned green hands.

The initial reaction was to safeguard skills and status against
these green hands. Local unions of edge-setters, trimmers, and
cutters appeared but did not last long. The Knights of St. Crispin,
between its founding in 1867 and its near collapse in 1878, for-
bade members to "teach, or aid in teaching, any part or parts of
boot or shoe-making" without the agreement of three-fourths of
the local lodge. The Lasters' Protective Union came into being
for the same purpose. The lasters retained a privileged position
in the factory, but the Crispins could not withstand increasing
mechanization, and lockouts and strikes quickly exhausted a
limited treasury. By the early 1880's the erstwhile skilled and unskilled comprehended alike "that in the age of collective capital
there must be a larger co-operation among the wage-workers
than the isolated local union. . ."[2]

Together with the awareness of the need for concerted class action was a mood of nostalgia. The new economy came with such sudden swiftness and awful consequences that the shoemakers sought comfort in the reveries of a recent past that had been pleasant. Their historian recalled that once "almost every New England shoe shop was a lyceum," which although not as "romantic, possibly, as the academic groves where the Grecian seekers after truth gathered," was altogether expressive of the "Yankee combination of utility with . . . inquiry into all things mundane and celestial." There it had been usual for cobblers to employ a boy to read aloud philosophical and theoretical works, which were discussed amid tasks uninterrupted. In days of old, too, there had been neither cleavage between artisan and small shopowner nor cutthroat competition among workers: there was solidarity. Admittedly sentimental, the artisans of the "gentle craft of leather" asked to "be pardoned a memory of regret for that time when the man was more than a tender to the machine, and the military rule of our present industrial system did not oppose a perpetual menace to the individuality of the operative." [3]

The values of the shoemakers were those of old New England. Increased factory production meant progress to census takers, economists, and manufacturers — but retrogression to the man who yearned to work skillfully by hand and with quality rather than quantity in mind. Similarly, division of labor made output more efficient and rapid, but what of the loss of status that placed cobbler on the same level with mill hand? The shoemaker had come from farm, village, and small town, where he had been nurtured on the old ideal of self-reliance and on the equally old virtue that workers ought not to constitute a permanent class. The new factory system, by its very organization, gave validity to traditional beliefs. Before the age of the elaborate front office — of public relations men, of sales forces, of large secretarial staffs, of imposing managerial suites — the workers saw none but themselves, and believed that they, and they alone, created wealth. The labor theory of value and the longing for a golden age led shoemakers to look to the coöperative: it would destroy the new class structure, recreate the fraternity of the shop, and restore a cherished status. Shoe workers fixed their eyes on the New England of 1850, and they joined, indeed made up the bulk of, the Knights of Labor in Massachusetts.[4]

The leaders of Massachusetts District Assembly 30 of the Knights of Labor shared the shoemakers' objective to replace competitive capitalism with coöperative enterprise, and hoped to rally all producers in the state to this objective. Old, professional hands at labor reform, they had been working for the coöperative commonwealth for years. Most of them — and here Charles Litchman, A. A. Carlton, and Robert Howard were representative figures — had themselves been cobblers, who in the 1860's and 1870's became labor organizers. Passage from the Knights of St. Crispin, which had endorsed the producer coöperative, to the Knights of Labor was like taking another try at a course that one had failed. There was, too, ancient but vigorous John Orviss, ex-abolitionist, ex-Brook-Farmerite, and Fourierist evangelist for over four decades. Like him were two self-taught social theoreticians, George E. McNeill and Ira Steward, who for some twenty years had been in possession of a sure-fire scheme for coöperative regeneration, but had been unable to keep an organization together long enough to realize the scheme. The old guard reformers, no longer belonging to the ranks of wage-earners, regarded themselves as Christian soldiers for the good society rather than spokesmen for a single class. Undiscouraged by the failures of coöperatives from Brook Farm to the Sovereigns of Industry, they embraced the Noble and Holy Order of the Knights of Labor as the long-dreamt-for agency of social salvation.[5]

The chief propagandist and organizer for the Bay State Knights was George E. McNeill. A prototype of the universal reformer, he came of age in the 1850's. As a mid-century idealist, he believed in perfecting mankind and in realizing America's divine mission

> To build foundations strong for Freedom's home,
> To shelter the oppressed of every clime.[6]

He also believed in the Puritan's passion in chasing out evil, the evil of "ancient foes, Mammon's priests," who tempted the nation to sin for gold against the Indian, then the Negro, and then the worker. In the last part of his life a large, stooped figure with a shaggy beard, heavy eyebrows, bald head, and rough but attractive homeliness, the reformer reminded friends of an Old Testament prophet. McNeill, serving God and opposing Satan, supported until his death in 1906 nearly every ism that would build the earthly heaven in the New World. It was characteristic of the man to name his eldest son after Ira Steward, the labor reformer, who was, he thought, a modern saint in the industrial age.

McNeill's life began in 1837 in an abolitionist, Scotch-Irish Amesbury home, frequented by John Greenleaf Whittier and responsive to the humanitarian impulses of the day. Out of school and in the mill at the age of fourteen, he led an unsuccessful strike that taught him the evil of unchecked capital. "I hereby swear," the youth is reported to have said, "to fight this thing till I die." In 1856, he made his way to Boston and found work as a shoe worker. Immediately he embraced the anti-slavery, temperance, utopian socialist, and labor movements. His contemporaries were Theodore Parker, Albert Brisbane, George Ripley, Wendell Phillips, and he emerged with the latter by the 1870's as Boston's chief labor reformer. The great divide in his life came during the Civil War, when he met Ira Steward, Boston machinist and originator of the eight-hour-day philosophy. Converted to that philosophy, McNeill thereafter championed it so long and so vigorously that he and not Steward was known as the "father of the eight-hour movement." This he did as labor newspaper editor, historian, pamphleteer, statistician for the Massachusetts Bureau of Statistics of Labor, labor organizer, and executive of the Grand Eight-Hour League of Boston, the Order of the People, the Industrial Congress, and the Sovereigns of Industry. He also wrote poetry on his pet subject. In the years 1884–1886, as Secretary-

Treasurer of District Assembly 30, he was still championing the Steward ideology, as well as a number of currency, tax, land, and public utility reforms he had picked up from Henry George.[7]

Leaving the ranks of wage-earners in 1883 to form his own insurance company, McNeill was, like other Knights leaders, an Emersonian jack-of-all-trades predisposed to reject the idea that the worker must remain a worker. The worker must become his own employer. This objective the Boston reformer wrote into the principles of the Knights of Labor, as well as the methods to achieve it. Government in a democracy, he wrote, must legislate against extreme wealth: it must nationalize natural monopolies; withhold land from speculators; deny private banks the privilege to issue money; and tax unearned increment. Democratic government should also help the underdog by abolishing child labor and incorporating trade unions. While the people's political representatives checked the plutocracy, their economic congress — the one big union of the Knights — was to land the knockout blow. They were to agitate for the eight-hour day so as to achieve "co-operative institutions such as will tend to supercede the wage-system." [8]

Coöperative institutions and the eight-hour day — here was the heart of McNeill's position. From Steward he learned that wages were paid according to the worker's needs, not, as the classical economists instructed, according to the law of supply and demand. Steward phrased the controlling assumption in a couplet quoted by coöperators up and down the land:

> Whether you work by the piece or work by the day,
> Decreasing the hours increases the pay.

Reducing the time at the mill to eight hours, the Steward-McNeill thesis ran, would give the workingman strength and leisure and time to develop the desires of the business and professional classes — for books, plays, and newspapers, for decent housing, furnishings, and clothing. A worker with such tastes would demand and receive wages necessary to sustain them. The eight-hour day, however, was only a first step; one must further reduce hours of labor, and therefore increase wages, until the capitalist was denied all profit. At that point employees of mill and mine and factory would buy out their employers and thereby achieve "Co-operation . . . the final result. . ." [9]

The coöperative society was defended on the grounds that, by removing the "wage-labor system," it would eliminate the anomaly in a free society of feudal employers on the one side and "serfs of the mill, the workshop, and the mine" on the other. Also, coöperation was as logical as it was equitable: for labor, and only labor, "produces wealth . . . makes civilization possible. . ." It was logical, too, that workers should be compensated according to need, for the machine removed the line separating skilled from unskilled. All workers were equal. When critics charged that economic equality would discourage initiative, the Knights replied that equal leisure and means would enable men to pursue a variety of pursuits to excel in the things of the mind. As important as the secular defense was the claim that the coöperative harmonized with "the Gospel that all men are of one blood." The conclusion: "the new Pentecost will come, when every man shall have according to his needs." [10]

Massachusetts District Assembly 30, staffed by universal reformers and supported originally by the shoemakers of Brockton, Lynn, Haverhill, and Milford, developed by the mid-eighties into a fraternity of enthusiastic crusaders. In the great upsurge of those years more than 5000 Bostonians rallied to the standard. They were of every sort and condition, for McNeill's philosophy transcended class and nationality, and the Noble Order welcomed all who worked for a living except for such "non-producers" as lawyers, gamblers, bankers, and bartenders. Enrolled in the ranks were the radical clergymen Jesse Jones and W. D. P. Bliss and the Theosophist journalist Cyrus Field Willard. When the Order repealed the oath of secrecy in 1881, Irish Catholics joined and rubbed shoulders with Yankees. Unskilled and skilled wage-earners recognized for a time a like identity as printers made common cause with mill hands. Even wives of "producers" were admitted, who, according to Willard, sought men at outings, picnics, dances, and discussion groups to satisfy sexual desires outside the nuptial bond. The Noble and Holy Order was not a trade union. Rather it was a club to promote socialism and sociability, a bright light in the lives of men and women who grasped the opportunity for solidarity in an age of individualism.

The very eclecticism of the Order contained the germs of its destruction. Apart from certain artisans, the Knights were organized geographically in mixed assemblies, not in craft unions, or as they were called, "trade districts." Presumably everyone had faith in the eight-hour day as a means toward coöperation, but there were in the ranks direct political actionists, Single-Taxers, Christian Socialists, Fabian Socialists, Marxian Socialists, Theosophists. More serious, there were business unionists who, at the Order's high point in 1886, were also members of the emerging American Federation of Labor. Skilled workers responsive to the enthusiasm of the times, they had reservations about an organization held together by sex and idealism, and were ready to bolt in case the Knights of Labor failed.[11]

In the years 1884–1886, it seemed that the Noble and Holy Order, expanding its membership at an incredible rate (71,326 to 729,677) and planning to storm the citadels of capitalism by way of strikes and political action, could not fail. In Boston, the assemblies multiplied thirty fold, while Massachusetts' D. A. 30 grew so rapidly as to lead to "the suspension of the initiation of new members." Assemblies were even organized in England, Belgium, Ireland, Australia, and New Zealand. In an age when most strikes failed, the Knights did the impossible when Joe Buchanan forced Jay Gould, labor's *bête noire*, to capitulate in the Wabash strike; and planned for May 1, 1886 (but without T. V. Powderly's endorsement) was a grand demonstration for the eight-hour day. Also, in that year George E. McNeill and Henry George were running for mayor respectively in Boston and New York on the United Labor Party ticket with K. of L. support. Rejoicing over all this activity, John Swinton, the veteran labor newspaperman, cried: "Never in all history has there been such a spectacle as the march of the Order of the Knights of Labor as the present time." George E. McNeill, after tracing the progress of the workers from slavery through feudalism to contract, prophesied: "The year 1886 will be known as the year of the great uprising of labor." [12]

The uprising fizzled, and the Noble and Holy Order deflated as quickly as it had expanded. In a return engagement Jay Gould smashed the Knights to bits; and the professional politicians routed George E. McNeill and Henry George. As for the eight-hour-day demonstration, it backfired miserably, resulting indirectly in the Haymarket Affair and the discrediting of the K. of L. as a dangerous and irresponsible organization. More important, within the Order trade unionists and universal reformers quarreled over basic issues of polity and policy. The latter wished to continue the idea of one big union of *all* "producers," and disapproved the strike. The former championed the cause of skilled workers, and hoped to organize artisans in craft unions with autonomous control over apprenticeship rules, strikes, boycotts, and dues. Not even George McNeill, who tried to effect a compromise at both the national and district levels, could bring the warring elements together. By 1890 District Assembly 30 was a ghost of its former self, its Boston support gone, and it's shoeworkers in the factory towns quiescent; 1886 was the year of blighted hopes: fiasco.[13]

The universal reformers, experiencing familiar defeat, continued undismayed the quest for the millennium. Orviss and Litchman attempted to regroup dazed Knights, Bliss and Jones organized the Society of Christian Socialists, and Willard sparked the Nationalist movement. George E. McNeill joined and became a warden of Bliss's Church of the Carpenter, and throughout the 1890's carried on as a true son of New England's age of newness. He composed an ode to Count Tolstoi, hailed William Jennings Bryan as a savior, and agitated for Russian, Irish, Negro, female,

and Filipino freedoms. He was a principal in the Anti-Tenement
House League, a member of the International Peace Society, and
a mover in the Anti-Imperialist League. At the General Court, he
argued for free textbooks, employers' liability and weekly pay-
ment bills, and the abolition of the poll tax. And until he died in
1906, he continued to believe and write that Samuel Gompers
and the American Federation of Labor, leading the common man,
would crush the feudal masters of industry and democratize the
economy through coöperatives. McNeil remained and died a
universal reformer, thinking that soon "Christ's eternal reign will
dawn"; that it was a question of time before "we . . . cleansed our
hearts from Mammon's lust." [14]

The Boston crusader failed to recognize that the Knights of
Labor marked the end of a road that had started at Brook Farm.
In August 1887, the trade unionists of Massachusetts, sparked by
Boston's printers, lasters, and cigar makers, founded a state
branch of the American Federation of Labor. A younger generation of leaders replaced McNeill and his sort. They rejoiced that
the "Hurrah" phase of the labor movement was dead: that the
day was done when skilled and unskilled were organized promiscuously in geographical districts and led by "professional labor
reformers" in pursuit of an unattainable goal. For the remainder
of the century these younger men would recall with anguish the
crushing disappointment of 1886. As one wrote, in the "first enthusiasm of their conversion," they expected to achieve the "radical" objective of "coöperation in the loftiest sense." The year 1886
came and went; and "the wage system remained, the factory
whistle blew early in the morning, the machine and its tender
ran all the day, the envelope was scantily filled on Saturday
night. . ." The lesson: "it was found necessary to treat of present
conditions instead of with future millenniums." [15]

II

Like modern proponents of Neo-Orthodoxy, the 1890's trade unionists of Boston were disillusioned radicals who rejected beliefs they once held regarding the nature of man and society. Man was not perfectible, they argued, but dual in his capacity for good and evil. Therefore, it was quixotic to plan on a final outcome for history that did not take human selfishness into account. Yet for all their hardheadedness, the trade unionists did not abandon the liberal's faith in human intelligence to make life better or doubt that the industrial revolution would ultimately confer blessings on mankind. The humanitarianism of the Knights of Labor lingered. Products of the frustrated hopes of the New England Renaissance, the trade unionists pitched their sights lower than the Coöperators. They accepted the economic system of private property, competition, and the profit motive, but agitated for the improvement of that system so as to include themselves in its benefits. They were individualists.

Their individualism was rooted in self-respect, self-confidence, and self-reliance. Except for garment workers in factories displaced by the sweatshop, they were skilled workers of *old* crafts unaffected by major technological changes. Masons and carpenters, painters and plasterers, bakers, brewers, and printers, they knew that they were not the wage-slaves the Coöperators and Marxians told them they were. To have admitted otherwise would have denied them the superior status they thought they enjoyed among the general class of wage-earners. They were poor but not degraded, and they by-passed the dismal North End for respectable working-class neighborhoods in Dorchester, Roxbury, and Cambridge, the South and West Ends. Unlike the illiterate charges of Robert A. Woods, they were men of some education who supported labor journals and joined political and educational clubs. They dressed respectably, had rugs on their living-room floors, pictures on their walls — or hoped to. Whereas the intellectuals spoke for immigrants fresh from Europe, these artisans, born in America and often products of the villages and farms of New England, spoke for themselves.[16]

They wanted a little more, and thought that privileged wealth got too much. The conception that they had of their class and of society paralleled that of the Jacksonian workers. The trade unionists of both the 1830's and 1890's, as skilled hands in old crafts, were more interested in themselves than in the larger class of wage-earners embraced in the factory system. Yet they resented what passed for the status quo, and this resentment catapulted them into a social reform that looked to basic changes in government and economy. Alike, they objected to the favors which businessmen solicited from government, for these privileges concentrated wealth in the hands of the few. The workers of the thirties and the nineties inveighed against combination in business and business in government; they demanded competition and impartial government. They revived the Jeffersonian tradition of anti-statism, and while those of the 1830's buttressed that tradition with Adam Smith, those of the 1890's found a more than adequate substitute in Herbert Spencer.[17]

Herbert Spencer caught on in Boston in the 1890's for the same reason that he caught on at Yale in 1883: the skilled artisan was William Graham Sumner's "Forgotten Man." It is often overlooked that, in *What Social Classes Owe to Each Other*, the Yale professor domesticated the individualistic philosophy of Herbert Spencer in the interests of the humble person who was neither poor nor rich enough to make special claims on the state. It was the middle-class worker who paid for the "jobbery" of the tariff and the franchise, the monopoly and the land grant, for every piece of class legislation that the lobbyist bought. Sumner called attention to the peril in America of the "plutocrats . . . trying to do what the generals, nobles, and priests have done in the past — get the power of the State into their hands. . ." He looked to voluntary associations, such as trade unions, to check the "insolence of wealth," as once the landed aristocrats had done. Boston's artisans, like Sumner, appreciated Herbert Spencer's con-

ception that free society must have impartial government, and
"increase, multiply, and extend the chances" to acquire wealth
through competition. Resenting plutocracy, as the Jacksonian
worker had resented neo-Mercantilism, Boston's artisans were
forgotten men on the make who championed the liberalism of
the individualistic school.[18]

The collectivist school, however, would not down. A small and
ineffectual German-speaking section of the Socialist Labor Party,
which had been founded in Boston in the 1870's, received important strength from the cigar makers in the 1880's and 1890's. The
latter were immigrants from Central and Eastern Europe, whose
hard lives in Boston read like a page out of the works of Karl
Marx and Laurence Gronlund, whom they read and quoted. Once
theirs had been the proud trade of journeymen, until the mold
enabled manufacturers to utilize cheap labor operating in tenement house apartments. The blue label had been directed against
this competition, but to no avail. The cigar makers concluded
with Marx and Gronlund that machinery benefited the bourgeoisie
but increased the misery of the proletariat. Life was truly a struggle between classes, and since Boston would not outlaw the tenement house, it was clear that the ruling class controlled the state.
The Marxians were therefore right in believing that trade unionists must organize a political party, capture the government, and
run industry. Then, and only then, would there be an end to
surplus value and the degradation resulting from it.

The cigar makers constituted a minority in Boston, but a lo-
quacious minority, and certain of their leaders were strategically
placed. They were instrumental in founding the Massachusetts
branch of the American Federation of Labor, and their own
Henry Abrahams was elected president in 1888. A tireless propagandist, Abrahams was persistent in bringing up the question
of direct political action, especially at the Central Labor Union
of Boston, a clearinghouse for the city's working-class ideologies.
There gathered remnants of the Knights of Labor, Communist
Anarchists, Single-Taxers, Fabian Socialists, Populists, Philoso-

phical Anarchists — "about every 'ist and 'ism that the mind can conceive." In particular, there was the Reverend W. D. P. Bliss, representing a local assembly of the Knights of Labor, who together with Abrahams kept things in a boil. Finally, in the American Federation of Labor, as Samuel Gompers well knew, about one-third of the membership approved socialist ideas and political action; and Thomas J. Morgan of Chicago and Daniel De Leon of New York hoped to make the A. F. of L. the backbone of the Socialist Labor Party.[19] Abrahams, in league with De Leon and Morgan, was a menace.

By common consent, Frank K. Foster of Typographical Union 13 was the chief individualist and opponent to Marxian collectivism. Born December 18, 1855, in Thorndike, Massachusetts, where he was educated through the academy, he learned the printer's trade in Hartford, and came to Boston at the age of twenty-five. An idealistic young artisan, he joined the Noble and Holy Order, rose by 1883 to executive rank in both D.A. 30 and the General Assembly, and by 1884 assumed the editorship of the Order's official journal in Massachusetts. In the uprising of 1886, young Foster ran for Lieutenant Governor on the Democratic ticket, only to lose. By this time Secretary of the A. F. of L., he joined forces with Samuel Gompers, P. J. McGuire, and Adolphe Strasser — fellow disillusioned craftsmen — to build up the successor to the K. of L. He played a leading role in the founding of the Bay State Federation and, as debater, Secretary, and Chairman of its Legislative Committee, formulated the principles of craft unionism. Without the extra talent of a Benjamin Franklin or a Horace Greeley, fellow printers, the Boston artisan never graduated from his class. In the trade union movement, however, he became a labor statesman, skilled in speech, writing, and diplomacy.

Aged thirty-two in 1887, Foster started editing with George E. McNeill the *Labor Leader*, official paper for the Bay State and Boston trade unions. It was one of the few successful ventures of the labor press in the latter part of the nineteenth century.

Within a year McNeill retired and laid on hands, as it were, on young Foster. Like other organs in an age of personal journalism, Foster's was largely a one-man sheet; and through his editorials, short stories, and news articles, he took on George E. McNeill's role as Boston's philosopher of the labor movement. In his busy lifetime he also brought out a volume of verse, *The Karma of Labor*, which, while lacking the lyrical quality of John Boyle O'Reilly's or Edwin Markham's stanzas, belonged to the genre of their poetry, that of social protest. Thinking himself to be the American counterpart to the English Gerald Massey, a poet for labor, Foster captured the squalor of the mine, the torpor of overwork, and the void of life without hope. Finally, in the *Evolution of a Trade Unionist*, an autobiographical novel, he summed up the experience of his generation in groping for an adequate philosophy after the disillusionment of the 1880's.[20]

A prodigious reader and quoter, Frank K. Foster was a professed social reformer whose thought defies easy formulation. He took almost excessive pride in his hardheadedness, yet championed Wendell Phillips' ideal of the melting pot against Gompers' immigration restrictionist views. He thought Shakespeare great for cataloguing human vices, yet insisted that we "must have faith in the To Be. . ." He implored craft unionists to follow Samuel Gompers and concentrate on bread and butter questions, yet fought with eloquence and passion for women's rights. He deplored craft unions' going into politics, yet encouraged workers to take the ballot seriously. He remarked that "life is a puzzle beyond the analysis of cheap dogmatists," yet dogmatized with Herbert Spencer that the key to the cosmos was the working out of individualism. Loving paradox almost for its own sake, Foster cut through the monism of Henry Abrahams. Analyzing man, the state, and society he hoped to dismiss from the trade union movement "the hidden mysteries and heterogeneous nothingness of Karl Marx, the inspired ebullitions of Laurence Gronlund. . ."[21]

Foster derided the basic premise of the Marxians that men were sufficiently good to work for others rather than for self. In his youth he had been a socialist, and he had played a prominent role in the coöperative upheaval of 1886, only to learn that few men were idealistic enough to place altruism above egoism. In the trade union movement he had encountered prejudice, stubbornness, inertia, and the most vulgar kind of ambition for place and reputation. He knew the faces of the North End — "bleary-eyed, sodden, stamped with vice, graven with iniquity, prematurely aged, cunning, leering, sensual, vicious, bloated, hardened, — human driftwood with the humanity gone. . ." Was this the sort of stuff one could build the coöperative commonwealth on? Yet Foster recognized the good in men, too, the good that encouraged trade unionists to believe that some improvement was possible. He wrote, like modern believers in Neo-Orthodoxy: "the individual is part angel and part beast." To Henry Abrahams, who claimed that only capitalists embodied the beast, Foster retorted that it "is but a species of inane imbecility . . . to attempt the canonization of the shovel, hoe, pick, or other implement of labor." [22]

Since men were capable of evil, the monolithic state would be the perfect instrument for doing evil. Jefferson and Spencer had so written, as well as every clear thinking individualist from Adam Smith down. American experience confirmed the observations of the philosophers. Alexander Hamilton and the Federalists used the central government to destroy local autonomy, and President Grover Cleveland colluded with businessmen to jail Eugene Debs. Since 1865 the Congress gave land grants to railroads, manipulated coinage in the interests of stock-jobbers, and raised tariff schedules for persuasive and bribing lobbyists. The entire history of Tammany Hall should be proof that the politician with absolute power is as preying a beast as the greediest monopolist. Foster also found fault in the logic that "monopoly is caused by governmental privileges; therefore competition is a crime" and state industry a corrective. He concluded by paraphrasing Spencer that government had been instituted to "control the evil in man" and, that as "a necessary evil . . . [must] be discarded as we progress." [23]

For ten years, Frank Foster matched Henry Abrahams' quotations and paraphrases from Karl Marx with appropriate text and passage from Herbert Spencer to disprove the Marxian interpretation of history. Spencer was right in describing the gradual up-lifting of the masses, and Marx was wrong in prophesying the increasing misery of the proletariat. Spencer was wise in noting the need for evolutionary growth, and Marx was mad in proposing revolutionary change. Spencer proved that progress resulted from increasing heterogeneity, and Marx was therefore fool to believe in forced homogeneity. Individualism, as Spencer argued, was the mark of progress, not collectivism, as Marx maintained. Not statism, not forced coöperation, not a unitary culture, but weak government, voluntary association (as in the trade unions), and increasing diversity — these were the lines of civilization; and the Socialists who thought otherwise would turn the cosmic process back on itself.[24]

Frank K. Foster's ultimate objective was a culture founded on Spencer's Law of Equal Freedom, which stated that every man should have the right to do what he would, provided he did not infringe on the right of others to do the same.[25] The objective was individualism; and in this connection the words of Emerson and Jefferson on liberty were revived. Translated for the trade union movement, Spencer's Law meant that workers must strip from the boss and the businessman advantages unfairly gained and monopolized. Concurrently, workers were to come into rights and privileges heretofore reserved for the few. The agencies for achieving the good society were both the state and the trade union.

Recognizing the limitations of Spencer's doctrinaireness, Foster would use the authority of the state to further the liberty of the greatest number of individuals. As head of the Massachusetts State Federation of Labor Legislative Committee, he formulated and presented a number of demands to the General Court. He called upon the legislature to prosecute with vigor police powers: to outlaw Pinkertonism, the sweatshop, and the yellow dog contract; to forbid manufacturers from working women and children (society's wards) more than fifty-eight hours a week; to make it illegal for manufacturers to fine employees for poor work. At the same time, he pressed for the initiative, referendum, and recall. Such measures, Foster argued, did not grant special favors to a few, but denied grasping businessmen and scheming politicians the exercise of powers withheld from the many. For industries which were by their very nature subject to monopoly, such as utilities, Foster urged municipal ownership — and hoped that a vigilant public would frustrate bureaucrats who might dip into the common purse. None of these reforms were to be achieved by direct political action. Rather workers were to vote for candidates of either of the two major parties — or of a third party — receptive to the Federation's legislative program.[26]

To win the culture and comfort already possessed by the business and professional classes, the skilled worker was to build up the trade union to the strength of an "army" so as to control the field of action — the market. The weapons, and Foster spoke of them as such, were not the pamphlets and resolutions of radical theorizers "which rarely crystallize into action." Rather they were apprenticeshop rules to fight off green hands, union labels to win allies among consumers, and high dues to assure the success of strikes against warring businessmen. Every local, while part of the larger whole, was a platoon in need of officers expert in the tactics and terrain of the locale. They must brief the men in the ranks on the objectives to be won, and create an *esprit de corps*. The latter was particularly important, for Foster recognized that too often workers hoped to leave the class of wage-earners for more "respectable" jobs.[27]

Under no circumstances were Socialists or Single-Taxers or Populists or Nationalists to attempt to merge the union with a political party. As trade unionists had learned to submerge ethnic, religious, and racial differences in consideration of the craft, so must they submerge political differences. Failing to do so, the American Federation of Labor would fall into the endless argumentation and pitiful fragmentation that had been the bane of the labor movement since the days of George Henry Evans and Robert Dale Owen. "The prime purpose of trade unionism," wrote the *Labor Leader* time and time again, is the achievement of a higher standard of living through "the regulation of wages and hours." [28]

Once certain that the trade unionists had beaten off the rival ideology of state socialism, Frank K. Foster summed up and defended his position against critics. He agreed that the A. F. of L. would not solve the entire social problem, but what single group would? He granted that the unions represented but a fraction of the discontent, but who would emancipate the workers if not themselves? As for the charge that he had no ideals, he asserted that he had them, but that he had modified them after his taste of radicalism so as to grapple more effectively with the conditions surrounding the "contracted multitude." Above all, he explained away what seemed to be a contradiction: his belief at the same time in individualism and working-class association. There was no contradiction, he believed, for trade union association was the *means* to promote the *end* of the well-being of the *individual* laborer. Foster called his ideology "collective-individualism," and on it he rested his claim to be known as a social reformer.[29]

The skilled workers, their ideals worked out by 1890, felt no compulsion at that time to rush into drastic social reformation, again reflecting Spencer. The chief exceptions were the clothing workers in factories who, by the late 1880's and early 1890's, faced extinction as a consequence of ruinous competition from Boston and New York sweatshops. Cruelly displaced or expecting to be, they prophesied industrial apocalypse if the sweaters were not driven from the land. Thus, in a short story that takes place in 1998, John Crowley, leader of the garment workers, described the consequences of a cholera plague that had its origin in the sweatshop.

Frenzied mobs, black; frowning and terrible, whose eyes blazed like the enraged lion's set fire to every clothing house and hunted down the owners, whom they slaughtered as a pack of wolves would their prey. . . Who shall attempt to describe these horrors; the desolation, waste, confusion, mortality, or the intense midsummer heat in which the air, poisoned by the stench of unburied corpses, quivered? Feeble is the fury of wild beasts beside that of maddened mobs. In ashes cities lie buried. Shut were the gates of mercy. . . Spoil, rapine, murder and villainy stalked hand in hand with the dreadful plague. . . the army, also plague stricken, . . . joined in the outbreak and confusion; . . Hell was vacant; the fiends were all on earth. . . Not until the country was blasted throughout the length and breadth of the land, and the flower of the nation had perished, did the pestilence, with its clustering woes pass away.

The non-factory workers — the carpenters, printers, masons, plasterers — sympathized with Crowley and his kind, and agreed to support his request that the General Court rid Boston of its sweatshops.[30] But they felt none of his panic — until the Panic of 1893.

The bitter winter of 1893–94 in Boston, as elsewhere, impressed many social reformers as being the beginning of those hard times preceding a secular day of judgment. In the ranks of skilled labor union membership fell off, unemployment rose, and the Massachusetts Federation of Labor as well as its official journal were hard put to survive. It was an ominous sign when Frank K. Foster, who opposed handouts, agreed to declare a moratorium on subscriptions to the *Labor Leader,* and print out-of-work ads for union men free of charge. Firebrands like Herbert Newton Casson and Morrison I. Swift descended on the General Court on February 24, 1894 with several thousands of the unemployed; theirs was a noisy, and fearsome, demonstration. Three weeks later at Faneuil Hall, the uninhibited Mr. Swift, author of a utopian socialist tract, cried: "We propose to take away the property of the rich — by law." Before long, Swift was on his way to join up with Coxey's army marching on Washington. From Kansas, Mary

Ellen Lease came to Boston to raise hell among Boston's working class. Weekly Foster's prose and poetry, as well as that of his contributors, grew bitter. The depression, he declared, came because "the joint product which has gone back to the laborer in wages is too small to enable him to buy these commodities." In his poem, "The Unemployed," he addressed the "sapient rulers" in the language of Henry Abrahams:

> Scan close historic story, Jack Cade of Peterloo,
> Choose you the olive branches or Revolution's rule? [31]

It was against the background of depression that the final showdown came between Collective Individualists and Marxian Socialists. T. J. Morgan of Chicago, at the 1893 Convention of the American Federation of Labor, forced Samuel Gompers to poll affiliated bodies on direct political action to promote a number of reforms, of which the chief, embodied in Plank 10, was "Collective ownership by the people of all means of production and distribution." As anticipated, warring factions contended for supremacy in St. Louis and Chicago, Brooklyn and New York, in Boston. At last, Henry Abrahams and the cigar makers seemed to have empirical proof for the Marxian theory of increasing misery, and many workers in Massachusetts were demanding a third party. After furious debates, at the Boston Central Labor Union, a special state conference of workers, and the Massachusetts Federation of Labor, Frank Foster and his colleagues defeated the Socialists. Plank 10 was voted down. Similarly, Bostonians contributed to the vote against Plank 10 at the national convention in 1894. Crowed Foster: "Tommy Morgan cracked his organ." [32]

However, the Collective Individualists, although loath to do so, conceded the need for political action. On the invitation of the Boston Central Labor Union, a conference of workingmen from Massachusetts met in the spring of 1894 to draft a platform for the November election. Shortly thereafter, the Massachusetts People's Party, which had been organized in 1891 by Nationalists, endorsed the platform; and the State Federation of Labor followed suit. The latter, refusing to run its own candidates, agreed to support the Populist ticket, and the *Labor Leader* was pledged to the cause. On the surface, 1894 seemed to be a repetition of 1886, as Eastern workers, Western farmers, and intellectuals joined in a "producers" movement to crush the "non-producers." [33]

But only on the surface. The platform did not advocate the producer coöperative. Rather, in the name of the Forgotten Man enraged over special privileges, it called for impartial government. Every one of the resolutions demanded the revocation of rights granted by government to the rich. Thus the platform declaimed against the tariff, Cleveland's deal with Morgan, government-sponsored monopoly, national banks, and the unfree coinage of silver. Massachusetts workers, feeling like identity with the forgotten men of the prairies, requested that land be withheld from speculators. They urged that, since the telegraph and railroad were monopolistic in nature, government must own them. They asked, too, for laws providing for the initiative, referendum, and recall so as to by-pass the caucus of political monopolists. Finally, objecting to disproportionate taxation, they favored a graded tax on income. Their goal was not the planned economy; they felt no kinship with the Marxians. Rather they shared with the Populist Tom Watson the hope for a society that would say: "The field is clear, the contest fair; come, and win your share if you can." [34]

The year 1894 was different from 1886 in strategy as well as ideology. The universal reformers had hoped to win and reconstruct society, whereas the Collective Individualists expected to lose and strengthen the labor movement. The latter offered angry workers Populism as an alternative to Marxian Socialism; and anticipated that the defeat of the People's Party would prove conclusively that salvation for the workingman lay not in politics but in the trade union. As expected, the Populists won only 1 per cent of the Boston vote, and did only slightly better in the shoe towns of the state. Significantly, Foster and his kind refused to incorporate the Boston Central Labor Union and the Massachusetts Federation of Labor in the People's Party or to expend union funds in its behalf. They foresaw that the Catholics would go Democratic and the Protestants Republican, and recognized in the People's Party the familiar formula for failure: enthusiasm without the money, machinery, candidates, and publicity essential for triumph at the ballot box. Although Foster wrote in defense of Populist candidates, he concentrated his editorial energies to promote Congressman Michael J. McEttrick, an Independent who had sponsored the Federation's legislative demands while a member of the General Court. Shortly before November 6, Frank K. Foster revealed his true thoughts in reminding the readers of the *Labor Leader* that, after the votes were counted, they would rejoice that they still had their trade unions.[35] The year 1894 was then a double *tour de force*: the defeat of the twin enemies of direct political action and Marxian Socialism.

Their points won, the Collective Individualists entered politics in a way calculated to bring the most results with the least amount of risk. In 1894 Boston's artisans founded the Workingmen's Political League. A combination club and nonpartisan pressure group, the League admitted individuals, not unions, interested in city government. It invited reformers, such as Professor Frank Parsons, to speak on municipalism, and held debates on the issues of the day. On occasions it nominated one of its own for office — Harry Lloyd ran for the School Committee and lost — but more commonly it endorsed pro-labor candidates. Thus the League supported Josiah Quincy for mayor in 1895 rather than Parsons, who ran on a third-party ticket advocating municipal socialism. Henry Abrahams and the cigar makers tried throughout the 1890's to rally the working class to the Socialist Labor Party, only to meet increasing indifference; Abrahams was dismissed as a bore and a pest.[36] By 1900, the trade unions of Boston, due in large measure to the generalship and polemics of Frank Foster, were numerically strong and ideologically tough: they had weathered the depression of 1893, the fever of 1894, and the Marxian trio of De Leon, Morgan, and Abrahams.

III

As among other groups in Boston, social reformers among workers were generally of Old American stock and Protestant persuasion. Henry Abrahams was the exception, Frank K. Foster the norm. Irish Catholic trade unionists were largely confined to the building trades and were conservative. Apart from the cigar makers who applied the catechism of Marx to America, Boston's working-class liberals operated within the framework of indigenous traditions. The shoemakers and universal reformers of the Knights of Labor, sharing the values of reformist mid-century New England, attempted through the producer coöperative to restore (so they thought) the classless society that had existed before the mill. The artisans of Foster's sort enjoyed skills not yet made obsolete, and built an ideology for the machine age out of the assumptions scattered throughout "Self-Reliance." McNeill and Foster abhorred the class hatred of Marxism. The one embodied the New England of George Ripley, the other the New England of Ralph Waldo Emerson.

Frank K. Foster, although recognized by contemporaries as a figure of first rank, has received scant attention from modern scholars. In part, his neglect derives from the historian's usual neglect of reformers of the 1880's other than the figures already known. In part, it derives from the fact that Foster died (1909) long before the other founders of the A. F. of L., and hence did not have the opportunity, as did the others, to claim lion's share in placing the first permanent trade union group on its feet. He was editor of the Knights of Labor's Massachusetts newspaper and Secretary of the A. F. of L. before that organization received its name in 1886. He was a pioneer. When McNeill chose a successor, he chose Foster. When Gompers selected a partner to negotiate with the Knights of Labor on the question of dual unionism, it was again Foster; and he turned to him for help against the New York Marxians, especially Daniel De Leon. It was also Foster who was given the task of debating President Eliot of Harvard on the right to strike. Upon learning of Foster's death, James Duncan, who was high in the councils of the A. F. of L., lamented the passing of truly creative spirit. In 1947, an anonymous writer for the electrical workers revived Frank Foster's memory and all but canonized him.[37]

The Boston printer gave vigor and intellectual order to the aspirations of skilled artisans. Like Samuel Gompers and Adolphe Strasser, the Bostonians hoped to raise the standard of living within the framework of capitalism. But the Bostonians were idealists, where Strasser and Gompers were not. While Strasser boasted, "We have no ultimate ends," Frank K. Foster championed the ultimate end of "collective-individualism." Gompers was a racist who led the Federation to restrict immigration, but Foster and fellow Bostonians opposed restriction in the name of the melting pot. Gompers questioned the nation's capacity for economic experimentation and growth, and Foster urged a reformation after the model of Tom Jefferson and Herbert Spencer. Frank K. Foster did not accept the monopoly capitalism of his day. Gompers and Strasser were pure and simples; Foster and fellow Bostonians were pure and simples plus.[38]

The plus came from the usable heritage of New England; 1776, the reform movements of the second quarter of the century, Transcendentalism, the religion of social justice of George E. McNeill and Wendell Phillips — in these, the Boston wage-earners took regional pride. Further, there was the personality of Frank K. Foster. By his own admission, he was a frustrated intellectual denied an academic career because he did not go to college. Given his New England idealism, though somewhat tarnished by 1886, and "compelled," as he wrote of his hero in *The Evolution of a Trade Unionist*, "to win his own livelihood under conditions which tend to callous both hands and intellect, he had whether he willed it or not, been forced to join the protestants against a social order where so much of good material is wasted on unnecessary friction and one-sided competition." Of the workers, Foster thought himself somewhat above them; and this thought enabled him to share the sense of stewardship — of helping those below and directing society from above — that was so crucial in the make-up of the middle-class reformers. Thus, in his efforts against the immigration restrictionists, he wrote, not like an artisan in fear of the green hand, but with the security of a Phillips, a Higginson, a Hale:

> If Democracy's aught but a fancy, fear not for the final test;
> Let the races fuse in the crucible; welcome each coming guest.
> Your danger is not from the lowly of whatever creed or tongue,
> Whose voice swells a mightier anthem than e'er the world heard sung.
> Welcome the Jew and Gentile, all the human brotherhood;
> From out the present chaos shall come a greater good.
> Stand close in the bonds of labor, in its great fraternity,
> And hasten the time the wide world o'er when all men shall be free.[39]

In the 1890's, when combination in business and business in government was the status quo, the trade unionists' demand for competition and impartial government was a demand calculated to benefit, not only themselves, but the nation at large. Only the myopia of the liberalism of the 1930's would blur the importance of the individualistic philosophy, including that of Adam Smith and Herbert Spencer, in the history of American social reform. To be sure, big business has used this philosophy to rationalize the status quo, but the artisans behind Jackson, the farmers behind Jefferson, and the small businessmen behind Wilson also employed it to challenge the status quo. When championed by groups who have been on the make and who have resented special privilege, the individualistic philosophy has promoted social reform. Boston's skilled workers were one such group, and its feminists another.

Chapter Nine

THE NEW AND THE NEWER WOMEN

As Reformers

The changes made in the laws which affect women, during these thirty years, the new industries open to them, and their higher education have made so great a difference in the life to which every growing girl looks forward that it seems hardly the same world to her that it was to her mother. But the grand safeguard for all that is gained, and all that remains to be secured, the ballot, is still beyond our reach. The work, therefore, is not done. — Lucy Stone

Into this world . . . life with bewildering and contradictory theories, yet bent, as no other age has ever been, in the analysis of social evil and the right of social wrong — into this world we are born — we, the first generation of college women. In a sense, we represent a new factor in the social order. . . Surely, I may at least say, that we make ourselves significant if we will. — Vida D. Scudder[1]

To the Boston feminists of 1880 the society in which they lived was a comfort and a challenge: a comfort because they enjoyed rights denied their sex for centuries; a challenge because they smarted from political and legal disabilities reducing them to the status of lunatics and criminals. Society was also paradoxical to them. There were, on the one hand, the equalitarian principles of the nation, and, on the other, the less than equal position of wives and mothers and sisters in the national life.[2] In the 1840's a band of ardent female agitators began a crusade for equal rights which, by 1880, had made spectacular gains and which, by 1920, would win the cherished general suffrage. Boston's emancipated women in the years 1880–1900 recognized that they were in the middle of an unfinished job; and they contemplated the continuation of the struggle against the ruling sex with the aim of battering down the remaining impediments of law, custom, inertia, and prejudice. As objects of the reforms' for which they agitated, they brought to their task the insider's knowledge, tenacity, and caution. As a persecuted half of the nation, they also brought to other oppressed portions of the population the sympathy born out of humiliation and frustration.

The generation that grew up after the death of Margaret Fuller lived in a society dreamt of by Margaret but unknown to her. Between the first National Woman's Rights Convention of 1850 and the election of James Garfield, come-outers swept away many but not all the centuries-old discriminations embodied in the Common Law and custom. If married, women could own property, retain their earnings, sue and be sued, make contracts, serve as executrixes, and engage in business. Whereas Harriet Martineau had observed that American women could engage in but a handful of menial occupations, Lord Bryce noted that careers were open in medicine, college teaching, law, journalism, the arts, and the ministry. In 1878 the Boston Girls Latin School was founded. By 1880, one hundred fifty-three colleges admitted female students, among them Boston University, the Massachusetts Institute of Technology, the Harvard Annex, and Wellesley. Early in the 1870's Boston's women could run for the School Committee; in 1879 they were given the right to vote for it. However, in 1880, few girls actually went to college, office jobs were harder to come by than factory work, the law discriminated against married women as regards the inheritance of property and custody of children, and the municipal, state, and national suffrage was still the firm prerogative of men.[3]

Notwithstanding her less than absolute equality with the American male, the new woman had arrived. "Do something, be of worth in yourself, form opinions, is the imperative mood in which the times address the modern woman. . . ," noted Kate Gannett Wells, a Back Bay lady, in 1880. Henry James in *The Bostonians* and Robert Grant in *Unleavened Bread* mercilessly caricatured the strong-minded girl, and Mrs. Wells warned that the emerging type might destroy the gentle female virtues. A male friend of hers, she reported, complained to her that he "could not see a Boston woman without her wishing to aid him. Can't they just be themselves, and let us like them, and not eternally have objects, views?" Mrs. Wells cautioned her sex that a future day might look upon their likeness as having the "Woman's-mission look," and that they would appear like a "gallery of photographed 'causes.'" While the apprehensive Back Bay lady lamented the excesses of the transitional woman, other matrons rejoiced in the changing order. The Association for the Advancement of Women hailed Ibsen's plays for portraying the emancipated woman sympathetically; and the *Woman's Column* and the *Woman's Journal* carried short stories and playlets that idealized the new type. If married, she stood up to her husband and demanded to be treated as a person of consequence and sense; if single, she was independent, educated, and either earning her own living or aspiring to a career in business or the professions.[4]

All this had been anticipated by such oldster come-outers as Lucy Stone, Julia Ward Howe, and Mary Ashton Livermore — the heroines of the middle-class, *avant-garde* woman. Lucy Stone was the first New England woman to receive a college education, the first to retain her maiden name on marrying, a pioneer in speaking on the public platform, and a career journalist of international reputation. At her marriage ceremony in 1853 (Thomas Wentworth Higginson officiated), she and her reformer-husband, Henry Brown Blackwell, published a manifesto which became a model for modern marriage and the blueprint for the equal rights movement. In it they agreed that Lucy would have equal custody of the children, keep her property, retain her earnings, and will her belongings as she saw fit. In the 1880's Professor Ellen Hayes

of Wellesley College often took her students to the Stone-Black-
well home in Dorchester to show them the workings of an ideal
marital union.[5] The feminists of the 1880's and 1890's were little
different from Lucy Stone; they simply had caught up to her in
some respects. However, they were not subject to the ridicule,
contempt, and ostracism (she was read out of her church for
speaking in public against slavery) which she had encountered;
and because industrialization made housekeeping less time-ab-
sorbing, they were far more numerous than those like Lucy in
her younger days. Literally thousands of housewives in the Boston area had come out of the kitchen and nursery to play their
role in the life of their city, state, and nation. Throughout the
1880's and 1890's young college graduates joined the ranks of
emancipated women.

The new women, in their new-found freedom, turned toward
being active, and between 1880 and 1900 a multitude of organizations sprouted forth for one purpose or another. As professional and business women grew in number, so there came into
being societies in law, journalism, and business. The women's
clubs, numbering a dozen in 1880 and more than fifty by the
turn of the century, drew housewives eager for self-improvement.
Of some culture and hungering for more, middle-aged matrons
explored the mysteries of Dante and social science, thrilled to
Browning and Shakespeare, organized crusades against cruelty
to birds and children, and listened to famous lecturers on all sorts
of topics. Neither the professional nor social sororities showed
much interest in reform; this task was left to the suffrage, educational, and temperance societies. So numerous had female associations become by 1896 that Alice Stone Blackwell declared:
"We are organized to death." In 1881, however, Harriet Robinson, whose memory went back to the unfree days of the 1850's,
was so impressed with the new privileges and societies for women
that she rejoiced: "Never in the history of civilization, has woman
held the political, legal or social position that she does in Massachusetts to-day!" [6]

II

Organized, optimistic, facing outward, and feeling their oats, Boston's emancipated women were a force for good in proportion to their dissatisfaction with the status quo. The majority did not object to the basic economic and political structure of the American community, but to the irrational and undemocratic rules regulating the relationship of the sexes. Like the leaders of twentieth-century unassimilated minority groups that aspire upwards, the emancipated members of the gentle sex were educated middle-class Americans who wanted to dissipate anti-democratic custom and law impeding their entrance into a culture otherwise acceptable to them. They also had allies among the privileged group — men. In its basic assumptions, goals, arguments, and organization, the women's rights movement resembles the activities of the National Association for the Advancement of Colored People. Indeed, at the outset and up to the Civil War, the crusades against slavery and female bondage were twin movements of the same spirit; and the leaders of the one were the guiding hands of the other. With the passage of the Fifteenth Amendment the oldster come-outers believed that, since the Negro had had his day, the time had come for woman.[7]

As Negroes have had recourse to anthropology, so the feminists turned to biology and genetics to rout the opposition's claim that they were congenitally inferior to men. When the Surgeon General of the Army, Dr. A. W. Hammond, declared that the female brain was of a lower order than the male's, Helen H. Gardener went to the laboratory and came forth with the announcement that woman's brain was no different from man's with respect to weight and convolutions. When the exponents of male superiority boasted of the active role of the sperm and deprecated the passive role of the egg in reproduction, the feminists retorted that modern genetics "demonstrates the absolute equality of the nuclei of the male and female germ-

cells. . ." When opponents to higher education and the suffrage
argued that Latin and the ballot would drive hypersensitive
woman mad, the equal righters answered that biology proved
that "from infusoria up to man, the female animal moves,
breathes, looks, runs, flies, swims, pursues its food, eats it, digests
it, in precisely the same manner as the male. . ." Apart from
parentage, "all instincts, all characteristics, are the same. . ." [8]

Four stout biographical dictionaries on famous women issued
forth from Boston pens between 1883 and 1904, each intent on
proving that, on the basis of achievement, women were entitled
to first-class citizenship. In her introduction to Annie Nathan
Meyer's *Woman's Work in America,* Julia Ward Howe wrote that
the volume would "confute calumny," disprove the notion that
the gentle sex had only "secondary capacities," and "furnish chapter and verse to substantiate what is claimed for the attainments
of women." In much the same spirit, the *Woman's Column* and
the *Woman's Journal* trumpeted the success of their sisters as
lawyers, doctors, engineers, artists, professors, philanthropists,
authors, scientists, inventors. Proud of their millionaires, the
feminists also revived the attainments of Helen of Troy, Joan of
Arc, and Catherine the Great to prove that their sex was equal
to the male. And annually the suffrage bazaars displayed handi-
crafts of one sort or another to vindicate female abilities. Like
modern minority groups bitter over their rejection, the feminists
indulged in the most obvious kind of self-congratulatory works,
distorting the achievements of women so that it seemed that men
had done little for American civilization. [9]

Again like twentieth-century minorities, the feminists asked for
fair play in the name of democracy, humanity, and Christianity.
As Charlotte Perkins Stetson put it in her poem, "Women to Men":

> O Man-at-large! Friend! Comrade!
>   Fellow-worker!
> I am a Human Being like yourself!

Lucy Stone, who allegedly went to college to learn the Bible in

Greek so that she could read for herself whether it was true that
Scripture sanctioned male superiority, wrote that Jesus made no
invidious distinctions between the sexes, that all were brethren
unto one another. The American paradox of professing equalitarian sentiments and fostering unequal practices being perfectly
clear to the equal righters, they reminded the dominant sex that
it was not playing the game according to the hallowed rules of
the Declaration of Independence and the Bill of Rights. For a
democracy to deny equal rights to women simply because they
are women, wrote Thomas Wentworth Higginson, is a contradiction so monstrous and apparent "that it cannot last forever, without new discoveries in logic." [10]

Through speech, essay, pamphlet, legislative petition, book,
and weekly (*Woman's Journal* and *Woman's Column*),[11] the
feminists insisted on absolute equality as an end in itself, on the
final abolition of the double standard in law, education, the economy, love, and politics. Their arguments rested on the basic
assumption that America tolerates no privileged class, race, section, religion, or sex, and that all Americans have the natural
right to engage in the struggle for life on terms of equality and
freedom. The leaders of the equal rights movement understood
this good mid-century ideal; they had helped to formulate it.
They were the surviving come-outers and groaners of the pre-
Civil War reform era — Lucy Stone and her husband Henry B.
Blackwell, Mary A. Livermore and Abby Morton Diaz, Ednah D.
Cheney and Julia Ward Howe, Thomas Wentworth Higginson,
Samuel May, and many more. From oldster liberal stock, moreover, came reinforcements: Alice Stone Blackwell, Louisa May
Alcott, Frederick and William Lloyd Garrison, Jr.[12] Blessed with
amazing longevity and loyal progeny, buoyed up by past success,
and bent on finishing the job begun in Seneca Falls in 1848, the
equal righters intended to batter and exasperate the opposition
into submission through sheer persistence.

Steadfast, the elderly come-outers were also conservative in
their tactics and bent on being respectable. They were advanced

in age, their eccentric days were behind them, and their success from 1850 to 1880 had sobered them. Lucy Stone was done with wearing bloomers, she was no longer met with the epithet of "shrieking Lucy," and she was past the stage of fearing bodily harm for speaking on the platform in behalf of so unpopular a cause as abolition. By 1880, the woman's rights movement with which she was identified enjoyed, if not popularity, at least grudging and growing respect. It was out of the phase of eccentricity, in the stage of argument, and with wise tactics might soon be in the realm of achievement. The newspapers reported the proceedings of the suffrage conventions without malice; Governor Long favored the cause of female enfranchisement; and such perfectly safe, venerated, and proper Bostonians as Edward Everett Hale and James Freeman Clarke espoused equal rights sentiments. So respectable had the movement become that Julia Ward Howe, searching for a new activity after the Civil War, joined the company of Lucy Stone. Whereas for some three decades she had regarded the antics of equal righters as grotesque, she "now found a sphere of action . . . which . . . no longer appeared singular or eccentric, but simple, natural, and, under the circumstances, inevitable." And the presence of Mrs. Howe, the Beacon Hill lady who charmed foreign nobles with her *gentillesse*, gave further seemliness to a movement grown proper through the years. As Tom Appleton, a long-standing conservative, told one of the Howe girls: "Your mother's great importance to this cause is that she forms a bridge between the world of society and the world of reform." [13]

The split between the suffragists in 1869 into the New York-dominated National Woman's Suffrage Association (N.W.S.A.) and the Boston-controlled American Woman's Suffrage Association (A.W.S.A.) reveals the cautiousness of the latter. Led by Susan B. Anthony and Elizabeth Cady Stanton, the feminists of the Empire City were more strident in their manifestoes, carrying on as if they were engaged in a deadly battle of the sexes. They refused to include men in their organization, whereas the Bostonians welcomed both sexes of good will. The Anthony-Stanton group wanted the suffrage immediately and through federal amendment, while the Stone-Howe people would seek it slowly through state law. The N.W.S.A. fought against the Fifteenth Amendment because it did not enfranchise women, but the A.W.S.A. refused to stand in the way of the Negro. Whereas the New Yorkers denounced the "rulers in the state . . . the anointed leaders in the church . . . the capitalist in the world of work . . . the autocrat in the home . . . ," [14] the Bostonians appealed to the sense of chivalry of the dominant sex. Sobered by success, Lucy Stone and her people were possibilists, wary of needlessly antagonizing the opposition, eager to get what they could, and not so recalcitrant as to deny others what they could not achieve. They knew that eventually they must win.

They were particularly anxious to avoid entangling their movement with "extraneous radical issues" and eccentric reformers, again differing from the New Yorkers. The latter, to the dismay of the Bostonians, championed paper currency and easy divorce laws. Even more reprehensible was the willingness of Mrs. Anthony to accept the aid of George Train, a self-nominated presidential candidate known to be insane, and Mrs. Victoria C. Woodhull and her sister, Tennessee Claflin, the firebrands of the 1870's. The latter two edited *Woodhull and Claflin's Weekly*, an organ devoted to anarchy and free love, especially the latter. On the public platform Victoria declared that a woman had the "right to take a new lover every day. . ." Her own conquests included, according to her own testimony, Commodore Vanderbilt, Henry Ward Beecher, Theodore Tilton, and Benjamin R. Tucker. Stephen Pearl Andrews, a frequent contributor to her journal, also opposed monogamy and spoke knowingly of how diverse liaisons produced "variation and compound harmony." Like Train, Mrs. Woodhull also ran for president.[15]

It was just this sort of notoriety that the Bostonians wished to avoid; for they recognized that the die-hards of the opposition wanted to believe that the new woman was queer, that she desired "to vote and smoke cigars, and wear bloomers, and all that sort of thing, you know." Mrs. Howe, for example, took special care to point out that she and her co-workers were not, like the New Yorkers, "a frantic, shrieking mob . . . contemners of marriage, . . . neglectors of home and offspring. . . ." Rather they were respected and respectable persons of moderate wealth who had much to gain from society as then constituted. She wrote: "We have had, or hope to have, our holy fireside, our joyful cradle, our decent bank account." Not until the N.W.S.A. outran its radicalism in 1890 did the A.W.S.A. coalesce with it to form the National-American Woman Suffrage Association.[16]

Its fundamentalism dissipated, the Boston equal rights movement still carried on with religious enthusiasm. Julia Ward Howe, having been brought up in Transcendentalism, regarded the cause as conforming to divine plan. At their annual conventions, the suffragists emblazoned their hall with gay banners, sang songs of female significance, and prophesied the coming of their particular millennium. As the faithful passed to the Great Beyond with the roll of time, they were duly canonized in the obituaries of the *Woman's Journal*. When Lucy Stone died in 1893, more than a thousand persons attended her funeral, which blazed with the suffrage colors, yellow and white, in roses and chrysanthemums. The "services were not like a funeral but like a solemn celebration and a coronation," noted the Reverend Charles G. Ames, who officiated. And shortly before her death, Lucy, the female pope of the woman's rights church, laid on hands, so to speak, on daughter Alice. Her parting whisper was, "Make the world better." Lucy Stone was so religiously devoted to the great God progress that, even in death, she became a pioneer; on her request she was cremated, which, her daughter and husband quietly and proudly noted, made her the first New England woman to be so disposed of.[17]

The equal righters watched with satisfaction as the barriers of prejudice continued to crumble in the economy, law, education, and religion in the years 1880–1900, victories due to their own agitation and enlightened public opinion. Long the proponents of coeducation, they applauded the Yale (1892) and John Hopkins (1893) graduate schools and Tufts College (1896) for throwing open their doors to students irrespective of sex. Incensed over the refusal of various Protestant lay conferences to seat women, they rejoiced by 1900 in the almost complete reversal of that policy. Eager to compete with men in all occupations, they welcomed the gradual opening of once forbidden fields and protested job discrimination. As guardians of social purity, they pressured the General Court to raise the age of consent from ten to thirten and finally to sixteen years of age (1893); separate the sexes at the houses of detention; and appoint police matrons to the Boston Force (1887). As a result of their annual descent on the Massachusetts legislature, they succeeded in getting a law that gave married women possession of their clothing (1881) and another that equalized the descent of real estate and personal property of husband and wife (1899). In 1893, nonsupport was made a criminal offense in the Bay State.[18]

Desirous first of municipal suffrage and then the franchise for state and federal officials, the Boston feminists ran into stubborn opposition. Francis Parkman, Louis D. Brandeis, John Boyle O'Reilly, William Norton Eliot, Octavius Brooks Frothingham, Edward W. Bok, Charles Dudley Warner, and the Reverend Lyman Abbott constituted but a few of the distinguished men who insisted that woman's place was in the home. A Massachusetts legislator, after orating that women did not want the vote, concluded his speech by stating: "Grant suffrage to women, and you will have to build insane asylums in every county, and establish a divorce court in every town. Women are too nervous and hysterical to enter into politics." Housewives pledged against disturbing the status quo also opposed political equality. Such was the case of the wife of a Baptist minister from Newton, who lamented before the General Court that "Sockless" Jerry Simpson went sockless because Mrs. Simpson was too busy campaigning to take care of her husband. The stiffest resistance to the franchise emanated from the parlors of the Beacon Hill ladies, many of whom, like Mrs. Kate Gannett Wells, had done practical reform work through Boston's Woman's Education Association in promoting the Harvard Annex in 1878 and the playground movement early in the 1890's.[19]

Margaret Deland, the sort of strong-minded woman in whom the feminists took pride, was a Beacon Hiller opposed to political equality. Brought up in Pennsylvania by a devout Presbyterian foster-mother and an old-fashioned foster-father, she rebelled against middle-class mores by seeking economic independence as an instructor at New York's Hunter College in the 1870's. She shocked her parents by her preference for "freedom and New York to conventionality and Parnassus." Margaret sickened at the theology of Jonathan Edwards, upon which she had been raised, and after she married Lorin Deland, a Boston Unitarian, she and her husband joined Trinity Church because of the humane preaching of Phillips Brooks. The Delands surprised the respectables by taking fallen women into their own home and rehabilitating them. Settled firmly on Beacon Hill by the middle of the 1880's, they opened their Mt. Vernon Street house to a meeting for Russian freedom at which the revolutionist, Stepniak, was the chief speaker.[20]

Mrs. Deland's chief contribution to the ferments of the 1880's was her novel, *John Ward, Preacher,* published in 1888. In it she made a plea for liberal Christianity by painting Calvinism in its darkest and harshest shades; she argued for an equitable solution of the labor problem that would take account of the baleful influence of poverty on the morals of workers; and she sympathized with the modern woman who insisted on reasoning out religion for herself rather than following her husband's lead. Like Dickens, whom she admired, Mrs. Deland believed that the "great value" of novels was to "awaken sympathy." Despite her rebellion against polite literature, parental authority, female submission, and ancestral religion, and her adoration of Julia Ward Howe and her daughter, Laura, Mrs. Deland stopped short of

wishing to enfranchise her sex. "We have suffered many things at
the hands of Patrick," she explained, "and now the New Woman
would add Bridget!" Mrs. Kate Gannett Wells also disapproved
the extension of the suffrage on the grounds that the wrong kind
of voter would go to the polls.[21]

The suffragists countered this argument by claiming that
native-born women in Boston and Massachusetts outnumbered
immigrant women, indeed promising that female suffrage would
diminish the power of the ignorant foreigner in the city.[22] They
scolded the wealthy ladies for forsaking their reform-minded
sisters out of selfish contentment with their own status. To those
like Mrs. Wells and Mrs. Deland, Julia Ward Howe asked whether
they would have the courage of Esther, who defied Haman to
help her Hebrew people, or fail in their Christian duty to lead
their sex upward. Moreover, since women owned property, the
equal righters asked, was it not reasonable for them to vote for
representatives to protect it? After all, they recalled, the men of
Bunker Hill fought a revolution because they refused to entrust
the safeguarding of their wealth to a government not of their
own choosing. (As Yankee Doodle exclaimed in one of the equal
rights playlets: "Good heavens! These girls of 1886 talk like the
men of 1776.") And if the gentle sex could vote for the school
board, by what reasoning could one deny them the right to choose
their own mayor, legislators, governor, and president? Logic,
noted wise old Thomas Wentworth Higginson, was on the side
of the suffragist. "Admit, in the slightest degree, her right to
property or education, and she must have the ballot to protect
the one and use the other. And there are no objections to this,
except such as would equally hold against the whole theory of
republican government." [23]

The Western states, the suffragists continued, gave empirical
proof that women purified politics and were not contaminated by
the ballot box, as such opponents as John Boyle O'Reilly alleged.
It was nonsense to believe that husbands represented their wives,
for the latter had an entirely different set of interests centering

in morals, education, temperance, and their own persons and property. True, they agreed, women did not do military service, but neither did ministers, and they voted. Nor need the republic fear the breakup of the home if mother went to the polls; for Mary A. Livermore, Julia Ward Howe, and Lucy Stone demonstarted that one could have love, husband, children, and grandchildren, and still have outside interests. The whole drift of Western democracy, the equal righters maintained, had been the inclusion of more and more classes into political rights: first the nobility followed by the bourgeoisie, and then the workers. Mrs. Livermore, in an article that Benjamin Orange Flower called the best of its kind, argued that her sex had the intelligence to play its political role; and only reactionaries like the English Tories who had opposed enfranchising the Jews would refuse woman her rightful place in the body politic.

In 1895, after yearly remonstrations to the General Court for nearly half a century, the equal righters faced a showdown on the question of municipal suffrage. The opposition prepared a state referendum on the issue, believing they would win and thereby embarrass the persistent Stones and Livermores and Howes and Diazes into silence. The women's clubs, trade unions, college faculties, Christian Temperance Union, and reformers of all shades rallied behind the Massachusetts Suffrage Association, sparked by Mary A. Livermore, and organized down to the precinct level. The anti-suffragists comprised a substantial number of Catholics and Beacon Hill gentlefolk of both sexes, both of whom organized as well as the feminists. The latter lost but not so badly as they or their enemies expected. Immediately they pressed for a state amendment that would grant what the referendum had denied. Still barred from voting for city officials in 1900, they remained undaunted, confident that the promise of the wonderful century just passed would reach fulfillment in the immediate years to come.[24]

Good mid-century idealists, the equal righters, while primarily concerned with themselves, also spoke against oppression in foreign lands and racial and religious bigotry at home and abroad. They did so, however, outside the suffrage society. In 1882, Mrs. Howe urged the Association for the Advancement of Women to condemn the California sand-lotters, declaring that "the case of the Chinese should be ours, as women are the natural friends of the oppressed." Twelve years later, Boston's feminists formed the Friends for Armenia, and Mrs. Livermore, Alice Stone Blackwell, and Julia Ward Howe called for American intervention to call off the Turkish attacks on the Middle Eastern Christians. The same persons headed the list of American Friends of Russian Freedom, formed in 1891, to "aid by all moral and legal means" Russian constitutionalists fighting for "political freedom and self-government." Through the *Woman's Column*, those who wished to free political prisoners in Italy got ample space. And when the Cretans rebelled against the Turks in 1897, Mrs. Howe, whose husband earlier had labored for Greek freedom, rejoiced in the fashion of her family.[25]

The Boston feminists *qua* feminists refused to load down their cause with so heavy a burden as the problems deriving from the new city and the new industry. As individuals, however, they took a stand. Julia Ward Howe, saturated with German idealism, inveighed against materialism, vulgarity, social climbing, and the new rich, but without proposing concrete reform measures. Abby Morton Diaz, as head of the Women's Industrial and Educational Union, pioneered in a new philanthropy. Her organization, a combination working girls' club and college, also carried protests to the General Court of illegal treatment of factory and shop women. She joined the Nationalist and Christian Socialist societies with Mary A. Livermore, but neither contributed anything new to socialist theory, their writings abounding rather in abstractions on justice and goodness.[26]

Henry B. Blackwell and family, nourished on the ethos of semi-industrialized mid-century America and supported by Blackwell's modest competence industriously earned in a small business, failed to understand the seriousness of concentrated wealth and the hostility between capital and labor in the 1880's and 1890's. Following the strikes of the late 1870's, the *Woman's Journal* condemned socialism as un-American, declared that there were no real economic inequalities, and proclaimed that America's mobile, free economy was the poor man's hope. Shocked by Homestead, Lucy Stone nevertheless saw no real cause for conflict between labor and capital. Workers, she thought, should leave their jobs when dissatisfied and form coöperatives rather than dissipate their savings in strikes. Lucy Stone rebuked Frances Willard for cavorting with the dangerous Knights of Labor; and husband Henry refused to recognize William Jennings Bryan as a rallying point around which progressives could gather to subdue privileged wealth. Blackwell's hero in politics was the Reverend Samuel J. Barrows, editor of the *Christian Register*, who stood for election to Congress in 1896 on a platform of woman suffrage, civil service and prison reform, and justice to Indians and Armenians.[27]

Of pre-Civil War origin, the Boston equal rights movement was both Emersonian and Jacksonian in its philosophy, having in mind the removal of impediments to the competitive world. As abolitionism sought to remove legal servitude, and Jacksonian democracy, monopoly and unfair lien, militia and conspiracy laws, so feminism desired to remove restrictions on the fair sex. Each looked forward to allowing the able to enjoy the privileges of middle-class America regardless of birth and unhindered by anti-democratic law and custom. In the words of Thomas Wentworth Higginson the objective was: "*La Carrière ouverte aux talents.* Every man for himself, every woman for herself. . ."[28] Because their job remained unfinished during the last decades of the nineteenth century, the crusaders for female equality pushed on in the same manner year after year. The vestiges of an earlier age whose objective should have terminated with the Fifteenth Amendment, their liberalism appeared anachronistic to the younger generation of women reformers facing up to the challenge of the machine age.

III

The Boston females who kept abreast of the problems created by the dislocations of industrialization and urbanization were conscience-stricken maidens of the college generation of the 1880's and 1890's. They were not preoccupied with the inferior status of women in America, as were the feminists, for they enjoyed equal opportunities in higher education and the professions. Assimilated, they had practically all the rights of first-class citizenship, and educated, they overflowed with the humane heritage of Western culture. By the late 1880's they came to realize that their problem as women was not the further extension of equal rights (that would come with time), but the humanitarian use of their learning; what the feminists had fought for as an ultimate end now became a means for social and economic regeneration. The rise of the city, coming at the same time as the Boston college girls' quest for usefulness, channeled their activities into helping the laboring poor.

The leader of this newer kind of emancipated woman was Vida Dutton Scudder. She was as different from Lucy Stone as Lucy Stone had been from Mrs. Harrison Gray Otis. Lucy had to overcome her father's prejudice to go to college; Vida took undergraduate and graduate work with her family's blessing. Lucy learned at Oberlin that the Bible taught that women were equal to men; Vida discovered at Oxford that the proletariat bore the brunt of capitalism. Lucy liked *Ramona* and *Ten Times One is Ten;* Vida preferred *A Traveller from Altruria* and *The Fabian Essays.* Lucy was a lax churchgoer who suspected Christianity of denying her sex its natural rights; Vida was a devout Episcopalian who wanted Christianity to socialize the world. Lucy struggled long for every right she had; Vida tasted leisurely the fruits of feminist achievement. Whereas Lucy Stone, the farmer's daughter, wanted the privileges of middle-class America, Vida D. Scudder, the Back Bay girl, fled from them as sinful to identify herself with the tenement-house population.

Partly hostile to and partly bored with feminism, Vida D. Scudder criticized the equal rights movement for its limited objective. It was not enough, she wrote, for woman to be free; she must be useful. The free woman was the central theme in the feminist plays, but the female as social engineer was the type Miss Scudder idealized in her drama. Thus, in her *Nora's Return, A Sequel to "The Doll's House" of Henry Ibsen*, Ednah D. Cheny reconciles Nora and her husband when the latter, recognizing that his wife must cultivate her individuality, welcomes her back to a library and bank account of her own. In Miss Scudder's *Mitsu-Yu Nissi, Or A Japanese Wedding*, the heroine, a Japanese girl educated in America, returns to Japan to find herself out of step with her native feudal culture. Her choice is to stay at home and uplift her countrymen (presumably through education) or to flee to the New World and the emancipated but unobligated life. She chooses the first alternative.[29]

The suffrage bazaars filled the Boston girl with repugnance, what with their second-rate handicraft exhibitions to justify the "gorgeous banners covered with high-sounding inscriptions: 'Our powers demand our rights,' and the like." Did it not occur to the feminists, she asked, that the "dreary, futile, and petty array" of doilies, sachet-bags, crocheted mats, and hand-painted screens proved to the masculine world that women *were* solely interested in homemaking? And where was the suffragist sense of balance? "Here is a world of suffering needing to be healed, of ignorance longing to be enlightened; and here are women, the heaven-appointed powers to illumine and to heal, devoting their energies to the embroidery of doilies, while they mourn the narrowness of their lives." Concluding that the franchise would come with time, Miss Scudder urged the equal righters to overcome their parochialism by studying the new economics and supporting movements for greater economic "equality and fairness in the social order."[30]

These ideas came to fruition by the middle of the 1880's, and behind them lay the personal security, cosmopolitan experience, and select education made possible by inherited wealth. Vida was a Scudder, of lineage which even the most genealogical-minded Bostonian respected. She traced her descent from John Winthrop, and Uncle Horace Scudder was editor of the *Atlantic Monthly*. Her father chose missionary work in India, where she was born in 1861. One year later he died from drowning, and Mrs. Scudder returned to Boston with her baby daughter, never to remarry, financially well-off, and intent on giving her girl every cultural advantage. Vida attended an aristocratic private grade school, joined the Episcopal Church with her mother, as did so many Congregationalists who were swept off their feet by Phillips Brooks. She traveled in Europe, read widely, dabbled in painting, cultivating her artistic and bookish tastes. In 1878 she entered the first class of Boston Girls' Latin School, was graduated two years later, and then went on to Smith for a Bachelor's degree. In 1884, she was at Oxford for graduate studies in English literature.[31]

Professor John Bates Clark at Smith and her reading of Frederick Denison Maurice had made Vida Scudder sensitive to social problems, but before embarking for England she was essentially a literary, introverted, and well-to-do Puritan girl whose impulses for social good were satisfied, at best, through Christian philanthropy. The North End lay close to her Back Bay home, yet Vida was ignorant of the conditions of Boston's worst slum. She knew that there were poor folk and that, as a good and prosperous Episcopalian, she must share an occasional Thanksgiving dinner with them. That she could pursue a career in letters without feeling any obligation toward the underprivileged seemed perfectly just. In the quiet of Oxford, however, John Ruskin fully awakened her to the responsibility of the educated rich toward the ignorant poor. His lectures mark the watershed of her career as scholar and reformer. Years later she wrote of them:

> Listening, dreaming, an entirely new order of questions began to form in the hearer's minds. Were political economy and art so far separated, after all? . . . Could a nation play

beautifully that did not as a whole work healthfully? . . .
Is it delicate, is it courteous, is it Christian, is it even just,
to rejoice contentedly in pretty descriptions of nature or in
the contemplation of art, while vast throngs of those to whose
labor we owe our fine sensibilities and the leisure to indulge
them are shut off from art and nature alike? What ought
idealism to play upon, — dreams, abstractions, the study of
the past, or the big crude world of modern fact? [32]

Heretofore having thrilled to *Stones of Venice* and *Modern
Painters*, the Boston maiden now became a votary of art for
humanity's sake. Music, she wrote, was utterly useless, for it
"arouses emotion without furnishing any hint of an end to which
the emotion shall be directed." Literature, she believed, was no
better when written for art's sake or studied through *explication
du texte*. As Professor in English Literature at Wellesley after
1887, she broke ground in approaching prose and poetry as social
documents relating to the ages out of which they came. This she
did in a little volume on Ruskin, another on Shelley, and still
another on the nineteenth-century British poets. Whereas at Oxford she took examinations on the most minute points in English
literature, she quizzed her own students on "the differing effects
of the democratic ideal on the poetry of Burns, Blake, Words-
worth, Coleridge, and Shelley." A trinitarian Christian as well
as a democrat, she picked holes in the agnostic writings of
Frederick Harrison and Herbert Spencer, arguing that the Christianity of Maurice's and Kingsley's works was both rational and
a force for good.[33] In 1898, her speculations and scholarship came
to ripe fulfillment in *Social Ideals in English Letters*, the outstanding example in the 1890's of literary criticism as social reform.

The Wellesley professor surveyed English literature from *Piers
Plowman* and the Peasant Revolution of 1381 to the *Fabian
Essays* and the London Dock Strike of 1889, on the lookout for
social criticism, social delineation, and social reconstruction.
Langland was significant because he laid bare the soul of the
peasant, Sir Thomas More because he would liberate the poor

from poverty to enjoy the things of the mind, and Jonathan Swift because he exposed the barbarous follies of his day. Following the age of Swift came the French and industrial revolutions, the catalysts of the modern world, Miss Scudder explained, and to which she traced the origins of nineteenth-century thought. She thrilled to Shelley in spite of his agnosticism, because his *Prometheus Unbound* embodied the 1789 ideal of setting mankind free from evil and oppression. She thought dimly of Keats for fleeing from the Revolution's passion for humanity to a dream world, and abused the Pre-Raphaelites for escaping from industrialism to medieval fantasy. Carlyle, Ruskin, and Arnold, Miss Scudder's chief heroes, showed up laissez-faire capitalism for what it was: predatory and anti-Christian. Few would disagree, the Wellesley professor wrote, with Arnold's indictment of Britain's economy: "Our inequality materializes our upper class, vulgarizes our middle class, brutalizes our lower class. . . We owe our uncivilizedness to our inequality."

Disraeli and Kingsley, Thackeray and Dickens, Reade and Besant — they did for the novel what Carlyle, Ruskin, and Arnold did for the essay. Their novels exposed the materialism, vulgarity, inhumanity, and spiritual poverty of competitive industrialism. George Eliot impressed the Wellesley academician as being the most significant English writer of fiction; she was the first to create well-born characters to suffer "with atoning pain for the sorrows of the world," as in *Daniel Deronda*. Daniel is an indecisive well-bred Englishman who is torn between worldly ambition and sacrificial service. At the point of marrying well, entering into the fellowship of the English nobility, and taking a seat in Parliament, he suddenly learns that he is a Jew. He voluntarily renounces his plans, Miss Scudder rejoiced, "to ally himself with a race vulgar and despised. We leave him fearing that he is embarked in a hopeless cause, — the restoration of the Jews to Palestine, — but confident that he has found the emancipation which brings life, in the service of an ideal such as a commercial civilization sighed for in vain."

American novelists, poets, and essayists did not produce a literature of economic protest comparable to that of England in the years 1840–1880, Miss Scudder observed, for the single reason that there was nothing to protest against. Whereas in Britain economic liberalism was a selfish bourgeois ethic, in America it was an inclusive and democratic ethos. Whittier, Emerson, and Whitman had pointed to economic individualism, equality of opportunity, and private property as showering blessings on the masses of men. Matthew Arnold desired the downfall of the theory of *La Carrière ouverte aux talents;* Lowell regarded it as "the last word of civilization." That ideal was splendid for our fathers because it worked, Miss Scudder agreed, but America has since vastly changed, as the contrast between Lucy Larcom's *A New England Girlhood* and Sidney Lanier's *The Symphony* will reveal. Since 1880 we have become like the Old World, what with our slums, our very rich, our very poor; "Disraeli's 'two nations' are among us. . ." In fact, because our proletariat in the cities consists almost entirely of immigrants, our problem is vastly more complicated than Europe's. This complication Miss Scudder wrote into *A Listener in Babel.*

The pre-1880 generation of Americans and Englishmen who wrote under the long reach of the Enlightenment and capitalism, the Wellesley professor concluded, should instruct her own generation. One cannot return with Ruskin and Carlyle to the pre-industrial handicraft system, nor should one view social democracy as timidly as Arnold. Weak on prescriptions, the three Britishers willed the late nineteenth century an indictment of capitalism that economists have not bettered but rather added statistics to. From George Eliot, the liberal must learn to suffer and sacrifice himself for the underdog. As for Emerson and his generation, let us remember, she noted, their passion in opposing Negro slavery and their expectation that "America should have no privileged class with a monopoly of luxuries. . . A plutocracy was assuredly the last result of their hopes. . ." [34] For the realization of mid-century American ideals, however, Miss Scudder

again turned to England, to the post-1880 England of Fabian
Socialism and the settlement house.

Overwhelmed by a desire to "expiate her worldly prosperity,"
Miss Scudder took to the slums and settlement work. In an article
in the *Christian Union* she rebuked Florence Wichnewitzky for
preaching hatred against capitalists instead of noting that they,
like the proletariat, were the products of an economy sanctioned
by the value of the survival of the fittest. Christian brotherhood,
not socialist violence, is required to bridge the awful chasm
separating classes; and the wealthy must see that the reformation come "from above and not from below." In 1887, together
with Helen Thayer, Jean Fine, and other Smith alumnae, Miss
Scudder hatched plans for a settlement of college women which
led to the opening of the Rivington Street House Settlement in
1889, the founding of the College Settlements Association in 1890,
and the establishing of Boston's Denison House in 1892. Emily
Greene Balch, instructor in economics at Wellesley and later to
win the Nobel Prize for peace, was selected as first head of
Denison House.

Modeled on Toynbee Hall, anticipating Jane Addams' Hull
House by only a few weeks, and similar to Robert Woods's
Andover House, Miss Scudder's project nevertheless had a
peculiar twist of its own. She and her comrades believed that,
as the "first-generation of college women," they must justify
America's granting them an education by demonstrating that
they did "not mean . . . to shut themselves up in complacent en-
joyments of their advantages. . ." Something of the self-consciousness of that generation is revealed in Miss Scudder's manifesto:
"We stand here as a new Fact — new, to all intents and purposes,
within the last quarter of a century. Our lives are in our hands.
. . . What is the relation which these lives should bear to the needs
and demands of the time?" [35]

The girls at Denison House, including alumnae as well as
undergraduates at Boston's colleges, were in search of diverse
things. Some wished to improve philanthropic methods, others

to organize clubs, classes, and dispensaries, still others to supplement their studies in economics, and a few to preach socialism. The House, like others, established a bath, gymnasium, public library, reading room, and summer school. During the depression winter of 1893–94 it engaged in relief work. It called Mary Kenney O'Sullivan from Hull House to organize women's trade unions, opened a social science club to be attended by employers and employees, and sent a delegate to Boston's Central Labor Union. Unlike Andover House, the woman's settlement did not produce a social survey of the neighborhood.[36]

And it is here that we touch on a crucial difference between Robert A. Woods and Vida D. Scudder. Woods believed that the well-situated must identify themselves with and uplift the poor, but the *sine qua non* of the settlement was to reclaim a blighted neighborhood. It would collect data on the life of the area, discover the causes of poverty, coöperate with trade unions, serve as a neighborhood center of public pressure, and above all, recommend at the end of ten years how to eliminate want and woe from American cities. Miss Scudder regarded all of this as fine, but the settlement "should feel that it vindicates its existence, though it give not a statistic to the world, if only, in these difficult and sorrowful days, it renders possible life among the people for those whose heart belongs to the people." [37]

Through the settlement the Boston girl wanted to live the simple life of the worker, through socialism she hoped that the worker would live the life of ease of her own class. Kingsley, Maurice, Lammenais, Ruskin, and Tolstoi had opened her heart to socialism, and the *Fabian Essays* completed the conversion. Of Edward Bellamy's philosophy she had doubts, disliking the emphasis on material ease, fearing the removal of struggle from human life. A Christian, she believed that struggle was good for the soul and, an evolutionist, she thought that the next stage in existence would be man's struggle to push back the frontiers in science, philosophy, and art. These were precisely the views of W. D. P. Bliss, whose Society and Church of the Carpenter she

joined. In her *Socialism and Spiritual Progress,* she defended the
coöperative commonwealth, without delineating its structure, as
a means to unburden men from excessive toil and want to pursue
the higher things of life. In addition to her socialist activities,
she joined the Church Social Union (Episcopal study group)
and the Society of the Companions of the Holy Cross (Episcopal
fellowship group which prays for social reform).[38]

Having tried her hand variously at short stories, Platonic dia-
logues, and plays, Vida D. Scudder summed up the experience
of her generation in a semi-autobiographical novel, *A Listener
in Babel.* With the Boston slums as its background, the work is
a minor *Pilgrim's Progress* as it describes the search for a modern
faith in a world of social sin. Hilda Lathrop, the heroine, gives up
a promising art career, as well as her love for a man of whom
her best friend is enamored, and joins a settlement. Bent on
finding "Calvary . . . close to the metropolis," she rejoices in the
knowledge that "instinctive recoil from happiness" shapes her
life. The novel is a talk-fest, as persons of all conditions, nationalities, and religions appear on the pages to describe their pet
schemes of social salvation. The wealthy characters ache with
Hilda's urge for social penitence; for wherever they look they
feel that they are in part responsible for prevailing violations of
democracy and Christianity — of "cleavage of classes, cleavage of
races, cleavage of faiths! an inextricable confusion. And the voice
of democracy, crying aloud in our streets: 'Out of all this achieve
brotherhood! achieve the race to be.' "

Their solutions vary. One woman wants to melt all immigrants
down to the New England Yankee mold through the public
school, while another hopes that America will profit from the gifts
of its newcomers — that the Irish will give us warmth, the Italians
art, the Germans music, the Slavs dreams, and the Jews ideals.
Neither examined what the immigrants thought about their own
adjustment. The labor leader looked to economic salvation through
high wages and the short-hour day, whereas the anarchist pledged
himself to violence and anarchism. The devout Christian agreed

to renounce $10,000 a year and live in Christian fellowship and simplicity with others like herself, as did St. Francis. The Fabian Socialist prophesied the triumph of gradual collectivism in a generation, meanwhile urging radicals to be patient and tolerant of the defenders of the status quo who live honorably. Hilda's choice, a blend of Tolystoyan and Ruskinesque principles, is to go among factory workers in the hope of discovering how modern productive processes can be made aesthetic to the workers. The reformers, or the "children of the future" as Miss Scudder called them, seemed to be more concerned with the effect of reform on the reformer than on the intended reformed.[39]

IV

The emancipation of women, almost complete by 1900, stands as a supreme achievement of nineteenth-century liberalism and at the same time testifies to the enduring appeal of the ideals of the Enlightenment. It ranks in importance with the abolition of Negro slavery and the enfranchisement of Jews and Catholics. Like them it rested on the vision of equality and liberty, at the heart of which lay the crucial concept of the Enlightenment that all human beings, irrespective of surface differences, shared a common humanity. Similarly, those who wished to free Negroes, Jews, Catholics, and women appealed to the good eighteenth-century doctrine of natural rights. They regarded the state, not as an instrument for economic planning, but as a means of blasting out the accretions of discriminatory laws and customs violating the equalitarian principles of the Heavenly City. The liberalism of feminism, thus, rested on individualistic and not collectivistic assumptions.

Vida D. Scudder understood the difference between the two sets of assumptions because she profited from the personal freedoms and the higher education that the equal righters had won for her generation. A member of the first class at Girls' Latin and of the fourth class at Smith, she was also one of the first American women to study at Oxford, and a professor at the first girls' college in the Boston area. Protesting against the narrowness of her class background and the parochialism of the leaders of her sex, she charted new paths for women to follow. Her associates included Mary Kingsbury Simkhovitch (head of Greenwich House), Jean Fine (head of Rivington House), Katherine Coman (who later won fame as an historian), Emily Greene Balch (economics instructor at Wellesley and later prominent in the peace movement), and Jane Addams.[40] All these women the modern American will recognize as completely modern, whereas the feminists, whether Lucy Stone or Alice Stone Blackwell, Julia Ward Howe or Elizabeth Stuart Phelps, savor of an age unlike our own.

Many Wellesley students from the 1880's until her retirement in 1926 followed Miss Scudder's lead into social reform. The most striking example is Florence Converse (class of 1892), who dedicated several of her books to her mentor and, by the 1920's, became her lifetime companion. Miss Converse's *The Burden of Christopher*, a novel published by Houghton Mifflin in 1900, bears the Christian socialist imprint of Miss Scudder's ideas. Full of indignation against Christian charity as a remedy for the social problem, the book tells how a young New England shoe manufacturer, Christopher Kenyon, tried the Christian experiment of coöperative enterprise in his factory. Competitive and wicked capitalism drive him to the wall and he commits suicide. In his very failure and death, however, he achieves victory; for he shared the idea of his good friend, a reform-minded Episcopalian minister, that "martyrdom is success." [41]

The successor to the National-American Woman Suffrage Association is the League of Women Voters, the heirs of Miss Scudder's ideas are the Christian socialists. In the twentieth century Vida D. Scudder's ideas matured and caught fire in the left-wing movements of her Episcopalian church, especially among the Anglo-Catholics. Her two books on St. Francis, her studies on the Anglican concept of poverty, and her splicing of Marxism and Trinitarian Christianity in *Socialism and Character* (1912) are acknowledged parts of the Episcopalian Social Gospel. To her was dedicated *Christianty and Property* in 1947, a collection of papers contributed by leading American Anglican socialists. Professor Joseph Fletcher, of the Episcopal Theological School in Cambridge, noted in the dedication that:

> There is no other person in the American scene to whom a book on Chistianity and property could so rightly be dedicated. She and her work, for all these years since she published *Social Ideals in English Letters* (in 1898, the first of many great contributions to Christian social thought), have enormously influenced us all. Hosts of her former students brighten when her name is mentioned. To know her now is to have a lively foretaste of the communion of saints. Her wisdom, her faith in social redemption, her vast learning and mature sense of humor, have been towers of strength in the Church League for Industrial Democracy, the Society of Companions of the Holy Cross, and other fellowships that look forward to a new day.[42]

Scornful of the feminists, Vida D. Scudder curiously proved their point that woman can do as well as man if given an equal chance.

Up to 1900, however, Vida D. Scudder and the newer of the new women were different from their social settlement counterparts of the opposite sex. They did not share Frederick Bushée's contempt for immigrants, and they did not agree with Robert A. Woods that the primary function of the social settlement was to be a laboratory of social science. The first generation of college women were more concerned with the profitable use of their time than with the effect of their progressivism on the masses. While not as belligerent about their sex as the feminists, they did not quite take themselves for granted like men. Their type was in transition in the 1880's and 1890's. In 1951, Miss Scudder remembered neither her rebellion against feminism nor the self-consciousness of her generation.[43] A half century of freedom made her forget the anxious beginnings of the modern woman.

of science and industry, the progeny of the Puritans refashioned their religion to mean more the promotion of democracy and less exclusively the preparation for the eternal Sabbath. As their covenant-making forefathers lacked nothing in devotion to the Divine Being, so they faltered not in their dedication to *Homo Sapiens*. Like their ancestors they regarded themselves as God's stewards on earth.

Solomon Schindler, the Jew, and John Boyle O'Reilly, the Catholic, similarly found nourishment for their reform aspirations. Schindler's God was the eighteenth-century's disinterested First Cause and Clockmaker, but He was rational; and the ethics of the Ten Commandments gave no sanction to the dog-eat-dog philosophy of Social Darwinism. O'Reilly's God was loving and kind, not the sort to tolerate materialism, exploitation of labor, and concentrated wealth. *Rerum Novarum* cut short a budding Catholic radicalism in Boston, but it contained enough holy declamatory remarks against predatory businessmen to allow the followers of the Bishop of Rome to support William Jennings Bryan. In the brief moment of the 1880's and 1890's, Boston's Protestant, Catholic, and Jewish reformers had come to agree that the Kingdom of Heaven, the City of God, and the Messiah meant the salvation of industrial man on earth through a more humane social system, and salvation in the immediate future.

The belief in the earthly redemption of mankind also derived from the heritage of the Enlightenment. In a deep sense, reform movements in America have been an *obiter dictum* on the Declaration of Independence, and significantly, attacks on reform have centered on the assumptions of eighteenth-century humanitarianism. The doers-of-good of the 1880's and 1890's knew the principles of the eighteenth century as transmitted by Emerson and his generation, and proudly compared themselves to the abolitionists. As grandchildren of the *Philosophes* they assumed that man counted for much, that he was capable of good, that no human beings ought to be condemned to permanent degradation, and that society could progress through reason and will.

Nineteenth-century science and technology strengthened the Enlightenment's legacy of progress. As Newton and the French Revolution had inspired Condorcet to prophesy limitless improvement, so Darwin and the Industrial Revolution fired Benjamin Orange Flower to behold a glorious future for the human race. Machinery made life more abundant, and Evolution promised that mankind would continue to pull itself up from the depths. Regarding themselves as playing a role of cosmic proportions, the progressives of the late nineteenth century believed that, by including more and more people in the benefits of civilization, they would lead mankind another step up the evolutionary ladder.

Because it was disposed to regard life as growth through experimentation, the reform mind rejected deduction as a means to understand society. Only the anarchists persisted in the deductive method, and they were the kinsmen of Adam Smith. The other progressives championed institutional economics over Manchester dogma. They also looked to the observable past, to history, in order to determine the truth of things. George E. McNeill wrote a history of labor; W. D. P. Bliss a history of socialism; B. O. Flower a history of British reform; Vida D. Scudder a sociological history of English literature; Nicholas P. Gilman a history of American character and profit-sharing. Robert A. Woods chronicled contemporary British social reform. W. D. P. Bliss compiled an encyclopedia of social good. By the 1890's the survivors of Boston's age of newness flooded the market with biographies, autobiographies, and histories dealing with the ferments of 1830–1865. Historical-mindedness derived from a climate of opinion heavy with evolution, but even more important, from the liberal's urgent need to see himself in relationship to the past. If one did not know history, one could not predict the future.

Historically and empirically oriented to regard society as being in the making and as something to master through manipulation, the Boston progressives showed a lively interest in social reform abroad. Europe, Great Britain, Australia, and New Zealand, they reasoned, should serve as the laboratory of American liberalism; for they were ahead of the New World in trying out methods of social reconstruction. They were experimenting — the crucial and appealing item of nineteenth-century science. Assuming that conditions in this country were like those overseas, the reformers asked, if a measure works over there, why should it not work here? Thus Solomon Schindler championed Bismarck's social welfare state; W. D. McCrackan the Swiss referendum and re-call; W. D. P. Bliss the French Postal Savings Bank; Alice Stone Blackwell the Scotch municipal franchise for women; George Hodges the English Social Gospel; Robert A. Woods the British settlement house; George E. McNeill the Australian eight-hour day; and Frank Parsons the New Zealand nationalization and municipalization of basic utilities. Birmingham and Glasgow held particular fascination for the reformer, for they had solved the problems of the city through public housing, parks, gymnasiums, bathhouses, and transportation. W. D. P. Bliss's *Encyclopedia of Social Reform* was encyclopedic in its use of data from foreign countries. Aside from the reform *experience* of foreign nations, some reformers imbibed deeply from the European ideological draughts of Marxism, Fabian Socialism, and Anarchism. All these influences from the outside were as stimulating to the late-nine-teenth-century progressive mind as the Reform Act of 1832, Chartism, the repeal of the corn laws, and the revolutions of 1830 and 1848 had been to the groaners and come-outers of the second quarter of the century.

Marxian Socialism attracted a handful of trade unionists and Christian Socialists (who trimmed it to their ministerial liking), but its chief importance for the 1880's and 1890's was to spur the reformers of that age to find alternate solutions for the social problem. Frank K. Foster felt compelled to argue the merits of pure and simple trade unionism in order to combat the influence of the Socialist Labor Party in the ranks of labor. Francis Green-wood Peabody viewed his own moderate reforms as a means to head off socialist revolution, and Joseph Cook interested himself in social reform because of the menace he perceived in the Socialist Labor Party. Nicholas Paine Gilman, the only reformer of the late nineteenth century to analyze American character as a first step toward reforming it, did so out of the desire to prove that socialism and American ideals were incompatible. Edward Bellamy deliberately chose to call his system Nationalism because he disliked Marxian Socialism. At the same time, practically all the reformers thought that they were socialists in the sense that Webster defined socialism as being an ideal system. In fine, the drift of the 1880's and 1890's was to find the right kind of socialism, one that would avoid the class hatred involved in Marxian polemics and conserve the open society.

Some reformers were moderates and some were radicals, some were progressives in the pre-Civil War sense, and others of the postwar kind. The moderates did not regard American society as being totally bad and they wished to patch its defective parts. The radicals looked at their culture as if it were a complete abomination and called for a sharp break. The moderates, such as Francis Greenwood Peabody, Robert A. Woods, Edwin D. Mead, Benjamin O. Flower, Nicholas Paine Gilman, and Minot J. Savage, proposed coöperatives, the short work day, trade unions, the public ownership of utilities, an income tax, direct legislation. The radicals, such as Edward Bellamy, Solomon Schindler, W. D. P. Bliss, Jesse H. Jones, Laurence Gronlund, and Hamlin Garland, proposed various socialisms or the Single Tax. The pre-Civil War vintage reformer, such as the feminists, looked to state action to obtain greater individual freedom and equality. The majority of the post-Civil War reformers, however, thought less of the state as an instrument to negate prejudicial laws than as a positive force for planning. Both streams of liberalism exist at mid-century, in the New and Fair Deals, which have used the state for economic planning and as a power to curb racial and religious prejudices.

Whether radical or moderate, of the pre- or post-Civil War generation, the reform mind abhorred the contemplative ideal and acted vigorously in defense of its principles. Samuel Gridley Howe's observation of Theodore Parker's activist urge applies equally well to the crusaders of Benjamin Orange Flower's day. "How lucky it is," Howe wrote to Parker, "that there are evil institutions and wicked men in the world . . . or you would have smote the good. . ." [2] Similarly, the late-nineteenth-century progressives were so full of combat, so full of enthusiasm to fight for good, that one wonders how they would have behaved, could they have lived in the perfected societies for which they agitated. The example of the settlement house residents going to live with the poor of the slums illustrates the need of that generation to *do* something about its convictions and not merely talk and think about them. Bostonians, moreover, organized themselves into all sorts of societies to agitate for Nationalism and Christian Socialism, women's rights and justice to Armenians, peace and anti-imperialism, clean government and direct legislation, the Single Tax and the public ownership of utilities, the eight-hour day and the abolition of the sweatshop. Frank Parsons carried the cult of activism to the point of declaring that it was "a moral duty to perspire at least once every day."

Moral duty led to the hair shirt in the case of the Christian Socialists and Benjamin Orange Flower. The writings of W. D. P. Bliss and his disciples and the editor of the *Arena* contained a non-Utilitarian calculus by which they measured pleasure by the amount of pain they suffered in helping mankind. The desire for self-sacrifice derived in part from the reformers' abhorrence of worldly success, which the exploits of Jay Gould, Jim Fisk, and Andrew Carnegie had identified with wealth and fame wrung from the jungle-like, and therefore, anti-Christian world of the competitive economy. Even more important, the Christian Socialists believed that as disciples of Christ they must follow the Nazarene's example of earthly failure as a means of regenerating the race. Their credo was: "Blessed are they who suffer for righteousness' sake; for theirs is the kingdom of heaven." [3] Finally, the reformers who looked forward to their own cross were convinced by their reading of history that progress had resulted from the efforts of a creative ethical minority, from men ranging from Socrates to Luther through Garrison, who had announced a truth, been persecuted for it, and eventually heralded as its champions. The martyrs therefore welcomed public indifference or hostility as a sign that their ideas were predestined to prevail in the future. In their eagerness to travel the lonely road to the mountain top of virtue and vision, men like Bliss and Flower practiced an inverted snobbism.

Prophetic revelation in Christian Socialist thought was part of a Christian eschatology secularized by the frightening urgency of the times. The violent strikes of the 1880's and 1890's, the spread of the slums, the depression of 1893, Coxey's Army and the wrathful uprising of the Populists — all these suggested that Americans were fast approaching a day of judgment. W. D. P. Bliss reasoned that in the beginning America had had a golden age of freedom and plenty and equality, which by his time had been cut short by the original sin of plutocracy. Through the use of science and sentiment one could return to God's way. The church had the special function of leading the nation to salvation, of purifying Americans from capitalist sin and preparing them to live like brothers in the earthly kingdom of heaven. In their desire to chase out evil, the Christian Socialists seized on the simplest means: the routing of the plutocracy through collective enterprise.

An articulate minority of Bostonians were social reformers. The mass of the citizens were indifferent or hostile to liberalism. The minority, however, represented all sections of the population. They approached social problems with the sensitivity that derived from their particular position in society. Thus the feminists, Jews, Catholics, and trade unionists regarded social reforms as vitally affecting their position in society, whereas writers, artists, college professors and students, and Protestant ministers looked upon themselves as responsible for leadership in time of crisis. They all met on common ground in the smelting pot of

American equalitarianism. In varying degrees the product of religious idealism, the Enlightenment, and nineteenth-century science and technology, they all spoke the same language of making life more meaningful for the underprivileged — the language of the American dream.

The reformers' interpretation of the American dream derived from their sensitivity to evil, which, in turn, was determined by their role in the Boston community. Protestant ministers, unlike Catholic priests and Jewish rabbis, inherited a reformist tradition and felt guilty in ministering to the rich. They were therefore more active than the other two in contributing to the Social Gospel. The colleges and the seminaries, as centers of Western learning and training grounds for leaders in society, placed social science in the service of humanity. The settlement house institutionalized the urge of the academic community to do good, symbolizing the Christian and experimental approach to human affairs. The free-lance intellectuals, without a solid footing in the community, were the most radical of the reformers — the anarchists, the socialists, the Single-Taxers, the Populists. Feminists and trade unionists, as objects of the reforms for which they agitated, were conservative in their tactics and limited in their aims: conservative because they did not wish to alienate well-wishers by radical affiliations; and limited because they accepted the basic economic and political structure of the American community, wanting only to share the benefits of middle-class civilization. They believed in self-help.

The descendants of the Puritans led the way in social reform, but the native Bostonians of wealth and culture failed to meet the problems of the day in a constructive way. Excepting the pre-Civil War reformers, and Francis Greenwood Peabody and Vida D. Scudder of the younger generation, every progressive of importance came originally from the outside — from New England, the Middle States, the West, and from such faraway places as Denmark, Ireland, and Germany. They came to Boston because they regarded it as a center of culture and liberal aspirations;

Boston to them was the city of the Tea Party and the Breakfast Table, of Brook Farm and the Over-Soul. With the fervor of converts they kept the faith. The natives, on the other hand, resigned to losing power to the newer immigrant groups, turned to a different past: to the past of their English forebears and merchant grandfathers, from which they excluded the new arrivals. Henry Adams went as far back as medieval France, sunk as low as racism, and lamented that he could not do what father Charles, grandfather John Quincy, and great-grandfather John had done.

Vida D. Scudder is the most conspicuous example of the native Bostonian who embraced the newer kinds of social reform, going as far to the left as Christian Socialism. She represented a type more common to England than America during the 1880's and 1890's, but which has become since then not at all rare in this country. That type is the person of inherited wealth who, suffering from a sense of guilt in enjoying money earned by one's ancestors, is driven to identify one's self with the laboring masses. Significantly, she learned of her duty to the poor in England, through John Ruskin, and all her life she has practiced her liberalism in the semi-English bosom of the American Anglo-Catholic church. Perhaps it is the English, and almost aristocratic, origin of her liberalism, its self-conscious *noblesse oblige*, and its medieval romanticism of the joys of simplicity and poverty that explain its failure to catch on among many Americans. It was a liberalism for the rich, or at least, the very comfortable.

The most authentic American, in a deep sense, was Thomas Wentworth Higginson. The causes he embraced have all been realized: the abolition of slavery, the emancipation of women, the municipal and national ownership of some but not all basic utilities, the referendum and recall. He grew up in the age of Emerson, when Americans believed that one could bring out the good in man by tinkering with the environment. He never once renounced that basic assumption. Scholars have interpreted America as being significant for its glorification of the capitalist virtues, but Higginson stands as proof that America is even more significant as that area on the globe where men have dedicated themselves to realize the ideals of the Enlightenment. To him capitalism was but one means toward these ideals, not an end. Blessed with an almost natural propensity to remonstrate, he kept alive the notion that freedom is not to be won at once, but rather to be pursued endlessly as unfreedoms crop up. He also recognized that the post-Civil War reformers needed the social sciences to grapple with the complex problems of the day, whereas their predecessors had only to grasp the simple fact of the wickedness of slavery to combat it.

Frank Parsons illustrates the difference between the pre- and post-Civil War reformer. Engineer, lawyer, economist, and believer in applied Christianity, he brought to his study of complex industrial problems the requisites of his day. He started out as a radical, as a Mutualist, which was the American counterpart of Fabian Socialism except for its hope for economic equality in the future. He ended his life as an Independent Roosevelt Republican, having come to accept the American's penchant for piecemeal reform. His refutation of Spencer's arguments for laissez faire bordering on anarchy compares to that of Lester Ward. In his two-decade-long liberal career he espoused all of the reforms endorsed by his contemporaries: the eight-hour day, slum clearance, and public works; coöperatives and the municipal and national ownership of public utilities; woman suffrage, the initiative, referendum, recall, and direct primary; the income tax and an elastic currency. He perceived clearly that the problem of the century was the problem of the city.

Radical or moderate in their proposals, the Boston progressives were conservative in their assumptions. They wished to preserve the older ideas of American life wrapped up in the one idea of the open society. Fearful that America would follow Europe in developing a class-ridden society, they cherished the ancient doctrine of the oneness of the human race. In an age characterized by Social Darwinist ethics, jurisprudence, economics, and business, this particular idea fed on continuous challenge. When viewed as a reaction to predatory individualism, the doctrine of all is One is not puzzling, as William James believed, but perfectly understandable. It afforded "a welcome sense of freedom, arising from a triumph over, or an absolution from, the troublesome cleavages and disjunctions of things." [4] Nourished on the organic conception of society, which was Spencerian, Transcendental, Theosophist, and Christian in origin, and strengthened by the tying together of continents by improved methods of transportation and communication, the idea that all is One gave the reformers a metaphysical doctrine of mystical appeal.

In the case of some of the intellectuals, metaphysics presented contradictions left unresolved. On the one hand, they were rationalists, believing in science, the inductive method, the social laboratory. On the other hand, they were Theosophists or spiritualists, having faith in the unseen world. The Theosophist ethic of universal brotherhood was not incompatible with the ultimate goals of Nationalism, and the hope of Hamlin Garland and Benjamin Flower to find proof for the existence of the hereafter through mediums did not contravene the Populism and Bryanism of the *Arena*. The paradox was in method: the intuitionism of the occult versus the empiricism of secular conceptions of social reform. Romanticism and rationalism were inadvertently blended in the architecture of the reform intellect.

The decades of the eighties and nineties produced no giant intellectual as reformer; there was no Socrates, no St. Augustine, no Luther, no Galileo, no Auguste Comte, no Karl Marx. The most distinguished man of letters was William Dean Howells, and he left for New York before his liberal ideas matured. Except for the interested scholar, few today read the works of Boston's late-nineteenth-century progressives. Rather we read their contemporaries who were either indifferent or antagonistic to reform: Henry James, Josiah Royce, Henry Adams, and Oliver Wendell Holmes, Jr. It is precisely because the reformers were not the first-rate writers of their day, however, that they are of vital concern to the historian of ideas. Professor Palmer explains why:

> The tendencies of an age appear more distinctly in its writers of inferior rank than those of commanding genius. These latter tell of past and future as well as present. They are for all time. . . But in the sensitive responsive souls, of less creative power, current ideals record themselves with clearness.[5]

In Boston's reformers one can follow the level of aspiration of the generation of 1880–1900.

The last twenty-five years of the nineteenth century were the seed bed of modern America. Boston's reformers met the challenges raised by the forces remaking their nation: industry, science, and immigration. They did not regard Boston's intellectual life as passing through an "Indian Summer"; nor do they give proof to Edmund Wilson's judgment that their age was "perhaps the most provincial and uninspired moment in the history of American society." [6] On the contrary, with an optimism and zeal reminiscent of the age of Ralph Waldo Emerson and Bronson Alcott, they rejuvenated the languishing spirit of reform to meet the problems of the modern, urban-industrial culture. Together with fellow liberals in other American cities they created a new climate of opinion that stimulated urban dwellers to rally behind the progressive creeds of Theodore Roosevelt and Woodrow Wilson. As in the case of Jacksonian democracy, the twentieth-century progressive movements fed on both the liberalism of eastern cities and western farmers.

Urban and agrarian reformers of the last part of the nineteenth century were alike in several respects. They opposed monopoly and concentrated wealth, and proposed that the national income filter down in a more equitable way. Neither farmer nor city man understood that one of their obscure planks, the tax on personal income, would in the future revolutionize the distribution of wealth more than any other single reform or combined reforms. During the depression of the 1890's there was a rough kind of agreement as to how to rout the plutocracy between, on the one hand, the trade unionists, Nationalists, *Arena* and *New England Magazine* people, and Irish Catholics, and on the other hand, western Populists. City and prairie joined for the most part in rejecting Marxian Socialism.

There were also differences. The railroad was for the farmer a personally felt problem; for city folk it was one example of how big business controlled the nation. The worker pursued the eight-hour day reform, while for the farmer, the major objective was a stable price structure guaranteed by the ever-normal granary and free-silver or paper money. Farmers were like women and trade unionists in wishing to help themselves by perfecting the rules of competition, but different from other city reformers who had nothing personal to gain from changing the structure of American society. Nowhere in the Populist platform was there so thorough-going a socialism as municipal socialism. Urban reformers knew they must live with the city; agrarians would ostracize it.

Today it is fashionable to find fault with the reform mind. We are told of its naïve faith in the perfection of man and mankind, of its simple-minded approach to the nature of evil. Its eight-eenth-century assumptions, it has been suggested, are no more substantial than the foundations of revealed religion. Yet the generation of 1880–1900 was not unsophisticated; its ideal of making America a better place in which to live was simple to grasp but by no means simple-minded. Some of the socialists were inclined to regard men as being angelic, but Frank K. Foster, Nicholas P. Gilman, and Robert A. Woods spoke more typically for their generation in pointing out mankind's capacity for evil. There was no idealization or idolization of the dirt farmer and factory worker. Again excepting the socialists, the reformers did not believe in the magic of environment. Progress would come through education and experimentation and re-experimen-tation, through pain and struggle and compromise over a long period of time. They knew better than the reactionaries that man was not brute, and better than the conservatives that man was not the prisoner of himself but that he could break the cake of custom if only he willed it.

The Yankee reformers of the last part of the nineteenth century belong to the long line of men and women in Western civilization who have fixed their eyes on what-ought-to-be. Their unique function has been to supply the community, since its secularization in the past two hundred years, with a tension that religion gives to the truly religious person: the tension that derives from contemplating the difference between what one is and what one should be. Our age, disillusioned by Buchenwald and the Cominform, appalled by Nagasaki and Hiroshima, and attracted to T. S. Eliot and Franz Kafka, is too stunned and hurt to hope in the grand reforming manner. Yet it would be intolerant and unhistorical to condemn an earlier generation for such optimism as not to anticipate current calamities, or to blame them for the flabbiness of some contemporary liberal thinking. Limited and fallible — like all men — the liberals of the 1880's and 1890's saw well the evils of their own age. Frank Foster, the most hardheaded of the Yankee reformers and the one who most nearly embodies the now emerging semi-pessimistic, semi-optimistic temper, justifies the credo of his contemporaries:

> A plea for the dreamer, who sees the mass
> No longer despoiled by greed for gold,
> No longer ruled by the pride of class,
> No longer slaves to be bought and sold.[7]

**BIBLIOGRAPHICAL
NOTE**

NOTES

INDEX

Bibliographical Note

Yankee Reformers in the Urban Age is, in a sense, a bibliographical essay in itself, and the notes, which grew like Topsy, demonstrate the relationship of text to sources. The main body of this study rests on written materials, yet residence in Boston and interviews with the survivors and their descendants and friends gave me something of a feeling for the city and also for a past reforming generation. For the complete bibliography, see the manuscript copy in the Widener Archives of Harvard University. The following is a brief description of the pattern of my research and of my larger indebtedness to certain of the more helpful materials.

Authors had little trouble in getting published in the 1880's and 1890's, which, apart from the need to go reforming, accounts for the prodigious and embarrassingly rich sources. And the men and women of that day, brought up on the written word, may well have had a compulsion to break into print. Modern America does not have a Frank K. Foster who, in addition to his job, administrative duties, and editorial chores, published a book of verse and a novel. Nor is there a contemporary clergyman comparable to the Reverend Minot J. Savage in the technique of the one-man assembly line. Weekly, Savage delivered his sermons extemporaneously, which were taken down stenographically, and then rushed to the printer to be made available for distribution the following Sunday. His sermons go on, understandably, volume on volume (*Unity Pulpit.* 17 Vols. Boston, 1879–1896). And so it was, in varying degrees, for the prolific others. George Hodges, by retiring to his study mornings, wrote more than thirty books before he died in his late fifties. A forty-page catalogue was required to list the published works of Thomas Wentworth Higginson.

Most of the books and pamphlets were polemical, but certain of them have perspective and perception that afford insights into the period and the subject as a whole. They are four. W. D. P. Bliss's *Encyclopedia of Social Reform* (New York, 1897) lives up to its title, and a number of articles stand up well alongside contemporary scholarship. Benjamin Orange Flower's *Progressive Men, Women, and Movements of the Past Twenty-Five Years* (Boston, 1914) is the best over-all coverage of that generation by a contemporary. William Jewett Tucker saw his age clearly and steadily in his *My Generation* (Boston, 1919); the first eighteen pages contain as penetrating an analysis of the middle class religious reformer as is to be found. Frank K. Foster's *The Evolution of a Trade Unionist* (Boston, 1903), full of the sights, smells, and ideologies of reform Boston, is the best of the period fictional pieces. The big book of the day, *The Autobiography of Henry Adams*, is lacking in the stuff that forms the substance of this study.

Magazines as well as books and pamphlets were a major reference source. Although research followed Bostonians into non-Boston periodicals, the bulk of the fortnightlies, monthlies, and quarterlies consulted issued from New England's capital. For the most part, they were polemical and provincial, but there is useful general reform material in the *Andover Review, Nationalist, New Nation,* and *Dawn.* For the emerging difference in the last part of the nineteenth century between charity and reform, see *Lend A Hand* and the *Journal of Social Sciences.* Students of alienation, bohemia, and social reform would do well to consult the *Fly Leaf,* while those concerned with the relationship between academic freedom and liberalism should see the *Industrialist* (Manhattan, Kansas). The *American Fabian* (published in New York by W. D. P. Bliss) is a good starting place for studying the impact of English social thought on America. Aspects of denominational history can be followed in the Episcopalian *Publications of the Church Social Union;* the Congregationalist *Our Day, A Record and Review of Current Reform;* the Swedenborgian *New Church Review; Universalist Quarterly Review;* and the *Unitarian Review.* A reading of the *Arena* will provide a quite comprehensive view of what the middle class reform world was up to, and the same applies nearly as well to the *New England Magazine.* The journals of B. O. Flower and Edwin D. Mead — with attractive format, interesting book reviews, high literateness, and over-all sprightliness — reflect the taste of a once large reading middle class. They are rebuttal to the criticism that the liberal is without mind, and reminder to some present-day successors that reform journalism has not always been dull.

A major portion of three chapters and sections in others of this book derive from research in weekly newspapers. The Boston *Pilot,* available partly in microfilm and partly in the original at the Boston Public Library, is the bibliographical backbone of the chapter on the Catholics. The *Woman's Journal* and *Woman's Column,* housed appropriately at Radcliffe, have yet to be exploited for the history we need on women in America. The Massachusetts Institute of Technology has an almost unbroken file, most of it on microfilm, of the *Labor*

Leader, which is the indispensable source on the thought and character of Frank K. Foster and organized labor in Massachusetts in the last years of the nineteenth century. These four weeklies, despite parochial orientations, are useful in following the news of the day, for they were in competition with the general press. The same is true of the Unitarian *Christian Register* and the *Congregationalist*. Students of religious history have still to profit from the files of Solomon Schindler's *Hebrew Observer*, locked up in the New England Deposit Library, but made available by the Boston Public Library. Useful as documents in the history of social reform, the weekly press also helped considerably in piecing together the parts of the Boston community.

Newspapers, magazines, and books and pamphlets by reformers are the main reference tools of this work, but there are others. College catalogues tell much, especially when supplemented by the reminiscences of a Thodore Roosevelt and a Mary K. Simkhovitch, a Francis Greenwood Peabody and a Charles F. Dole. The statistics of Washington and the State House need to be used with caution, but there is much useful social and economic data in the *Annual Reports of the Massachusetts Bureau of Statistics of Labor*. The reform press is good on the activities of liberal groups, and there also exist the fuller and periodic reports of the women's associations and the social settlements. The latter, in conjunction with Robert A. Woods's and Albert J. Kennedy's *A Handbook of Settlements* (New York, 1912), are a convenient jumping-off point for an understanding of the beginnings of modern social work. Finally, to keep in mind the larger pattern of urban social reform, I found valuable the writings, and where available, the autobiographies, of such non-Bostonians as Washington Gladden, Josiah Strong, Jane Addams, Richard T. Ely, John R. Commons, Samuel Gompers, Terence V. Powderly, Henry George, and Henry Demarest Lloyd, to mention but the more prominent of them.

Although the bulk of this monograph rests on research in materials found on the library shelf, reference to personal collections yielded satisfying results. Thumbing through scrapbooks, letters, and miscellanea of yesteryear somehow gave me a sense of contemporaneousness with the past. And it was convenient, too, as in the case of the well-ordered *Scrapbooks* of Julia Ward Howe and Solomon Schindler, the one deposited at Radcliffe and the other in the possession of Mrs. Claire Schindler Hamburger, of Brookline, Massachusetts. The George Hodges *Papers*, unassorted and resting in the basements of the Cambridge Episcopal Theological School, is an unusually rich and as yet unexploited store of information on the social and intellectual history of Boston. Relevant materials in the *Papers* of Thomas Wentworth Higginson (Harvard) and the unused *Papers* of William Jewett Tucker (Dartmouth) were few, but the Frank Parsons *Papers* (Yale) are worth while the attention of the historian of social reform. The Francis Greenwood Peabody *Quinquennial File* (Harvard) is most valuable for the notebooks of two of his students in Social Ethics. Available for general use at Harvard since last year are the Robert A. Woods *Papers;* the letters, but more especially the *Diary*, although amply reproduced by his wife-biographer, reveal the inner life of one of the Yankee Reformers. Thanks to Arthur E. Morgan, Harvard has a fine collection of manuscripts on Edward Bellamy and the Nationalist movement, which Mr. Morgan's published researches, however, make nearly superfluous. Cyrus Field Willard's "Autobiography" one of the unpublished manuscripts, is a firsthand account by a labor reporter and organizer of the Knights of Labor in Massachusetts of that organization, and might also interest students who are curious about the relationship between sex and reform. Vida D. Scudder's autobiographies are revealing, but her *Papers*, kept at home in her intriguing attic-study, will reward the scholar interested in the progression of her thought. Primary materials on the feminist movement are ample, but students of that movement must await the final assembling of the voluminous *Papers* of the Blackwell family, in which Mrs. Guy Stantial of Melrose is engaged. I wish to thank Professor Howard Quint for sendng me relevant microfilm from the reform mine of the Wisconsin Historical Society.

Happily, I built on the labors of others. *Fifty Years of Boston, A Memorial Volume* (Boston, 1932), edited by Elisabeth M. Herlihy, is uneven in quality; and there remains the task of doing for post-1880 Boston what Justin Winsor and his staff did for pre-1880 Boston in the superlative *The Memorial History of Boston*, 4 vols. (Boston, 1881). The latter, together with Oscar Handlin's *Boston's Immigrants, 1790–1865* (Cambridge, 1941), carried this researcher to the point from which he jumped into his own study. The footnotes reveal the special indebtedness to the intellectual histories of a number of fine scholars that touched my field. Since this book was revised in final form in the winter of 1953, Howard Quint's *The Forging of American Socialism* (Columbia, South Carolina, 1953) has appeared. His learning and insight would have eased my way had I seen it earlier.

Notes

Chapter I. The Social Milieu: 1800-1900

1. Helen Keller, "My Recollections of Boston. — The City of Kind Hearts," in Elisabeth M. Herlihy, ed., *Fifty Years of Boston, A Memorial Volume* (Boston, 1932), p. xviii; Vida D. Scudder, *A Listener in Babel. Being a Series of Imaginary Conversations Held at the Close of the Last Century* (Boston, 1903), p. 74.

2. Herlihy, *Fifty Years of Boston*, p. 715.

3. Herlihy, *Fifty Years of Boston*, pp. 230, 231, 233, 234; William W. Lincoln, "Boston Commerce and Trade, 1880–1898" (mss. deposited in Boston Athenaeum, 1899), pp. 20–31; Horace G. Wadlin, "The Manufacturing Industries of Boston" (mss. deposited in Boston Athenaeum, 1899), pp. 29–31 and *passim*; Henry Adams, *The Education of Henry Adams* (Modern Library ed., New York, 1931), p. 338; *Seventeenth Annual Report of the Massachusetts Bureau of Statistics of Labor* (Boston, 1886), pp. 66, 116; W. D. P. Bliss, *A Handbook of Socialism* (New York, 1895), p. 257; Frank Parsons, *The City for the People* (Philadelphia, 1901), pp. 64, 73, 77–81, 228; Alpheus T. Mason, *Brandeis, A Free Man's Life* (New York, 1946), pp. 106–117; *Dawn*, IV (Dec. 31, 1892); Horace G. Wadlin, "The Sweating System in Massachusetts," *Journal of Social Science*, XXX (Oct. 1892), 86–102.

4. Frederick A. Bushée, "The Growth of the Population of Boston," *American Statistical Association*, VI (June 1899), 240–263; Robert H. Lord, *History of the Archdiocese of Boston in the Various Stages of Its Development, 1604–1943* (New York, 1944), III, 64 ff.; Frederick A. Bushée, "Ethnic Factors in the Population of Boston," *Publications of the American Economic Association*, IV (March 1903), 147; Solomon Schindler, *Israelites in Boston* (Boston, 1889), chap. I; Herlihy, *Fifty Years of Boston*, pp. 715, 726; Boston *Pilot*, Dec. 30, 1882, Jan. 5, April 5, Aug. 23, 1884, Sept. 25, 1886; Albert Bushnell Hart, ed., *Commonwealth History of Massachusetts* (New York, 1930), IV, 613; James Jeffrey Roche, *The Life of John Boyle O'Reilly* (New York, 1891), pp. 301–302; *Labor Leader*, May 9, 1891; Robert A. Woods, ed., *Americans in Process, a Settlement Study* (Boston, 1902), pp. 11–70; Woods, ed., *The City Wilderness, a Settlement Study* (Boston, 1898), pp. 33–57; Edward Everett Hale, *If Jesus Came to Boston* (Boston, 1894), pp. 25–39; *Twenty-Third Report of the Massa-*

chusetts Bureau of Statistics of Labor (Boston, 1893), pp. 435–437.

5. *Twenty-Third Report*, pp. 194–195; Woods, *Americans in Process*, pp. 5, 24–30, 40, 41–42, 56.

6. Woods, *Americans in Process*, pp. 1–3, 94–95, 190–223, and *passim*; *Twenty-Third Report*, pp. 85–86.

7. Woods, *City Wilderness*, pp. 82–113, 176–200, and *passim*.

8. Walter Blackburn Harte, "The Back Bay, Boston's Throne of Wealth," *Arena*, X (June 1894), 6; M. A. DeWolfe Howe used the term "city wilderness" for the first time in an article in *The Atlantic Monthly* (Jan. 1896) and suggested to Robert Woods that it be used for his book, *The City Wilderness*. Woods, *City Wilderness*, p. v.

9. Woods, *City Wilderness*, p. 31; Bushée, "The Growth of the Population of Boston," *loc. cit.*, p. 266; Charles F. Dole, *My Eighty Years* (New York, 1927), p. 199; *Thirty-First Annual Report of the Bureau of Statistics of Labor* (Boston, 1901), p 62; Harte, "The Back Bay," *loc. cit.*, pp. 1–22; Herlihy, *Fifty Years of Boston*, pp. 337, 342–343.

10. Harte, "The Back Bay," *loc. cit.*, pp. 1, 18; Benjamin O. Flower, *Civilization's Inferno; Or, Studies in the Social Cellar* (Boston, 1893), pp. 13–14, 229.

11. *Twenty-Third Report*, pp. 396–410; *Labor Leader*, April 16, 1892.

12. Van Wyck Brooks, *New England: Indian Summer 1865–1915* (New York, 1940), pp. 331, 424–430; Cleveland Amory, *The Proper Bostonians* (New York, 1947), p. 53; Arthur M. Schlesinger, *The Rise of the City, 1878–1898* (New York, 1938), pp. 410–411; Herlihy, *Fifty Years of Boston*, p. 304.

13. Quoted in Brooks, *New England: Indian Summer*, p. 409; Henry Adams, *The Life of George Cabot Lodge* (Boston, 1911), pp. 15–16, 129–130; Francis Parkman, *Montcalm and Wolfe* (Boston, 1890), II, 410–414; Christina Hopkinson Baker, ed., *Diary and Letters of Josephine Preston Peabody* (Boston, 1925), p. 73.

14. Brooks Adams, Introduction to Henry Adams, *The Degradation of the Democratic Dogma* (New York, 1919), p. 93.

15. Henry Adams, *Degradation*, pp. vii, 78–86, 105–107.

16. Brooks Adams, *The Law of Civilization and Decay* (New York, 1896), pp. vii, ix, 313 ff.; Henry Adams, *Degradation*, pp. viii, 101. Henry and Brooks were silverites in 1896, but feared what Bryan and "the people behind him would not do, supposing they got into power." Thornton Anderson, *Brooks Adams, Constructive Conservative* (Ithaca, 1951), p. 59. On loss of faith in democracy, *ibid.*, p. 190.

17. Henry Adams, *Degradaton*, p. 108; Henry Adams, *History of the United States of America During the Administration of James Madison* (New York, 1930), IX, 241–242.

18. Henry Adams, *Democracy, An American Novel* (New York, 1880), p. 10.

19. Henry Adams, *Democracy*, p. 37.

20. Henry Adams, *Degradation*, pp. 98, 101–102, 140 ff.; Henry Adams, *The Education*, pp. 379 ff. For the fruit of Adams' labors in medievalism, see Henry Adams, *Mont-Saint-Michel and Chartres* (Boston, 1936), esp. pp. 87–103, 342–378.

21. Interest in pre-Civil War reformers and reform movements was at its height in the last quarter of the nineteenth century. See, for example, Thomas Wentworth Higginson, *Cheerful Yesterdays* (Boston, 1898), *Contemporaries* (Boston, 1899), *Margaret Fuller Ossoli* (Boston, 1884); Octavius Brooks Frothingham, *Transcendentalism in New England* (Boston, 1876), *Memoir of William Henry Channing* (Boston, 1886); Joseph Henry Allen, *Our Liberal Movement in Theology, Chiefly as Shown in Recollections of the History of Unitarianism in New England* (Boston, 1882); Julia Ward Howe, *Margaret Fuller (Marchesa Ossoli)* (Boston, 1882); *Works of Edward Everett Hale* (Boston, 1898–1903), 10 vols.; Edward Everett Hale, *James Russell Lowell and His Friends* (Boston, 1899), *James Freeman Clarke* (Boston, 1891); Franklin B. Sanborn, *A. Bronson Alcott: His Life and Philosophy* (Boston, 1893), *The Genius and Character of Emerson* (Boston, 1895), *Henry David Thoreau* (Cambridge, 1882), *The Life and Letters of John Brown* (Boston, 1885); *Letters of Lydia Maria Child*, Introduction by John Greenleaf Whittier, Appendix by Wendell Phillips (Boston, 1883); *William Lloyd Garrison, 1805–1879; the Story of his Life Told by his Children* (New York, 1885–1889), 4 vols. These are but a sample of the literature on the New England Renaissance. In addition, there were a number of autobiographies, some of which are cited in the footnotes of this chapter.

22. Julia Ward Howe, *Modern Society* (Boston, 1880), pp. 40, 64; Hale, quoted in Herlihy, *Fifty Years of Boston*, p. 304.

23. Thomas Wentworth Higginson, *Part of a Man's Life* (Boston, 1905), pp. 288–290, 300–301; Wendell Phillips, *The Scholar in a Republic* (Boston, 1881), pp. 1–36. Cf. Thomas Wentworth Higginson, *The Afternoon Landscape* (Cambridge, 1889), p. 67.

24. Mary Thatcher Higginson, *Thomas Wentworth Higginson, The Story of His Life* (Boston, 1914), pp. 142–151, 241–252; Carlos Martyn, *Wendell Phillips: The Agitator* (New York, 1890), p. 230; Frank-

lin B. Sanborn, *Recollections of Seventy Years* (Boston, 1909), I, 224; Julia Ward Howe, *Reminiscences, 1819–1899* (Boston, 1899), pp. 442–444; Mary Ashton Livermore, *The Story of my Life* (Hartford, 1897), pp. 143 ff.; Edwin D. Mead, "Boston Memories of Fifty Years," in Herlihy, *Fifty Years of Boston*, p. 28. For Mrs. Livermore's work with the Sanitation Commission, see especially her *My Story of the War* (Hartford, 1889). For Higginson's own account of his Civil War fighting days, see his *Army Life in a Black Regiment* (Boston, 1870).

25. Edward Everett Hale, *New England Boyhood and Other Bits of Autobiography* (Boston, 1900), p. 243; Howe, *Modern Society*, pp. 46–47; Wendell Phillips, *Speeches, Lectures, and Letters* (Boston, 1863), p. 53; Quoted in Edwin D. Mead, "Thomas Wentworth Higginson," reprint, *New England Magazine*, p. 11.

26. Martyn, *Wendell Phillips: The Agitator*, 133, 386 ff.; Thomas Wentworth Higginson, "On the Outskirts of Public Life," *Atlantic Monthly* LXXXI (Feb. 1898), 194; Mead, "Thomas Wentworth Higginson," *loc. cit.*, pp. 3, 11–12; Mary T. Higginson, *Thomas Wentworth Higginson*, 320, 335–336; Edward E. Hale, Jr., *The Life and Letters of Edward Everett Hale* (Boston, 1917), II, 122.

27. Parsons, *City for the People*, pp. 218, 239–240, 554; Edward Everett Hale, *Addresses and Essays* (Boston, 1900), pp. 371, 377–378, 380, 393–394; Hale, a book review of Edward Bellamy's *Looking Backward, Lend a Hand*, III (Oct. 1888), 551–554; Hale, "The Erie Canal," *Nationalist*, I (Nov. 1889), 244; Hale, "The Best Government," *ibid.*, I (June 1889), 37–40; Thomas Wentworth Higginson, "Step by Step," *ibid.*, I (Sept. 1889), 147–148; Franklin B. Sanborn, "The Social Sciences. Their Growth and Future," *Journal of Social Science*, XXI (Sept. 1886), 10.

28. Higginson, "Step by Step," *loc. cit.*, p. 147; Higginson, "The Heirs of Time," I, *Nationalist* (May 1889), 5.

29. Wendell Phillips, *Speeches, Lectures, and Letters* (Second Series, Boston, 1894), pp. 152, 163, 170.

30. Edward Everett Hale, *How They Lived at Hampton, a Study in Practical Christianity* (Boston, 1888), *passim; Lend a Hand*, IV (April 1889), 74.

31. For purpose of the journal, see *Lend a Hand*, I (Jan. 1886), 1–2. For the journal's occasional interest in profit-sharing, postal savings banks, temperance, labor arbitration, coöperative building associations, German social insurance laws, the municipal ownership of public utilities, and English settlement houses, see respectively I (June

1886), 380–381; I (April 1886), 246–248; II (Jan. 1887), 1–3; III (June 1888), 309; IV (April 1889), 251–254; III (June 1888), 340–341; extra-entire issue, IV (March 1889); IV (May 1889), 330–337. Cf. Edward Everett Hale, *Ten Times One and Other Stories* (Boston, 1899), pp. v–vi and *passim*.

32. For the activities of the American Social Science Association, see Franklin B. Sanborn, "History of the American Social Science Association," *Journal of Social Science*, XLVI (Dec. 1909), 2–6. For estimate of Sanborn, see Alexander Johnson, "An Appreciation of Franklin Benjamin Sanborn," *Survey*, XXXVII (March 10, 1917), 656–657. For representative samples of Sanborn's philosophy, see Franklin B. Sanborn, "The Work of Social Science," *Journal of Social Science*, VIII (May 1876), 26; Sanborn, "The Social Sciences. Their Growth and Future," *Journal of Social Science*, XXI (Sept. 1886), 6, 10; Sanborn, "The Commonwealth of Social Science," *ibid.*, XIX (Dec. 1884), 7; Sanborn, "Address of the Chairman," *ibid.*, XXII (June 1887), 98, 104, 105, 106; Sanborn, "Socialism and Social Science," *ibid.*, XXX (Jan. 1894), xii–xlvii; Sanborn, "Society and Socialism," *ibid.*, XXXI (Nov. 1895), 22, 23, 24, 25, 27; Sanborn, "Social Relations in the United States," *ibid.*, XXXVII (Dec. 1899), 74; Sanborn, "Social Changes in the United States in the Half Century, 1850–1900," *ibid.*, XXXVIII (Dec. 1900), 141.

33. Thomas Wentworth Higginson, *Contemporaries* (Boston, 1899), pp. 275–276.

34. Higginson, "On the Outskirts of Public Life," *loc. cit.*, p. 188; Franklin B. Sanborn, "Social Changes in the United States," *loc. cit.*, p. 141; Thomas Wentworth Higginson to William Jennings Bryan, Cambridge, Nov. 4, 1901, Thomas Wentworth Higginson Papers. Cf. Bryan to Higginson, Lincoln, Nebraska, Nov. 15, 23, Dec. 3, 1901, *ibid.*

35. John Boyle O'Reilly, "Wendell Phillips," *In Bohemia* (Boston, 1886), p. 20. For other tributes to Phillips, see George Lowell Austin, *The Life and Times of Wendell Phillips* (Boston, 1884), pp. 388–431. For description of the memorial meeting, see Lilian Whiting, *Boston Days* (Boston, 1902), pp. 66, 71. For desire to build temple of reform in honor of Phillips, see *Dawn*, III (Oct. 1891).

36. Benjamin O. Flower, *Progressive Men, Women, and Movements of the Past Twenty-Five Years* (Boston, 1915), pp. 42–46.

37. James Bryce, *The American Commonwealth* (London, 1891), II, 484.

38. Henry Adams, *Esther*, Facsimile Reprint of W. E. Gurney Copy (New York, 1938), p. 273. For importance of John Fiske, see Richard Hofstadter, *Social Darwinism in American Thought, 1860–1915* (Philadelphia, 1945), pp. 1, 2, 3, 73, 75, 76, 77, 78. For Fiske's chief work, see John Fiske, *Outlines of Cosmic Philosophy* (15th ed., Boston, 1894), I, 326–355; II, 3–31, 133 ff. For impact of science on religion, see Schlesinger, *The Rise of the City*, p. 322.

39. W. D. P. Bliss, "Hints Toward a Scientific Sociology," *Dawn*, IV (Nov. 2, 1892).

40. For change in American social science scholarship in the latter part of the nineteenth century, see Joseph Dorfman, *The Economic Mind in American Civilization, Volume III, 1865–1918* (New York, 1949), pp. 82 ff.; Ralph Henry Gabriel, *The Course of American Democratic Thought; An Intellectual History Since 1815* (New York, 1940), pp. 293–307; Henry F. May, *Protestant Churches and Industrial America* (New York, 1949), pp. 136–147; Hofstadter, *Social Darwinism*, 52–67, 124–133; Henry Steele Commager, *The American Mind* (New Haven, 1950), pp. 199 ff.

41. Helen M. Winslow, *Literary Boston of Today* (Boston, 1903), *passim*; Brooks, *New England: Indian Summer*, p. 379; Boston *Pilot*, April 28, 1887; Herlihy, *Fifty Years of Boston*, pp. 480–486, 505–521, 716.

Chapter II. Irish Catholic Liberalism: The Spirit of 1848

1. Quoted in Katherine Conway, "John Boyle O'Reilly," *Catholic World*, LIII (May 1891), 206; Conway, *Watchwords from John Boyle O'Reilly* (Boston, 1891), p. xxvii; Boston *Pilot*, Dec. 15, 1883.

2. John Herman Randall, *The Making of the Modern Mind* (Cambridge, 1940), pp. 544–545, 546–547.

3. Oscar Handlin, *Boston's Immigrants 1790–1865, A Study in Acculturation* (Cambridge, 1941), pp. 128–155. For similar Catholic reaction to New York humanitarianism, see Robert Ernst, *Immigrant Life in New York City 1825–1863* (New York, 1949), pp. 152–153.

4. Boston *Pilot*, Nov. 27, 1880; Robert H. Lord, *History of the Archdiocese of Boston in the Various Stages of its Development, 1604–1943* (New York, 1944), III, 358–382. For background of personalism in Catholic social thought up to the Civil War, see Celestine Joseph Nuesse, M.A., *The Social Thought of American Catholics, 1634–1829* (Washington, D.C., 1945), pp. 276–280.

5. Maurice Dineen, *The Catholic Total Abstinence Movement in*

the *Archdiocese of Boston* (Boston, 1908), *passim;* Handlin, *Boston's Immigrants*, p. 138.

6. Quoted in Boston *Pilot*, July 7, 1883. For fear of anticlerical liberalism leading to the formation of the Catholic Social Union in 1873; the activities and their purpose and extent of the St. Vincent de Paul Society; and agitation against England, see Lord, *History of the Archdiocese of Boston*, III, 384–385, 390–391. For representative samples of the literary output of Boston's Irish intellectuals, see Katherine Conway, *The Color of Life* (Boston, 1927); *A Dream of Lilies* (Boston, 1893); Henry Bernard Carpenter, *Liber Amoris, Being the Book of Love of Brother Aurelius* (Boston, 1887); *A Poet's Last Songs*, Introduction by James Jeffrey Roche (Boston, 1891); Mary E. Blake, *Verses Along the Way* (Boston, 1890); Louise Imogen Guiney, *"England and Yesterday"; A Book of Short Poems* (London, 1898); *The Secret of Fougereuse; a Romance of the Fifteenth Century; . . .* (Boston, 1898); *The Sermon to the Birds and the Wolf of Gubbio; . . .* (Cambridge, 1898); Robert Dwyer Joyce, *Ballads of Irish Chivalry; . . .* (Boston, 1872).

7. James Jeffrey Roche, *The Life of John Boyle O'Reilly* (New York, 1891), pp. 3–9, 10–11, 68 ff.; Conway, "John Boyle O'Reilly," *loc. cit.*, pp. 198–206; Richard E. Connel, "A Citizen of the Democracy of Literature," *Catholic World*, LXV (Sept. 1891), 751–759.

8. *Harper's Weekly* XXXIV (Aug. 23, 1890), 664; Roche, *John Boyle O'Reilly*, pp. 106, 155; Boston *Pilot*, Jan. 10, 1891; Appolinaris W. Baumgartner, *Catholic Journalism: A Study of its Development in the United States, 1789–1930* (New York, 1931), pp. 13, 58, 65. For tributes to O'Reilly as a poet, see Conway, *Watchwords from John Boyle O'Reilly*, pp. xix, xxix, xxxix, xl; *Memorial of John Boyle O'Reilly From the City of Boston* (Boston, 1891), *passim*.

9. O'Reilly to J, quoted in *Atlantic Monthly*, LXVI (Oct. 1890), 574. Cf. George Parsons Lathrop, "John Boyle O'Reilly as a Poet of Humanity," *Century Magazine*, XLIII (Dec. 1891), 314.

10. Quoted in *Atlantic Monthly*, LXVI (Oct. 1890), 574. For O'Reilly's attitude toward religion, see Roche, *John Boyle O'Reilly*, p. 377; Boston *Pilot*, Dec. 30, 1882; Jan. 5, April 5, 1884.

11. Conway, *Watchwords from John Boyle O'Reilly*, p. xxviii.

12. John Boyle O'Reilly, *The Statues in the Block* (Boston, 1881), pp. 38, 42; O'Reilly, *In Bohemia* (Boston, 1886), pp. 70–76; Roche, *John Boyle O'Reilly*, p. 410. For O'Reilly's first poems, see John Boyle O'Reilly, *Songs From the Southern Seas* (Boston, 1873).

13. O'Reilly, *The Statues in the Block*, pp. 42–44.

14. O'Reilly, *The Statues in the Block*, pp. 45–51; "Pilgrim Fathers" and "Crispus Attucks," in Roche, *John Boyle O'Reilly*, pp. 403, 410; O'Reilly, *In Bohemia*, p. 19.

15. John Boyle O'Reilly, ed., *Poetry and Song of Ireland* (New York, 1887), pp. iii, v, viii.

16. O'Reilly, *Moondyne*, pp. 118, 119, 261, *passim*.

17. John Boyle O'Reilly, Robert Grant, Frederic J. Stimson, John T. Wheelwright, *The King's Men* (Boston, 1884), p. 270.

18. Quoted in Boston *Pilot*, Jan. 10, 1891.

19. Boston *Pilot*, June 23, 1883. *Ibid.*, Dec. 15, 1883.

20. Boston *Pilot*, March 24, 1883; Feb. 2, 1884; Feb. 19, 1887; April 7, 1888.

21. Boston *Pilot*, June 26, Aug. 21, Dec. 11, 1880; Dec. 15, 1883; Jan. 19, 26, Feb. 2, March 15, 1884; Feb. 28, 1885; April 3, 10, Oct. 30, Nov. 13, 1886.

22. Boston *Pilot*, March 19, 1887.

23. Boston *Pilot*, Dec. 15, 1883; March 24, 1884; May 14, 1887; March 31, 1888.

24. Boston *Pilot*, Sept. 25, 1890.

25. Boston *Pilot*, Feb. 28, April 17, 1880; Feb. 3, 1883; Jan. 12, 1884; Oct. 10, 1885; April 10, May 1, 15, 27, July 31, Oct. 16, 1886; March 5, June 18, 1887.

26. Boston *Pilot*, June 12, 19, Sept. 11, 18, Oct. 2, 1886.

27. Boston *Pilot*, May 15, 1880; July 28, 1883; Jan. 29, 1887; Jan. 28, 1888.

28. Roche, *John Boyle O'Reilly*, p. 302; Boston *Pilot*, June 19, 26, July 3, 31, Sept. 25, Oct. 9, 30, Nov. 6, 1880; May 31, June 14, 21, July 5, 22, 29, Aug. 16, Oct. 4, 18, Dec. 13, 1884; May 30, 1885; June 16, Oct. 27, 1888.

29. Boston *Pilot*, April 19, July 12, 1884; April 24, Sept. 26, 1886; July 12, 26, 1884.

30. Boston *Pilot*, Sept. 25, Oct. 16, Nov. 6, Dec. 18, 25, 1886; Jan. 22, Feb. 19, July 16, Aug. 6, 1887; Feb. 18, 1888.

31. Boston *Pilot*, July 31, 1880; Dec. 29, 1883. For difference between pre- and post-Civil War attitude toward melting pot, see Ralph Henry Gabriel, *The Course of American Democratic Thought; An Intellectual History Since 1815* (New York, 1940), p. 45; Richard Hofstadter, *Social Darwinism in American Thought, 1860–1915*, pp. 144–154.

32. John Boyle O'Reilly, "The Negro American," Speech to Massa-

chusetts Colored League, Boston, Dec. 17, 1885, in Roche, *John Boyle O'Reilly*, pp. 738–742; Boston *Pilot*, June 5, 1880; June 19, Sept. 22, 1883; June 28, 1884; Dec. 15, 1888; Jan. 12, 1889.

33. Boston *Pilot*, June 12, 1880; July 14, 1883; Jan. 5, 1884; Sept. 19, 1885; April 25, Aug. 25, Dec. 22, 1888.

34. Lord, *History of the Archdiocese of Boston*, III, 64 ff.; Boston *Pilot*, Aug. 23, 1884; July 9, 1887.

35. Boston *Pilot*, Aug. 28, Nov. 10, 1880; May 24, July 26, 1884; Sept. 18, 1886; quoted in Roche, *John Boyle O'Reilly*, p. 331.

36. *Memorial of John Boyle O'Reilly*, pp. 39–40.

37. *Memorial of John Boyle O'Reilly*, p. 43. For attitude of O'Reilly toward monarchy, see Boston *Pilot*, Nov. 28, Dec. 19, 1885. For division among American Catholics on the Knights of Labor, see Henry J. Browne, *The Catholic Church and the Knights of Labor* (Washington, D.C., 1949), *passim*.

38. Handlin, *Boston's Immigrants*, pp. 146–147; Roche, *John Boyle O'Reilly*, pp. 43, 334; Boston *Pilot*, Sept. 10, 1881; Sept. 19, 26, Oct. 3, 17, Nov. 14, 1885; Nov. 9, 1889; July 26, 1890. O'Reilly joined the First Nationalist Club of Boston, Arthur E. Morgan, *Edward Bellamy* (New York, 1944), p. 251. An excerpt from his "City Streets" appeared in *The Nationalist*, I (Sept. 1889), 168. Otherwise he was not connected with Nationalism.

39. Dumas Malone, ed., *Dictionary of American Biography* (New York, 1935), XVI, 63; Walter Lecky, *Down at Claxton's* (Baltimore, 1895), pp. 89–91.

40. James Jeffrey Roche, *Songs and Satires* (Boston, 1887), pp. 14, 15–16; Lecky, *Down at Claxton's*, p. 84.

41. Boston *Pilot*, May 30, 1891; July 18, 25, 1896; Nov. 7, 1898; Nov. 10, 1900.

42. Boston *Pilot*, April 30, 1892; Feb. 20, Oct. 2, 1897; June 25, 1898; July 28, 1900.

43. Boston *Pilot*, May 30, 1891; May 7, July 16, August 6, 1892; Sept. 18, 1897; Oct. 13, 1900.

44. Boston *Pilot*, Oct. 30, 1897.

45. Boston *Pilot*, June 13, 1891.

46. Boston *Pilot*, Aug. 27, 1898.

47. Boston *Pilot*, Jan. 1, 1898; April 29, 1899.

48. Boston *Pilot*, Dec. 31, 1898; Sept. 30, 1899.

49. Boston *Pilot*, March 3, 1900.

50. Boston *Pilot*, June 16, 1900.

Chapter III.   Judaism: Premature Radicalism Aborted

This chapter entitled "Solomon Schindler: Boston Radical" appeared in somewhat different form in the *New England Quarterly*, Dec. 1950. It is printed with the permission of the *New England Quarterly*.

1. Solomon Schindler, "The Position and Mission of the Liberal Jew in the Nineteenth Century," p. 10, mss. lecture at the Globe Theatre, Boston, Mass., Dec. 16, 1888, Solomon Schindler Papers; Schindler, "The Ideal and the Real," mss. sermon at Temple Adath Israel, Boston, Mass., 189?, *ibid.*

2. *Pirke Abot*, IV, 16 (21), (Translation by Professor Harry A. Wolfson of Harvard); Edward Everett Hale, *New England Boyhood and Other Bits of Autobiography* (Boston, 1900), p. 243.

3. Schindler, *Israelites in Boston* (Boston, 1889), chap. v. The pages are not numbered; references will be given hereafter according to chapters.

4. *The Boston Daily Globe*, probably in 1886, Schindler Papers; *The Transcript*, May 6, 1915; Benjamin O. Flower, *Progressive Men, Women and Movements of the Past Twenty-Five Years* (Boston, 1914), pp. 173–174; *Jewish Advocate*, May 7, 1915, Schindler Papers; J. C. Rand, *One of a Thousand* (Boston, 1890), pp. 541–542; Dumas Malone, ed., *Dictionary of American Biography* (New York, 1928–1937), XVI, 433–435; A. G. Daniels, *History of the Jews of Boston and New England* (Boston, 1892), pages unnumbered. See the Schindler Papers, which are in the possession of Mrs. Claire Schindler Hamburger, daughter of Solomon, for the various degrees and teaching licenses that her father received in Germany (original German copies and English translations by Dr. Arnold Weinberger of Houghton Library).

5. Minutes of Temple Adath Israel, July 5, 1874, p. 219; Schindler, *Israelites in Boston*, chap. ii.

6. "Notes and Announcements," *Arena*, VI (1892), lvii, lviii; *ibid.*, VII (1892–1893), xix; *Psychical Review*, I (Aug. 1892), 96 (for Schindler's writings on spiritualism see Schindler, "Report," *Psychical Review*, I (Aug. 1892), 39–41; Schindler, "Experiment on Psychography," *ibid.*, I (Nov. 1892), 131–135); Arthur E. Morgan, *Edward Bellamy* (New York, 1944), pp. 65, 251; Minot J. Savage, *Bluffton: A Story of Today* (New York, 1878); Interviews with Mrs. Claire Schindler Hamburger and Dr. John Haynes Holmes; Flower, *Progressive Men, Women, and Movements of the Past Twenty-Five Years*, pp. 173–174; *Index*, Nov. 5, 1885, Schindler Papers.

7. *Jewish Advocate*, May 7, 1915, Schindler Papers. For O'Reilly's

"The Treasure of Abram," see Solomon Schindler, ed., *The Illustrated Hebrew Almanac for the Year 5641* (New York, 1880), p. 55.

8. Schindler, "The Position and Mission of the Liberal Jew in the Nineteenth Century," p. 10; Schindler, *Israelites in Boston*, chap. i.

9. Schindler, "Shifting Thoughts of a Shifting Mind," *Jewish Advocate*, undated, Schindler Papers; Schindler, *Israelites in Boston*, chap. ii; *Boston Daily Globe*, probably in 1886, Schindler Papers; Stella D. Obst, *The Story of Adath Israel* (Boston, 1927), pp. 16–17; Schindler, "Mistakes I've Made," Sermon at Temple Adath Israel, reprinted in *Jewish Advocate*, March 31, 1911. For comparable changes in other synagogues, see David Philipson, *The Reform Movement in Judaism* (New York, 1907), pp. 461–512 and *passim*.

10. For the ferment in American religion during Schindler's time, see Arthur M. Schlesinger, "A Critical Period in American Religion, 1875–1900," *Massachusetts Historical Society Proceedings* LXIV (1932), 523–547.

11. Minot J. Savage, Preface to Solomon Schindler, *Messianic Expectations and Modern Judaism* (Boston, 1886), p. ix; *Boston Daily Globe*, April 7, 1886, Schindler Papers; *Transcript*, April 7, 1886, *ibid.*

12. Schindler, "Jesus of Nazareth," mss. lecture, delivered for the first time in 1886 at the Free Congregational Society of Florence, Mass., Schindler Papers; *Boston Daily Globe*, March 8, May 24, 1886, *ibid.*

13. For Schindler's attacks on Orthodox Judaism, which were frequent, see particularly the following reprinted sermons in *Boston Daily Globe*, Jan. 23, May 24, Nov. 6, 1886, Schindler Papers; *Philadelphia Times*, Nov. 29, 1886, *ibid.*

14. Schindler, sermons at Temple Adath Israel, reprinted in *Boston Herald*, March 13, 1886, Schindler Papers; *Boston Daily Globe*, Oct. 23, Nov. 6, 1886, *ibid.*

15. Schindler, *Messianic Expectations and Modern Judaism*, pp. 3, 8, 10, 11, 13, 15 ff.

16. Schindler, *Messianic Expectations and Modern Judaism*, p. 166.

17. Schindler, *Messianic Expectations and Modern Judaism*, p. 167.

18. Schindler, "Modern Judaism," sermon at Philadelphia's Temple Keneseth Israel, reprinted in *Philadelphia Times*, Nov. 29, 1886, Schindler Papers; Schindler, *Messianic Expectations and Modern Judaism*, pp. 4–5; Schindler, *Israelites in Boston*, chap. ii.

19. Schindler, *Dissolving Views in the History of Judaism* (Boston, 1888), pp. 299–313 and *passim*; Schindler, *Messianic Expectations and Modern Judaism*, pp. 170–205.

20. *Christian Endeavor,* Jan. 27, 1887, Schindler Papers; *Transcript,* Nov. 14, Dec. 23, 1885, April 7, 1886, *ibid.; Index,* Dec. 24, 1885, *ibid.; Boston Daily Globe,* Nov. 9, 1885; Savage, Preface to *Messianic Expectations and Modern Judaism,* p. x; Schindler, "The Position and Mission of the Liberal Jew in the Nineteenth Century," p. 1.

21. Schindler, *Israelites in Boston,* chap. vii. For the Boston clergymen in the Nationalist movement, see James Dombrowski, *The Early Days of Christian Socialism in America* (New York, 1936), pp. 93–94; Charles Howard Hopkins, *The Rise of the Social Gospel in American Protestantism, 1865–1915* (New Haven, 1940), pp. 173–174.

22. Morgan, *Edward Bellamy,* pp. 65, 251.

23. Schindler, "Individualism and Socialism," p. 19, mss. lecture delivered first (repeated thereafter many times) in Cleveland, Ohio, Nov. 20, 1892, Schindler Papers; Schindler, "Nationalism Versus Individualism," *Arena,* III (April 1891), 601–607; Hamlin Garland, "A New Declaration of Rights," *ibid.,* III (Jan. 1891), 159–184.

24. Schindler, "What is Nationalism?" *New England Magazine,* VII (Sept. 1892), 56; Schindler, "Nationalism as a Religion," pp. 19–20, 24, mss. lecture delivered first at Tremont Temple, Boston, Nov. 21, 1890, Schindler Papers. Of "What is Nationalism?" Mary A. Livermore, feminist and Nationalist, wrote that of all the articles she had read on the subject none was so "well adapted to popular comprehension" as the one by Schindler. Livermore to Schindler, undated, "Notes and Announcements," *Arena,* V (1892–93), xlviii. For the use of Spencer by liberal clergymen, see Richard Hofstadter, *Social Darwinism in American Thought, 1860–1915* (Philadelphia, 1945), pp. 88–91.

25. *Boston Daily Globe,* July 17, 1889, Schindler Papers; Schindler, "The Use of Public Ways by Private Corporations," *Arena,* V (May 1892), 688; Schindler, "Natural Monopolies and the State," *ibid.,* IX (Jan. 1894), 234–237.

26. Schindler, *Young West* (Boston, 1894), pp. 83–84, 149–150.

27. Schindler, *Young West,* p. 283. For Schindler's faith in progress see his "Dr. Leete's Letter to Julian West," *Nationalist,* III (Sept. 1890), 81–86.

28. Edward Bellamy, *Looking Backward* (Modern Library ed., New York), pp. 221–239; Schindler, *Young West,* pp. 81–120; Schindler, sermon at Temple Adath Israel, reprinted in *Boston Daily Globe,* Dec. 25, 1886, Schindler Papers.

29. Bellamy, *Looking Backward,* p. 112; Schindler, *Young West,* pp. 221, 225–226, 245–250, 254–258.

30. Schindler, "Friends and Foes of Socialism," pp. 10, 13, 17, mss. lecture delivered in New York, undated, Schindler Papers; Schindler, "What is Nationalism?" *loc. cit.* 61; Schindler, "First Steps to Nationalism," *Arena*, XIII (June 1895), 29; Schindler, "Nationalization of the Railroads," *ibid.*, VII (Jan. 1893), 209–212; Schindler, "The Use of Public Ways by Public Corporations," *ibid.*, I (May 1892), 687–693; Schindler, "National Monopolies and the State," *ibid.*, IX (Jan. 1894), 234–237; Schindler, "The Nationalization of Electricity," *ibid.*, X (June 1894), 84–90; Schindler, "Insurance and the Nation," *ibid.*, X (Aug. 1894), 384.

31. For coverage of Schindler's dismissal, see the clippings in the Schindler Papers of Boston newspapers for April and May of 1893.

32. For Jewish charities, see *Hebrew Observer*, Dec. 27, 1882; *Jewish Chronicle*, Oct. 16, Dec. 18, 1891; Feb. 5, 26, 1892. In the twentieth century Louis D. Brandeis and Lincoln Filene, both Jews, were active Boston reformers. There was, however, nothing Jewish in the derivation of their reform. For the activities of the trade unionist, Henry Abrahams, see Chap. VIII. Again, there was nothing Jewish in Abrahams' social reform. A Marxian, he was an extreme secularist.

Chapter IV. Protestant Gospels of Social Redemption

1. Aug. 1896. Quoted in Aaron I. Abell, *The Urban Impact on American Protestantism, 1865–1900* (Cambridge, 1943), p. 63; Jesse H. Jones, *The Bible Plan for the Abolition of Poverty and the New Political Economy Therein* (Boston, 1873), pp. 40–41.

2. Arthur M. Schlesinger, *The American as Reformer* (Cambridge, 1950), p. 12.

3. Schlesinger, *The American as Reformer,* pp. 12–13; Charles Howard Hopkins, *The Rise of the Social Gospel in Amercan Protestantism, 1865–1915* (New York, 1940), pp. 3–5; Henry F. May, *Protestant Churches and Industrial America* (New York, 1949), pp. 30–32; Daniel Aaron, *Men of Good Hope, A Story of American Progressives* (New York, 1951), pp. 21–54.

4. Preface by Phillips Brooks to *Faith and Action* (Boston, 1886) — a compilation of Frederick Denison Maurice's writings; Minot J. Savage, *My Creed* (Boston, 1890), pp. 10, 12, 14; William Jewett Tucker, *My Generation, an Autobiographical Interpretation* (Boston, 1919), pp. 61, 92–94, 99; Jesse H. Jones to the Editor of the *Century*, Halifax, Mass., March 7, 1903, The Century Collection; George C. Lorimer, "The Newer Heresies," *Arena*, IV (Sept. 1891), 385–390;

Benjamin O. Flower, *Progressive Men, Women, and Movements of the Past Twenty-Five Years* (Boston, 1915), pp. 162–173; *Christian Register*, March 18, 1886. C. F. Elisabeth M. Herlihy (ed.), *Fifty Years of Boston, A Memorial Volume* (Boston, 1932), pp. 588–616; Charles Howard Hopkins, *The Rise of the Social Gospel*, pp. 5, 7; May, *Protestant Churches and Industrial America*, pp. 84–87; Stow Persons, *Free Religion, an American Faith* (New Haven, 1947), pp. 150–156; James Dombrowski, *The Early Days of Christian Socialism in America* (New York, 1936), pp. 18, 64; Abell, *The Urban Impact on American Protestantism*, pp. 224–232, 234–236, 239.

5. Abell, *The Urban Impact on American Protestantism*, pp. 62–66, 153–154, 160–161, 167, 174–175, 176, 180, 249; Charles Dickinson, "The Problem of the Modern City Church," *Andover Review*, XII (Oct. 1889), 355; Charles F. Dole, *My Eighty Years* (New York, 1927), pp. 198–199; Walter Blackburn Harte, "The Back Bay: Boston's Throne of Wealth," *Arena*, X (June 1894), 15; *Philo Woodruff Sprague, The Collected Essays of Eight Associates With a Foreword by His Bishop for Forty Years* (Charlestown, 1927), pp. 20–21, 41, 42; Editorial, "Social Classes and the Church," *Andover Review*, II (Sept. 1884), 290–297; Richard T. Ely, "Socialism," *ibid.*, V (Feb. 1886), 151; Newman Smyth, "Social Problems in the Pulpit," *ibid.*, III (April 1885), 300–301; John C. Kimball, "The Church as a Mediator Between the Different Classes of Society," *Unitarian Review*, XVII (June 1882), 481–499; *Dawn*, I (July 15, 1889), 4; George R. Lewis, "A Plea for the Poor," *The Unitarian*, I (May 1886), 126–127.

6. Abell, *The Urban Impact on American Protestantism*, pp. 27, 31–34, 35, 38, 56, 84; May, *Protestant Churches and Industrial America*, pp. 136–137; Tucker, *My Generation*, pp. 16–17.

7. *Christian Register*, March 25, 1886; Philo W. Sprague, *Christian Socialism, What and Why* (New York, 1891), p. 5; George Batchelor, *Social Equilibrium and Other Problems Ethical and Religious* (Boston, 1887), p. 29; Joseph Cook, *Socialism with Preludes on Current Events* (Boston, 1880), pp. vi, 50, 55–57, 67, 76, 79, 83; Minot J. Savage, *Social Problems* (Boston, 1886), p. 106; William J. Tucker, book review of John Rae, *Contemporary Socialism* (New York, 1884), *Andover Review*, II (Dec. 1884), 621; Ely, "Socialism," *ibid.*, V (Feb. 1886), 149; Newman Smyth, "The Claims of Labor," *ibid.*, III (April 1885), 303–305, 309. For the varied and conflicting definitions of socialism given by lexicographers, see Benjamin R. Tucker, *Instead of a Book, by a Man Too Busy to Write One* (New York, 1893), pp. 366–369.

8. *Dawn*, IV (Nov. 16, 1892), 2.

9. *Christian Register*, Feb. 21, 1884; *Congregationalist*, Jan. 10, 1884; *Unitarian Review*, VIII (Oct. 1877), 441; Editorial, *ibid.*, XIII (March 1880), 281; Nicholas Paine Gilman, "The Reaction Against Individualism," *ibid.*, XXV (March 1886), 218–234; E. H. Capen, "Some Modern Phases of Social Economy," *Universalist Quarterly*, XXIV (April 1887), 161–176; Nicholas Paine Gilman, "Realizable and Unrealizable Ideals," *ibid.*, XXXI (June 1889), 563; Editorial, *ibid.*, XXVIII (Nov. 1887), 457–464; William B. Weeden, "The Social Side of Massachusetts," *ibid.*, XV (June 1881), 496; William B. Weeden, "Mr. Heber Newton's Communism," *ibid.*, XVII (Feb. 1882), 150–160; book review of Laurence Gronlund, *The Coöperative Commonwealth*, *ibid.*, XXIV (Sept. 1885), 277–281; John C. Learned, "Capitalism and Communism," *ibid.*, XXVIII (Nov. 1887), 425–443; Savage, *Social Problems*, 106.

10. *Congregationalist*, Dec. 30, 1886; April 6, 1881; Feb. 11, 18, 25, March 4, 11, 1886; Jan. 13, 20, 1887; *Unitarian Review*, XXVI (Aug. 1886), 175–176; XXVIII (July 1887), 69–77; "Our Boston Anniversaries," *The Unitarian*, II (June 1887), 144; *Christian Register*, March 25, April 15, 1886; Jan. 19, 1888; July 9, 1896. For an example of ecclesiastical muckraking, see Louis A. Banks, *White Slaves, or The Oppression of the Worthy Poor* (Boston, 1892). *Lend A Hand*, I (Jan. 1886), 9–13; W. D. P. Bliss, ed., *The Encyclopedia of Social Reform* (New York, 1897), pp. 275–276. For representative pamphlets, of the Church Social Union, see Philo W. Sprague, "The Slums of Great Cities," No. 7 (Oct. 15, 1896); George Hodges, "Christian Socialism and the Social Union," No. 30 (Oct. 15, 1897); James Yeames, "Social Righteousness: II, The Law of Love as Set Forth by Jesus Christ," No. 61 (May 15, 1899); W. D. P. Bliss, "American Trade Unions," No. 10 (Jan. 15, 1896); W. D. P. Bliss, "Poverty and Its Causes," No. 25 (May 15, 1896).

11. *Congregationalist*, Jan. 12, Feb. 23, March 9, 1881; April 20, 1882; May 10, Nov. 22, Dec. 6, 1883; Jan. 10, April 3, 1884; Sept. 13, 1888; Dec. 7, 1893; March 1, 1894; Editorial, *Unitarian Review*, XIV (Oct. 1880), 369; *ibid.*, XVI (Dec. 1881), 558–561; Editorial, *ibid.*, XVII (April 1882), 363–365; *ibid.*, XXVI (July 1886), 88; *The Unitarian*, IX (April 1894), 177–178; *Christian Register*, Feb. 14, 1884; March 4, Dec. 9, 1886; Dec. 15, 1892; Julius H. Ward, *The Church in Modern Society* (Boston, 1889), *passim*; Batchelor, *Social Equilibrium*, *passim*; Phillips Brooks, *Addresses*, introduction by Julius H. Ward (Boston, 1893), pp. 70–95; Banks, *White Slaves*, pp. 201–208; 234–

238; Persons, *Free Religion*, pp. 74, 148; *Christian Register*, Feb. 9, 1888.

12. Cook, *Socialism with Preludes on Current Events*, pp. vi, 117, 164–166, 197, 306, and *passim*.

13. *Our Day*, I (Jan. 1888), 80; Louis A. Banks, "Crimes against Working Girls," *ibid.*, VIII (Oct. 1891), 252–258; W. E. Blackstone, "May the United States Intercede for the Jews?" *ibid.*, pp. 241–251; Florence Kelley Wischnewetzky, "Our Toiling Children," *ibid.*, VI (Sept. 1890), 192–197; Editorial, *ibid.*, V (March 1890), 254–257; Editorial, *ibid.*, II (Dec. 1888), 524, 525; Joseph Cook, "Edward Bellamy's Nationalism," *ibid.*, V (April 1890), 344.

14. Persons, *Free Religion*, pp. 74 ff.

15. Minot J. Savage, *The Religion of Evolution* (Boston, 1876), pp. 64 ff. For development of Savage's ideas from orthodoxy to advanced Unitarianism, see his autobiographical novel, *Bluffton: A Story of To-Day* (Boston, 1889), *passim;* Savage, *My Creed*, pp. 13–27. For his social views, see Savage, *Social Problems*, pp. 21–23, 106–112; Savage, *The Signs of the Times* (Boston, 1889), pp. 177, 185, 186; Savage, "Tyranny of Nationalism," *Arena*, IV (Aug. 1891), 315, 318, 320, 321; Savage, "Present Conflict for Larger Life," *ibid.*, X (Aug. 1894), 303, 305–306; Savage, "Mr. Bellamy's Nationalism," *Unity Pulpit*, XI, No. 20 (Feb. 21, 1890), 5–19; Savage, "Other Social Dreams," *ibid.*, XI, No. 22 (March 7, 1890), 5–8.

16. Minot J. Savage, "The Glory of a Common Life," *Unity Pulpit*, XIV, No. 31 (April 28, 1893), 5–6; Savage, "Jesus as to Wealth and Poverty," *ibid.*, XIV, No. 21 (Feb. 17, 1893), 14; Savage, "God in the City," *ibid.*, XVII, No. 1 (Sept. 27, 1895), 3–15.

17. Nicholas Paine Gilman, *Socialism and the American Spirit* (Boston, 1893), pp. 14, 46 ff.

18. Gilman, *Socialism and the American Spirit*, pp. 252 ff.; Gilman, *Proft Sharing Between Employer and Employee* (Boston, 1889), pp. 10, 412–445 and *passim*.

19. Gilman, *Socialism and the American Spirit*, pp. 16–24, 100–117, 350; Gilman, book review of Richard T. Ely's *French and German Socialism in Modern Times* and William Graham Sumner's *What Social Classes Owe to Each Other*, *Christian Register*, Feb. 21, 1884; Gilman, *Profit Sharing*, p. 445.

20. Charles F. Dole, *The Citizen and the Neighbor; or, Men's Rights and Duties . . .* (Boston, 1884), p. 51. For Gilman, see Abell, *The Urban Impact on American Protestantism*, p. 242.

21. Jesse H. Jones, *Joshua Davidson Christian, The Story of the Life*

of One, Who in the Nineteenth Century, "Was Like Unto Christ"; as Told by His Body Servant (New York, 1907), p. 139. For biographical material on Jones, see Introduction by Halah H. Loud to *ibid.*; *Dawn*, V (1892), 1. Jones reported to Loud that he read Finney at eleven, joined the church at twelve, and that thereafter "his theological ideas were well set." Introduction, p. vii. For the importance of Finney in American social reform, see Whitney R. Cross, *The Burned-Over District; The Social and Intellectual History of Enthusiastic Religion in Western New York* (Ithaca, 1950), pp. 158 ff.; Gilbert Hobbs Barnes, *The Anti-Slavery Impulse, 1830–1844* (New York, 1933), pp. 7–12; Alice Felt Tyler, *Freedom's Ferment; Phases of American Social History to 1860* (Minneapolis, 1944), pp. 41, 258, 490, 491.

22. Jones, *The Bible Plan for the Abolition of Poverty and the New Political Economy Involved Therein*, pp. 2, 5, 24–31, 37, 54–88; Jones, *Joshua Davidson*, pp. 34, 137–140, 183, 185–186, 188–189, 190, 222, 227.

23. Dombrowski, *The Early Days of Christian Socialism in America*, p. 83; Loud, Introduction, *Joshua Davidson*, p. xi.

24. Jones, *Joshua Davidson*, pp. v, 1–16, 21, 23, 114, 294, 308.

25. Ralph Henry Gabriel, *The Course of American Democratic Thought; An Intellectual History Since 1815* (New York, 1940), p. 315; W. D. P. Bliss, ed., *The New Encyclopedia of Social Reform* (New York, 1910), pp. 122–123; W. D. P. Bliss, *A Handbook of Socialism* (New York, 1895), pp. 209, 214; *Dawn*, III (Dec. 1890), inside page cover.

26. Hopkins, *The Rise of the Social Gospel*, p. 171; W. D. P. Bliss, "Socialism in the Church of England," *Andover Review*, X (Nov. 1888), 491–496; *Dawn*, I (May 15, 1899), 3; *ibid.*, II (June 1890), 100; W. D. P. Bliss, ed., James E. Thorald Rogers, *Six Centuries of Work and Wages, a History of English Labour* (New York, 1890), pp. 134, 160.

27. For support of Society, see *Dawn*, I (May 15, 1889), 4; *ibid.*, II (June 1890), 96–99; *ibid.*, I (June 15, 1889), 4; Hopkins, *The Rise of the Social Gospel*, pp. 175, 176, 177, 178.

28. *Dawn*, I (Aug. 15, 1889), 7; *ibid.*, II (May 1890); *ibid.*, I (Dec. 15, 1889), 3; *ibid.*, III (March 1892), 12; *ibid.*, III (April 1892), 9–12; *ibid.*, III (May 1, 1891), 2; *ibid.*, VI (Jan. 1894), 1; Philo W. Sprague, *Christian Socialism, What and Why* (New York, 1891), pp. 111, 113–114, 119, 120–129, 136, 138–146, 160–161; Bliss, *A Handbook of Socialism*, pp. 209, 232–233, 241–242.

29. Derivative rather than original thinkers, the Christian Socialists

were always editing someone's ideas. In the *Dawn*, see I (May 15, 1889), 6; II (Jan. 15, 1890), 2; II (June 1890), 103; II (May 1890), 4; III (May 1, 1891), 3; I (July 15, 1889); I (Sept. 15, 1889); III (Dec. 4, 1890), 11. In the *Handbook of Socialism*, see especially Appendices A and B. The Society, further, sold pamphlets and books of the major "socialist" thinkers, and as editor of the Humboldt Social Science Series, Bliss brought out *The Communism of John Ruskin* (New York, 1890); *William Morris, Poet, Artist, Socialist* (New York, 1891); Thorald Rogers, *Six Centuries of Work and Wages.*

30. *Dawn*, I (May 15, 1889), 1; *ibid.*, I (Aug. 15, 1889), 4; I (Jan. 15, 1890), 4.

31. *Dawn*, I (May 15, 1889), 2–3, 4; *ibid.*, I (Aug. 15, 1889), 7; *ibid.*, I (Oct. 15, 1889), 3; Gilman, *Socialism and the American Spirit*, p. 231.

32. Sprague, *Christian Socialism*, pp. 21–25; Philip Moxom, "Christian Socialism," *New England Magazine*, X (March 1894), 21–29; *Dawn*, I (Jan. 15, 1890), 1–3; Bliss, *A Handbook of Socialism*, p. 16.

33. *Dawn*, I (Jan. 15, 1890), 2; Bliss, *A Handbook of Socialism*, pp. vii, viii, 21–23, 193–194.

34. *Dawn*, I (Sept. 15, 1889), 5, 6; *ibid.*, I (Oct. 15, 1889), 5; *ibid.*, III (Dec. 4, 1890), 2; *ibid.*, III (Jan. 1, 1891), 11; *ibid.*, III (June 1, 1891), 1–4; *ibid.*, III (Oct. 1891), 2; *ibid.*, IV (April 1892), 5–9; *ibid.*, VII (Oct. 1895), 5. For description of Bliss's church, see *Dawn*, III (Dec. 4, 1890), 9; *ibid.*, III (March 21, 1891), 2; *ibid.*, III (Sept. 1891), 13; IV, *ibid.* (May 1892), 13; IV, *ibid.* (June 1892), 13.

35. *Dawn*, III (March 26, 1891), 2; *ibid.*, IV (June 1892), 4; *ibid.*, IV (Dec. 31, 1892), 2; Vida D. Scudder, *On Journey* (New York, 1937), p. 165.

36. Bliss, *A Handbook of Socialism*, p. 217; Herbert Newton Casson, *What We Believe* (Lynn, 1898), p. 5.

37. Casson, *What We Believe*, p. 2; Casson, *God Wills It* (n.p., n.d.), p. 2. For Casson's murky thinking on socialism, see Herbert Newton Casson, *The Socialism of Nature* (Lynn, 1895), *passim.*

38. Casson, *What We Believe*, pp. 3, 11; Casson, *God Wills It*, p. 8; Casson, *Who Is the Anarchist, Bryan or Hanna?* (Lynn, 1896), pp. 5, 8–9.

39. W. D. P. Bliss, "The Church of the Carpenter and Twenty Years After," *The Social Preparation for the Kingdom of God*, IX (Jan. 1922), 13.

40. Abell, *The Urban Impact on American Protestantism*, pp. 153–154, 160–161, 174–175, 176, 180, 249.

41. Bliss, Preface to Rogers, *Six Centuries of Work and Wages*, p. vi.

42. Gilman, *Socialism and the American Spirit*, p. 246.

43. For Bliss's admiration of the Anglican Church, its official position and some of its medieval ideas, see Bliss, "Socialism in the Church of England," *loc. cit.*, pp. 491–496, and his article in *The Encyclopedia of Social Reform* (New York, 1897).

44. For appeals for unity, see Ward, *The Church in Modern Society*, pp. 157 and *passim*; *Dawn*, III (Dec. 4, 1890), 8. For bickering among Social Gospelers, see *Dawn*, I (June 15, 1889), 3; Nicholas Paine Gilman, "Christian Socialism in America," *Unitarian Review*, XXXII (Oct. 1889), 345–357; Casson, *What We Believe*, pp. 3, 9, 11. For agreement on denominational level see May, *Protestant Churches and Industrial America*, pp. 182–203; Abell, *The Urban Impact on American Protestantism*, pp. 88–111.

Chapter V.   The Higher Learning: The Inductive Method and the Gentleman's Burden

1. Quoted in Samuel A. Eliot, "Francis Greenwood Peabody, His Work and Hopes for Hampton," *Southern Workmen*, LXVI (March 1937), 77; Robert A. Woods, "University Settlements as Laboratories in Social Science," address delivered in 1893 at the Chicago World's Fair, reprinted in Woods, *The Neighborhood in Nation-Building, the Running Comment of Thirty Years at the South End House* (Boston, 1923), p. 31.

2. Francis Greenwood Peabody, *The Religion of an Educated Man* (New York, 1903), p. 77; Elting E. Morison, ed., *The Letters of Theodore Roosevelt* (Cambridge, 1951), I, 42; Theodore Roosevelt, *An Autobiography* (New York, 1920), p. 25. For course offerings at the Boston schools, see *Harvard University Catalogue 1880–1881*, p. 119; *A Catalogue of the Officers and Students of Tufts College 1880–1881* (Boston, 1880), pp. 34–35; *Boston University Year Book* (Boston, 1880), pp. 78–79.

3. Roosevelt, *Autobiography*, p. 22; Owen Wister, *Philosophy Four* (New York, 1903) *passim*; Mary Kingsbury Simkhovitch, *Here is God's Plenty, Reflections on American Social Advance* (New York, 1949), p. 12. For experience of ministers, see Francis Greenwood Peabody, *Reminiscences of Present-Day Saints* (Boston, 1927), pp. 29, 66; William Jewett Tucker, *My Generation, an Autobiographical Interpretation* (Boston, 1919), pp. 55–58; Charles F. Dole, *My Eighty*

Years (New York, 1927), p. 107; Minot J. Savage, "The Irresistible Conflict Between Two World-Theories," *Unity Pulpit*, XII, No. 17, pp. 4–5; Savage, *My Creed* (Boston, 1890), p. 19.

4. *Harvard University Catalogue 1880–1881* (Cambridge, 1880), p. 97; Morison, *Letters of Roosevelt*, I, 25–26; Francis A. Walker, *Discussions in Economics and Statistics*, Davis R. Dewey, ed. (New York, 1899), I, 328.

5. Richard T. Ely, "Socialism," *Andover Review* V (Feb. 1886), 162; Carlos Martyn, *Wendell Phillips: The Agitator* (New York, 1890), pp. 520–605; quoted in Richard Hofstadter, *The American Political Tradition and the Men Who Made It* (New York, 1948), p. 161.

6. F. Spencer Baldwin, "Ideals of a College Education," *New England Magazine*, XVII (Jan. 1898), 573. Andover, while removed from Greater Boston, was tied to the city's intellectual and moral life. The Board of Overseers were often Bostonians; the Congregationalist ministers were frequently trained there; and the denominational newspapers looked to the seminary for formulations on sociology and theology. The heresy trial, resulting from the faculty's supporting Progressive Orthodoxy, involved Bostonians. Tucker, *My Generation*, pp. 100 ff.

7. James Phinney Munroe, *A Life of Francis Amasa Walker* (New York, 1923), pp. 11–26; Peabody, *Reminiscences*, pp. 1–21, 29, 49, 94, 181–204; Julia Shelley Hodges, *George Hodges, A Biography* (New York, 1926), pp. 13–15; Tucker, *My Generation*, pp. 7, 20–30.

8. Peabody, *Reminiscences*, pp. 117–118, 120–122, 157–167; *The Plummer Professor and University Preachers 1860–1904*, Peabody Quinquennial File; Tucker, *My Generation*, pp. 53, 90 ff.; Julia Hodges, *George Hodges*, p. 129; George Hodges, *Faith and Social Service, Eight Lectures Delivered Before the Lowell Institute* (New York, 1896), p. 100; James Arthur Muller, *The Episcopal Theological School, 1867–1943* (Cambridge, 1943), pp. 113–120; William Jewett Tucker, *The New Movement in Humanity from Liberty to Unity* (Boston, 1892), *passim*.

9. For the fame and activities of the Boston four, see the autobiographies and biographies already cited and the following of George Hodges' Scrapbooks, which contain memoranda of all sorts on clubs, philanthropies, and important people: *In Cambridge, January–June, 1894; In Cambridge, July–December, 1894; In Cambridge, July–December, 1895; In Cambridge, January–June, 1895*. For attitude toward mere wealth, see Munroe, *Walker*, p. 48; Julia Hodges, *George Hodges*, pp. 29, 30, 31, 32, 64, 108–115; Hodges, *Faith and Social*

Service, p. 71; William Jewett Tucker, "The Gospel of Wealth," *Andover Review,* XV (June, 1891), 636–637.

10. Walker, *Discussions,* II, 275 ff.; Francis Greenwood Peabody, *Jesus Christ and the Social Question* (New York, 1901), pp. 4, 14, 16 ff., 109, 298, 302; Peabody, "The Philosophy of the Social Questions," *Andover Review,* VIII (Dec. 1887), 562; Tucker, "The Gospel of Wealth," *loc. cit.,* p. 640; Hodges, *Faith and Social Service,* pp. 108–114; Ralph C. Larrabee, *Philosophy 5, Lectures by Professor F. G. Peabody, 1892–1893, Part I, October to January,* closing line, Peabody Quinquennial File.

11. Walker, *The Wages Question* (New York, 1876); Walker, *Discussions,* I, 305–306, 312–315, 316–317; II, 326, 328–329; Joseph Dorfman, *The Economic Mind in American Civilization, 1865–1918* (New York, 1949), III, 36–37.

12. Tucker, *My Generation,* pp. 97, 177–185; "Social Economics," I, "The Outline of an Elective Course of Study," *Andover Review,* XI (April 1889), 424–427; Larrabee, *Philosophy 5;* George Hodges, *Faith and Social Service,* p. 159.

13. Richard T. Ely, *Ground Under Our Feet, an Autobiography* (New York, 1938), p. 163. For the background of the American Economic Association and its professionalization, see L. L. Bernard, Jessie Bernard, *Origins of American Sociology, The Social Science Movement in the United States* (New York, 1943), pp. 527 ff. For representative articles in the *Andover Review,* see E. Benjamin Andrews, "Political Economy Old and New," X (Aug. 1888), 137–145; Edward W. Bemis, "Recent Economic Literature, " X (Nov. 1888), 555–559; Ely, "Socialism," V (Feb. 1886), 146–163.

14. Dorfman, *The Economic Mind,* III, 105–106; Walker, *Discussions,* II, 275 ff.; Peabody, *Jesus Christ and the Social Question,* 183 ff.; Tucker, "The Gospel of Wealth," *loc. cit.,* pp. 640–644; George Hodges, *Faith and Social Service,* pp. 217–241; George Hodges, *The Heresy of Cain* (New York, 1894), p. 202.

15. Peabody to Franklin B. Sanborn, undated, in Franklin B. Sanborn, "The Social Sciences. Their Growth and Future," *Journal of Social Science* XXI (Sept. 1886), 7–8; Tucker, *My Generation,* pp. 172–177; also see for Tucker's outline of Social Economics, *Andover Review* (1889–1892). For the kind of original research one such as Peabody undertook, see Francis Greenwood Peabody, *et al., The Liquor Problem, a Summary of Investigations Conducted by the Committee of Fifty, 1893–1903* (Boston, 1905), pp. 1–14. Cf. *Lend A Hand,* III (Jan. 1888), 33–34.

16. Munroe, *Walker*, p. 219; *Harvard University Catalogue 1900–1901* (Cambridge, 1900), p. 386; James Ford, "Social Ethics," in Samuel Eliot Morison, ed., *The Development of Harvard University Since the Inauguration of President Eliot, 1869–1929* (Cambridge, 1930), p. 224; Tucker, *My Generation*, p. 176; Tucker to those who would contribute funds to Andover House, Andover, Oct. 9, 1891, *Andover Review*, XVII (Jan.–June, 1892), 85; Edward Everett Hale, "The Kind of Church Needed in the Present Age," *Unitarian*, V (Jan. 1890), 10; Muller, *The Episcopal Theological School*, p. 137. Robert A. Woods gave the course at Cambridge Episcopal. For description, see *Episcopal Theological School Catalogues* (Cambridge, 1895–96), p. 23; (1897–98), p. 22; (1898–99), p. 21; (1899–1900), p. 22.

17. Peabody, *The Religion of an Educated Man*, pp. 36–37; Larrabee, *Philosophy 5*; *Harvard Advocate*, 1888, Peabody Quinquennial File. It is significant that Tucker sent his favorite student (Robert A. Woods) to England, and that Hodges named his Pittsburgh settlement house after Charles Kingsley.

18. *Harvard Advocate*, 1888, Peabody Quinquennial File; Sanborn, *loc. cit.*, pp. 7–8; James Dombrowski, *Early Days of Christian Socialism in America* (New York, 1936), pp. 67–68; Tucker, *My Generation*, p. 169; Eleanor H. Woods, *Robert A. Woods, Champion of Democracy* (Boston, 1929), pp. 18–19, 20, 26–27.

19. *The Mail and Express*, Dec. 4, 1897, Peabody Quinquennial File. Cf. Robert A. Woods, Albert J. Kennedy, *Handbook of Settlements* (New York, 1911), pp. 136–137; Robert E. Ely, "The Work of the Prospect Union," *Publications of the Church Social Union*, No. 31 (Nov. 1896), pp. 1–24; Larrabee, *Philosophy 5*; Peabody, *Jesus Christ and the Social Question*, pp. 337–338; Peabody, "The Privilege of the Scholar," *Christian Register*, Nov. 19, 1896.

20. Eleanor H. Woods, *Woods*, pp. 13, 18–23, 24, and *passim*.

21. Robert A. Woods, *Diary*, April 27, 1890, Robert A. Woods Papers; Eleanor H. Woods, *Woods*, pp. 21–22, 24, 31–32.

22. Woods, *Diary*, April 1, 1890; Eleanor H. Woods, *Woods*, pp. 33–44.

23. Robert A. Woods, *English Social Movements* (New York, 1891), pp. vi, 263–265 and *passim*; Woods, "The Social Awakening in London," in *Scribner's Magazine*, ed., *The Poor in Great Cities* (New York, 1895), pp. 1–42; Woods, book review of Charles Booth's *Labor and Life of the People, Andover Review*, XVII (Feb. 1892), 222; Woods, book review of Charles Booth's *Pauperism and the Endowment of Old Age, ibid.*, XIX (Nov.–Dec. 1893), 774; Woods, book review

of W. G. Collingwood's *The Life of John Ruskin, ibid.*, p. 763; Woods, " 'In Darkest England, and the Way Out' — General Booth's Social Plans," *ibid.*, XIV (Nov. 1890), 485–490.

24. Eleanor H. Woods, *Woods*, pp. 39, 47–49; Woods, book review of *Labor and Life, loc. cit.*, p. 222.

25. Robert A. Woods, "The University Settlement Idea," Address delivered in the Summer School of Ethics at Plymouth, 1892, reprinted in Woods, *The Neighborhood in Nation-Building*, pp. 1–29; Woods to Miss Dawes, Dec. 20, 1892, Woods Papers.

26. Robert A. Woods, *English Social Movements*, p. 37; Woods, "The University Settlement Idea," p. 26; Woods, "University Settlements as Laboratories in Social Science," pp. 30–46. Cf. Tucker, "The Work of the Andover House in Boston," *The Poor in Great Cities*, pp. 180–181; "Articles of Association," *Andover Review*, XVII (Jan. 1892), 87; Editorial, *ibid.*, XVII (Jan. 1892), 82–83.

27. Eleanor H. Woods, *Woods*, pp. 62, 68–69, 71–74, 84–85, 91–93, 103–104, 109; Woods and Kennedy, *Handbook of Settlements*, pp. 126–127.

28. Robert A. Woods, "Settlement Houses and City Politics," *Municipal Affairs*, June 1900, reprinted in Woods, *The Neighborhood in Nation-Building*, pp. 68–71; Eleanor H. Woods, *Woods*, pp. 120–121, 126–127, 140.

29. Quoted in Eleanor H. Woods, *Woods*, pp. 152, 156. For the bibliography of Andover House, see Woods and Kennedy, *Handbook of Settlements*, pp. 128–130.

30. Robert A. Woods, "University Settlements as Laboratories in Social Science," pp. 31, 43; *Boston University Year Book* (Boston, 1891), p. 121. For activities of Radcliffe, Wellesley, Boston University, Harvard, and Andover, see Woods and Kennedy, *Handbook of Settlements*, pp. 105, 109, 113.

31. See for example, Robert A. Woods, ed., *The City Wilderness, a Settlement Study* (Boston, 1898), pp. 58–81; Woods, ed., *Americans in Process. A Settlement Study* (Boston, 1902), pp. 40–70. For the later activities of settlement workers in the restriction movement, see Barbara Solomon's Ph.D. Dissertation (Harvard), *New England Pride and Prejudice: A Study in the Origins of Immigration Restriction.*

32. See, for example, *Harvard University Catalogue* for 1893–94, pp. 95–97; 1896–97, p. 106; 1897–98, p. 346; 1898–99, p. 352; *Catalogue of the Officers and Students of Boston College* (Boston, 1899), pp. 34–38; *A Catalogue of the Officers and Students of Tufts College 1899–1900* (Boston, 1899). Cf. Aaron I. Abell, *The Urban Impact on*

American Protestantism (Cambridge, 1943), pp. 235, 236, 239, 241, 243.

33. F. Spencer Baldwin, *Die Englischen Bergwerksgesetze, Ihre Geschichte von ihren Anfängen bis zur Gegenwart* (Stuttgart, 1894), p. 258; *Boston University Year Book* (Boston, 1895), pp. 67, 68.

34. Baldwin, "The United States and the Philippines," *Arena*, XXII (Nov. 1899), 575; Baldwin, "Ideals of College Education," *loc. cit.*, p. 577.

35. Baldwin, "The Present Position of Sociology," *Popular Science*, LV (Oct. 1899), 817; Hugo R. Meyer, *Municipal Ownership in Great Britain* (New York, 1906), p. 330. Cf. his *The British State Telegraphs; A Study of the Problem of a Large Body of Civil Servants in a Democracy* (New York, 1907), pp. 390–392; *Government Regulation of Railway Rates, a Study of the Experience of the United States, Germany, France, Austria-Hungary, Russia and Australia* (New York, 1905), pp. viii, 449 ff.; *Public Ownership and the Telephone in Great Britain* (New York, 1907), pp. 348–364. All four books were in preparation since 1892. Meyer, *Municipal Ownership*, p. vii. For radicalism in universities, see "Academic Freedom: A Symposium," *Arena*, XXII (Oct. 1899), 463–482; Thomas E. Will, "A College for the People," *ibid.*, XXVI (July 1901), 15–20; Will, "A Menace to Freedom: The College Trust," *ibid.*, XXVI (Sept. 1901), 244–257.

Chapter VI. Frank Parsons: The Professor as Radical

This chapter, entitled "Frank Parsons: The Professor as Crusader," appeared in somewhat different form in the *Mississippi Valley Historical Review* (December 1950). It is printed with the permission of the *Mississippi Valley Historical Review*.

1. Quoted in Benjamin O. Flower, "Professor Frank Parsons, Ph.D.: An Appreciation," *Arena*, XL (Nov. 1908), 498; Flower, "An Economist with Twentieth Century Ideals: Professor Frank Parsons, C. E., Ph.D., Educator, Author, and Economist," *ibid.*, XXVI (Aug. 1901), 157.

2. Flower, *Progressive Men, Women, and Movements of the Past Twenty-Five Years* (Boston, 1915), p. 113; Interview with Philip Davis, associate of Frank Parsons in settlement work, Boston, April 15, 1949; Interview with Ralph Albertson, Parsons' best friend and literary executor, Washington, D. C., April 1, 1949; "Edwin D. Mead's Tribute to Professor Frank Parsons," *Arena*, XL (Dec. 1908), 640; Frank Parsons, "The Philosophy of Mutualism," *ibid.*, IX (May 1894), 783; Parsons, "Youth and the World," chap. II, 6, Frank Parsons Papers.

3. Flower, "Economist with Twentieth Century Ideals," *loc. cit.*, pp. 157–160; *Industrialist* (Manhattan, Kan.), XXII (July 15, 1897), 164; handbill advertising Parsons' lectures, Parsons Papers; Francis Parkman to Parsons, May 2, 1890, *ibid.*; Phillips Brooks to Parsons, Oct. 1, 1889, *ibid.* For Parsons' outlines and teaching techniques at Boston University, see scattered memoranda, *ibid.*

4. Frank Parsons, *Our Country's Need, or, the Development of a Scientific Industrialism* (Boston, 1894), pp. xvii–xix. For Parsons' social criticism, see also the following series of articles in the *Arena*: "The Wicked Fact and the Wise Possibility," XXV (May 1901), 526–530; "Great Movements in the Nineteenth Century," XXVI (July–Aug. 1901), 1–14, 141–153; "Political Movement of the Nineteenth Century," XXVI (Sept. 1901), 258–273; "Causes of the Political Movements of Our Time," XXVI (Nov. 1901), 466–480.

5. Charles F. Taylor, "The Past Work of Equity Series," *Equity Series* (Philadelphia), VIII (Jan. 1906); *Arena*, XXXVI (Nov. 1906), 568. For a falling out between Parsons and Taylor over a personal quarrel, see Parsons to Taylor, undated; Taylor to Albertson, July 2, 1908, Parsons Papers. For Parsons' work for Bliss, see his "Municipal Railways," *Dawn* (Boston), VII (Jan. 1895), 8–9; "National Ownership of Railroads," *ibid.*, VII (Feb. 1896), 10–11; "Municipal Street Cars," *American Fabian* (Boston), I (Jan. 1895), 5; "Gabriel's Trumpet," *ibid.*, III (Oct. 1897), 3; "The Wisdom of Glasgow," *ibid.*, II (Dec. 1896), 1; "Compulsory Arbitration," *ibid.*, III (March 1897), 6–11. For work with N.C.F., see Frank Parsons, "History of the British Tramways," *Report of the National Civil Federation Commission on Public Ownership*, 3 vols. (New York, 1907), I, 261–303. For events leading up to the report, see Parsons, "The National Civic Federation and Its New Report on Public Ownership," *Arena*, XXXVIII (Oct. 1907), 401–408.

6. The following lecture notes have been preserved in the Parsons Papers: Fanny G. Noyes, "Notes on Nineteenth Century History"; Harriet A. Nichols, "Notes on Chapel Lectures"; "Civics Lectures for Winter Term, 1899." For character of Kansas State Agricultural College, see Frank Parsons, "The Regents' Investigation," *Industrialist*, XXV (June 1899), 381–382; *Industrialist*, XXII (July 15, 1897), 164–165. Thomas E. Will tried to make the college a center for liberal aspirations and turned the *Industrialist*, the college agricultural journal, into a reform organ. Parsons' contributions to the *Industrialist* reveal the general tenor of the magazine: an attack on Spencerian laissez faire called "The Functions of Government," XXIV (Jan. 1898), 22–

35; XXIV (Feb. 1898), 100–107; XXIV (March 1898), 162–175; XXIV (May 1898), 289–299; "Parties and the People," XXIV (Nov. 1898), 589–595; "Municipal Liberty," XXV (Jan. 1899), 3–11; XXV (May 1899), 267–275; XXV (June 1899), 372–377; "Glimpses of the Future," XXV (July 1899), 438–444. For Parsons and the Oxford movement, see President George McArthur Miller of Ruskin College, "To Whom it May Concern" (given to Parsons when he went abroad in 1901), June 22, 1901, Parsons Papers.

7. Interview with Albertson, April 1, 1949; interview with Davis, April 15, 1949; John M. Brewer, *History of Vocational Guidance* (New York, 1942), pp. 57–61.

8. Flower, "Economist with Twentieth Century Ideals," *loc. cit.*, p. 157; George H. Shibley, "Memorial Services in Memory of Professor Parsons in the Nation's Capital," *ibid.*, XL (Dec. 1908), 638; "Edwin D. Mead's Tribute to Professor Frank Parsons," *ibid.*, XL (Dec. 1908), 640–641.

9. For influence of Holmes, see Frank Parsons, *Legal Doctrine and Social Progress* (New York, 1911), dedication page. For that of Brooks, see Parsons, "My Philosophy of Life," manuscript lecture, Parsons Papers. Parsons revered Phillips Brooks and stated that Brooks's "splendid genius inspired" him. "Youth and the World," dedication page, *ibid.* For influence of Social Gospel on Parsons, see his praise of Josiah Strong, in Frank Parsons, F. E. Crawford, and H. T. Richardson, *The World's Best Books* (Boston, 1889), pp. 40, 46, 68. For Parsons' estimate of Herbert Spencer, *ibid.*, pp. 21–22, 41, 49, 68. For influence of economic nationalists, see Parsons, *The City for the People; or, the Municipalization of the City Government and of Local Franchises* (Philadelphia, 1901), *passim.*

10. Flower, "Economist with Twentieth Century Ideals," *loc. cit.*, p. 161; Brewer, *History of Vocational Guidance*, p. 53; Parsons, *Our Country's Need*, p. 154.

11. Parsons, *Our Country's Need*, pp. 8, 86–91; Parsons, Crawford, and Richardson, *World's Best Books*, p. 64; *New Nation*, II (April 16, 1892), 250.

12. *The Bibliotheca Sacra* (Oberlin, Ohio) L. (Jan. 1899), 120–121, 125, 138–139. The elements of the new political economy are scattered throughout Parsons, *Our Country's Need*. See also "Course in the New Political Economy," 1895, place where given unknown, Parsons Papers.

13. Parsons to Miss Holley, Nov. 24, 1890, Parsons Papers; Parsons, "Philosophy of Mutualism," *loc. cit.*, pp. 801–802, 812.

14. Parsons, "Philosophy of Mutualism," *loc. cit.*, pp. 798, 799; Parsons, *Our Country's Need*, pp. viii–x, 2, 5, 174, 176–186; Parsons, *The Drift of Our Time* (Chicago, 1898), pp. 7–10; Parsons, *Government and the Law of Equal Freedom* (Boston, 1892), p. 23.

15. Parsons, *Government and the Law of Equal Freedom*, pp. 1–11, 29; "Civic Lectures for Winter Term, 1899," Parsons Papers, *passim*; Parsons, *Our Country's Need*, pp. 160–162; Parsons, "The People's Highways," *Arena*, XII (April 1895), 218.

16. Parsons, "The Great Coal Strike and Its Lessons," *Arena*, XXIX (Jan. 1903), 3–7; Parsons, "The Truth at the Heart of Capitalism and of Socialism," *ibid.*, XXXVII (Jan. 1907), 7–10; Parsons to Dr. W. F. Warren, president of Boston University, June 7, 1902, Parsons Papers.

17. Parsons, *Drift of Our Time*, p. 7; Parsons, "The New Political Economy," *loc cit.*, p. 137; Parsons, "Philosophy of Mutualism," *loc. cit.*, p. 815; Parsons, "Parties and the People," *loc. cit.*, p. 594.

18. Parsons, *Rational Money* (Philadelphia, 1898), pp. iii–iv, 126–128, *passim*.

19. See Parsons' articles, "Chicago's Message to Uncle Sam," *Arena*, X (Sept. 1894), 494–496; "Compulsory Arbitration," *ibid.*, XVII (March 1897), 663–676; "Great Coal Strike and Its Lesson," *ibid.*, XXIX (Jan. 1903), 1–7; "The Abolition of Strikes and Lockouts," *ibid.*, XXXI (Jan. 1904), 1–11; Parsons, "Philosophy of Mutualism," *loc. cit.*, pp. 808, 810; Parsons, *Rational Money*, p. iv; "The Eight-Hour Movement Endorsed by Eminent Men," address before Boston Central Labor Union, Jan. 7, 1906, Parsons Papers. See special folder on the details of the campaign, *ibid.*

20. Parsons, *Our Country's Need*, p. 4; Parsons, "Philosophy of Mutualism," *loc. cit.*, p. 809. Parsons kept writing in this vein up to the time when he went into the slums. See, for example, Parsons, *The Story of New Zealand* (Philadelphia, 1904), p. 472; Parsons, "Australasian Methods of Dealing with Immigration," *Annals of the American Academy of Political and Social Science* (Philadelphia), XXIV (July 1904), 209–220.

21. Parsons, *City for the People*, pp. 251–253; Parsons, *The Railroads, the Trusts, and the People* (Philadelphia, 1905), pp. 451–462 (This work is a good example of scholarly muckraking. Parsons toured the country for information, went abroad and consulted with officials, businessmen, and such reformers as G. B. Shaw, Keir Hardie, and Sidney Webb. Ralph Albertson aided him in the research. *Ibid.*, pp. iii–iv. Out of his researches Parsons came to believe that discriminatory rates lay at the bottom of the problem and argued this view in

The Heart of the Railroad Problem (Boston, 1906), which Little, Brown and Company published after Parsons fell out with Taylor); Parsons, The Public Ownership of Monopolies (Boston, 1894), 5. Louis D. Brandeis criticized Parsons' approach in the public utilities struggles of Boston. Alpheus T. Mason, Brandeis, A Free Man's Life (New York, 1946), p. 136.

22. Parsons, "Legal Aspects of Monopoly," Edward W. Bemis, ed., Municipal Monopolies (New York, 1899), pp. 466–476; Parsons, The Telegraph Monopoly (Philadelphia, 1899), pp. 21–23, 69–77; Parsons, "The Telephone," Bemis, ed., Municipal Monopolies, p. 354; Parsons, Railroads, the Trusts, and the People, Pt. II, chaps. xxi–xxx; Parsons, "Reasons for Public Ownership of the Telephone," Municipal Affairs (New York), VI (Winter, 1902–03), 683–700; Parsons, "Glasgow's Great Record," Arena, XXXII (Nov. 1894), 461–471. These are only a sample of Parsons' works on the subject, the complete list being too extensive to enumerate. Railroads, the Trusts, and the People is perhaps the best sample of Parsons' approach to the economics of public monopoly. For Parsons' identification of equal sharing and coöperative labor with Mutualism, see in the Arena, "The Rise and Progress of Co-operation in Europe," XXX (July 1903), 27–36; "Co-operative Undertakings in Europe and America," XXX (Aug. 1903), 159–167; and "The City of the Future," lecture at the Filene's Coöperative Association meeting, June 10, 1904, Parsons Papers. Parsons was very active in the movement, helped to organize the Coöperative Association of America, and lost money in the project. Interview with Albertson, April 1, 1949. The profit-sharing plan of Filene's Boston department store aroused his warmest support; he made valuable suggestions to Filene and spoke many times to the Association. Mary La Dame, The Filene Store; a Study of Employees' Relation to Management in a Retail Store (New York, 1930), p. 430.

23. Parsons, Direct Legislation; or, The Veto Power in the Hands of the People (Philadelphia, 1900), passim; Parsons, City for the People, p. 328.

24. Parsons, City for the People, pp. 5, 7, passim; Parsons, The Bondage of Cities (Philadelphia, 1900), a reprint of Parsons' charges against city corruption. City for the People came out in expanded form in 1901; citations throughout this paper are to the later edition. The entire book is devoted to a factual description of these reforms — the obstacles confronting them, practical measures to attain them, and the benefits deriving from them.

25. Flower, Progressive Men, Women, and Movements, p. 134.

26. Parsons, *Story of New Zealand*, pp. x, xi, 347, 503, 510, 646, 710, 806. Henry Demarest Lloyd was a friend as dear to Parsons as Phillips Brooks had been. *Ibid.*, p. x.

27. Brewer, *History of Vocational Guidance*, p. 52; Roy W. Kelly, *Hiring the Worker* (New York, 1918), pp. 1–17.

28. Interview with Davis, April 15, 1949.

29. Brooks and James Russell Lowell letters to Parsons, in Parsons, *Our Country's Need*, pp. xiii–xv; Thomas E. Will, in "Memorial Services in Memory of Professor Frank Parsons in the Nation's Capital," *Arena*, XL (Dec. 1908), 637; "Testimony of Frank Parsons," *Report of the Industrial Commission* (Washington), No. IX (Aug. 6, 1901), 883–890; Parsons, "A Postal Telegraph," *Senate Documents*, No. 65 (Jan. 8, 1900), 56 Cong., 1 Sess., 1–170; Parsons, "Public Ownership," *ibid.*, No. 69 (Jan. 10, 1900), 56 Cong., 1 Sess., 1–20; Parsons, "Nationalization of the Railways," *ibid.*, No. 420 (May 18, 1900), 56 Cong., 1 Sess., 28–59; Parsons, *City for the People*, pp. 218, 611–613. In the Parsons Papers there is a box of letters written by eminent people to either Parsons or Taylor praising the book. See also the critical but favorable book reviews of Charles Zueblin, *International Journal of Ethics* (Philadelphia, Chicago), XI (Jan. 1901), 268–269; Samuel E. Sparling, *Municipal Affairs*, IV (June 1900), 405–406; Edward W. Bemis, *Annals of the American Academy of Political and Social Science* (Jan. 1901), 124–126. Benjamin O. Flower's review, *Arena*, XXV (Feb. 1901), 234–236, is laudatory.

Chapter VII. Writers and Artists in the Battalions of Reform

1. Hamlin Garland, *Under the Wheel, a Modern Play in Six Scenes* (Boston, 1890), Scene I, no page numbers; Edwin D. Mead, *The Philosophy of Carlyle* (Boston, 1881), p. 130; Benjamin O. Flower, *Gerald Massey: Poet, Prophet and Mystic* (Boston, 1895), p. 77.

2. Cf. Robert E. Spiller, Willard Thorp, Thomas H. Johnson, Henry Seidel Canby, eds., *Literary History of the United States* (New York, 1948), III, 331; Vernon L. Parrington, *Main Currents in American Thought* (New York, 1930), III, 54–60; Edwin D. Mead, "Boston Memories of Fifty Years," Elisabeth M. Herlihy, ed., *Fifty Years of Boston, A Memorial Volume* (Boston, 1932), p. 35.

3. The intellectuals did not create a myth. For role of writers in reform, see Arthur M. Schlesinger, *The American as Reformer* (Cambridge, 1950), pp. 6, 7, 12–17, 51; Boyd C. Shafer, "The American Heritage of Hope," *Mississippi Valley Historical Review*, XXXVII

(Dec. 1950), 427–450; Charles Madison, *Critics & Crusaders* (New York, 1947), pp. 3 ff.; Arthur M. Schlesinger, Jr., *The Age of Jackson* (New York, 1946), pp. 159–176, 306–321, 361–390.

4. Cf. Frank K. Foster, *The Evolution of a Trade Unionist* (Boston, 1901), pp. 64–68.

5. Cf. Spiller, Thorp, Johnson, Canby, *Literary History of the United States*, II, 895.

6. Victor S. Yarros, "Philosophical Anarchism, Its Rise, Decline, and Eclipse," *American Journal of Sociology*, XLI (Jan. 1936), 470, 472; Madison, *Critics & Crusaders*, pp. 195–198; Eunice M. Schuster, *Native American Anarchism, a Study of Left-Wing American Individualism* (Northampton, 1933), p. 140; Benjamin R. Tucker, *Instead of a Book, By a Man Too Busy to Write One* (New York, 1897), dedication page, and p. 30. This volume, consisting of selections from *Liberty*, Tucker's chief organ, is his only attempt to present his ideas systematically. His selections are arranged conveniently under the following headings: State Socialism and Anarchism, The Individual, Society and the State, Money and Interest, Land and Rent, Socialism, Communism, Methods.

7. Yarros, "Philosophical Anarchism," *loc. cit.*, p. 472. For examples of the controversies among Tucker and his staff, Henry Appleton, C. M. Hammond, Dyer D. Lum, J. William Lloyd, Gertrude P. Kelley, A. P. Kelly, Sarah E. Holmes, and Victor S. Yarros, see *Liberty*, IV (Feb. 26, 1887), 5; (March 12, 1887), 4; (March 26, 1887), 5; (Aug. 13, 1887), 7; (Aug. 27, 1887), 5; VI (Oct. 13, 1888), 5. Controversies ranged from the finer points of free love to the distinctions between opposing the state in general to a particular state.

8. Tucker, *Instead of a Book*, pp. 14, 15, 31, 40; Yarros, "Philosophical Anarchism," *loc. cit.*, p. 472; Madison, *Critics & Crusaders*, p. 194; Schuster, *Native American Anarchism*, pp. 140–156.

9. Tucker, *Instead of a Book*, pp. 6, 9, 11–18, 362, 363–365, 474, 476–480.

10. Tucker, *Instead of a Book*, pp. 14, 371–374, 414; *Liberty*, IV (Feb. 12, 1887), 4; *ibid.*, IV (Feb. 26, 1887), 5.

11. Tucker, *Instead of a Book*, pp. x, 7–8, 316–322, 375–378, 383–403, 412, 421–434, 439–449, 455–456.

12. *Liberty*, VII (March 21, 1891), 8.

13. Madison, *Critics & Crusaders*, p. 197; Schuster, *Native American Anarchism*, pp. 152–156; Yarros, "Philosophical Anarchism," *loc. cit.*, pp. 477–478; Tucker, *Instead of a Book*, advertisement of *Liberty*, next to last page; *Liberty*, IV (July 2, 1887), 4. Spooner was a tireless

worker for anarchism. His chief works during the 1880's, which were advertised in *Liberty*, are: *Natural Law or the Science of Justice* (Boston, 1882); *A Letter to Thomas F. Bayard* (Boston, 1882); *A Letter to Grover Cleveland* (Boston, 1886). In his works, Spooner argued that man was free by nature and that government was usurpation. Victor S. Yarros, Tucker's lieutenant, abridged Spooner's chief work, *Free Political Institutions* (Boston, 188?).

14. W. D. P. Bliss, *A Handbook of Socialism* (New York, 1895), p. 227; Dumas Malone, ed., *Dictionary of American Biography* (New York, 1932), VIII, 14; Arthur E. Morgan, *Edward Bellamy* (New York, 1944), pp. 251, 389; W. D. P. Bliss, *The Encyclopedia of Social Reform* (New York, 1897), p. 674.

15. Laurence Gronlund, *The Coöperative Commonwealth* (Boston, 1884), pp. 7, 8, 10, 11.

16. Gronlund, *The Coöperative Commonwealth*, pp. 8, 9, 12–74, 88, 89, and *passim*; Malone, ed., *Dictionary of American Biography*, VIII, 15.

17. Morgan, *Edward Bellamy*, 389–392; Malone, ed., *Dictionary of American Biography*, VIII, 15. For Gronlund's best statement on Christianity and socialism, see his *Our Destiny* (Boston, 1891), *passim*. See also his following articles: "The Misapprehensions of Socialism," *Dawn*, I (June, 1889), 2; "The Today of Labor," *ibid.*, I (Jan. 15, 1890), 7; "Nationalism," *Arena*, I (Jan. 1890), 153–165.

18. Bliss, *A Handbook of Socialism*, p. 257; *Dawn*, IV (May 1892), 10–12. Cf. Vernon Louis Parrington, Jr., *American Dreams, a Study of American Utopias* (Providence, 1947), pp. 131, 132, 134.

19. For Bellamy's contradictory claims, see Edward Bellamy, "How I Came to Write 'Looking Backward,'" *The Nationalist*, I (May 1889), 1; Bellamy, "How I Wrote 'Looking Backward,'" *Ladies Home Journal* (April 1894), reprinted in *Edward Bellamy Speaks Again* (Kansas City, 1937), p. 217. Bellamy's critics were quick to point out, after Bellamy first confessed that he wrote *Looking Backward* as a fantasy, that Nationalism was impractical. See Nicholas Paine Gilman, *Socialism and the American Spirit* (Boston, 1893), p. 210; Minot J. Savage, "Mr. Bellamy's Nationalism," *Unity Pulpit*, XI, No. 20 (Feb. 21, 1890), 10. For utopia and Peru, see Arthur E. Morgan, *Plagiarism in Utopia; a Study of the Continuity of the Utopian Tradition, with Special Reference to Edward Bellamy's Looking Backward* (Yellow Springs, Ohio, 1944), *passim*. For Morgan's view that utopian writers were thinking of lost civilizations, not dreaming, see his *Nowhere Was Somewhere, How History Makes Utopias and*

How Utopias Make History (Chapel Hill, 1946), pp. 8–9, and *passim*. Cf. John Hope Franklin, "Edward Bellamy and the Nationalist Movement," *New England Quarterly*, XI (Dec. 1938), 740–745.

20. Morgan, *Edward Bellamy*, pp. 31–32, 35, 41, 63, 145, 165, 254–255, 368, 372; Bellamy, "How I Wrote 'Looking Backward,'" p. 217; Bellamy, *The Religion of Solidarity* (Antioch, 1940), pp. 1–43. This is a published excerpt from Bellamy's journal by Arthur E. Morgan. For the outcrop of utopian literature in late nineteenth-century America, see Allyn B. Forbes, "The Literary Quest for Utopia, 1880–1900," *Social Forces*, VI (Dec. 1927), 180 ff.

21. Edward Bellamy, *Looking Backward* (Modern Library, New York), *passim*; Morgan, *Edward Bellamy*, pp. 247–252, 260–287, 295.

22. Cf. C. C. Regier, *The Era of the Muckrakers* (Chapel Hill, 1932), pp. 17–19, 23.

23. Edwin D. Mead, "Boston Memories of Fifty Years," *loc. cit.*, pp. 8, 10, 40. For Mead's veneration of the age of newness, see Mead, *The Influence of Emerson* (Boston, 1903), pp. 35–36, 72–74, and *passim*; Mead, *A Memorial of John Greenleaf Whittier* (Haverhill, 1893), pp. 71, 96–97, and *passim*; Mead, "Thomas Wentworth Higginson," Reprint from *New England Magazine*, pp. 1–15; Mead, "A Monument to Wendell Phillips," *ibid.*, III (Dec. 1890), 535–539; "Editor's Table," *ibid.*, VI (July 1892), 679–683; "Editor's Table," *ibid.*, VI (Aug. 1892), 820; "Editor's Table," *ibid.*, XVII (Dec. 1897), 510–516; "Editor's Table," *ibid.*, XV (Dec. 1896), 508–514. Cf. Mead, *The Philosophy of Carlyle*, pp. 41–44, 130, 131. See also the following articles in the *New England Magazine* which Mead solicited: Archibald H. Grimké, "Anti-Slavery Boston," III (Dec. 1890), 441–459; Franklin B. Sanborn, "Emerson and his Friends in Concord," III (Dec. 1890), 411–431; William M. Salter, "Emerson's Views on Reform," IV (July 1891), 656–664. For interest in non-Boston intellectuals, see Sylvester Baxter, "Walt Whitman in Boston," VI (Aug. 1892), 719, 721; Walter Blackburn Harte, "Walt Whitman's Democracy," VI (Aug. 1892), 721, 722.

24. "Editor's Table," *New England Magazine*, VI (April 1892), 267.

25. "Editor's Table," *ibid.*, XIII (Oct. 1895), 380–384; Mead, "Academic Freedom in America: The Collision at Brown University" (Boston, 1897), Reprint from the "Editor's Table" of the *New England Magazine*; "Editor's Table," *New England Magazine*, IV (June 1891), 539; "Editor's Table," *ibid.*, XIX (Nov. 1898), 387–392; "Editor's Table," *ibid.*, XIV (Oct. 1896), 256.

26. Mead, "Boston Memories of Fifty Years," *loc. cit.*, p. 33; "Edi-

tor's Table," *New England Magazine*, IX (Dec. 1893), 539–542; "Editor's Table," *ibid.*, XVII (Feb. 1898), 774–778; "Editor's Table," *New England Magazine*, X (May 1894), 387–392; "Editor's Table," *ibid.*, IV (June 1891), 539; "Editor's Table," *ibid.*, IX (Dec. 1893), 540.

27. Charles Welsh, "Workmen's Homes and Workmen's Trains," *ibid.*, XX (Aug. 1899), 764–766; "Editor's Table, *ibid.*, I (May 1890), 359–360; "Editor's Table, *ibid.*, IX (Jan. 1894), 667; "Editor's Table," *ibid.*, XIII (Oct. 1895), 254–255.

28. "Editor's Table," *New England Magazine*, XIV (March 1896), 123; "Editor's Table," *ibid.*, XIV (June 1896), 508–514; "Editor's Table," *ibid.*, XIV (July 1896), 636–640; "Editor's Table," *ibid.*, XX (April 1899), 253–259; "Editor's Table," *ibid.*, XX (July 1899), 636–648; "Editor's Table," *ibid.*, XIX (Oct. 1898), 259–268; "Editor's Table," *ibid.*, XIX (Sept. 1898), 130–136; "Editor's Table," *ibid.*, XIX (Dec. 1898), 520; Mead, "Boston Memories of Fifty Years," *loc. cit.*, pp. 32, 33, 34, 35.

29. Mead, "Boston Memories of Fifty Years," *loc. cit.*, p. 32; "Editor's Table," *New England Magazine*, V (Dec. 1891), 549. For an example of Foss's poetry of social significance, see his anti-war "Arbitration," *New England Magazine*, XVI (April 1897), 177. Mead boasted that he introduced and gave more space in his journal than any other American magazine to William Clarke, the English Fabian. For a representative sample of Clarke's essays in the *New England Magazine*, see his "William Morris," III (Feb. 1890), 740–749; "Carlyle and Ruskin and Their Influence on English Social Thought," IX (Dec. 1893), 473–488; "The Fabian Society," X (March 1894), 89–99; "The Life of the London Working Classes," X (July 1894), 572–584.

30. Editorial, *Arena*, III (Dec. 1890), 127. For biographical material, see Dumas Malone, ed., *Dictionary of American Biography* (New York, 1932), VI, 477–478; Regier, *The Era of the Muckrakers*, pp. 17–18; Howard F. Cline, "Benjamin Orange Flower and the Arena, 1889–1909," *Journalism Quarterly*, XVII (June 1940), 140–141.

31. Benjamin O. Flower, *The Century of Sir Thomas More* (Boston, 1896), pp. 183–184; Flower, "Guiseppe Mazzini," *Arena*, XXIX (March 1903), 264; Flower, *Gerald Massey, Poet, Prophet and Mystic*, pp. 47–48, 49–50; Flower, *Whittier; Prophet, Seer and Man* (Boston, 1896), *passim;* Flower, "Some of Civilization's Silent Currents," *Arena*, VI (Nov. 1892), 768; Flower, "There Dawned a Light in the East," *ibid.*, X (Aug. 1894), 342–352; Flower, "Social Ideals of Victor Hugo,"

ibid., X (June 1894), 104–109; Flower, "John Ruskin," *ibid.*, XVII (July 1897), 77.

32. Flower, *The Century of Sir Thomas More*, pp. 55, 91, 128, 285.

33. Flower, *Progressive Men, Women, and Movements of the Past Twenty-Five Years* (Boston, 1914), pp. 47–58; Flower, *The Century of Sir Thomas More*, p. 156; Flower, "The Menace of Plutocracy," *Arena*, VI (Sept. 1892), 509–516; Flower, "Religious Intolerance To-Day. Persecuted for Conscience Sake," *ibid.*, IV (Oct. 1891), 633. Cf. the following books published by the Arena Publishing Company: Henry L. Call, *The Coming Revolution* (Boston, 1895), *passim;* Dr. F. S. Billings, *How Shall the Rich Escape?* (Boston, 1893), *passim;* Frank Parsons, *Our Country's Need, or, the Development of a Scientific Industrialism* (Boston, 1894), pp. xvii-xix.

34. Flower, *The Century of Sir Thomas More*, p. 128; Flower, *Progressive Men, Women, and Movements*, p. 220; Flower, *Civilization's Inferno, or Studies in the Social Cellar* (Boston, 1893), *passim;* Editorial, *Arena*, I (April 1890), 629–630; Editorial, *ibid.*, III (Feb. 1891), 375–384; Editorial, *ibid.*, IV (Nov. 1891), 761–768; Editorial, *ibid.*, IV (Aug. 1891), 382–384; Flower, "An Epoch Making Drama," *ibid.*, IV (July 1891), 247; Lyman Abbott, "What is Christianity?" *ibid.*, III (Dec. 1890), 36–46; Helen Campbell, "Certain Convictions as to Poverty," *ibid.*, I (Dec. 1889), 101–113. This is but a sample of the muckraking indulged in by the *Arena*, the list being too long to enumerate.

35. Editorial, *Arena*, III (Jan. 1891), 250; Benjamin O. Flower, "The Coming Religion," *ibid.*, VIII (Oct. 1893), 647–656.

36. Editorial, *Arena*, II (Sept. 1890), 508.

37. Flower, *Progressive Men, Women, and Movements*, p. 18.

38. Flower, *Progressive Men, Women, and Movements*, pp. 76–78, 162–173, 223; W. D. McCrackan, "The Swiss Referendum," *Arena*, III (May 1891), 458–464; McCrackan, "The Swiss and American Constitutions," *ibid.*, V (July 1891), 172–179; McCrackan "Proportional Representation," *ibid.*, VII (Feb. 1893), 291, 294–297; McCrackan, "How to Introduce the Initiative and Referendum," *ibid.*, VII (May 1893), 696–700; McCrackan, "The Initiative in Switzerland," *ibid*, VII (April 1893), 549; Joseph Rhodes Buchanan, "Development of Genius by Proper Education," *Arena*, I (Dec. 1889), 55–68; Buchanan, "The New Education and Character Building," *ibid.*, VII (Feb. 1893), 268–278; Flower, Editorial, *Arena*, IV (Aug. 1891), 382–384; Flower, "Wellsprings and Feeders of Immorality," *ibid.*, XI (Dec. 1894), 56; Flower, "Lust Fostered by Legislation," *ibid.*, XI (Jan. 1895), 167–175;

Flower, "Social Conditions as Feeders of Immorality," *ibid.*, XI (Feb. 1895), 399–412; Carlos Martyn, "Churchianity vs. Christianity," *Arena*, II (July 1890), 154–155; George C. Lorimer, "The Newer Heresies," *ibid.*, IV (Sept. 1891), 385–390; Minot J. Savage, "Agencies That Are Working a Revolution in Theology," *ibid.*, I (Dec. 1889), 1–14.

39. Flower, *Progressive Men, Women, and Movements*, pp. 284–287.

40. For Garland in Boston, see Hamlin Garland, *A Son of the Middle Border* (New York, 1937), pp. 318 ff.; Garland, *Roadside Meetings* (New York, 1930), pp. 1 ff. For Garland's ideas, see Garland, *Crumbling Idols* (Chicago, 1894), pp. 43, 45, 52; Garland, "Mr. Howells' Latest Novels," *New England Magazine*, II (May 1890), 245–246, 249; Garland, "Ibsen as a Dramatist," *Arena*, II (June 1890), 82.

41. Garland, *Crumbling Idols*, pp. 52–53; Garland, "The Land Question and Its Relation to Art and Literature," *Arena*, IX (Jan. 1894), 173; Garland, "A New Declaration of Rights," *ibid.*, III (Jan. 1891), 166.

42. Flower, "Pure Democracy Versus Vicious Governmental Favoritism," *Arena*, VIII (July 1893), 261–269; Flower, "Four Epochs in the History of Our Republic," *ibid.*, XVI (Nov. 1896), 934. Cf. the following editorials in the *Arena*, XVI (June–Oct. 1896), 338–352, 524–528, 695–705, 1044–1050.

43. Flower, *Progressive Men, Women, and Movements*, p. 153; Cline, "Benjamin Orange Flower," *loc. cit.* p. 139; Editorial, *Arena*, III (Feb. 1891), 375; Editorial, *Arena*, III (April 1891), 632; Flower, *How England Averted a Revolution of Force* (Trenton, 1903), pp. 9–12.

44. For Harte's early career, see Mead, "Boston Memories of Fifty Years," *loc. cit.*, p. 32. For Harte's essays, see his *Meditations in Motley; a Bundle of Papers Imbued with the Sobriety of Midnight* (Boston, 1894). For admiration of Whitman, see Harte, "Walt Whitman's Democracy," *loc. cit.*, p. 722. For typical Bohemian articles see Harte, "Bubble and Squeak," *Fly Leaf*, I (Jan. 1895), 32; L. Lemmah, "The New God," *ibid.*, I (Jan. 1896), 21; Claude Fayette Bragdon, "The School of Necessity," *ibid.*, I (Jan. 1896), 23–24; Harte, "A Modest Proposal," *ibid.*, I (Feb. 1896), 2–12; Jonathan Penn, "A Little Commentary on Europe," *ibid.*, I (April 1896), 11; Harte, "The Apotheosis of the Harlot," *ibid.*, I (April 1896), 3–4; Harte, "Bubble and Squeak," *ibid.*, I (March 1896), 30–31.

45. Frank Parsons, *City for the People* (Philadelphia, 1901), pp. 218, 611–613. Flower, *Progressive Men, Women, and Movements*, pp. 128–130. For news of the Union for Practical Progress, see the *Arena*, IX–XIV (1893–1895).

46. Mead, "Boston Memories of Fifty Years," *loc. cit.*, pp. 36, 37. For typical program, see Twentieth Century Club, Announcement of Topics, Sept. 27, 1895, George Hodges, *In Cambridge: July–December, 1895*, George Hodges Papers.

47. Foster, *Evolution of a Trade Unionist*, pp. 15, 46, 67, 114, 163; *Labor Leader*, Aug. 27, 1887; April 4, Aug. 1, Nov. 14, Dec. 26, 1891; Feb. 13, May 14, Aug. 13, Nov. 26, Dec. 10, 1892; March 24, May 12, 1894; Sept. 28, Nov. 2, Dec. 7, 21, 1895; March 28, 1896.

Chapter VIII. The Workers: Coöperators and Collective Individualists

1. George E. McNeill, ed., *The Labor Movement: The Problem of To-Day* (Boston, 1887), p. 483; *Labor Leader*, Aug. 1, 1891.

2. McNeill, *The Labor Movement*, p. 198.

3. McNeill, *The Labor Movement*, pp. 195–196.

4. McNeill, *The Labor Movement*, p. 196.

5. For short accounts of these men and Boston labor movement, see *Labor Leader*, Jan. 15, 1887, March 6, 1897; McNeill, *The Labor Movement*, pp. 606, 611–612; Norman J. Ware, *The Labor Movement in the United States, 1860–1895* (New York, 1929), pp. 16, 20–21; John R. Commons *et al.*, *History of Labour in the United States* (New York, 1926), pp. 138–144.

6. George E. McNeill, *Unfrequented Paths* (Boston, 1903), p. 62.

7. W. D. P. Bliss, "The Church of the Carpenter Thirty Years After," *The Social Preparation for the Kingdom of God*, IX (Jan. 1922), p. 13; Bliss, *The Encyclopedia of Social Reform* (New York, 1897), p. 865; Frank K. Foster, "George E. McNeill," *Massachusetts Labor Bulletin*, XII (July–Dec. 1907), pp. 83–84, 87–89; McNeill, *The Labor Movement*, pp. 611–612; McNeill, *Unfrequented Paths*, pp. 63–64. For description of McNeill under the fictional guise of Ralph McLaren, see Frank K. Foster, *The Evolution of a Trade Unionist* (Boston, 1903), p. 40.

8. "Preamble of the Knights of Labor," in Richard T. Ely, *The Labor Movement in America* (New York, 1886), pp. 85–87; McNeill, *The Labor Movement*, pp. 38, 483–496. John R. Commons credits McNeill with writing the principles of the Knights of Labor. Dumas Malone, ed., *The Dictionary of American Biography* (New York, 1932),

XII, 151. Cf. Ware, *The Labor Movement*, p. 18, who credits the principles to Robert Schelling. For the social mobility of McNeill and such Knights as Terence V. Powderly, James L. Wright, and Charles H. Litchman, see McNeill, *The Labor Movement*, pp. 611–612; Ware, *The Labor Movement*, pp. 20–21; 28, 81–84; Foster, "McNeill" *loc. cit.*, p. 83.

9. Quoted in Selig Perlman, *A History of Trade Unionism in the United States* (New York, 1922), p. 45; McNeill, *The Labor Movement*, pp. 139–147, 482, 483. Cf. Ware, *The Labor Movement*, pp. 4–5, who thinks that Stewart believed in the eight-hour day as an end in itself.

10. McNeill, *The Labor Movement*, pp. 455, 456, 465–468, 469.

11. *Labor Leader*, Jan. 8, Jan. 15, Aug. 13, Aug. 20, Aug. 27, Sept. 17, Dec. 13, 1887; April 14, Sept. 8, 1888; Cyrus Field Willard mss. "Autobiography" (1938), pp. 7, 8, chap. ix; pp. 13–17, chap. x; T. V. Powderly, *Thirty Years of Labor, 1859–1889* (Columbus, 1889), pp. 289–295, 526–558; McNeill, *The Labor Movement*, pp. 169, 607–608; Ely, *The Labor Movement in America*, p. 78; Ware, *The Labor Movement*, pp. xvi-xvii, 104–105, 362–364; Ralph Henry Gabriel, *The Course of American Democratic Thought; An Intellectual History Since 1815* (New York, 1940), pp. 193–194.

12. McNeill, *The Labor Movement*, pp. 170, 423; Ely, *The Labor Movement in America*, p. 82; Joseph R. Buchanan, *The Story of a Labor Agitator* (New York, 1903), pp. 142 ff.; Donald L. Kemmerer, Edward D. Wickersham, "Reasons for the Growth of the Knights of Labor in 1885–1886," *Industrial and Labor Relations Review*, III (Jan. 1950), 213–220; Nathan Fine, *Labor and Farmer Parties in the United States, 1828–1928* (New York, 1928), p. 38; Ware, *The Labor Movement*, pp. 65–66, 68–69, 362–364; Commons, "George E. McNeill," *The Dictionary of American Biography*, p. 151.

13. For struggle in Boston between trade unionists and Knights see *Labor Leader*, Jan. 8, 15, 22, Aug. 27, Sept. 10, 17, 1887; Feb. 11, May 19, June 2, Sept. 8, 1888; McNeill, *The Labor Movement*, pp. 423–425; Ware, *The Labor Movement*, p. 115; Foster, "McNeill," *loc. cit.*, pp. 87–88. Cf. Samuel Gompers, *Seventy Years of Life and Labor, An Autobiography* (New York, 1925), I, 241–263; T. V. Powderly, *Thirty Years of Labor*, pp. 498–499, 639–641, 575, 576; *The Path I Trod, The Autobiography of Terence V. Powderly*, eds., Harry J. Carman, Henry David, Paul N. Guthrie (New York, 1940), pp. 47, 142, 234.

14. For Jones's attempts to revive the K. of L., see H. W. K. East-

man, *The Science of Government, A True Assay of the Crude Ore of Political Economy* (Lawrence, 1888), a murky millennial scheme which Jones helped to prepare. For McNeill's steadfastness see Foster, "McNeill," *loc. cit.*, pp. 90, 91, 92, 96; McNeill, *Unfrequented Paths*, p. 94. For his belief that Gompers was the heir of the eight-hour philosophy of Steward, see the pamphlet he wrote for Gompers for eight-hour agitation, 1888–1890: George E. McNeill, *The Eight-Hour Primer, The Fact, Theory and the Argument* (Washington, 1907), *passim*. For background, see Gompers, *Seventy Years of Life and Labor*, I, 288–310. Cf. McNeill, "The Great Federation of Labor," *American Federationist*, XI (Jan. 1904), 54; McNeill, "Labor's Advance. From the Old to the New Philosophy," *ibid.*, XI (Nov. 1904), 973–975; Anonymous, "The Late George E. McNeill," *ibid.*, XIII (July 1906), 470; McNeill, "The Trade Unions and the Monopolies," *ibid.*, III (Dec. 1896), 208–209; McNeill, "The Philosophy of the Labor Movement," a Paper read before the International Labor Congress, Chicago, Sept. 1893.

15. *Labor Leader*, Jan. 15, Aug. 27, Sept. 10, 17, 1887; Jan. 14, 21, Feb. 4, 11, 1888.

16. For the character of Boston's workers, see *Fourth Annual Report of the Bureau of Labor Statistics* (Boston, 1873), pp. 250–251; *Thirtieth Annual Report of the Bureau of Labor Statistics* (Boston, 1900), pp. 169–181; *Labor Leader*, Aug. 20, 1887; July 4, Aug. 8, Sept. 26, 1891; May 28, Oct. 8, 1892; Dec. 23, 1893; April 7, Sept. 22, Oct. 6, May 5, 1894; May 11, Dec. 21, 1895; March 7, 14, 28, 1896.

17. For the character of the Jacksonian worker, cf. Arthur M. Schlesinger, Jr., *The Age of Jackson* (New York, 1946), pp. 134, 306–317, 510–515; Joseph F. Blau, ed., *Social Theories of Jacksonian Democracy, Representative Writings of the Period 1825–1850* (New York, 1947), pp. xi-xii, xxiii-xxvii, 211–219; Oscar Handlin, Mary Flug Handlin, *Commonwealth, a Study of the Role of Government in the American Economy: Massachusetts, 1774–1861* (Cambridge, 1947), pp. 204–205, 282.

18. William Graham Sumner, *What Social Classes Owe to Each Other* (New York, 1883), pp. 36, 87–97, 101–111, 140–152, 168.

19. For a pen portrait of Abrahams, see Foster, *Evolution of a Trade Unionist*, p. 56. For description of Boston Central Labor Union, *ibid.*, p. 54; *Labor Leader*, April 13, 1895. For the cigar makers, *ibid.*, May 1, 1891. For socialist ideas, *ibid.*, July 21, 1894; Jan. 5, March 30, July 13, Sept. 21, 1895; Feb. 15, 1896; March 6, 1897. For threat of Marxians to Samuel Gompers, see Donald Drew Egbert, Stow Persons, eds., *Socialism and American Life* (Princeton, 1952), I, 244–253.

20. Biographical material for Foster is scarce. See *Leaves of History from Archives of the Boston Typographical Union* (Boston, 1898), pp. 27–29; Willard, "Autobiography," pp. 6, 7, 9, chap. ix; p. 5, chap. xi; McNeill, *The Labor Movement*, pp. 169, 607–608; Albert M. Heintz *et al.*, *History of the Massachusetts Federation of Labor, 1887–1935* (n.p., n.d.), pp. 18, 21, 34; "Beside Gompers Worked a Poet and Thinker," *Journal of Electrical Workers and Operators* (July 1947), pp. 264, 265, 291.

21. *Labor Leader*, Aug. 13, 1887; April 4, 25, 1891; May 12, 1892; Sept. 14, 1895; Aug. 7, 14, 1897.

22. *Labor Leader*, May 5, 1888; May 16, 1891; Nov. 5, 1892; Feb. 29, 1896; Foster, *Evolution of a Trade Unionist*, pp. 4–7, 9, 15, 46, 169, 173.

23. *Labor Leader*, Jan. 3, May 1, 1891; Nov. 5, 1892; June 16, 1894; June 8, Sept. 14, Oct. 12, 1895; Feb. 29, 1896.

24. *Labor Leader*, Feb. 18, 1888; Jan. 17, March 28, April 25, May 30, July 11, Aug. 15, Oct. 10, 1891; Aug. 13, Nov. 5, 1892; Sept. 14, Nov. 9, 1895; July 31, Sept. 4, 1897. Cf. Foster, *The Evolution of a Trade Unionist*, p. 117; Foster, *The Karma of Labor and Other Verses* (Boston, 1903), pp. 7, 116.

25. *Labor Leader*, Nov. 9, 1895.

26. *Labor Leader*, Feb. 18, 1888; Jan. 16, Aug. 6, 1892.

27. *Labor Leader*, Jan. 5, April 18, Sept. 17, 1887; Jan. 24, Feb. 14, March 7, April 4, May 1, May 8, 1891; Jan. 9, May 7, July 16, Oct. 8, Dec. 24, 1892; Jan. 25, Feb. 29, March 14, 1896; Sept. 4, 1897; Foster, *Evolution of a Trade Unionist*, p. 14.

28. *Labor Leader*, Jan. 31, May 16, June 13, July 11, Aug. 15, Sept. 26, 1891; Jan. 25, 1896.

29. Foster, *Evolution of a Trade Unionist*, p. 118. Cf. Foster, "Labor Politics, Policies and Platforms," *American Federationist*, I (March 1894), 5; Foster, "A Word About Trade Unionism," *ibid.*, IV (Sept. 1897), 148–150; Foster, "Trade Unionism and Social Reform," *ibid.*, VII (March 1900), 64–67; Foster, "The March of Labor," *ibid.*, VIII (July 1901), 249–252; Foster, "Spirit of the Labor Movement," *ibid.*, VIII (Sept. 1901), 342; Foster, "Condition of the American Working-Class: How Can It Be Benefited?" *Forum*, XXIV (Feb. 1898), 711–722. For Frank K. Foster's swan song, written before he left for California, see "Word About Trade Unionism," *Labor Leader*, Sept. 4, 1897.

30. *Dawn*, Dec. 7, 1892; *Labor Leader*, May 9, 1891; Oct. 8, 1892.

31. *Labor Leader*, Dec. 30, 1893; Jan. 6, 13, Feb. 17, 24, March 3, 10, 1894.

32. *Report of Proceedings of the Thirteenth Annual Convention of the American Federation of Labor* (Chicago, 1893), pp. 37–38; *Report of Proceedings of the Fourteenth Annual Convention of the American Federation of Labor* (Denver, 1894), pp. 36–37; *Labor Leader*, March 10, April 21, 28, June 23, July 28, Aug. 11, 25, Sept. 8, 22, Dec. 15, 22, 1894.

33. *Labor Leader*, Sept. 22, 1894.

34. Quoted in C. Vann Woodward, *Tom Watson*, (New York, 1938), p. 217. For the platform see *Labor Leader*, Sept. 29, 1894.

35. *Labor Leader*, June 2, 16, Sept. 8, Nov. 3, 10, 1894.

36. *Labor Leader*, Dec. 1, 8, 1894; Nov. 2, 9, 23, June 1, 8, Aug 3, Nov. 30, Dec. 14, 1895; Jan. 25, Feb. 22, 1896; March 6, 1897.

37. James Duncan, "The Passing of Frank K. Foster," *American Federationist*, XVI (Aug. 1909), 688–689; "Beside Gompers Worked a Poet and Thinker," *loc. cit.*, p. 264; Heintz, *History of the Massachusetts Federation of Labor*, p. 34.

38. For the Strasser quote see Eric F. Goldman, *Rendezvous With Destiny* (New York, 1952), p. 57. For the views of Foster and Gompers on immigration, compare Foster, *The Karma of Labor*, pp. 206–210; Gompers, *Seventy Years of Life and Labor*, II, 151–173; Arthur Mann, "Gompers and the Irony of Racism," *Antioch Review* (Summer, 1953), pp. 203–214.

39. Foster, *Evolution of a Trade Unionist*, p. 47; Foster, *The Karma of Labor*, pp. 209–210.

Chapter IX. The New and Newer Women as Reformers

1. *Woman's Journal*, July 17, 1880; Vida D. Scudder, "The Relation of College Women to Social Need," A Paper presented to the Associates of Collegiate Alumnae, Oct. 24, 1890, Vida D. Scudder Papers.

2. Mary A. Livermore, for example, whose "heart was so full of bitterness" for not being able to go to Harvard, never forgave the Cambridge institution. *Woman's Column*, May 7, 1898. Also, the feminists often quoted from Abigail Adams' wifely letter to husband John which, on the occasion of the Declaration of Independence, lamented: "I cannot say that I think you are very generous to the ladies, for, whilst you are proclaiming peace and good-will to men, emancipating all nations, you insist upon retaining an absolute power over wives." Quoted in Ednah D. Cheney, "The Women of Boston," Justin Winsor, ed., *The Memorial History of Boston* (Boston, 1881), IV, 340.

3. Cheney, "The Women of Boston," Winsor, ed., *The Memorial History of Boston*, pp. 343–348, 354; Harriet H. Robinson, *Massachusetts in the Woman Suffrage Movement* (Boston, 1881), pp. 117–165; James Bryce, *The American Commonwealth* (London, 1891), II, 600–601; *Woman's Column*, April 10, 1897; Francis G. Curtis, "Woman's Widening Sphere," Elisabeth M. Herlihy, ed., *Fifty Years of Boston* (Boston, 1932), pp. 627, 633; Susan B. Anthony and Ida Husted Harper, eds., *The History of Woman Suffrage* (New York, 1902), IV, 745.

4. Kate Gannett Wells, "The Transitional American Woman," *Atlantic Monthly*, XLVI (Dec. 1880), 820, 821. For Ibsen, see *Eighteenth Report of the Association for the Advancement of Women* (Fall River, 1891), p. 23. This association, organized in 1872, had among its more prominent members the following Bostonians: Julia Ward Howe, Abby May, Ednah D. Cheney, Kate Gannett Wells, Lillian Whiting, Dr. Zakrzewska. Mrs. Howe was president for many years. Highly respected by the male world for its moderation, the Association stimulated women to organize clubs, especially in the cities where it held conventions, at which time it discussed public problems. The philosophy of the Association was: "All girls should consider it disgraceful to be idlers. . . " *Tenth Annual Report* (Worcester, 1882), p. 7. For plays and playlets in women's press, see as examples, *Woman's Journal*, May 23, 1885; *Woman's Column*, Feb. 15, 1890; Jan. 13, 1894; Feb. 23, 1895; June 8, 1895. For a full-length equal rights drama, see Ella Cheever Thayer, *Lords of Creation* (Boston, 1883).

5. Alice Stone Blackwell, *Lucy Stone, Pioneer of Woman's Rights* (Boston, 1930), pp. vii, 161–168, and *passim*. For Lucy Stone's fame as an independent woman in a place as far away as Armenia, see *Woman's Column*, Jan. 6, 1894. For comparable widespread activities in pre-1880 days of Mary A. Livermore and Julia Ward Howe, see Mary A. Livermore, *My Story of the War* (Hartford, 1897), pp. 1 ff.; Julia Ward Howe, *Reminiscenses, 1819–1899* (Boston, 1899), pp. 1 ff. For the less famous but very important personages of Abby Morton Diaz and Ednah D. Cheney, see their autobiographies, respectively, *Bybury to Beacon Street* (Boston, 1887), *passim*; *Reminiscences* (Boston, 1902), *passim*.

6. For quotations, see *Woman's Column*, July 30, 1898; Robinson, *Massachusetts in the Woman Suffrage Movement*, p. 171. For associations, see Mrs. J. C. Croly, *The History of the Woman's Club Movement in America* (New York, 1898), pp. 600–674; Kate Gannett Wells, "The Boston Club Woman," *Arena*, VI (July 1892), 371; Henrietta

T. Wolcott, "Legislation to Prevent Cruelty to Children," *Papers Read Before the Association for the Advancement of Women at is Eleventh Annual Convention* (Buffalo, 1884), pp. 81–92; Julia A. Sprague, *History of the New England Women's Club from 1868 to 1893* (Boston, 1894), pp. 56, 87–99 and *passim*; Mrs. Walter A. Hall, Mrs. Joseph S. Leach, Mrs. Frederick G. Smith, *Progress and Achievement, a History of the Massachusetts State Federation of Women's Clubs, 1893–1931* (Norwood, 1932), pp. 5, 22, and *passim*.

7. Cf. Gunnar Myrdal, *An American Dilemma, The Negro Problem and Modern Democracy* (New York, 1944), pp. 1073–1079; Robinson, *Massachusetts in the Woman Suffrage Movement*, p. 50; Howe, *Reminiscences*, p. 373; Carrie Chapman Catt, Netti Rogers Shuler, *Woman Suffrage and Politics* (New York, 1926), pp. 13–18.

8. *Woman's Column*, Dec. 25, 1897; Thomas Wentworth Higginson, *Women and the Alphabet* (Boston, 1900), p. 21; "Helen H. Gardener," Dumas Malone, ed., *Dictionary of American Biography* (New York, 1931), VII, 135. Mrs. Gardener left her own brain to Columbia University, and it was evaluated by J. U. Papez, "The Brain of Helen H. Gardener," *American Journal of Physical Anthropology* (Oct.–Dec., 1927). Mrs. Gardener joined the ranks of Boston feminism in 1895, when her husband left New York to become business manager of the *Arena*. *Woman's Column*, Jan. 5, 1895.

9. *Our Famous Women*, no editor but contributions mostly by Bostonians and on Bostonians (Hartford, 1884); Frances E. Willard, Mary A. Livermore, eds., *A Woman of the Century. Fourteen Hundred-Seventy Biographical Sketches Accompanied by Portraits of Leading American Women in All Walks of Life* (Buffalo, 1893); Sarah Knowles Bolton, ed., *Famous Leaders Among Women* (Boston, 1895); Julia Ward Howe, ed., *Representative Women of New England* (Boston, 1904); Annie Nathan Meyer, ed., *Woman's Work in America* (New York, 1891), p. 2. Cf. Elizabeth Cady Stanton, Susan B. Anthony, Matilda Joslyn Gage, *The History of Woman Suffrage* (Rochester, 1886), III, iv.

10. *Woman's Column*, Feb. 1, 1896; *Woman's Journal*, June 18, 1881; Higginson, *Women and the Alphabet*, p. 35.

11. The *Woman's Journal*, started in 1870, and the *Woman's Column*, begun in 1887, were in the possession of the Blackwell family but served as the organs for the American Woman Suffrage Association and its New England and Massachusetts affiliates. The journals carried news of the movement at home and abroad, presented articles from William Lloyd Garrison, Jr., Elizabeth Stuart Phelps, Louisa May

Alcott, Julia Ward Howe, Mary A. Livermore, Charlotte Perkins Gilman, and many others. The *Journal* also printed the proceedings of the annual suffrage conventions.

12. The feminist movement attracted the interest of the younger generation of male reformers by the late 1880's (the Reverend Drs. Charles G. Ames, Minot J. Savage, John Graham Brooks, Philip Moxom, among others), but did not reach Boston's college girls until the late 1890's. *Woman's Column*, April 7, 1900.

13. Robinson, *Massachusetts in the Woman Suffrage Movement*, pp. 55, 67–89, 103–105; Howe, *Reminiscences*, p. 376; Madame Blanc, *The Condition of Woman in the United States*, Abby Langdon Alger, tr. (Boston, 1895), p. 105; Laura E. Richards, Maud Howe Elliott, assisted by Florence Howe Hall, *Julia Ward Howe, 1819–1910* (Boston, 1916), I, 360.

14. Blackwell, *Lucy Stone*, pp. 206–231; Stanton, Anthony, Gage, *The History of Woman Suffrage*, III, vi.

15. Blackwell, *Lucy Stone*, p. 222; Emanie Sachs, *"The Terrible Siren,"* Victoria Woodhull *(1838–1927)* (New York, 1928), pp. 65–74, 243, 252; *Woman's Journal*, March 11, 1899. The New York group accused the Bostonians of being ultra-conservative; and Sachs, *Victoria Woodhull*, p. 67, and Anna Garlin Spencer, *The Council Idea and Mary Wright Sewall* (New York, 1930), p. 2, agree with the charge. Actually, the Bostonians were limited, rather than conservative in their objectives — desirous only of female equality.

16. Thayer, *Lords of Creation*, p. 15; *Woman's Journal*, Feb. 5, 1887, *Julia Ward Howe Scrapbook*, I (AH85), 8–9; *Woman's Journal*, March 11, 1899.

17. Julia Ward Howe, *The Walk with God*, Laura E. Richards, ed. (New York, 1919), p. 78; Florence Howe Hall, ed., *Julia Ward Howe and the Woman Suffrage Movement* (Boston, 1913), p. 14. For the semi-religious atmosphere of the 1880 convention which celebrated the thirtieth anniversary of the first Massachusetts Woman Rights Convention, see Robinson, *Massachusetts in the Woman Suffrage Movement*, pp. 60–61, 228–229. For Lucy Stone, see Anthony and Harper, eds., *The History of Woman Suffrage*, IV, 712; Blackwell, *Lucy Stone*, p. 285; *Woman's Column*, Jan. 6, 1894.

18. *Woman's Column*, Jan. 2, Feb. 6, April 2, Dec. 3, March 26, 1892; Jan. 21, 1893; Jan. 30, 1897; Anthony and Harper, eds., *The History of Woman Suffrage*, IV, 744–746.

19. *Woman's Column*, Feb. 4, 1893; March 9, 1895. For the activities of the Woman's Education Association (formed in 1873) in higher

education and playgrounds, see *Twenty-Eighth Annual Report of the Woman's Education Association* (Boston, 1900), pp. 8–10, 16, 17.

20. Margaret Deland, *Golden Yesterdays* (New York, 1941), p. 73; Maud Howe Elliott, *Three Generations* (Boston, 1923), pp. 226–227. Lorin Deland's mother, a good Unitarian shocked by her son's conversion, was not reassured when he explained: "I assure you, he [Phillips Brooks] never said a word in his sermons that James Freeman Clarke himself could object to! (Dr. Clarke was a distinguished Unitarian minister.)" Deland, *Golden Yesterdays*, p. 118.

21. Deland, *John Ward, Preacher* (Boston, 1888), pp. 84, 85, 98, 140, 173–174, 190, 193, and *passim*. (Mrs. Deland's Social-Gospel novel followed on the heels of those by Olive Schreiner, a South African, *The Story of an African Town*, and Mrs. Humphry Ward, an Englishwoman, *Robert Elsmere*. All three shook up orthodox Calvinism. Deland, *Golden Yesterdays*, p. 222); *Woman's Column*, Nov. 16, 1895; Deland, *Golden Yesterdays*, p. 290; *Woman's Journal*, Feb. 5, 1887, *Julia Ward Howe Scrapbook*, I (AH85).

22. *Woman's Journal*, March 27, 1880. The A.W.S.A. and its New England affiliates avoided the bigotry of Eliza Trask Hill, head of the Independent Women Voters, which was formed in 1889, served through the *Woman's Voice*, and purporting to defeat Roman Catholics running for the School Board. Cf. Blackwell, *Lucy Stone*, p. 241. Nevertheless the equal righters often made the claim that intelligent native-born Protestant women would offset the foreign-born Catholic vote.

23. Julia Ward Howe, "Benefits of Suffrage for Women," *Papers Read Before the Association for the Advancement of Women at Its Eleventh Annual Congress Held at Chicago, Illinois, October, 1883* (Buffalo, 1884), p. 29; *Woman's Journal*, Feb. 15, 1890; Oct. 17, 1896.

24. Mary E. Livermore, "Centuries of Dishonor," *Arena*, I (Dec. 1889), 82 (this article was read widely, and in Portugal, Alice Moderno, editor of the *Diaro de Annuncios*, translated and circulated it as a tract. *Woman's Column*, Jan. 13, 1894); *Woman's Journal*, Feb. 11, 1882, Feb. 18, 1882; May 29, 1886; *Woman's Column*, Sept. 8, 1894; Jan. 29, 1896; Feb. 19, 1898; *Woman's Column*, June 2, 1900. For account of referendum, see *Woman's Column*, Sept. 14–Nov. 16, 1895.

25. *Tenth Annual Report of the Association for the Advancement of Women* (Worcester, 1882), pp. 7–8; *Woman's Journal*, Jan. 7, 1893; Jan. 4, 1896; Richards, Elliott, Hall, *Julia Ward Howe*, II, 187, 228;

Woman's Column, Jan. 25, 1896; Oct. 22, 1898; Jan. 14, 1899. During the height of the Armenian atrocities, Alice Stone Blackwell published *Armenian Poems* (Boston, 1896), sixty poems which she translated.

26. Julia Ward Howe, *Modern Society* (Boston, 1880), pp. 28, 32, 40, 44–45, 48; Croly, *The History of the Woman's Club Movement in America*, pp. 620–621. For examples of Livermore-Diaz writings, see Mary A. Livermore, "Along the Road," *Dawn*, I (July 15, 1889), 7; Livermore, "What is Christian Socialism?" *ibid.*, II (Oct. 1890), 221–223; Abby Morton Diaz, letter to the editor, *ibid.*, I (July 15, 1889), 5.

27. *Woman's Journal*, Jan. 17, 1880; Nov. 7, 1896; *Woman's Column*, July 23, 1892; Mary Earhart, *Frances Willard, From Prayer to Politics* (Chicago, 1944), pp. 246–247.

28. Higginson, *Women and the Alphabet*, pp. 21–22.

29. Vida D. Scudder, "The Effect on Character of a College Education," *Christian Union*, April 7, 1887, Scudder Papers; Ednah D. Cheney, *Nora's Return, a Sequel to "The Doll's House," of Henry Ibsen* (Boston, 1890), pp. 8, 60–61; Scudder, *Mitsu Yu Nissi, or a Japanese Wedding* (Boston, 1887), pp. 18 and *passim*.

30. Scudder, "The Educated Woman as a Social Factor," *Christian Union*, April 21, 1887, Scudder Papers. Of this article Hamilton W. Mabie, editor of the *Christian Union* wrote: "I have seen nothing so good." Mabie to Vida D. Scudder, May 9, 1887, New York, Scudder Papers.

31. *Boston Budget*, July 6, 189?, Scudder Papers; Scudder, *On Journey* (New York, 1937), pp. 15–96.

32. Scudder, *On Journey*, pp. 39, 43, 69, 72; Interview with Miss Vida D. Scudder, Spring, 1951, Wellesley, Mass.; Scudder, "The Contributor's Club," *Atlantic Monthly* (April 1890), p. 570, Scudder Papers.

33. Scudder, "The Moral Dangers of Musical Devotees," *Andover Review*, VII (Jan. 1887), 52; Wellesley College Midyear Examination, Jan. 1892, Scudder Papers; Scudder, *The Witness of Denial* (New York, 1895), pp. 87, 89, 151, and *passim*. For Miss Scudder's social approach to literature, see her *An Introduction to the Writings of John Ruskin* (Boston, 1890); *Prometheus Unbound, A Lyrical Drama by Percy Bysshe Shelley* (Boston, 1892); *The Life of the Spirit in the Modern English Poets* (Boston, 1897). For other examples of Miss Scudder's sociological interest in art, see her *The Grotesque in Gothic Art* (Boston, 1887). At the same time, Miss Scudder knew the contents as well as the significance of the literature she studied, as evidenced

by her lecture at the Browning Society: "Is Aprile a type of the Italian Renaissance?" Programme of the Boston Browning Society, 1892–93, Scudder Papers.

34. For the quotations, see Scudder, *Social Ideals in English Letters* (Boston, 1898), pp. 187, 191, 203, 205, 207, 257.

35. As stated in interview with Miss Scudder, Spring, 1951, Wellesley, Mass.; Scudder, "A Protest," June 16, 1887, Scudder Papers; Scudder, "The College Settlement Movement," *Smith College Monthly* (May 1900), pp. 447–454, *ibid.*; Scudder, "Appeal for a New Work," Feb. 12, 1889, *ibid.*, Scudder, "The Relation of College Women to Social Need," A Paper presented to the Association of Collegiate Alumni, Oct. 24, 1890, p. 3, *ibid.*

36. Robert A. Woods, Albert J. Kennedy, *Handbook of Settlements* (New York, 1911), pp. 109–111.

37. Woods, "The University Settlement Idea," *Andover Review*, XVIII (Oct. 1892), 317–339; Scudder, "The Place of the College Settlement," *ibid.*, XVIII (Oct. 1892), 345. Cf. Scudder, "College Settlements," *Far and Near*, IV (Dec. 1893), 24.

38. Scudder, *On Journey*, pp. 162, 165, 380; Scudder, *Social Ideals in English Letters*, pp. 60–62; Scudder, *Socialism and Spiritual Progress* (Boston, March, 1891), pp. 4, 7, 13, 15, 17, 18, 19. For Miss Scudder's contributions to the *Christian Social Union*, see her following pamphlets: "Christian Simplicity," No. 52 (Aug. 15, 1898); "Socialism and Spiritual Progress," No. 10 (Jan. 1896).

39. Scudder, *A Listener in Babylon. Being a Series of Imaginary Conversations Held at the Close of the Last Century* (Boston, 1903), pp. 4, 74, 292, and *passim*.

40. Scudder, *On Journey*, pp. 109–111, 135, 150.

41. Florence Converse, *The Burden of Christopher* (Boston, 1900), p. 6. Among Miss Converse's many books, see her *Efficiency Expert* (New York, 1934), a long poem attacking the evils of the Depression. Dedicated to Miss Scudder, the book has the sharply Ruskinesque social criticism expounded by the Wellesley professor.

42. Joseph Fletcher, ed., *Christianity and Property* (Philadelphia, 1947), p. 5. Miss Scudder contributed the section, "Anglican Thought on Property," to the volume. Cf. her *The Christian Attitude Toward Private Property* (Milwaukee, 1934); *Brother John — A Tale of the First Franciscans* (Boston, 1927); *The Franciscan Adventure* (Toronto, 1931). Miss Scudder also won scholarly recognition in the twentieth century, editing the following works on request for Everyman's Li-

brary: *Works of John Woolman* (1910); *Bede's History of England* (1911).

43. Interview with Miss Scudder, Spring, 1951, Wellesley, Mass.

Chapter X. Conclusion: "A Plea for the Dreamer"

1. Quoted in Thomas Wentworth Higginson, *Contemporaries* (Cambridge, 1900), p. 342.

2. Quoted in Daniel Aaron, *Men of Good Hope, A Story of American Progressives* (New York, 1951), p. 49.

3. As quoted by Miss Vida D. Scudder in interview with her, Spring, 1951, Wellesley, Mass.

4. Arthur O. Lovejoy, *Great Chain of Being, a Study of the History of an Idea* (Cambridge, 1936), p. 13.

5. Quoted in Lovejoy, *Great Chain of Being*, p. 20.

6. Quoted in Arthur M. Schlesinger, *The Rise of the City, 1878–1898* (New York, 1938), p. 439.

7. Frank K. Foster, *The Karma of Labor and Other Verses* (Boston, 1903), pp. 185–186.

Index

harper ☙ torchbooks

HUMANITIES AND SOCIAL SCIENCES

American Studies: General

THOMAS C. COCHRAN: The Inner Revolution: *Essays on the Social Sciences in History*   TB/1140
EDWARD S. CORWIN: American Constitutional History. △ *Essays edited by Alpheus T. Mason and Gerald Garvey*   TB/1136
CARL N. DEGLER, Ed.: Pivotal Interpretations of American History   TB/1240, TB/1241
A. HUNTER DUPREE: Science in the Federal Government: *A History of Politics and Activities to 1940*   TB/573
A. S. EISENSTADT, Ed.: The Craft of American History: *Recent Essays in American Historical Writing*
Vol. I   TB/1255;   Vol. II   TB/1256
OSCAR HANDLIN, Ed.: This Was America: *As Recorded by European Travelers in the Eighteenth, Nineteenth and Twentieth Centuries. Illus.*   TB/1119
MARCUS LEE HANSEN: The Atlantic Migration: 1607-1860. *Edited by Arthur M. Schlesinger*   TB/1052
MARCUS LEE HANSEN: The Immigrant in American History. *Edited with a Foreword by Arthur M. Schlesinger*   TB/1120
JOHN HIGHAM, Ed.: The Reconstruction of American History △   TB/1068
ROBERT H. JACKSON: The Supreme Court in the American System of Government   TB/1106
JOHN F. KENNEDY: A Nation of Immigrants. △ *Illus.*   TB/1118
RALPH BARTON PERRY: Puritanism and Democracy   TB/1138
ARNOLD ROSE: The Negro in America: *The Condensed Version of Gunnar Myrdal's An American Dilemma*   TB/3048
MAURICE R. STEIN: The Eclipse of Community: *An Interpretation of American Studies*   TB/1128
W. LLOYD WARNER and Associates: Democracy in Jonesville: *A Study in Quality and Inequality* ¶   TB/1129
W. LLOYD WARNER: Social Class in America: *The Evaluation of Status*   TB/1013

American Studies: Colonial

BERNARD BAILYN, Ed.: The Apologia of Robert Keayne: *Self-Portrait of a Puritan Merchant*   TB/1201
BERNARD BAILYN: The New England Merchants in the Seventeenth Century   TB/1149
JOSEPH CHARLES: The Origins of the American Party System   TB/1049
LAWRENCE HENRY GIPSON: The Coming of the Revolution: 1763-1775. † *Illus.*   TB/3007

LEONARD W. LEVY: Freedom of Speech and Press in Early American History: *Legacy of Suppression*   TB/1109
PERRY MILLER: Errand Into the Wilderness   TB/1139
PERRY MILLER & T. H. JOHNSON, Eds.: The Puritans: *A Sourcebook*   Vol. I   TB/1093;   Vol. II   TB/1094
EDMUND S. MORGAN, Ed.: The Diary of Michael Wigglesworth, 1653-1657: *The Conscience of a Puritan*   TB/1228
EDMUND S. MORGAN: The Puritan Family: *Religion and Domestic Relations in Seventeenth-Century New England*   TB/1227
RICHARD B. MORRIS: Government and Labor in Early America   TB/1244
KENNETH B. MURDOCK: Literature and Theology in Colonial New England   TB/99
WALLACE NOTESTEIN: The English People on the Eve of Colonization: 1603-1630. † *Illus.*   TB/3006
LOUIS B. WRIGHT: The Cultural Life of the American Colonies: 1607-1763. † *Illus.*   TB/3005

American Studies: From the Revolution to 1860

JOHN R. ALDEN: The American Revolution: 1775-1783. † *Illus.*   TB/3011
MAX BELOFF, Ed.: The Debate on the American Revolution, 1761-1783: *A Sourcebook* △   TB/1225
RAY A. BILLINGTON: The Far Western Frontier: 1830-1860. † *Illus.*   TB/3012
EDMUND BURKE: On the American Revolution. ‡ *Edited by Elliott Robert Barkan*   TB/3068
WHITNEY R. CROSS: The Burned-Over District: *The Social and Intellectual History of Enthusiastic Religion in Western New York, 1800-1850*   TB/1242
GEORGE DANGERFIELD: The Awakening of American Nationalism: 1815-1828. † *Illus.*   TB/3061
CLEMENT EATON: The Freedom-of-Thought Struggle in the Old South. *Revised and Enlarged. Illus.*   TB/1150
CLEMENT EATON: The Growth of Southern Civilization: 1790-1860. † *Illus.*   TB/3040
LOUIS FILLER: The Crusade Against Slavery: 1830-1860. † *Illus.*   TB/3029
DIXON RYAN FOX: The Decline of Aristocracy in the Politics of New York: 1801-1840. ‡ *Edited by Robert V. Remini*   TB/3064
FELIX GILBERT: The Beginnings of American Foreign Policy: *To the Farewell Address*   TB/1200
FRANCIS GRIERSON: The Valley of Shadows: *The Coming of the Civil War in Lincoln's Midwest: A Contemporary Account*   TB/1246
FRANCIS J. GRUND: Aristocracy in America: *Social Class in the Formative Years of the New Nation*   TB/1001
ALEXANDER HAMILTON: The Reports of Alexander Hamilton. ‡ *Edited by Jacob E. Cooke*   TB/3060

---

† The New American Nation Series, edited by Henry Steele Commager and Richard B. Morris.
‡ American Perspectives series, edited by Bernard Wishy and William E. Leuchtenburg.
* The Rise of Modern Europe series, edited by William L. Langer.
¶ Researches in the Social, Cultural, and Behavioral Sciences, edited by Benjamin Nelson.
§ The Library of Religion and Culture, edited by Benjamin Nelson.
Σ Harper Modern Science Series, edited by James R. Newman.
° Not for sale in Canada.
△ Not for sale in the U. K.

THOMAS JEFFERSON: Notes on the State of Virginia. ‡
    Edited by Thomas P. Abernethy   TB/3052
JAMES MADISON: The Forging of American Federalism:
    Selected Writings of James Madison. Edited by Saul
    K. Padover   TB/1126
BERNARD MAYO: Myths and Men: Patrick Henry, George
    Washington, Thomas Jefferson   TB/1108
JOHN C. MILLER: Alexander Hamilton and the Growth of
    the New Nation   TB/3057
RICHARD B. MORRIS, Ed.: The Era of the American Revo-
    lution   TB/1180
R. B. NYE: The Cultural Life of the New Nation: 1776-
    1801. † Illus.   TB/3026
FRANCIS S. PHILBRICK: The Rise of the West, 1754-1830. †
    Illus.   TB/3067
TIMOTHY L. SMITH: Revivalism and Social Reform:
    American Protestantism on the Eve of the Civil War
    TB/1229
FRANK THISTLETHWAITE: America and the Atlantic Com-
    munity: Anglo-American Aspects, 1790-1850 TB/1107
A. F. TYLER: Freedom's Ferment: Phases of American
    Social History from the Revolution to the Outbreak
    of the Civil War. 31 illus.   TB/1074
GLYNDON G. VAN DEUSEN: The Jacksonian Era: 1828-
    1848. † Illus.   TB/3028
LOUIS B. WRIGHT: Culture on the Moving Frontier
    TB/1053

American Studies: The Civil War to 1900

THOMAS C. COCHRAN & WILLIAM MILLER: The Age of Enter-
    prise: A Social History of Industrial America TB/1054
W. A. DUNNING: Essays on the Civil War and Reconstruc-
    tion. Introduction by David Donald   TB/1181
W. A. DUNNING: Reconstruction, Political and Economic:
    1865-1877   TB/1073
HAROLD U. FAULKNER: Politics, Reform and Expansion:
    1890-1900. † Illus.   TB/3020
HELEN HUNT JACKSON: A Century of Dishonor: The Early
    Crusade for Indian Reform. ‡ Edited by Andrew F.
    Rolle   TB/3063
ALBERT D. KIRWAN: Revolt of the Rednecks: Mississippi
    Politics, 1876-1925   TB/1199
ROBERT GREEN MC CLOSKEY: American Conservatism in
    the Age of Enterprise: 1865-1910   TB/1137
ARTHUR MANN: Yankee Reformers in the Urban Age:
    Social Reform in Boston, 1880-1900   TB/1247
WHITELAW REID: After the War: A Tour of the Southern
    States, 1865-1866. ‡ Edited by C. Vann Woodward
    TB/3066
CHARLES H. SHINN: Mining Camps: A Study in American
    Frontier Government. ‡ Edited by Rodman W. Paul
    TB/3062
VERNON LANE WHARTON: The Negro in Mississippi:
    1865-1890   TB/1178

American Studies: 1900 to the Present

RAY STANNARD BAKER: Following the Color Line: Ameri-
    can Negro Citizenship in Progressive Era. ‡ Illus.
    Edited by Dewey W. Grantham, Jr.   TB/3053
RANDOLPH S. BOURNE: War and the Intellectuals: Col-
    lected Essays, 1915-1919. ‡ Ed. by Carl Resek TB/3043
A. RUSSELL BUCHANAN: The United States and World War
    II. † Illus.   Vol. I TB/3044; Vol. II TB/3045
ABRAHAM CAHAN: The Rise of David Levinsky: a docu-
    mentary novel of social mobility in early twentieth
    century America. Intro. by John Higham   TB/1028
THOMAS C. COCHRAN: The American Business System:
    A Historical Perspective, 1900-1955   TB/1080
FOSTER RHEA DULLES: America's Rise to World Power:
    1898-1954. † Illus.   TB/3021
JOHN D. HICKS: Republican Ascendancy: 1921-1933. †
    Illus.   TB/3041
SIDNEY HOOK: Reason, Social Myths, and Democracy
    TB/1237
ROBERT HUNTER: Poverty: Social Conscience in the Pro-
    gressive Era. ‡ Edited by Peter d'A. Jones   TB/3065

WILLIAM L. LANGER & S. EVERETT GLEASON: The Challenge
    to Isolation: The World Crisis of 1937-1940 and
    American Foreign Policy
    Vol. I TB/3054; Vol. II TB/3055
WILLIAM E. LEUCHTENBURG: Franklin D. Roosevelt and
    the New Deal: 1932-1940. † Illus.   TB/3025
ARTHUR S. LINK: Woodrow Wilson and the Progressive
    Era: 1910-1917. † Illus.   TB/3023
GEORGE E. MOWRY: The Era of Theodore Roosevelt and
    the Birth of Modern America: 1900-1912. †   TB/3022
RUSSEL B. NYE: Midwestern Progressive Politics TB/1202
WALTER RAUSCHENBUSCH: Christianity and the Social
    Crisis. ‡ Edited by Robert D. Cross   TB/3059
JACOB RIIS: The Making of an American. ‡ Edited by
    Roy Lubove   TB/3070
PHILIP SELZNICK: TVA and the Grass Roots: A Study in
    the Sociology of Formal Organization   TB/1230
IDA M. TARBELL: The History of the Standard Oil Com-
    pany. Briefer Version. ‡ Edited by David M. Chalmers
    TB/3071
GEORGE B. TINDALL, Ed.: A Populist Reader ‡   TB/3069
TWELVE SOUTHERNERS: I'll Take My Stand: The South
    and the Agrarian Tradition. Intro. by Louis D. Rubin,
    Jr. Biographical Essays by Virginia Rock   TB/1072
WALTER E. WEYL: The New Democracy: An Essay on Cer-
    tain Political Tendencies in the United States. ‡ Edited
    by Charles B. Forcey   TB/3042

Anthropology

JACQUES BARZUN: Race: A Study in Superstition. Re-
    vised Edition   TB/1172
JOSEPH B. CASAGRANDE, Ed.: In the Company of Man:
    Portraits of Anthropological Informants   TB/3047
W. E. LE GROS CLARK: The Antecedents of Man: Intro.
    to Evolution of the Primates. ○ △ Illus.   TB/559
CORA DU BOIS: The People of Alor. New Preface by the
    author. Illus.   Vol. I TB/1042; Vol. II TB/1043
RAYMOND FIRTH, Ed.: Man and Culture: An Evaluation
    of the Work of Bronislaw Malinowski ¶ ○ △ TB/1133
DAVID LANDY: Tropical Childhood: Cultural Transmis-
    sion and Learning in a Puerto Rican Village ¶ TB/1235
L. S. B. LEAKEY: Adam's Ancestors: The Evolution of
    Man and His Culture. △ Illus.   TB/1019
ROBERT H. LOWIE: Primitive Society. Introduction by
    Fred Eggan   TB/1056
EDWARD BURNETT TYLOR: The Origin of Culture. Part I
    of "Primitive Culture." § Intro. by Paul Radin   TB/33
EDWARD BURNETT TYLOR: Religion in Primitive Culture.
    Part II of "Primitive Culture." § Intro. by Paul Radin
    TB/34
W. LLOYD WARNER: A Black Civilization: A Study of an
    Australian Tribe. ¶ Illus.   TB/3056

Art and Art History

WALTER LOWRIE: Art in the Early Church. Revised Edi-
    tion. 452 illus.   TB/124
EMILE MÂLE: The Gothic Image: Religious Art in France
    of the Thirteenth Century. § △ 190 illus.   TB/44
MILLARD MEISS: Painting in Florence and Siena after the
    Black Death: The Arts, Religion and Society in the
    Mid-Fourteenth Century. 169 illus.   TB/1148
ERICH NEUMANN: The Archetypal World of Henry
    Moore. △ 107 illus.   TB/2020
DORA & ERWIN PANOFSKY: Pandora's Box: The Changing
    Aspects of a Mythical Symbol. Illus.   TB/2021
ERWIN PANOFSKY: Studies in Iconology: Humanistic
    Themes in the Art of the Renaissance. △ 180 illustra-
    tions   TB/1077
ALEXANDRE PIANKOFF: The Shrines of Tut-Ankh-Amon.
    Edited by N. Rambova. 117 illus.   TB/2011
JEAN SEZNEC: The Survival of the Pagan Gods △ TB/2004
OTTO VON SIMSON: The Gothic Cathedral △   TB/2018
HEINRICH ZIMMER: Myths and Symbols in Indian Art and
    Civilization. 70 illustrations   TB/2005

ERNST CASSIRER: The Individual and the Cosmos in Renaissance Philosophy. △ Translated with an Introduction by Mario Domandi TB/1097

FEDERICO CHABOD: Machiavelli & Renaissance △ TB/1193

EDWARD P. CHEYNEY: The Dawn of a New Era, 1250-1453. * Illus. TB/3002

G. CONSTANT: The Reformation in England: The English Schism, Henry VIII, 1509-1547 △ TB/314

R. TREVOR DAVIES: The Golden Century of Spain, 1501-1621 ○ △ TB/1194

DESIDERIUS ERASMUS: Christian Humanism and the Reformation: Selected Writings. Edited and translated by John C. Olin TB/1166

WALLACE K. FERGUSON et al.: Facets of the Renaissance TB/1098

WALLACE K. FERGUSON et al.: The Renaissance: Six Essays. Illus. TB/1084

JOHN NEVILLE FIGGIS: The Divine Right of Kings. Introduction by G. R. Elton TB/1191

JOHN NEVILLE FIGGIS: Political Thought from Gerson to Grotius: 1414-1625 TB/1032

MYRON P. GILMORE: The World of Humanism, 1453-1517. * Illus. TB/3003

FRANCESCO GUICCIARDINI: Maxims and Reflections of a Renaissance Statesman (Ricordi) TB/1160

J. H. HEXTER: More's Utopia: The Biography of an Idea. New Epilogue by the Author TB/1195

HAJO HOLBORN: Ulrich von Hutten and the German Reformation TB/1238

JOHAN HUIZINGA: Erasmus and the Age of Reformation.△ Illus. TB/19

JOEL HURSTFIELD, Ed.: The Reformation Crisis △ TB/1267

ULRICH VON HUTTEN et al.: On the Eve of the Reformation: "Letters of Obscure Men" TB/1124

PAUL O. KRISTELLER: Renaissance Thought: The Classic, Scholastic, and Humanist Strains TB/1048

PAUL O. KRISTELLER: Renaissance Thought II: Papers on Humanism and the Arts TB/1163

NICCOLÒ MACHIAVELLI: History of Florence and of the Affairs of Italy TB/1027

ALFRED VON MARTIN: Sociology of the Renaissance. Introduction by Wallace K. Ferguson △ TB/1099

GARRETT MATTINGLY et al.: Renaissance Profiles. △ Edited by J. H. Plumb TB/1162

MILLARD MEISS: Painting in Florence and Siena after the Black Death: The Arts, Religion and Society in the Mid-Fourteenth Century. △ 169 illus. TB/1148

J. E. NEALE: The Age of Catherine de Medici ○ △ TB/1085

ERWIN PANOFSKY: Studies in Iconology: Humanistic Themes in the Art of the Renaissance △ TB/1077

J. H. PARRY: The Establishment of the European Hegemony: 1415-1715 △ TB/1045

J. H. PLUMB: The Italian Renaissance: A Concise Survey of Its History and Culture △ TB/1161

A. F. POLLARD: Henry VIII. ○ △ Introduction by A. G. Dickens TB/1249

A. F. POLLARD: Wolsey. ○ △ Introduction by A. G. Dickens TB/1248

CECIL ROTH: The Jews in the Renaissance. Illus. TB/834

A. L. ROWSE: The Expansion of Elizabethan England. ○ △ Illus. TB/1220

GORDON RUPP: Luther's Progress to the Diet of Worms ○ △ TB/120

FERDINAND SCHEVILL: The Medici. Illus. TB/1010

FERDINAND SCHEVILL: Medieval and Renaissance Florence. Illus. Volume I: Medieval Florence to the Age of the Medici TB/1090 Volume II: The Coming of Humanism and the Age of the Medici TB/1091

G. M. TREVELYAN: England in the Age of Wycliffe, 1368-1520 ○ △ TB/1112

VESPASIANO: Renaissance Princes, Popes, and Prelates: The Vespasiano Memoirs: Lives of Illustrious Men of the XVth Century TB/1111

History: Modern European

FREDERICK B. ARTZ: Reaction and Revolution, 1815-1852. * Illus. TB/3034

MAX BELOFF: The Age of Absolutism, 1660-1815 △ TB/1062

ROBERT C. BINKLEY: Realism and Nationalism, 1852-1871. * Illus. TB/3038

ASA BRIGGS: The Making of Modern England, 1784-1867: The Age of Improvement ○ △ TB/1203

CRANE BRINTON: A Decade of Revolution, 1789-1799. * Illus. TB/3018

D. W. BROGAN: The Development of Modern France. ○ △ Volume I: From the Fall of the Empire to the Dreyfus Affair TB/1184 Volume II: The Shadow of War, World War I, Between the Two Wars. New Introduction by the Author TB/1185

J. BRONOWSKI & BRUCE MAZLISH: The Western Intellectual Tradition: From Leonardo to Hegel △ TB/3001

GEOFFREY BRUUN: Europe and the French Imperium, 1799-1814. * Illus. TB/3033

ALAN BULLOCK: Hitler, A Study in Tyranny ○ △ TB/1123

E. H. CARR: The Twenty Years' Crisis, 1919-1939 ○ △ TB/1122

GORDON A. CRAIG: From Bismarck to Adenauer: Aspects of German Statecraft. Revised Edition TB/1171

WALTER L. DORN: Competition for Empire, 1740-1763. * Illus. TB/3032

FRANKLIN L. FORD: Robe and Sword: The Regrouping of the French Aristocracy after Louis XIV TB/1217

CARL J. FRIEDRICH: The Age of the Baroque, 1610-1660. * Illus. TB/3004

RENÉ FUELOEP-MILLER: The Mind and Face of Bolshevism TB/1188

M. DOROTHY GEORGE: London Life in the Eighteenth Century △ TB/1182

LEO GERSHOY: From Despotism to Revolution, 1763-1789. * Illus. TB/3017

C. C. GILLISPIE: Genesis and Geology: The Decades before Darwin § TB/51

ALBERT GOODWIN: The French Revolution △ TB/1064

ALBERT GUÉRARD: France in the Classical Age: The Life and Death of an Ideal △ TB/1183

CARLTON J. H. HAYES: A Generation of Materialism, 1871-1900. * Illus. TB/3039

J. H. HEXTER: Reappraisals in History: New Views on History & Society in Early Modern Europe △ TB/1100

STANLEY HOFFMANN et al.: In Search of France TB/1219

A. R. HUMPHREYS: The Augustan World: Society, Thought, and Letters in 18th Century England ○ △ TB/1105

DAN N. JACOBS, Ed.: The New Communist Manifesto & Related Documents. Third edition, Revised TB/1078

HANS KOHN: The Mind of Germany △ TB/1204

HANS KOHN, Ed.: The Mind of Modern Russia: Historical and Political Thought of Russia's Great Age TB/1065

FRANK E. MANUEL: The Prophets of Paris: Turgot, Condorcet, Saint-Simon, Fourier, and Comte TB/1218

KINGSLEY MARTIN: French Liberal Thought in the Eighteenth Century TB/1114

L. B. NAMIER: Personalities and Powers: Selected Essays △ TB/1186

L. B. NAMIER: Vanished Supremacies: Essays on European History, 1812-1918 ○ △ TB/1088

JOHN U. NEF: Western Civilization Since the Renaissance: Peace, War, Industry, and the Arts TB/1113

FREDERICK L. NUSSBAUM: The Triumph of Science and Reason, 1660-1685. * Illus. TB/3009

JOHN PLAMENATZ: German Marxism and Russian Communism. ○ △ New Preface by the Author TB/1189

RAYMOND W. POSTGATE, Ed.: Revolution from 1789 to 1906: Selected Documents TB/1063

PENFIELD ROBERTS: The Quest for Security, 1715-1740. * Illus. TB/3016

4

PRISCILLA ROBERTSON: Revolutions of 1848: *A Social History*   TB/1025
LOUIS, DUC DE SAINT-SIMON: Versailles, The Court, and Louis XIV. △ *Introductory Note by Peter Gay* TB/1250
ALBERT SOREL: Europe Under the Old Regime. *Translated by Francis H. Herrick*   TB/1121
N. N. SUKHANOV: The Russian Revolution, 1917: *Eyewitness Account.* △ *Edited by Joel Carmichael*
      Vol. I TB/1066; Vol. II TB/1067
A. J. P. TAYLOR: From Napoleon to Lenin: *Historical Essays* ○ △   TB/1268
A. J. P. TAYLOR: The Habsburg Monarchy, 1809-1918 ○ △   TB/1187
G. M. TREVELYAN: British History in the Nineteenth Century and After: 1782-1919. △ *Second Edition*
      TB/1251
H. R. TREVOR-ROPER: Historical Essays ○ △   TB/1269
JOHN B. WOLF: The Emergence of the Great Powers, 1685-1715. * *Illus.*   TB/3010
JOHN B. WOLF: France: 1814-1919: *The Rise of a Liberal-Democratic Society*   TB/3019

Intellectual History & History of Ideas

HERSCHEL BAKER: The Image of Man   TB/1047
R. R. BOLGAR: The Classical Heritage and Its Beneficiaries △   TB/1125
RANDOLPH S. BOURNE: War and the Intellectuals: *Collected Essays, 1915-1919.* ‡ △ *Edited by Carl Resek*
      TB/3043
J. BRONOWSKI & BRUCE MAZLISH: The Western Intellectual Tradition: *From Leonardo to Hegel* △   TB/3001
ERNST CASSIRER: The Individual and the Cosmos in Renaissance Philosophy. △ *Translated with an Introduction by Mario Domandi*   TB/1097
NORMAN COHN: Pursuit of the Millennium △   TB/1037
C. C. GILLISPIE: Genesis and Geology: *The Decades before Darwin* §   TB/51
G. RACHEL LEVY: Religious Conceptions of the Stone Age and Their Influence upon European Thought. △ *Illus. Introduction by Henri Frankfort*   TB/106
ARTHUR O. LOVEJOY: The Great Chain of Being: *A Study of the History of an Idea*   TB/1009
FRANK E. MANUEL: The Prophets of Paris: *Turgot, Condorcet, Saint-Simon, Fourier, and Comte*   TB/1218
PERRY MILLER & T. H. JOHNSON, Editors: The Puritans: *A Sourcebook of Their Writings*
      Vol. I TB/1093; Vol. II TB/1094
MILTON C. NAHM: Genius and Creativity: *An Essay in the History of Ideas*   TB/1196
ROBERT PAYNE: Hubris: *A Study of Pride. Foreword by Sir Herbert Read*   TB/1031
RALPH BARTON PERRY: The Thought and Character of William James: *Briefer Version*   TB/1156
GEORG SIMMEL et al.: Essays on Sociology, Philosophy, and Aesthetics. ¶ *Edited by Kurt H. Wolff*   TB/1234
BRUNO SNELL: The Discovery of the Mind: *The Greek Origins of European Thought* △   TB/1018
PAGET TOYNBEE: Dante Alighieri: *His Life and Works. Edited with Intro. by Charles S. Singleton*   TB/1206
ERNEST LEE TUVESON: Millennium and Utopia: *A Study in the Background of the Idea of Progress.* ¶ *New Preface by the Author*   TB/1134
PAUL VALÉRY: The Outlook for Intelligence △   TB/2016
PHILIP P. WIENER: Evolution and the Founders of Pragmatism. △ *Foreword by John Dewey*   TB/1212
BASIL WILLEY: Nineteenth Century Studies: *Coleridge to Matthew Arnold* ○ △   TB/1261
BASIL WILLEY: More Nineteenth Century Studies: *A Group of Honest Doubters* ○ △   TB/1262

Literature, Poetry, The Novel & Criticism

JACQUES BARZUN: The House of Intellect △   TB/1051
W. J. BATE: From Classic to Romantic: *Premises of Taste in Eighteenth Century England*   TB/1036
RACHEL BESPALOFF: On the Iliad   TB/2006

R. P. BLACKMUR et al.: Lectures in Criticism. *Introduction by Huntington Cairns*   TB/2003
JAMES BOSWELL: The Life of Dr. Johnson & The Journal of a Tour to the Hebrides with Samuel Johnson LL.D: *Selections.* ○ △ *Edited by F. V. Morley. Illus. by Ernest Shepard*   TB/1254
ABRAHAM CAHAN: The Rise of David Levinsky: *a documentary novel of social mobility in early twentieth century America. Intro. by John Higham*   TB/1028
ERNST R. CURTIUS: European Literature and the Latin Middle Ages △   TB/2015
GEORGE ELIOT: Daniel Deronda   TB/1039
ÉTIENNE GILSON: Dante and Philosophy   TB/1089
ALFRED HARBAGE: As They Liked It: *A Study of Shakespeare's Moral Artistry*   TB/1035
STANLEY R. HOPPER, Ed.: Spiritual Problems in Contemporary Literature §   TB/21
A. R. HUMPHREYS: The Augustan World: *Society in 18th Century England* ○ △   TB/1105
ALDOUS HUXLEY: Antic Hay & The Giaconda Smile. ○ △ *Introduction by Martin Green*   TB/3503
ALDOUS HUXLEY: Brave New World & Brave New World Revisited. ○ △ *Introduction by Martin Green*   TB/3501
HENRY JAMES: The Tragic Muse   TB/1017
ARNOLD KETTLE: An Introduction to the English Novel
    Volume I: *Defoe to George Eliot*   TB/1011
    Volume II: *Henry James to the Present*   TB/1012
RICHMOND LATTIMORE: The Poetry of Greek Tragedy △
      TB/1257
J. B. LEISHMAN: The Monarch of Wit: *An Analytical and Comparative Study of the Poetry of John Donne* ○ △
      TB/1258
J. B. LEISHMAN: Themes and Variations in Shakespeare's Sonnets ○ △   TB/1259
ROGER SHERMAN LOOMIS: The Development of Arthurian Romance △   TB/1167
JOHN STUART MILL: On Bentham and Coleridge. △ *Introduction by F. R. Leavis*   TB/1070
KENNETH B. MURDOCK: Literature and Theology in Colonial New England   TB/99
SAMUEL PEPYS: The Diary of Samuel Pepys. ○ *Edited by O. F. Morshead. Illus. by Ernest Shepard*   TB/1007
ST.-JOHN PERSE: Seamarks   TB/2002
V. DE S. PINTO: Crisis in English Poetry, 1880-1940 ○ △
      TB/1260
GEORGE SANTAYANA: Interpretations of Poetry and Religion §   TB/9
C. K. STEAD: The New Poetic: Yeats to Eliot ○ △   TB/1263
HEINRICH STRAUMANN: American Literature in the Twentieth Century. △ *Third Edition, Revised*   TB/1168
PAGET TOYNBEE: Dante Alighieri: *His Life and Works. Edited with Intro. by Charles S. Singleton*   TB/1206
DOROTHY VAN GHENT: The English Novel   TB/1050
E. B. WHITE: One Man's Meat   TB/3505
BASIL WILLEY: Nineteenth Century Studies: *Coleridge to Matthew Arnold* ○ △   TB/1261
BASIL WILLEY: More Nineteenth Century Studies: *A Group of Honest Doubters* ○ △   TB/1262
RAYMOND WILLIAMS: Culture and Society, 1780-1950 △
      TB/1252
RAYMOND WILLIAMS: The Long Revolution. △ *Revised Edition*   TB/1253
MORTON DAUWEN ZABEL, Editor: *Literary Opinion in America*   Vol. I TB/3013; Vol. II TB/3014

Myth, Symbol & Folklore

JOSEPH CAMPBELL, Editor: Pagan and Christian Mysteries. *Illus.*   TB/2013
MIRCEA ELIADE: Cosmos and History: *The Myth of the Eternal Return* §   TB/2050
MIRCEA ELIADE: Rites and Symbols of Initiation: *The Mysteries of Birth and Rebirth* § △   TB/1236

DORA & ERWIN PANOFSKY: Pandora's Box: *The Changing Aspects of a Mythical Symbol.* △ *Revised Edition. Illus.* TB/2021
TB/2021
HELLMUT WILHELM: Change: *Eight Lectures on the I Ching* △ TB/2019
HEINRICH ZIMMER: Myths and Symbols in Indian Art and Civilization. △ *70 illustrations* TB/2005

Philosophy

G. E. M. ANSCOMBE: An Introduction to Wittgenstein's Tractatus. º △ *Second Edition, Revised* TB/1210
HENRI BERGSON: Time and Free Will º △ TB/1021
H. J. BLACKHAM: Six Existentialist Thinkers º △ TB/1002
CRANE BRINTON: Nietzsche TB/1197
ERNST CASSIRER: The Individual and the Cosmos in Renaissance Philosophy △ TB/1097
FREDERICK COPLESTON: Medieval Philosophy º △ TB/376
F. M. CORNFORD: Principium Sapientiae: *A Study of the Origins of Greek Philosophical Thought* TB/1213
F. M. CORNFORD: From Religion to Philosophy: *A Study in the Origins of Western Speculation* § TB/20
WILFRID DESAN: The Tragic Finale: *An Essay on the Philosophy of Jean-Paul Sartre* TB/1030
A. P. D'ENTRÈVES: Natural Law △ TB/1223
HERBERET FINGARETTE: The Self in Transformation: *Psychoanalysis, Philosophy and the Life of the Spirit* ¶ TB/1177
PAUL FRIEDLÄNDER: Plato: *An Introduction* △ TB/2017
ÉTIENNE GILSON: Dante and Philosophy △ TB/1089
WILLIAM CHASE GREENE: Moira: *Fate, Good, and Evil in Greek Thought* TB/1104
W. K. C. GUTHRIE: The Greek Philosophers: *From Thales to Aristotle* º △ TB/1008
F. H. HEINEMANN: Existentialism and the Modern Predicament △ TB/28
ISAAC HUSIK: A History of Medieval Jewish Philosophy JP/3
EDMUND HUSSERL: Phenomenology and the Crisis of Philosophy TB/1170
IMMANUEL KANT: The Doctrine of Virtue, *being Part II of the Metaphysic of Morals* TB/110
IMMANUEL KANT: Groundwork of the Metaphysic of Morals. *Trans. & analyzed by H. J. Paton* TB/1159
IMMANUEL KANT: Lectures on Ethics § △ TB/105
IMMANUEL KANT: Religion Within the Limits of Reason Alone. § *Intro. by T. M. Greene & J. Silber* TB/67
QUENTIN LAUER: Phenomenology TB/1169
GABRIEL MARCEL: Being and Having △ TB/310
GEORGE A. MORGAN: What Nietzsche Means TB/1198
PHILO, SAADYA GAON, & JEHUDA HALEVI: Three Jewish Philosophers. *Ed. by Hans Lewy, Alexander Altmann, & Isaak Heinemann* TB/813
MICHAEL POLANYI: Personal Knowledge △ TB/1158
WILLARD VAN ORMAN QUINE: Elementary Logic. *Revised Edition* TB/577
WILLARD VAN ORMAN QUINE: From a Logical Point of View: *Logico-Philosophical Essays* TB/566
BERTRAND RUSSELL et al.: The Philosophy of Bertrand Russell Vol. I TB/1095; Vol. II TB/1096
L. S. STEBBING: A Modern Introduction to Logic △ TB/538
ALFRED NORTH WHITEHEAD: Process and Reality: *An Essay in Cosmology* △ TB/1033
PHILIP P. WIENER: Evolution and the Founders of Pragmatism. *Foreword by John Dewey* TB/1212
WILHELM WINDELBAND: A History of Philosophy
Vol. I: *Greek, Roman, Medieval* TB/38
Vol. II: *Renaissance, Enlightenment, Modern* TB/39
LUDWIG WITTGENSTEIN: Blue and Brown Books º TB/1211

Political Science & Government

JEREMY BENTHAM: The Handbook of Political Fallacies. *Introduction by Crane Brinton* TB/1069
KENNETH E. BOULDING: Conflict and Defense TB/3024

CRANE BRINTON: English Political Thought in the Nineteenth Century TB/1071
EDWARD S. CORWIN: American Constitutional History. *Essays edited by Alpheus T. Mason and Gerald Garvey* TB/1136
ROBERT DAHL & CHARLES E. LINDBLOM: Politics, Economics, and Welfare TB/3037
F. L. GANSHOF: Feudalism △ TB/1058
G. P. GOOCH: English Democratic Ideas in Seventeenth Century TB/1006
J. H. HEXTER: More's Utopia: *The Biography of an Idea. New Epilogue by the Author* TB/1195
SIDNEY HOOK: Reason, Social Myths and Democracy △ TB/1237
ROBERT H. JACKSON: The Supreme Court in the American System of Government △ TB/1106
DAN N. JACOBS, Ed.: The New Communist Manifesto *and Related Documents. Third edition, Revised* TB/1078
DAN N. JACOBS & HANS BAERWALD Eds.: Chinese Communism: *Selected Documents* TB/3031
ROBERT GREEN MC CLOSKEY: American Conservatism in the Age of Enterprise, 1865-1910 TB/1137
KINGSLEY MARTIN: French Liberal Thought in the Eighteenth Century △ TB/1114
ROBERTO MICHELS: First Lectures in Political Sociology. *Edited by Alfred de Grazia* △ TB/1224
JOHN STUART MILL: On Bentham and Coleridge. △ *Introduction by F. R. Leavis* TB/1070
BARRINGTON MOORE, JR.: Political Power and Social Theory: *Seven Studies* ¶ TB/1221
BARRINGTON MOORE, JR.: Soviet Politics—The Dilemma of Power ¶ TB/1222
BARRINGTON MOORE, JR.: Terror and Progress—USSR: *Some Sources of Change and Stability in the Soviet Dictatorship* ¶ TB/1266
JOHN B. MORRALL: Political Thought in Medieval Times △ TB/1076
JOHN PLAMENATZ: German Marxism and Russian Communism. º △ *New Preface by the Author* TB/1189
KARL R. POPPER: The Open Society and Its Enemies △
Vol. I: *The Spell of Plato* TB/1101
Vol. II: *The High Tide of Prophecy: Hegel, Marx, and the Aftermath* TB/1102
HENRI DE SAINT-SIMON: Social Organization, The Science of Man, and Other Writings. *Edited and Translated by Felix Markham* TB/1152
JOSEPH A. SCHUMPETER: Capitalism, Socialism and Democracy △ TB/3008
CHARLES H. SHINN: Mining Camps: *A Study in American Frontier Government.* ‡ *Edited by Rodman W. Paul* TB/3062

Psychology

ALFRED ADLER: Individual Psychology of Alfred Adler △ TB/1154
ALFRED ADLER: Problems of Neurosis. *Introduction by Heinz L. Ansbacher* TB/1145
ANTON T. BOISEN: The Exploration of the Inner World: *A Study of Mental Disorder and Religious Experience* TB/87
HERBERT FINGARETTE: The Self in Transformation ¶ TB/1177
SIGMUND FREUD: On Creativity and the Unconscious. § △ *Intro. by Benjamin Nelson* TB/45
C. JUDSON HERRICK: The Evolution of Human Nature TB/545
WILLIAM JAMES: Psychology: *Briefer Course* TB/1034
C. G. JUNG: Psychological Reflections △ TB/2001
C. G. JUNG: Symbols of Transformation △
Vol. I TB/2009; Vol. II TB/2010
C. G. JUNG & C. KERÉNYI: Essays on a Science of Mythology: *The Myths of the Divine Child and the Divine Maiden* TB/2014
JOHN T. MC NEILL: A History of the Cure of Souls TB/126
KARL MENNINGER: Theory of Psychoanalytic Technique TB/1144

ERICH NEUMANN: Amor and Psyche △ TB/2012
ERICH NEUMANN: The Archetypal World of Henry
Moore. *107 illus.* TB/2020
ERICH NEUMANN: The Origins and History of Consciousness △ Vol. I *Illus.* TB/2007; Vol. II TB/2008
C. P. OBERNDORF: A History of Psychoanalysis in America
TB/1147
RALPH BARTON PERRY: The Thought and Character of
William James: *Briefer Version* TB/1156
JEAN PIAGET, BÄRBEL INHELDER, & ALINA SZEMINSKA: The
Child's Conception of Geometry ° △ TB/1146
JOHN H. SCHAAR: Escape from Authority: *The Perspectives of Erich Fromm* TB/1155

Sociology

JACQUES BARZUN: Race: *A Study in Superstition. Revised
Edition* TB/1172
BERNARD BERELSON, Ed.: The Behavioral Sciences Today
TB/1127
ABRAHAM CAHAN: The Rise of David Levinsky: *A documentary novel of social mobility in early twentieth
century America. Intro. by John Higham* TB/1028
THOMAS C. COCHRAN: The Inner Revolution: *Essays on
the Social Sciences in History* TB/1140
ALLISON DAVIS & JOHN DOLLARD: Children of Bondage:
*The Personality Development of Negro Youth in the
Urban South* ¶ TB/3049
ST. CLAIR DRAKE & HORACE R. CAYTON: Black Metropolis:
*A Study of Negro Life in a Northern City. Revised
and Enlarged. Intro. by Everett C. Hughes*
Vol. I TB/1086; Vol. II TB/1087
EMILE DURKHEIM et al.: Essays on Sociology and Philosophy. *With Analysis of Durkheim's Life and Work.* ¶
Edited by Kurt H. Wolff TB/1151
LEON FESTINGER, HENRY W. RIECKEN & STANLEY SCHACHTER:
When Prophecy Fails: *A Social and Psychological Account of a Modern Group that Predicted the Destruction of the World* ¶ TB/1132
ALVIN W. GOULDNER: Wildcat Strike ¶ TB/1176
FRANCIS J. GRUND: Aristocracy in America: *Social Class
in the Formative Years of the New Nation* △ TB/1001
KURT LEWIN: Field Theory in Social Science: *Selected
Theoretical Papers.* ¶ △ *Edited with a Foreword by
Dorwin Cartwright* TB/1135
R. M. MACIVER: Social Causation TB/1153
ROBERT K. MERTON, LEONARD BROOM, LEONARD S. COTTRELL,
JR., Editors: Sociology Today: *Problems and Prospects* ¶ Vol. I TB/1173; Vol. II TB/1174
ROBERTO MICHELS: First Lectures in Political Sociology.
Edited by Alfred de Grazia ¶ ° TB/1224
BARRINGTON MOORE, JR.: Political Power and Social
Theory: *Seven Studies* ¶ TB/1221
BARRINGTON MOORE, JR.: Soviet Politics—The Dilemma
of Power: *The Role of Ideas in Social Change* ¶
TB/1222
TALCOTT PARSONS & EDWARD A. SHILS, Editors: Toward
a General Theory of Action TB/1083
JOHN H. ROHRER & MUNRO S. EDMONSON, Eds.: The Eighth
Generation Grows Up ¶ TB/3050
KURT SAMUELSSON: Religion and Economic Action: *A
Critique of Max Weber's The Protestant Ethic and
the Spirit of Capitalism.* ¶ ° *Trans. by E. G. French.
Ed. with Intro by D. C. Coleman* TB/1131
PHILIP SELZNICK: TVA and the Grass Roots: *A Study in
the Sociology of Formal Organization* TB/1230
GEORG SIMMEL et al.: Essays on Sociology, Philosophy,
and Aesthetics. ¶ *Edited by Kurt H. Wolff* TB/1234
HERBERT SIMON: The Shape of Automation △ TB/1245
PITIRIM A. SOROKIN: Contemporary Sociological Theories:
Through the First Quarter of the 20th Century ¶ TB/3046
MAURICE R. STEIN: The Eclipse of Community: *An Interpretation of American Studies* TB/1128
FERDINAND TÖNNIES: Community and Society: *Gemeinschaft und Gesellschaft. Translated and edited by
Charles P. Loomis* TB/1116

W. LLOYD WARNER & Associates: Democracy in Jonesville: *A Study in Quality and Inequality* TB/1129
W. LLOYD WARNER: Social Class in America: *The Evaluation of Status* TB/1013

RELIGION

Ancient & Classical

J. H. BREASTED: Development of Religion and Thought in
Ancient Egypt TB/57
HENRI FRANKFORT: Ancient Egyptian Religion TB/77
G. RACHEL LEVY: Religious Conceptions of the Stone Age
and their Influence upon European Thought. △ *Illus.
Introduction by Henri Frankfort* TB/106
MARTIN P. NILSSON: Greek Folk Religion TB/78
ALEXANDRE PIANKOFF: The Shrines of Tut-Ankh-Amon. △
Edited by N. Rambova. 117 illus. TB/2011
H. J. ROSE: Religion in Greece and Rome △ TB/55

Biblical Thought & Literature

W. F. ALBRIGHT: The Biblical Period from Abraham to
Ezra TB/102
C. K. BARRETT, Ed.: The New Testament Background:
Selected Documents △ TB/86
C. H. DODD: The Authority of the Bible △ TB/43
M. S. ENSLIN: Christian Beginnings △ TB/5
M. S. ENSLIN: The Literature of the Christian Movement △
TB/6
JOHN GRAY: Archaeology and the Old Testament World. △
Illus. TB/127
JAMES MUILENBURG: The Way of Israel: *Biblical Faith
and Ethics* △ TB/133
H. H. ROWLEY: The Growth of the Old Testament △
TB/107
D. WINTON THOMAS, Ed.: Documents from Old Testament
Times △ TB/85

The Judaic Tradition

LEO BAECK: Judaism and Christianity. *Trans. with Intro.
by Walter Kaufmann* JP/23
SALO W. BARON: Modern Nationalism and Religion
JP/18
MARTIN BUBER: Eclipse of God: *Studies in the Relation
Between Religion and Philosophy* △ TB/12
MARTIN BUBER: For the Sake of Heaven TB/801
MARTIN BUBER: The Knowledge of Man: *Selected Essays.* △ *Edited with an Introduction by Maurice Friedman. Translated by Maurice Friedman and Ronald
Gregor Smith* TB/135
MARTIN BUBER: Moses: *The Revelation and the Covenant* △ TB/827
MARTIN BUBER: The Origin and Meaning of Hasidism △
TB/835
MARTIN BUBER: Pointing the Way. △ *Introduction by
Maurice S. Friedman* TB/103
MARTIN BUBER: The Prophetic Faith TB/73
MARTIN BUBER: Two Types of Faith: *the interpenetration
of Judaism and Christianity* ° △ TB/75
ERNST LUDWIG EHRLICH: A Concise History of Israel:
*From the Earliest Times to the Destruction of the
Temple in A. D. 70* ° △ TB/128
MAURICE S. FRIEDMAN: Martin Buber: *The Life of Dialogue* △ TB/64
GENESIS: The NJV Translation TB/836
SOLOMON GRAYZEL: A History of the Contemporary Jews
TB/816
WILL HERBERG: Judaism and Modern Man TB/810
ARTHUR HERTZBERG: The Zionist Idea TB/817
ABRAHAM J. HESCHEL: God in Search of Man: *A Philosophy of Judaism* TB/807
ISAAK HUSIK: A History of Medieval Jewish Philosophy
JP/3

FLAVIUS JOSEPHUS: The Great Roman-Jewish War, *with* The Life of Josephus. *Introduction by William R. Farmer* TB/74
JACOB R. MARCUS: The Jew in the Medieval World TB/814
MAX L. MARGOLIS & ALEXANDER MARX: A History of the Jewish People TB/806
T. J. MEEK: Hebrew Origins TB/69
C. G. MONTEFIORE & H. LOEWE, Eds.: A Rabbinic Anthology JP/32
JAMES PARKES: The Conflict of the Church and the Synagogue: *The Jews and Early Christianity* JP/21
PHILO, SAADYA GAON, & JEHUDA HALEVI: Three Jewish Philosophers. *Ed. by Hans Lewey, Alexander Altmann, & Isaac Heinemann* TB/813
CECIL ROTH: A History of the Marranos TB/812
CECIL ROTH: The Jews in the Renaissance. *Illus.* TB/834
HERMAN L. STRACK: Introduction to the Talmud and Midrash TB/808
JOSHUA TRACHTENBERG: The Devil and the Jews: *The Medieval Conception of the Jew and its Relation to Modern Anti-Semitism* JP/22

Christianity: General

ROLAND H. BAINTON: Christendom: *A Short History of Christianity and its Impact on Western Civilization.* △ *Illus.* Vol. I TB/131; Vol. II TB/132

Christianity: Origins & Early Development

AUGUSTINE: An Augustine Synthesis. △ *Edited by Erich Przywara* TB/335
ADOLF DEISSMANN: Paul: *A Study in Social and Religious History* TB/15
EDWARD GIBBON: The Triumph of Christendom in the Roman Empire (*Chaps. XV-XX of "Decline and Fall," J. B. Bury edition*). § △ *Illus.* TB/46
MAURICE GOGUEL: Jesus and the Origins of Christianity. ° △ *Introduction by C. Leslie Mitton*
  Volume I: *Prolegomena to the Life of Jesus* TB/65
  Volume II: *The Life of Jesus* TB/66
EDGAR J. GOODSPEED: A Life of Jesus TB/1
ROBERT M. GRANT: Gnosticism and Early Christianity. △ *Revised Edition* TB/136
ADOLF HARNACK: The Mission and Expansion of Christianity *in the First Three Centuries. Introduction by Jaroslav Pelikan* TB/92
R. K. HARRISON: The Dead Sea Scrolls: *An Introduction* ° △ TB/84
EDWIN HATCH: The Influence of Greek Ideas on Christianity. § △ *Introduction and Bibliography by Frederick C. Grant* TB/18
ARTHUR DARBY NOCK: Early Gentile Christianity and Its Hellenistic Background TB/111
ARTHUR DARBY NOCK: St. Paul ° △ TB/104
ORIGEN: On First Principles. △ *Edited by G. W. Butterworth. Introduction by Henri de Lubac* TB/310
JAMES PARKES: The Conflict of the Church and the Synagogue: *The Jews and Early Christianity* JP/21
SULPICIUS SEVERUS et al.: The Western Fathers: *Being the Lives of Martin of Tours, Ambrose, Augustine of Hippo, Honoratus of Arles and Germanus of Auxerre.* △ *Edited and translated by F. R. Hoare* TB/309
F. VAN DER MEER: Augustine the Bishop: *Church and Society at the Dawn of the Middle Ages* △ TB/304
JOHANNES WEISS: Earliest Christianity: *A History of the Period A.D. 30-150. Introduction and Bibliography by Frederick C. Grant* Volume I TB/53
  Volume II TB/54

Christianity: The Middle Ages and The Reformation

JOHN CALVIN & JACOPO SADOLETO: A Reformation Debate. *Edited by John C. Olin* TB/1239

G. CONSTANT: The Reformation in England: *The English Schism, Henry VIII, 1509-1547* △ TB/314
CHRISTOPHER DAWSON, Ed.: Mission to Asia: *Narratives and Letters of the Franciscan Missionaries in Mongolia and China in the 13th and 14th Centuries* △ TB/315
JOHANNES ECKHART: Meister Eckhart: *A Modern Translation by R. B. Blakney* TB/8
DESIDERIUS ERASMUS: Christian Humanism and the Reformation: *Selected Writings. Edited and translated by John C. Olin* TB/1166
ÉTIENNE GILSON: Dante and Philosophy △ TB/1089
WILLIAM HALLER: The Rise of Puritanism △ TB/22
HAJO HOLBORN: Ulrich von Hutten and the German Reformation TB/1238
JOHAN HUIZINGA: Erasmus and the Age of Reformation. △ *Illus.* TB/19
A. C. MC GIFFERT: Protestant Thought Before Kant. △ *Preface by Jaroslav Pelikan* TB/93
JOHN T. MC NEILL: Makers of the Christian Tradition: *From Alfred the Great to Schleiermacher* △ TB/121
G. MOLLAT: The Popes at Avignon, 1305-1378 △ TB/308
GORDON RUPP: Luther's Progress to the Diet of Worms ° △ TB/120

Christianity: The Protestant Tradition

KARL BARTH: Church Dogmatics: *A Selection* △ TB/95
KARL BARTH: Dogmatics in Outline △ TB/56
KARL BARTH: The Word of God and the Word of Man TB/13
RUDOLF BULTMANN et al.: Translating Theology into the Modern Age: *Historical, Systematic and Pastoral Reflections on Theology and the Church in the Contemporary Situation. Volume 2 of Journal for Theology and the Church, edited by Robert W. Funk in association with Gerhard Ebeling* TB/252
WINTHROP HUDSON: The Great Tradition of the American Churches TB/98
SOREN KIERKEGAARD: Edifying Discourses. *Edited with an Introduction by Paul Holmer* TB/32
SOREN KIERKEGAARD: The Journals of Kierkegaard. ° △ *Edited with an Introduction by Alexander Dru* TB/52
SOREN KIERKEGAARD: The Point of View for My Work as an Author: *A Report to History.* § *Preface by Benjamin Nelson* TB/88
SOREN KIERKEGAARD: The Present Age. § △ *Translated and edited by Alexander Dru. Introduction by Walter Kaufmann* TB/94
SOREN KIERKEGAARD: Purity of Heart △ TB/4
SOREN KIERKEGAARD: Repetition: *An Essay in Experimental Psychology.* △ *Translated with Introduction & Notes by Walter Lowrie* TB/117
SOREN KIERKEGAARD: Works of Love: *Some Christian Reflections in the Form of Discourses* △ TB/122
WALTER LOWRIE: Kierkegaard: *A Life* Vol. I TB/89
  Vol. II TB/90
JOHN MACQUARRIE: The Scope of Demythologizing: *Bultmann and his Critics* △ TB/134
PERRY MILLER & T. H. JOHNSON, Editors: The Puritans: *A Sourcebook of Their Writings* Vol. I TB/1093
  Vol. II TB/1094
JAMES M. ROBINSON et al.: The Bultmann School of Biblical Interpretation: New Directions? *Volume 1 of Journal of Theology and the Church, edited by Robert W. Funk in association with Gerhard Ebeling* TB/251
F. SCHLEIERMACHER: The Christian Faith. △ *Introduction by Richard R. Niebuhr* Vol. I TB/108
  Vol. II TB/109
F. SCHLEIERMACHER: On Religion: *Speeches to Its Cultured Despisers. Intro. by Rudolf Otto* TB/36
PAUL TILLICH: Dynamics of Faith △ TB/42
EVELYN UNDERHILL: Worship △ TB/10
G. VAN DER LEEUW: Religion in Essence and manifestation: *A Study in Phenomenology.* △ *Appendices by Hans H. Penner* Vol. I TB/100; Vol. II TB/101

EDMUND W. SINNOTT: Cell and Psyche: *The Biology of Purpose* TB/546

C. H. WADDINGTON: How Animals Develop. △ *Illus.* TB/553

C. H. WADDINGTON: The Nature of Life: *The Main Problems and Trends in Modern Biology* △ TB/580

Chemistry

J. R. PARTINGTON: A Short History of Chemistry. △ *Illus.* TB/522

Communication Theory

J. R. PIERCE: Symbols, Signals and Noise: *The Nature and Process of Communication* △ TB/574

Geography

R. E. COKER: This Great and Wide Sea: *An Introduction to Oceanography and Marine Biology. Illus.* TB/551

F. K. HARE: The Restless Atmosphere △ TB/560

History of Science

MARIE BOAS: The Scientific Renaissance, 1450-1630 ° △ TB/583

W. DAMPIER, Ed.: Readings in the Literature of Science. *Illus.* TB/512

A. HUNTER DUPREE: Science in the Federal Government: *A History of Policies and Activities to 1940* △ TB/573

ALEXANDRE KOYRÉ: From the Closed World to the Infinite Universe: *Copernicus, Kepler, Galileo, Newton, etc.* △ TB/31

A. G. VAN MELSEN: From Atomos to Atom: *A History of the Concept Atom* TB/517

O. NEUGEBAUER: The Exact Sciences in Antiquity TB/552

HANS THIRRING: Energy for Man: *From Windmills to Nuclear Power* △ TB/556

LANCELOT LAW WHYTE: Essay on Atomism: *From Democritus to 1960* △ TB/565

Mathematics

E. W. BETH: The Foundations of Mathematics: *A Study in the Philosophy of Science* △ TB/581

H. DAVENPORT: The Higher Arithmetic: *An Introduction to the Theory of Numbers* △ TB/526

H. G. FORDER: Geometry: *An Introduction* △ TB/548

S. KÖRNER: The Philosophy of Mathematics: *An Introduction* △ TB/547

D. E. LITTLEWOOD: Skeleton Key of Mathematics: *A Simple Account of Complex Algebraic Problems* △ TB/525

GEORGE E. OWEN: Fundamentals of Scientific Mathematics TB/569

WILLARD VAN ORMAN QUINE: Mathematical Logic TB/558

O. G. SUTTON: Mathematics in Action. ° △ *Foreword by James R. Newman. Illus.* TB/518

FREDERICK WAISMANN: Introduction to Mathematical Thinking. *Foreword by Karl Menger* TB/511

Philosophy of Science

R. B. BRAITHWAITE: Scientific Explanation TB/515

J. BRONOWSKI: Science and Human Values. △ *Revised and Enlarged Edition* TB/505

ALBERT EINSTEIN et al.: Albert Einstein: Philosopher-Scientist. *Edited by Paul A. Schilpp* Vol. I TB/502
 Vol. II TB/503

WERNER HEISENBERG: Physics and Philosophy: *The Revolution in Modern Science* △ TB/549

JOHN MAYNARD KEYNES: A Treatise on Probability. ° △ *Introduction by N. R. Hanson* TB/557

KARL R. POPPER: Logic of Scientific Discovery △ TB/576

STEPHEN TOULMIN: Foresight and Understanding: *An Enquiry into the Aims of Science. △ Foreword by Jacques Barzun* TB/564

STEPHEN TOULMIN: The Philosophy of Science: *An Introduction* △ TB/513

G. J. WHITROW: Natural Philosophy of Time ° △ TB/563

Physics and Cosmology

JOHN E. ALLEN: Aerodynamics: *A Space Age Survey* △ TB/582

STEPHEN TOULMIN & JUNE GOODFIELD: The Fabric of the Heavens: *The Development of Astronomy and Dynamics.* △ *Illus.* TB/579

DAVID BOHM: Causality and Chance in Modern Physics.△ *Foreword by Louis de Broglie* TB/536

P. W. BRIDGMAN: The Nature of Thermodynamics TB/537

P. W. BRIDGMAN: A Sophisticate's Primer of Relativity △ TB/575

A. C. CROMBIE, Ed.: Turning Point in Physics TB/535

C. V. DURRELL: Readable Relativity. △ *Foreword by Freeman J. Dyson* TB/530

ARTHUR EDDINGTON: Space, Time and Gravitation: *An Outline of the General Relativity Theory* TB/510

GEORGE GAMOW: Biography of Physics Σ △ TB/567

MAX JAMMER: Concepts of Force: *A Study in the Foundation of Dynamics* TB/550

MAX JAMMER: Concepts of Mass *in Classical and Modern Physics* TB/571

MAX JAMMER: Concepts of Space: *The History of Theories of Space in Physics. Foreword by Albert Einstein* TB/533

G. J. WHITROW: The Structure and Evolution of the Universe: *An Introduction to Cosmology.* △ *Illus.* TB/504